ON THEIR OWN

ON THEIR OWN

Widows and Widowhood in the American Southwest 1848-1939

Edited by
ARLENE SCADRON

University of Illinois Press
Urbana and Chicago

Manufactured in the United States of America
C 5 4 3 2 1

This book is printed on acid-free paper.

Library of Congress Cataloging-in-Publication Data

On their own.

Bibliography: p.
Includes index.
1. Widows—Southwestern States—History—19th century.
2. Widows—Southwestern States—History—20th century.
I. Scadron, Arlene.
HQ1058.5.U505 1988 306.8′8 86-30850
ISBN 0-252-01439-1 (alk. paper)

TO HELEN S. CARTER,
friend and colleague
(June 20, 1926-January 5, 1985)

Contents

Preface

Widowhood is one of the most stressful experiences in a woman's life, and one that most modern women undergo. Its deleterious impact on increasing numbers of contemporary women—particularly older and poor women—evoked the fundamental scholarly question of this volume: what was it like to be a widow in one of the least developed, most ethnically diverse regions of the United States at a time when women's employment opportunities were severely limited, workers' pensions were almost nonexistent, insurance policies were rare, public and private charities offered minimal support to an impoverished few, and the modern welfare state was still in its infancy?[1]

The loss of a spouse is now, and over the past few centuries has often been, a critical problem for women, but its history remains to be written.[2] This collection of essays by twelve scholars—historians, sociologists, anthropologists, and an attorney—is designed to fill a major gap in the literature by examining significant aspects of widowhood within a specific historical context and presenting historical background for a topic that has been dominated by contemporary considerations. While this is not a conventional history book, these case studies are intended as models for using different methodological approaches and sources in writing about widowhood in the past. In addition, all of the essays included here, based on original research in primary historical sources, oral interviews, or fieldwork, offer insights into widowhood in the past and provide several building blocks toward a general history of widowhood in America. An interdisciplinary study, this collection extends beyond the subject of American and western women's history to other historical subdisciplines, including family and social history and the history of aging; it also addresses issues in women's studies, gerontology, sociology and social work, anthropology, psychology, and the law.

The initial stimulus for this work was a question posed by Deborah J. Baldwin, a historian and one of the contributors to this volume. A scholar of Mexican history, she wondered about the fate of hundreds of women who crossed the border from Mexico into Arizona and New Mexico between 1910 and 1920 to escape the turmoil of the Mexican Revolution. One result was that many of them were widowed and remained in the Southwest, often cut off from families, support networks, and visible means of sustenance. What happened to these women? How did they survive? And what happened to numerous other women who emigrated to the Southwest in the early twentieth century, often out of concern for their spouses' health, and found themselves widows in a strange land? Further, in recent times, this region has become a magnet for older, retired people for whom widowhood is a predictable prospect. These queries and observations provoked additional questions that became a collaborative research project funded by the National Institute on Aging.[3]

The comparative invisibility of widows and widowhood in American historical studies reflects in part the dominance of men until the last decade as both actors and chroniclers in historical writing, the discomfort of many Americans in confronting death and dying, and an underlying aversion to women alone, especially older women. Also, the emergence of a sizeable widowed and aging population commanding notice is a recent development, the result of a demographic revolution marked by increasing longevity of both sexes, particularly of women. A computerized bibliographic search of the literature on widowhood turned up numerous references to medical, psychological, and sociological aspects of contemporary widowhood, even a few to "black widow spiders," but very few to black widows and almost none to the history of widowhood or to the conditions of widows in the past. As for widowhood in the Southwest, virtually nothing has been written about the history of this topic.

Yet the Southwest, which has been relatively neglected in regional studies, provides a fascinating crucibile for examining some of the critical issues affecting widows—one of society's most vulnerable groups. Represented here are American Indian, Spanish-speaking, and Anglo populations, including Mormons, which allow us to examine the impact of diverse cultural traditions on the lives of widowed women. Description and analysis of institutions such as the family and church, the law, political structures, and informal social organizations relating to widows and widowhood illuminate the complexity of the widow's place in society while also establishing a basis for comparing this region with others.

The period under consideration begins in 1848, with the termination of hostilities between the United States and Mexico and U.S. acquisition of a vast new empire in the Southwest. It ends in 1939, when the U.S. Congress amended the 1935 Social Security Act to expand coverage of elderly wives, widows, and dependent children, assuming a national responsibility for many, though not all widows. During this century, the Southwest experienced dramatic political and economic changes that had a direct impact on women and widows. As a result of the Mexican War, the former Mexican provinces of New Mexico, Upper California, and Texas were transformed into American territories and eventually into states. Though the Southwest was less developed than many other sections of the country, its economic profile also changed, and the evolution of agricultural, mining, railroading, and urban commercial and industrial communities affected the options available to widowed women of different social classes.

While all of the chapters herein are set within this specific chronological framework, some focus on more limited time periods, while others, such as Helen Carter's examination of the changing legal status of widows, span the entire century. Using untapped, rich regional sources and traditional sources in new ways, the contributors explore selected aspects of the personal, social, and institutional dimensions of widowhood within this historical context. In the first six essays, authors illustrate the impact of ethnic diversity upon various groups of widows, beginning with those populations who settled the region first: American Indian and Spanish-speaking women, followed by studies of Mormon women. In the next three chapters, the contributors study institutional, economic, and social conditions of widows in Colorado and Arizona. And in the final two contributions, essayists, drawing upon sources from the entire region and time period, explore the psychological ramifications and legal aspects of widowhood.

In the introduction Arlene Scadron examines demographic, historiographic, and theoretical issues relating to widowhood. This section also includes a brief overview of southwestern history during the period under study. The first two chapters treat American Indian widowhood and offer a dramatic contrast with mainstream Western cultures. In "Widowhood and Autonomy in the Native-American Southwest" (chapter 1), the anthropologist Sarah M. Nelson explores the relationships between social structure and widowhood among major southwestern tribes. Noting the paucity of ethnographic information about widowhood and the differences among southwestern Indian cultures, Nelson finds that the greater the autonomy of widows, the fewer economic and social penalties they suffer; in most cases, widows in southwestern American Indian cultures do better than women in the dominant American culture. Alice Schlegel, also an anthropologist, studies Hopi widows and widowers in "Hopi Family Structure and the Experience of Widowhood" (chapter 2). She finds that certain constraints upon Hopi marriage—close links with kin, ties and obligations between siblings competitive with husband-wife relationships, and segregation of the sexes in most occupational and recreational activities—provide insurance against destitution, social isolation, and change of social status concomitant with widowhood in the larger society.

The historian Deena J. González examines the lives of Santa Fe's Spanish-Mexican widows within the larger community of unmarried women who were divorced, separated, or deserted in "The Widowed Women of Santa Fe: Assessments on the Lives of an Unmarried Population, 1850-80" (chapter 3). Following the Mexican War, there were numerous widows in Santa Fe, and González focuses on the specific characteristics of a widowed population as well as on the socioeconomic forces created by a changing society and an economy dominated by wealthy newcomers to the community. González relies primarily upon census data and the scanty evidence in folklore, legal and church documents, and family papers to describe the numbers, living arrangements, and kinship networks of Hispanic women in an essentially patriarchal society. The sociologist Martha Oehmke Loustaunau also deals with Hispanic widows of New Mexico in "Hispanic Widows and Their Support Systems in the Mesilla Valley of Southern New Mexico, 1910-40" (chapter 4), a rural agricultural environment. Combining various methodologies, such as demography, cross-cultural comparison, analysis of socioenvironmental conditions, and oral history, Loustaunau finds that most widows depended for support much more on individual initiative and a culturally based system of extended family than on formal institutions.

An analysis of the personal response to widowhood among Mormons is presented in "Widowhood among the Mormons: The Personal Accounts" (chapter 5), by the historians and literary scholars Maureen Ursenbach Beecher, Carol Cornwall Madsen, and Lavina Fielding Anderson. The authors probe ways that religious ideology and practices, polygamy and support systems ameliorated privations due to widowhood. Using three-hundred-odd collections of diaries, reminiscences, and letters by Mormon widows about their lives after the death of their spouses, the authors reveal the views of a literate, self-confident elite. A disproportionate number of these diarists lived in polygamy and defended the practice in their writings. Geraldine P. Mineau, a sociologist, also examines Mormon widows in "Utah Widowhood: A Demographic Profile" (chapter 6) through a statistical analysis of five ten-year cohorts of women born between 1830 and 1879, from marriage through death. Data derived from 180,000 computerized Utah genealogies collected through the Mormon Historical Demography Project allow longitudinal study, focusing on first marriages, circumstances and timing of termination, and subsequent demographic experiences, including remarriage, length of widowhood, residential change, and life expectancy of marriage survivors.

Joyce D. Goodfriend, a historian, in "The Struggle for Survival: Widows in Denver, 1880-1912" (chapter 7) analyzes economic problems attendant on the loss of a husband in the largest city of the region. She describes various strategies and their impact on family life when widows who did not remarry found reliance on accumulated personal resources and kin inadequate to ensure their survival. Menial labor and homework, assistance from community agencies, and poor relief were among the means widows used to cope with economic problems. Despite their desperate plight, policymakers were slow to recognize and remedy the destitution of widows; in fact, most Progressive Era legislative enactments benefiting widows were aimed directly at their children. Donna J. Guy, a historian, also examines economic issues in "The Economics of Widowhood in Arizona, 1880-1940" (chapter 8), as Arizona developed from a territory to a state. Focusing on employment in the paid labor force, and support provided by the public and private sectors, she illuminates various avenues for coping with the economic consequences of widowhood and some of the limitations imposed by primitive frontier conditions earlier in the period. Later, dislocations caused by rapidly changing technology, social mores, immigration patterns, and discriminatory practices against blacks, Hispanics, and the elderly rendered the state incapable of fulfilling its promises to vulnerable groups, including widows. Some Arizona widows had no need for public assistance or even wage-earning employment. The historian Deborah J. Baldwin delineates strategies available to a relatively secure group of middle-class widows—women whose spouses were members of the Arizona Pioneer Society—in "A Successful Search for Security: Arizona Pioneer Society Widows" (chapter 9). Through familial involvement in multiple businesses, investment in urban property, clear inheritance provisions, Hispanic traditions, and supportive kindred networks, they were insulated from the isolation and hardship commonly experienced by many widows.

Arlene Scadron, a historian, explores personal and psychological dimensions of widowhood in "Letting Go: Bereavement among Selected Southwestern Anglo Widows" (chapter 10). Relying upon contemporary bereavement scholarship and literary sources such as diaries, family correspondence, reminiscences, oral histories, and popular literature, Scadron looks closely at the first year or two following the death of the spouse to examine bereavement processes and adjustment to widowhood. Helen S. Carter, an attorney, presents a detailed description and analysis of the "Legal Aspects of Widowhood and Aging" (chapter 11) in the region during the entire period between 1848 and 1939. Readers interested in comprehensive coverage of the law may prefer to begin the book with this chapter, in which Carter compares and contrasts the Southwest's two major legal systems: civil law in Arizona and New Mexico and common law in Colorado and Utah. Analyzing statutes and case reports of the period, Carter reviews the disposition of intestate and testate deaths and such provisions for widows and aged persons as dower and property rights, homestead exemptions, widow's allowances, and rights of election. The concluding chapter by Arlene Scadron summarizes major findings and suggests possibilities for future study.

Widowhood is a universal experience, which tests a woman's identity, resourcefulness, and courage. Yet the experience of individual women in coping with this condition varies enormously and is affected by a multitude of historical, cultural, and personal factors. It is premature to write of long-range trends, models, or even common patterns of behavior among widows everywhere. But illuminating the perception of and response to a critical life-stage among a diverse population within a small, distinctive region of the country should add to our understanding of similarities, variations, and changes in widowhood over time and provide a broader perspective on the lives of women in the Southwest. By suggesting new directions for future research about widowhood under different historical conditions in other regions of the country, we hope these essays help lay the foundation for a general history of widowhood in America.

NOTES

1. A brief history of social welfare in America since colonial times can be found in Walter I. Trattner, *From Poor Law to Welfare State: A History of Social Welfare in America,* 2d ed. (New York: Free Press, 1979). For a more detailed discussion of the period since 1900, when the modern welfare state began to emerge, see James T. Patterson, *America's Struggle against Poverty, 1900-1980* (Cambridge, Mass.: Harvard University Press, 1981), and Edward Berkowitz and Kim McQuaid, *Creating the Welfare State: The Political Economy of Twentieth-Century Reform* (New York: Praeger Publishers, 1980). Also useful on social security legislation is Roy Lubove, *The Struggle for Social Security, 1900-1935* (Cambridge, Mass.: Har-

vard University Press, 1968); W. Andrew Achenbaum, *Social Security: Visions and Revisions* (Cambridge: Cambridge University Press, 1986).

2. For a brief historical and cross-cultural overview of widowhood focusing on support systems, roles, and status in several different societies including Europe and America, see Helena Z. Lopata, *Women as Widows: Support Systems* (New York: Elsevier, 1979), 13-46. A more recent summary of the history of women and children as economic dependents in Europe and the United States prior to the 1930s is offered by Helena Z. Lopata and Henry P. Brehm, *Widows and Dependent Wives: From Social Problem to Federal Program* (New York: Praeger Publishers, 1986), 1-55. They treat dependency resulting from widowhood and the development and impact of social security legislation on widows.

3. "Widowhood & Aging: The American Southwest, 1847-1939," Department of Health and Human Services, National Institute on Aging Social and Behavioral Research Program, Grant #5R01 AG03042-02, was written and directed by Arlene Scadron, principal investigator and the editor of this volume. The Southwest Institute for Research on Women (SIROW), Women's Studies Committee, University of Arizona, Tucson, sponsored the proposal. Each chapter is an original essay written specifically for the NIA study and modified for this collection by scholars whose research has focused on women or on the Southwest. During a working conference at the University of Arizona, the authors shared views about earlier drafts of these essays.

Acknowledgments

This book owes its being to the generous support of the National Institute on Aging Social and Behavioral Research Program, which funded a three-year project, "Widowhood & Aging: The American Southwest, 1847-1939." NIA's patronage in underwriting historical/interdisciplinary research that cannot promise immediately applicable results permitted us to explore unknown terrain. Matilda White Riley, associate director of the program, and Kathleen Bond, my program officer, were always cooperative and helpful.

A research stipend from the Newberry Library during the summer of 1980 assisted in the initial stages of research for the NIA proposal. I am grateful for the hospitality of Richard S. Brown of the Newberry and to Drs. Robert L. Middlekauff and Arlie Hochschild, both then of the University of California at Berkeley, who supported my Newberry application.

This book is also one of the first research projects undertaken through the Southwest Institute for Research on Women (SIROW), funded by the Ford Foundation at the University of Arizona. Myra Dinnerstein, chair of the Women's Studies Committee, University of Arizona, and SIROW director, offered financial support as a research associate during the early period of proposal development. The SIROW network of scholars in the region helped me identify colleagues who proved to be interested in pursuing research on widowhood. Dr. Dinnerstein and Dr. Janice Monk, SIROW's executive director, critiqued several drafts of the research proposal and provided funding for its processing through the university. Both also read an early version of the essays, and Dr. Monk provided administrative assistance during a conference of the contributors.

It is immediately apparent from a look at the table of contents that much of the work in this book was done by the contributors whose chapters follow. Despite the demands of busy professional schedules and other writing commitments, they cooperated by meeting deadlines and sharing information and constructive criticism with me and each other at crucial times.

A few, Sarah M. Nelson in Denver and Joyce D. Goodfriend in Denver and Manchester, Vt., went out of their way to provide hospitality and critical insights during research sojourns. Mitchel M. Carter, Helen Carter's husband, a retired professor of law, generously continued to cooperate with me after Helen's death, proofreading and correcting her manuscript at several stages. I was warned at the beginning of this project that coordinating the work of twelve other scholars could become a horrendous management task. It has been time-consuming, and occasionally more profitable to AT&T and the U.S. Post Office than to scholarship, but the benefits of our intellectual collaboration and the friendships that have developed far outweigh the tedium of administration.

I owe a great deal to Dr. Ann Kerwin, who provided intellectual and moral support during a particularly difficult passage through the life of this project. She also served as "manager-in-residence," handling a number of administrative tasks during a seven-month period when I was in India as a Fulbright scholar. In addition, she read and discussed innumerable drafts of many of the essays, offering invaluable advice and criticism. Without her help at critical junctures, this book would have taken much longer.

Other friends and scholars who shared their views and expertise about the widowhood project in its incipient stages, offered bibliographic information, or read and critiqued drafts of the grant proposal, book chapters, and related papers presented at professional meetings include: Drs. Rachel Fuchs, June Sochen, Joan Jensen, Janet Roebuck, Robert Schulzinger, Michel Dahlin, Kitty Sklar, Arlene Kaplan Daniels, Susan J. Kleinberg, Elizabeth Jameson, J. L. Reiff, Sue Sheridan Walker, Robert V. Wells, Constance Schulz, and Carol B. Stack. Marlys H. Witte, M.D., a friend and colleague of long standing, read a number of drafts of my chapters and offered advice and support throughout. By also providing part-time employment through the American Medical Women's Association Professional Resources Research Center, she enabled me to pursue the widowhood project.

During the course of research, I have benefited enormously from many conversations with a number of widows who helped me attain a realistic understanding of the academic and primary sources I was reading. They often questioned what they regarded as an "ivory tower" focus on "dead widows" instead of women of their own generation, but they have helped me appreciate a few "universals" of the experience and condition of widowhood. Genevieve Ginsburg, founder of Widowed to Widowed Services, Inc., in Tucson, was most helpful in this regard.

Most historians (and other scholars) are indebted to the research libraries and librarians who assist them at every turn, often uncovering new primary sources or pointing to particularly valuable documents within a manuscript collection. I appreciate the assistance of many librarians and have delighted in the opportunity to work in the following libraries: the Arizona Historical Society in Tucson and Phoenix; the University of Arizona Special Collections Library and Main Library; the Arizona Department of Library, Archives, and Public Records, Phoenix; the Sharlot Hall Museum, Prescott; the University of California at Berkeley Library and Berkeley's Bancroft Library (with special thanks to Annegret S. Ogden, Irene Morin, Peter Hanf, Anthony Bliss, and Richard Ogar); the California Historical Society Library, San Francisco; the Huntington Library and Art Gallery, San Marino, Cal. (where Director Robert L. Middlekauff was exceptionally hospitable); the New Mexico State Records Center and Archives, Santa Fe (where Stanley M. Hordes, state historian, lent valuable assistance); the Museum of New Mexico Library, Santa Fe; the University of New Mexico Special Collections Department of the General Library, Albuquerque; the Colorado Historical Society Library, Denver (where Maxine Benson, formerly historian of the society, provided important assistance); the University of Denver Library; and the Denver Public Library.

Catherine Dargel, Gary Hearn, and Dana Larson scoured local and state libraries for primary source materials, providing research assistance and uncovering enough leads to keep me busy studying widows for some time to come.

Elaine Segura, Sue Earley, and Barbara Bickel typed various portions of the manuscript, always efficiently and accurately, with nary a complaint about some of the circuitous communications that must have tried their patience. Laura Cardinal kept track of the financial accounts and paperwork required in managing the NIA grant while also maintaining a smile.

My editors at the University of Illinois Press have been efficient and encouraging throughout the long haul from initial idea to publication. Carole S. Appel, senior editor, supported this project from the start. Susan L. Patterson, Elizabeth Dulany, and Barbara E. Cohen have shepherded it through the final stages.

Having spent what seemed to be an inordinate amount of time studying how women dealt with the loss of "significant others" heightened my appreciation of a loving family. My husband, Michael, and my daughters, Kari and Lisa, no doubt felt at times that preoccupation with this book had imposed "widow(er)hood" on them. I am deeply grateful for their patience and support throughout this project, as I am to my parents, Mandel and Minnette Weininger, who have always encouraged my work.

Arlene Scadron
Tucson, Arizona
May, 1987

Introduction

ARLENE SCADRON

In many societies, including our own, widowhood is an experience that "penetrates the very heart of the individual," testing a woman's vitality as well as the strength of the social fabric.[1] Being widowed confronts most women, whatever their age, with unavoidable, historically persistent problems that severely try their ability to cope. These include: dealing with immediate grief and the crises of bereavement, new and usually reduced financial circumstances, responsibility for household, family, and business affairs, potential loss of an independent household and social status, loss of consortium, loneliness, isolation, and the need to forge a new identity and new social networks as a woman alone. Yet the problems and coping mechanisms of widowhood are not the same for all widows, nor have they ever been. Variations are discernible according to race, class, ethnic background, age, presence or absence of dependent and adult children, religious beliefs, availability of family, kinship, and other support networks, the degree of autonomy within marriage and the quality of marriage, previous work experience and skills, the nature and timing of the spouse's death, and emotional and economic preparation for death and widowhood.

Societal conditions including cultural values and practices also shape the experience of widowhood.[2] Among the most important are attitudes toward dying and death; the status and social roles available to married women, older women, and widows; constraints upon remarriage created by sex ratios and cultural proscriptions; informal and institutional provisions for the widowed poor, elderly women, and dependent children; legal regulations governing inheritance, the descent of property, testate and intestate deaths, and distribution of and control over marital property; and the role of women in the work force. Historical time is another important variable. Whether widowhood occurs during a depression, during a period of economic growth, or during a time when welfare exists on a broad scale or not at all affect coping and outcome in a fundamental way—as does the widow's past up to that point.[3]

Where patriarchal values have shaped traditional concepts of marriage, women were, and in many cases still are, expected to be subservient to their husbands and conform to double standards governing both the private and public spheres. Within this context, widowhood becomes, in the words of one social scientist, "a negatively evaluated social category where the individual loses the central source of identity, financial support and social relationships . . . a 'roleless role.' "[4] Thus, a woman whose major identity has been as wife and mother finds that "there is no comfortable role of widow available to her."[5] Redefining herself as a woman on her own, particularly if she is older, is one of the chief tasks facing a widow, whatever her economic or professional status. It is not surprising therefore that Lynn Caine, a successful career woman with two young children, described this poignant reaction to her husband's death:

> I felt like one of those spiraled shells washed up on the beach. Poke a straw through the twisting tunnel, around and around, and there is nothing there. No flesh. No life. Whatever lived there is dried up and gone.
>
> Our society is set up so that most women lose their identities when their husbands die. Marriage is a symbiotic relationship for most of us. We draw our identities from our husbands. We add ourselves to our men, pour ourselves into them and their lives. We exist in their reflection. And then . . . ? If they die . . . ? What is left? It's wrenching enough to lose the man who is your lover, your companion, your best friend, the father of your children, without losing yourself as well.[6]

This grim portrait reflects the historical failure of mainstream Western culture to develop adequate, socially approved models of widowhood[7] that provide for positive responses and changing circumstances. It reflects an ambiguity, even a repugnance, toward women alone and older women. In Anglo-American literature, we typically find two stereotypes of widowhood in the "sorrowing widow" and the "merry widow"—neither fully accurate representations of the experience of most widows nor useful guides to self-definition as independent individuals.[8] While Lynn Caine does not fit the stereotype of the completely subservient wife—the woman whose life is merged with her spouse's, who is totally dependent upon him emotionally, financially, and socially, and who finds herself wholly bereft, without an individual identity when he dies—her *cri de coeur* evokes the self-image of the sorrowing widow. By contrast, widowers, however grief-stricken, do not typically equate spousal loss with loss of personal identity, nor usually with loss of financial security. Although the notion of wifely subordination has never been extended in Western culture to the extreme of self-immolation on the husband's funeral pyre expected of a widow in the traditional Hindu practice of suttee,[9] current precepts still leave widows with few constructive models for independent living.

At the opposite end of the spectrum lies the "merry widow"—typically young, pretty, and wealthy, often childless, sought after eagerly by suitors after the briefest respectable mourning period. She usually remarries someone older, although she can afford to mate with a less affluent younger man. This type of widow, however, is more likely to be found in literary expressions and allusions[10] than in real life and bears little resemblance to the experience of the majority of widows now or in the past.

Another stereotype of widowhood revolves around the primary role of the family—particularly among Hispanics and American Indians—in providing "a safety net" for the protection of society's most vulnerable members, such as the elderly, the widowed, and dependent children. Whether living under one roof or within close proximity, the immediate household and the extended family kinship network has been viewed as a major source of emotional and material security for its members. While this allegedly idyllic kin-based world in which elderly women, usually widowed, were highly valued and cared for is sometimes romanticized, its erosion with increasing urbanization and industrialization does not negate its importance in the period prior to 1940.[11]

Attitudes toward widows are inseparable from attitudes toward death, and in contemporary Western culture, too many repress fears of mortality, deflecting hostility onto unhappy reminders of death's inevitable sting. Caine and others, detesting the label "widow," attribute much of their (undeserved) suffering to societal perceptions of widows as "carriers and transmitters of the reality of death." At a time when death has become taboo and the ill and dying are isolated physically and psychologically, widows become unwitting victims, alienated and often "disengaged" from much of society. They comprise "a subculture whose members live in relative oblivion, submerged in the despair of loneliness, chiding each other for self-pity, advising each other to keep busy, individually hoping for an avenue of escape, and collectively succumbing to an attitude of hopelessness."[12]

Widows also constitute a subculture of increasing size and importance in

American life. Of 12.6 million widowed persons in the United States in 1982, almost 10.8 million were women, and their numbers have been growing by at least 100,000 per year. About 12 percent of all women over age 15 are now widows, as are 50.4 percent of elderly women over 65, and 30 percent of *all elderly persons.* Approximately 75 percent of all married women in the United States will eventually become widows, and most of them will remain so for a lengthy period. The median age of a widow today is almost 69, and the average widow "who does not remarry and dies a natural death will have spent eighteen and a half years in this final stage of life." (For a widower, the comparable period is thirteen and one-half years.)[13] And for most, remarriage is not likely: fewer than one-third of widows ever remarry and the vast majority of those who do are under 40. Horace Greeley's remark, "A [white] widow of doubtful age will marry almost any sort of a white man," though crude, aptly describes the predicament of many older widows, then and now.[14]

In the past, widowhood was shorter and affected a greater proportion of young women with dependent children. Despite the rigors of childbearing, a white married woman in colonial and early nineteenth-century America had life chances roughly equal to her mate's; both spouses could expect their marriage to be severed by death before all of their children grew to adulthood. Prior to the widespread practice of family limitation and the significant rise in life expectancy beginning about 1880, a woman's normal adult life would be spent in bearing and rearing children, with the end of parenting and the onset of widowhood coinciding closely in time. For either husband or wife, widowhood would typically last three or four years until the death of the surviving spouse. The "empty nest" stage of the life cycle—a long period of companionship (averaging 12-15 years today) a married couple enjoys after their grown children have left home—was unusual in earlier times. So too was the situation facing married women today who can expect in the final stage of life to spend a substantial period of time alone, without dependent children or husbands.[15]

Since 1890, when marital status first began to be tabulated in the federal census,[16] there has been a significant shift in the age distribution of widows, with increasing percentages concentrated among older age groups. For example, the proportion of widows aged 35-44 among all widowed women over 14 has steadily declined from almost 14 percent in 1890 to only 3 percent in 1982, whereas the percentage of elderly widows has more than doubled over the same period, from 32 percent to almost 70 percent.[17] Thus, in contemporary American society widowhood has become a common segment of the last stage of life when women are also confronted with a host of physiological, psychological, and sociological problems concomitant with aging.[18]

By 1982 there were 7.5 million widows and 1.3 million widowers in the United States over age 65, almost a 6:1 difference, whereas in 1890 elderly widows outnumbered elderly widowers by only 2.4:1.[19] Comparing the experience of men and women, the proportion of male widowers to all males over 14 has dropped from 3.8 percent in 1890 to 2.2 percent in 1982, while the proportion of widows to all women over 14 has been consistently higher and has risen from 10.6 percent in 1890 to 12.3 percent in 1970, dropping off slightly to 11.7 percent in 1982.[20] Among some ethnic minorities, these trends are even more pronounced. Widowhood is the most common marital status of elderly America Indian women, and among Hispanic women 75 years and older, there has been a greater increase of widows in the last decade than for comparably aged Anglos.[21]

These imbalances reflect women's longer life expectancy, the relatively small number of eligible older males, differential remarriage rates, comparatively earlier deaths among minority males, and deep-seated cultural practices that encourage the marriage of older men to younger women.[22] One of the few culturally sanctioned exceptions to this mating pattern has been the occasional union of wealthy older widows to younger men, a partnership whose attractions Benjamin Franklin captured in his observation: "A rich widow is the only kind of second-hand goods that will sell at prime cost."[23]

Dramatic in themselves, these changes in the demographic patterns of widowhood are part of a worldwide transformation in the aging of the population. By the year 2000, the number of persons over 60 throughout the world will double; in the United States, 32 to 35 million Americans will be over 65, with the fastest population growth among those over 85. This revolution in life expectancy of both sexes represents a shift of illness and death from the earlier years of the life cycle to later years, what Robert N. Butler has called a "veritable triumph of survivorship," part of a "worldwide longevity revolution unprecedented in human history." Notable among the survivors, contend Butler and Myrna I. Lewis, are widowed women, who constitute the majority of pioneers in this century of old age.[24]

Prevailing bleak stereotypes of widows and older women inhibit their recognition as true social innovators who cope, survive, and sometimes thrive in the face of loss and economic and social disadvantage. Though social scientists and social workers, physicians, feminist reformers, and even politicians have begun to spotlight the plight and accomplishments of widowed women—especially older, impoverished widows and displaced homemakers—and while some widows have organized support networks to share their grief and build new friendships, historians have rarely studied widowhood. Whatever the reasons, family historians have primarily emphasized childhood, adolescence, and early adulthood; historians of old age have treated widowhood as an afterthought; and women's historians, while they have incorporated bits of information about widows into scholarly monographs and primary source collections, have provided no sustained book-length treatments of the subject. What we know about widowhood in the American past draws upon the findings of a few scholarly articles, most of them focused on legal issues, economic status, and demographic topics including remarriage and household arrangements. Perhaps because so much of the pioneering work in the new social history has been rooted in the colonial period, most of the historical literature on widowhood in America focuses on the first two centuries following settlement. Restricted by the nature of archival materials and the demands of quantitative methodology, many of these studies examine one colony or small community.

Quantitative studies of family life in the seventeenth-century Chesapeake region along the tobacco coast have noted the critical stabilizing role played by widows in demographically unstable situations.[25] Characterized by a severely imbalanced sex ratio in favor of men, high mortality among both sexes, and high immigration, especially of single men, marriages in late seventeenth-century Maryland were brief: one partner in a marriage was likely to die within seven years and only one-third of marriages lasted ten years. Frequent widowhood and successive remarriage were commonplace. In Charles County, Maryland, for example, "widows took new husbands three times more often than widowers took new wives." The remarried widow played a critical role as the lynchpin in a complex family comprised of her children from the first marriage, her new husband's children, and children of the new union, a role that also enhanced her power.

These circumstances may also explain the generosity and trust that characterized the wills of the deceased. According to Lois Green Carr and Lorena S. Walsh, "Only a handful of men left estates to their wives only for their term of widowhood or until the children came of age. When a man did not leave his wife a life estate, he often gave her land outright or more than her dower third of his movable property. Such bequests were at the expense of his children and showed his concern that his widow should have a maintenance which young children could not supply." Widows were usually named the executor of the estates of their deceased husbands, responsible for paying debts and maintaining the remaining assets. Although more than one-half the husbands who left a will also appointed overseers to ensure that its terms were followed, few authorized removal of children from the homes of stepfathers for abuse or waste of their property. This suggests that husbands were most concerned about the welfare of their widows and, despite their almost certain remarriage, trusted them with management of the estate and the future of offspring.

Research on the legal status and remarriage rates of widows in colonial Virginia, South Carolina, and New York demonstrates the critical importance of comparing the provisions of the law to its actual application. In a number of cases, widows were better off than a mere reading of the statutes would imply. Many husbands exceeded the traditional dower bequest consisting of a life interest in one-third the real property and a comparable portion of personal property forever. The autonomy and power of widows varied considerably according to demographic and other realities affecting the lives of couples and eventually the testamentary behavior of husbands. Several studies indicate an inverse correlation between a widow's age and her autonomy and authority over her husband's estate. Husbands were inclined to bequeath more power and autonomy to younger wives, presumably for the protection of dependent children, whereas older men with older wives and adult children were less inclined to do so.[26]

The few studies of widowhood in early New England communities[27] find an older group of widows who rarely remarried and whose property rights and opportunities for self-support were limited, confronting the family and community with the problem of providing economic support and constraining mobility among the younger generation.

The psychological components of widowhood have been more widely ignored by historians than other aspects of this condition. Yet what distinguishes widowhood from many other life course experiences—the multiple loss of role and status, economic security, and close companion/partner—can only be fully understood through examination of the psychological stress of bereavement and individual coping strategies.[28]

Researchers have also explored support for widows through expansion of veterans' pension legislation in the nineteenth century and widows' pensions (or mothers' compensation) beginning in the early twentieth century. These programs, in turn, established a precedent for federally supported old-age pensions and Aid to Families with Dependent Children (AFDC) eventually enacted by Social Security legislation.[29] The provision by local and state charities and private agencies of institutional support for elderly, formerly middle-class working women made destitute by widowhood and lack of kin support is illuminated in Carole Haber's study of old-age homes in nineteenth-century Philadelphia and Brian Gratton's discussion of the Home for Elderly Women in Boston.[30]

The literature on the history of aging and the elderly in America is growing and provides an important potential theoretical framework for the study of widowhood. However, little has been done to integrate the experience of women. Neither David Hackett Fischer nor W. Andrew Achenbaum[31] shed much light on the history of attitudes toward older women and even less on widows. They disagree about periodization, but both argue that conceptions about the elderly were transformed during the chronological period covered in this study (1848-1939) from veneration to denigration. Haber disagrees, believing, "There was never a golden age of senescence in which the old were treated with veneration." She argues, "For many individuals, even in colonial America, gray hair and wrinkles seemed reason for contempt instead of honor; their age alone was not deemed worthy of respect. Nor did attitudes toward the old ever veer sharply from adoration to contempt. The aged were not loved as a group at one moment, only to be hated collectively the next."[32] By the twentieth century the old were deemed obsolescent. Even campaigns for old-age pensions and social security were motivated in part by the presumed need to rid the work force of its least efficient members—understood to be those over 65—making room for younger workers.[33] Janet Roebuck, on the other hand, prods scholars to recognize older women as true revolutionaries whose resilience and innovation remains largely unnoticed and unrecorded.[34]

Until the last decade, much of the historical writing about America's western frontier has been dominated by male historians who have emphasized the values, fantasies, and experiences of male pioneers. Influential for at least fifty years after its publication in 1893, Frederick Jackson Turner's theory of the significance of the frontier on the development of the American character shaped most of the studies that followed. Turner's protean concept and agrarian orientation most frequently emphasized the frontier as "the hither edge of free land" and postulated its formative role in fostering nationalism, individualism, optimism, improvisation, self-reliance, and the democratization of family relations and other institutions. In time, the Turnerian thesis came under attack for ambiguity in defining critical terms such as "frontier," "democracy," and "individualism," for ignoring other kinds of frontiers—urban, industrial, technological—that in their own ways offered extensive if not greater economic opportunity and stimulated similar mobility, and for its contradictons and its implicit pessimism about the future of the country after the closing of the frontier in 1890.[35] Until 1964, however, when David Potter published his seminal essay, "American Women and the American Character,"[36] few seemed to notice that Turner had applied his ideas almost wholly to men.

The story of migration from East to West and South to North involved families as much as it involved single males—miners, fur trappers, traders, and cowboys—but including women in the story has been a direct result of the women's movement and its intention to recreate a usable past. Ultimately, this effort may well transform basic interpretations of western history. A number of recently published works on western women provide helpful background for this study.[37] Among them is an award-winning article by Joan M. Jensen and Darlis A. Miller,[38] who call for "a whole new infusion of cross-cultural comparison" of the relations among women of different cultures, of demography, and of the impact of industrialization on the lives and work patterns of women in the West.

Lillian Schlissel describes the omnipresence of mortality on the Oregon Trail as recorded in women's diaries. "The fact of death loomed large for the women, and they felt death to be a personal catastrophe." She finds that women meticulously recorded the personal details of each death along the trail, while men's accounts referred more generally to the aggregate numbers of dead. "No one who reads the diaries," she notes, "can escape feeling the intensity with which the women regarded the loss of life. Cholera, illness, accident—these were the central facts in the minds of the women who were the ritual caretakers of the dying and the dead." For the widows on the journey, there was no alternative but to continue the trip and file the claim alone. "No widow ever placed her wagon and her family under the protection of another family," according to Schlissel. "The expectation was that women would direct the family enterprise independently when need arose." Unlike widows in more settled regions, especially older ones, "all of the wives who were widowed at the end of the journey remarried, most of them quickly and two of them twice."[39] Stoicism, resourcefulness, dogged determination, and a strong sense of responsibility to provide for their families characterized many of these simple women who found themselves bereft and alone in a strange land. One can only speculate whether the instability of the family unit and the frequent exposure to death inured these women and their children to loss and prepared them for similar experiences later.

These few studies provide useful insights for improving our understanding of the western experience and the lives of Anglo widows on the West's many frontiers. But the historical literature on widows and aging women is sparse, and in the Southwest, even more scarce. This collection of essays examines widowhood in the Southwest[40] following the Mexican War in 1848, the expansion of Anglo settlement and institutions into the traditional American Indian and Hispanic territories, and the development of multicultural, partially urbanized societies, up to 1939, when the federal government through Social Security legislation assumed a large measure of responsibility for widowed women, dependent children, and the elderly.

The future Four Corners States comprised part of Spain's colonial empire in the New World, where outposts had been planted since the sixteenth century. Won by the newly formed Mexican Republic in 1821, after its war for independence from Spain, these American-Mexican borderlands, Mexico's northern provinces, were taken by the United States during the Mexican War, 1846-48.[41] The Treaty of Guadalupe-Hidalgo, signed February 2, 1848, ceded California and New Mexico to the United States for $15 million and confirmed America's title to Texas as far as the Rio Grande River, a vast region constituting about one-half of Mexico, and advancing the nation's boundaries to the Pacific Ocean. A few years later, with the Gadsden Purchase of 1853, remaining disputes over the southern boundary of the ceded territory were settled with the sale to the United States of the huge area now comprising the southern portions of Arizona and New Mexico and release from responsibility for damages inflicted by Indian raids on Mexico from the United States.[42]

During the period of this study, the American Southwest evolved politically from territories to independent states in the American union.[43] They shared and still share lengthy common boundaries, and many political, economic, military, and social problems. All four states have "similar soils, surface vegetation, watersheds, and climates." The overriding geographical feature of the region is its harsh environment marked by "aridity."[44] While it possessed several important physiographic differences, "the entire region had difficult mountains, broken plateaus, deserts, arid or semi-arid climates, and—once whites settled there—similar ranching, mining, and irrigated farming economies." Just as critical a "historical determinant" in the region was a permanent, Indian population divided into tribes (among them Apache, Navajo, Ute, and Comanche) often as hostile to each other as to whites.

Indian warfare, fear, and harassment also created barriers among Indians and Spanish-Mexicans that took generations to crumble.[45]

The territorial system of government imposed in 1850 put nearly all of present-day Arizona and part of future Colorado under New Mexican jurisdiction, while part of western Colorado, the future state of Nevada, and Utah were under Utah's authority. Only Colorado achieved statehood quickly, attaining the required population of 60,000 in 1876, within fifteen years of territorial status. A frontier mining society settled primarily by Anglo-Americans, Colorado was influenced by its close business connections with the East coast. The Latter-day Saints (Mormons) settled Utah in 1847, which only gained territorial status in 1850 and statehood in 1896, after a stormy period that culminated in the Mormons' renunciation of polygamy. Mormons "deliberately developed their own unique social and political systems" during these early years, and Mormon society has "remained so distinct that anthropologists still identify it as a separate American subculture, just as they do Spanish-American society in New Mexico."[46] Arizona Territory, created in 1863 primarily to counteract Confederate claims to the Southwest, attracted a diverse lot of settlers from the Confederate South, Sonoran Mexico, Mormon Utah, and the American Northeast—a melange quite different from the other three states. It gained statehood in 1912, as did New Mexico, which remained Spanish-American in culture, Roman Catholic in religion, and traditional in its habits throughout the territorial period.

The region's earliest Anglo settlers depended heavily on federal help and outside private capital to subdue Indians, exploit the land, and build roads and railroads; this assistance was also necessary to finance technical innovations, including irrigation and machinery, that encouraged profitable mining, ranching, and farming—industries indispensable to regional expansion. Between the end of the nineteenth century and World War I, further economic growth and eventual independence of the West, as well as the Southwest, followed expanded transportation links with the rest of the country. By 1914 the Santa Fe, the Denver and Rio Grande, and the Union Pacific railroads had completed many of their lines, and the Western Pacific extended from San Francisco to Salt Lake City. The major instrument of growth, railroads encouraged migration and facilitated export of minerals and produce to profitable urban markets in the East. Railroads also reduced physical and mental isolation of the region's populace and ultimately stimulated increasing demands for better roads and highways.[47] Cattle grazing and commercial agriculture requiring intensive capital investment, technology, and irrigation were less developed in the dry Southwest than in

California and some other western states; still, they stimulated growth of smaller but productive urban centers.

By the mid-1880s, fighting between Indians and whites in the Southwest ended, the reservation system was put in place, and federal statutes governing land distribution and citizenship had been enacted. Based on the theory that Indians ought to be assimilated into white society by weaning them from their tribal affiliations, measures were undertaken to turn Indians into property owners, provide them with public education, and win them over to Christianity (preferably Protestantism). Attempts to alter Indian landholding practices in the General Allotment Act of 1887 through dissolution of reservations were disruptive but failed; the rest of the government's Americanization program drove native religious celebrations and healing ceremonies underground, imposed bitterly resisted health measures, and removed school-aged children from their homes to boarding schools. Full citizenship was conferred on Indians, in part to reward their participation in World War I and in part to assure their religious freedom. With the Indian Reorganization Act of 1934, official policy reflected at least some awareness of "the damage done to the Indian's pride in the white man's attempt to eradicate his racial heritage," and the Indian Office encouraged native crafts and customs, communal landholding, and tribal government based on written constitutions.[48]

Whatever their heritage, for the vast majority of women everywhere, widowhood is one of the most traumatic crises in the life cycle. It is a multidimensional experience whose course and outcome vary widely depending on an array of personal, social, and institutional factors. Writing about widowhood has been one of the neglected topics in historical literature, even in the abundant new work in women's history, in part because so many variables shape the experience. It is a difficult subject for historians to treat without narrowing their focus to very discrete topics, thus limiting the potential for generalization. The essays that follow suggest several alternative approaches to recovering this history while at the same time enlarging our understanding of the Southwest and widowhood in the past. Using an interdisciplinary, cross-cultural perspective through individual case studies offers an opportunity to explore both similarities and differences as well as changes over time in this critical life stage. For the millions of women who are or will be widows, recalling the experience of those who preceded us is wrenching and sad, but also encouraging, and at times, truly ennobling.

NOTES

1. Herbert H. Hyman, *Of Time and Widowhood: Nationwide Studies of Enduring Effects* (Durham, N.C.: Duke University Press Policy Studies, 1983), 3.

2. Vivian C. Fox and Martin H. Quitt, *Loving, Parenting, and Dying: The Family Cycle in England and America, Past and Present* (New York: The Psychohistory Press, 1980), 51-61; Helena Z. Lopata, *Women as Widows: Support Systems* (New York: Elsevier, 1979), ch. 1.

3. Tamara K. Hareven, "Family Time and Historical Time," *Daedalus* 106 (1977):57-70.

4. Starr Roxanne Hiltz, "Widowhood: A Roleless Role," in Arlene Skolnick and Jerome H. Skolnick, eds., *Family in Transition*, 3d ed. (Boston: Little, Brown, 1980), 237; Lopata, *Women as Widows*, 13.

5. Lopata has studied urban widows in contemporary American society more extensively than any other scholar. *Women as Widows*, 32.

6. Lynn Caine, *Widow* (New York: William Morrow, 1974), 1.

7. This insight relies in part upon the unpublished commentary of Janet Roebuck, Department of History, University of New Mexico, Albuquerque, at the Western Social Science Association Meeting, Apr. 27-30, 1983, Albuquerque, for a panel on "Widowhood and Aging in the American Southwest."

8. For example, Christine H. Tompsett, "A Note on the Economic Status of Widows in Colonial New York," *New York History* 55 (1974):321*n*1 refers to the reinforcement, in several early works on colonial women and colonial law, of simple stereotypes of sought-after rich widows and of poor widows who along with orphans and cripples were objects of charity. Or see Charles Dana Gibson, *A Widow and Her Friends* (New York: R. H. Russell, 1901), a set of eighty-four drawings that depict an elegant young widow who moves from grieving and thoughts about entering a convent to a renewed social life that elicits gossip about her scandalously early emergence from mourning. Still other illuminating documents are a series of short stories in *Neal's Saturday Gazette* and *Godey's Lady Magazine* in the mid-nineteenth century. See Alice B. Neal, *The Widow Bedott Papers* (New York: Derby & Jackson, 1856), whose central character is a widow. A fruitful topic for future research would develop a fuller picture of community attitudes and prevalent stereotypes about widows during different time periods.

9. Lopata, *Women as Widows*, 8. Dorothy K. Stein, "Women to Burn: Suttee as a Normative Institution," *Signs* 4 (1978):253-68, and Vina Mazumdar, "Comment," ibid., 269-73, discuss the presence of this practice in other cultures, its origins and practice in India, and its significance for understanding the role of women and widows and the methods of controlling them in Hindu culture. For a fascinating discussion of the relation between grief and warfare, see Daniel K. Richter, "War and Culture: The Iroquois Experience," *William and Mary Quarterly*, 3d Ser., 4 (1983):528-59, esp. 528-59, esp. 528-37, on the "mourning-war"

and the practice of widows taking hostages and torturing them, or marrying them, as grief work.

10. See the sources cited in note 8, above.

11. The chapters by Alice Schlegel, Martha Loustaunau, and Deena González in this volume are instructive. Also see Nancie L. Gonzalez, *The Spanish-Americans of New Mexico: A Heritage of Pride* (Albuquerque: University of New Mexico Press, 1967), 58-63. Arizona's Hispanic Perspective," a research report prepared by the University of Arizona for Arizona's 38th Town Hall, Mar. 1981, 129-36, available in the University of Arizona library and its Special Collections Library, Tucson. Also useful on changes in the family is Edward H. Spicer and Raymond H. Thompson's *Plural Society in the Southwest* (Albuquerque: University of New Mexico Press, 1972), 276-77.

12. Carol J. Barrett, "Women in Widowhood: A Review Essay," *Signs* 2 (1977):856. There is an enormous literature on death and dying; a few useful studies on attitudes toward death in American culture include: David E. Stannard, ed., *Death in America* (Philadelphia: University of Pennsylvania Press, 1975); Stannard, *The Puritan Way of Death: A Study in Religion, Culture, and Social Change* (New York: Oxford University Press, 1977); Maris A. Vinovksis, "Angels' Heads and Weeping Willows: Death in Early America," in Tamara K. Hareven, ed., *Themes in the History of the Family* (Worcester, Mass.: American Antiquarian Society, 1978), 25-54, and Vinovksis, "The Influence of Death on the North American Family," World Conference on Records, Preserving Our Heritage, Aug. 12-15, 1980, Salt Lake City, Utah, Series 328, available at both the University of Arizona library and the Church of Jesus-Christ of Latter-day Saints, Salt Lake City. Also see Gerald F. Moran and Maris A. Vinovksis, "The Puritan Family and Religion: A Critical Reappraisal," *William and Mary Quarterly,* 31 Ser., 39 (1982):49-62. A sweeping overview of changing Western attitudes toward death is offered by Philippe Aries, *The Hour of Our Death* (New York: Alfred A. Knopf, 1981), esp. ch. 12, "Death Denied."

13. Unless otherwise stated, all statistics about marital status have been taken from U.S. Bureau of the Census, *Historical Statistics of the United States, Colonial Times to 1970. Part 1.* Bicentennial Ed. (Washington, D.C.: Government Printing Office, 1975), 20-21; and U.S. Bureau of the Census, Current Population Reports, Population Characteristics, Series P-20, No. 380, *Marital Status and Living Arrangements: March 1982* (Washington, D.C.: Government Printing Office, 1983), 8, hereafter cited as U.S. Bureau of the Census. The 1982 figures include all women (and all widows) 15 years and over. Lopata, *Women as Widows,* 34-43; Hiltz, "Widowhood," 238; Marilyn R. Block et al., *Uncharted Territory—Issues and Concerns of Women over 40* (College Park: University of Maryland Center on Aging, 1978), 115, 865.

14. In Elizabethan times, wealthy, often younger widows were pressured to remarry, and successive widowhood was not uncommon. See Fox and Quitt, *Loving,*

Parenting, and Dying, 49, 407-8. Where the sex ratio favored men and mortality was high among both sexes, similar remarriage patterns occurred. For a meticulous account of the legal status of women under conditions of demographic imbalance, see Lois G. Carr and Lorena A. Walsh, "The Planter's Wife: The Experience of White Women in Seventeenth-Century Maryland," *William and Mary Quarterly,* 3d Ser., 34 (1977):542-71. Also note the discussion in Edmund S. Morgan, *American Slavery, American Freedom: The Ordeal of Colonial Virginia* (New York: W. W. Norton, 1975), 164-67, for a characterization of Virginia women in the seventeenth century. Widowhood and successive remarriage permitted the concentration of wealth in female hands. Early Virginia was on the way to becoming an economic matriarchy or widowarchy," notes Morgan. A quantitative study of remarriage in later American history is provided by Susan Grigg, "Toward a Theory of Remarriage: A Case Study of Newburyport at the Beginning of the Nineteenth Century," *Journal of Interdisciplinary History* 8 (1977): 183-220.

15. This summary relies upon two suggestive articles: Janet Roebuck, "Grandma as Revolutionary: Elderly Women and Some Modern Patterns of Social Change," *International Journal of Aging and Human Development* 17 (1983): esp. 255-58, and Robert V. Wells, "Women's Lives Transformed: Demographic and Family Patterns in America, 1600-1970," in Carol Ruth Berkin and Mary Beth Norton, eds., *Women of America: A History* (Boston: Houghton Mifflin, 1979), 20-26. Wells focuses most closely on white couples but notes that black women never enjoyed marital stability to the same degree; rather, they experienced shorter marriages and earlier widowhood with dependent children more frequently than white women. In his more recent synthesis, *Revolutions in Americans' Lives: A Demographic Perspective on the History of Americans, Their Families, and Their Society* (Westport, Conn.: Greenwood Press, 1982), 43, 54-55, 157, 173, 246, Wells discusses widows and various aspects of widowhood. Also see Peter Uhlenberg, "Death and the Family," *Journal of Family History* 5 (1980):313-20, esp. 319; and the discussions in Donald M. Scott and Bernard Wishy, eds., *America's Families: A Documentary History* (New York: Harper & Row, 1982), 2-8; and Paul C. Glick, "Updating the Life Cycle of the Family," *Journal of Marriage and the Family* 39 (1977):5-13, esp. 6, Table I (7-9), and 11, for documentation on the "empty nest" phase of the life cycle among cohorts of mothers born in the eighty years between the 1880s and the 1950s.

16. Marital status was first specifically recorded by federal census-takers in 1880, but the results were not tabulated. Thus, the 1890 census data on marital status constitutes the baseline to which all statistics collected since are compared. Through painstaking counting and calculations from the manuscript schedules, marital status in 1880 can be tabulated for individual localities and states. In this volume Joyce D. Goodfriend, "The Struggle for Survival: Widows in Denver, 1880-1912," relies partly on analysis of the 1880 manuscript census. Prior to 1880, information about marriage was occasionally included in the census manuscript

schedules for different communities; historians have used these to make inferences and educated guesses, as from other types of records prior to the first federal census of 1790. A discussion of the methodological problems in studying widowhood posed by working with census materials before 1880 is provided herein by Deena González, "The Widowed Women of Santa Fe." These issues are also addressed by Goodfriend in "Sources and Methodologies for the Study of Widows in American History," the Sixth Berkshire Conference on the History of Women, Smith College, Northampton, Mass., June 3, 1984. Also see Conrad Taeuber and Irene B. Taeuber, *The Changing Population of the United States* (New York: John Wiley, 1958), 147.

17. U.S. Bureau of the Census.

18. In addition to widowhood, the major crises of old age include marital and sexual problems, retirement, sensory loss, chronic disease, pain, hospitalization, surgery, institutionalization, and dying. "They are difficult to face, especially if several occur simultaneously or closely follow one upon another" — as they often do. Robert N. Butler, *Why Survive? Being Old in America* (New York: Harper & Row, 1975), 418.

19. U.S. Bureau of the Census.

20. Ibid.

21. The author is grateful to Bette A. Ide for sharing a review of the literature about American Indian and Hispanic elderly widows in contemporary society, part of her study, "Coping and Health among Older Urban Widows," supported by the Department of Health and Human Services, National Institute on Aging.

22. The life expectancy of women in 1983 was 77.9 years compared with 70.3 for men; at the turn of the century, women outlived men by two years; by 2050, predictions are that women may live ten years longer. Robert N. Butler and Myrna Lewis, Keynote Address, American Medical Women's Association Annual Meeting, Nov. 11, 1983, Dearborn, Mich. See also Hiltz, "Widowhood," 238. One result: in 1982 there were 16.6 million women and only 10.7 million men over 65.

23. The Franklin quote is contained in Cora D. Willmarth, *Widows Grave and Otherwise* (N.d., n.p.), Bancroft Library, University of California, Berkeley. Also see, Fox and Quitt, *Loving, Parenting, and Dying,* 407-9; Laurel Thatcher Ulrich, *Good Wives: Image and Reality in the Lives of Women in Northern New England, 1650-1750* (New York: Alfred A. Knopf, 1982), 7, 38, 97.

24. In the United States, this is the first century in which a newborn child can expect to live out the full normal life cycle. Between 1900 and 1983, average life expectancy of Americans has increased 26 years — from 47 to 73 years — which almost equals the 29-year gain over the 5,000 years from the Bronze Age to 1900. This dramatic change reflects success in drastically reducing deaths in infancy, early childhood, and young adulthood from such major communicable diseases as tuberculosis, influenza, and pneumonia, killers of children over one year, and from gastroenteritis, the major cause of infant mortality in most societies around

1900. Consequently, these leading causes of death in the past have been replaced by the degenerative diseases associated with the aging process, including heart disease, cancer, and stroke as well as accidental injury. Louis Pasteur's germ theory of disease, which led to pasteurization and refrigeration of milk; successful campaigns by public health advocates around 1900 for proper sewage disposal, purified drinking water, sanitary food, and other reforms; and in the 1930s, medical developments including the discovery of sulfa, antibiotics, and other drugs; and the advancement of anesthesia and surgery were instrumental in this progress. While mortality rates for both sexes have declined substantially in the twentieth century, the rate of decline has been much sharper for females.

Though researchers continue to debate the proper weight to accord genetics and environment and the balance between them in explaining the remarkable longevity of women, current scientific argument attributes the differences more to sociocultural and health habits and environmental exposure than to genetic differences in the immune and hormonal systems of men and women. Perhaps as much as two-thirds or more of the difference in life expectancy between men and women may be due to such hazards as greater reliance by men on smoking and alcohol, exposure to carcinogens in the work environment, and hard-driving, stress-prone, competitive personalities than to genes, although the durability of the female body ought not to be underestimated. As women continue to enter the work force in substantial numbers and are subjected to similar conditions and as they adopt such habits as smoking with greater frequency, these figures might begin to change; recent statistics on increasing lung cancer deaths in women suggest this possibility. See Butler and Lewis, Keynote Address; Monroe Lerner, "When, Why, and Where People Die," in Edwin S. Schneidman, ed., *Death: Current Perspectives* (Palo Alto, Calif.: Mayfield Publishing, 1976), 138-61; Pamela T. Amoss and Stevan Harrell, eds., *Other Ways of Growing Old: Anthropological Perspectives* (Stanford, Calif.: Stanford University Press, 1981), xiii-xxi.

25. Carr and Walsh, "The Planter's Wife," 542-71, and Lorena S. Walsh, " 'Till Death Us Do Part': Marriage and Family in Seventeenth-Century Maryland," in Thad W. Tate and David L. Ammerman, eds., *The Chesapeake in the Seventeenth Century: Essays on Anglo-American Society* (Chapel Hill: University of North Carolina Press, 1979), 126-52.

26. Linda E. Speth, "Woman's Sphere: Role and Status of White Women in 18th-Century Virginia" (M.A. thesis, Utah State University, 1980), 43-61; Speth, "Southern Women and Probate Records: The Transfer of Property and Authority in Southside Virginia, 1735-1775," paper presented at Fifth Berkshire Conference on the History of Women, Vassar College, Poughkeepsie, N.Y., June 17, 1981; Speth, "More than Her 'Thirds': Wives and Widows in Colonial Virginia," *Women and History*, 4 (1982):5-41. I am grateful to Ms. Speth for clarifying certain issues raised in these manuscripts and for sharing them with me. Carol Berkin's introduction to the subject of women's status in "Women, Family, and Community in

Colonial America: Two Perspectives," *Women & History* (New York: Haworth Press, 1983), 1-3, is also useful. See, too, Marylynn Salmon, "Women and Property in South Carolina: The Evidence from Marriage Settlements, 1730 to 1830," *William and Mary Quarterly,* 3d Ser., 39 (1982):655-85, esp. 656, 659; and Salmon, *Women and the Law of Property in Early America* (Chapel Hill: University of North Carolina Press, 1986). For New York, see David E. Narrett, "Patterns of Inheritance and Family Life in Colonial New York, 1664-1775: A Comparative Perspective," paper presented at Conference on New Approaches to the History of Colonial and Revolutionary New York, New York Historical Society, May 20, 1983, and Tompsett, "Note on the Economic Status of Widows," 319-32, who questions the continued influence of Dutch customs and examines women's economic status through calculations of the value of widows' estates from colonial New York City tax lists. Lisa W. Waciega, "A 'Man of Business': The Widow of Means in Southeastern Pennsylvania, 1750-1850," *William and Mary Quarterly,* 3d Ser., 44 (1987):40-64, focuses on a later generation of propertied widows who improved their families' economic circumstances and provided effectively for their children.

27. John M. Faragher, "Old Women and Old Men in Seventeenth-Century Wethersfield, Connecticut," *Women's Studies* 4 (1976):11-31; Alexander Keyssar, "Widowhood in Eighteenth-Century Massachusetts: A Problem in the History of the Family," *Perspectives in American History* 8 (1974):83-119; also see James K. Somerville, "The Salem (Mass.) Woman in the Home, 1660-1770," *Eighteenth-Century Life* 1 (1974):11-14. For a procedure to rank individuals according to the relative likelihood of remarriage, see Grigg, "Toward a Theory of Remarriage," 183-220.

28. Though her intent was to compare the lives of several eighteenth-century women, Anne Firor Scott provides interesting insights on bereavement in her discussion of Eliza Lucas Pinckney's adaptation to widowhood. See "Self-Portraits: Three Women," in Richard Bushman, ed., *Uprooted Americans* (Boston: Little Brown, 1979), 43-76. Other brief glimpses of widows, including Pinckney, can be found in Mary Beth Norton, *Liberty's Daughters: The Revolutionary Experience of American Women, 1750-1800* (Boston: Little Brown, 1980), 132-38, 145-51, who also discusses widows' legal status and opportunities in the work force, and Catherine Clinton, *The Plantation Mistress: Woman's World in the Old South* (New York: Pantheon Books, 1982), 76-78, 129, 170-71.

29. Constance B. Schulz, "Revolutionary War Pension Applications: A Neglected Source for Social and Family History," *Prologue* 15 (1983):103-14. Examination of these applications should provide a myriad of details about the lives of ordinary women both before and after widowhood. The most substantive secondary work on veterans' pensions is William H. Glasson, *Federal Military Pensions in the United States* (New York: Oxford University Press, 1918). Also valuable is

Michel R. Dahlin, "From Poorhouse to Pension: The Changing View of Old Age in America, 1890-1929" (Ph.D. diss., Stanford University, 1983), 166-70, for a discussion of the military pension system, its expansion in 1890 and more explicitly in 1904 to include old-age disabilities, and its negligible, even negative, impact on public debate during the 1910s and 1920s over old-age pensions. An example of the importance of this source of support for wives, widows, widowed mothers, and dependent children in Massachusetts is provided in ibid., 169*n*7. Further information about mothers' pensions is available in Walter I. Trattner, *From Poor Law to Welfare State: A History of Social Welfare in America,* 2d ed. (New York: Free Press, 1979), 184-87; Mark H. Leff, "Consensus for Reform: The Mothers' Pension Movement in the Progressive Era," in Frank R. Breul and Steven J. Diner, eds., *Compassion and Responsibility: Readings in the History of Social Welfare Policy in the United States* (Chicago: University of Chicago Press, 1980), 244-64. Recent useful studies include Helena Z. Lopata and Henry P. Brehm, *Widows and Dependent Wives: From Social Problem to Federal Program* (New York: Praeger Publishers, 1986), 1-48; W. Andrew Achenbaum, *Social Security: Visions and Revisions* (Cambridge: Cambridge University Press, 1986), 1-37.

30. Carole Haber, "The Old Folks at Home: The Development of Institutionalized Care for the Aged in Nineteenth-Century Philadelphia," *Pennsylvania Magazine of History and Biography* 101 (1977):240-57. See also Haber, *Beyond Sixty-Five: The Dilemma of Old Age in America's Past* (Cambridge: Cambridge University Press, 1983), 82-107; Brian Gratton, "Labor Markets and Old Ladies' Homes," in Elizabeth W. Markson, ed., *Older Women: Issues and Prospects* (Lexington, Mass.: Lexington Books, 1983), 121-49. Admission to these homes was usually restricted on the basis of social status, ethnicity, religious affiliation, or occupation. On the plight of widowed women, many of them elderly, in Pittsburgh, see "Aging and Widowhood," a chapter in a manuscript by S. J. Kleinberg, "The Shadow of the Mills" (copy in my possession).

31. David Hackett Fischer, *Growing Old in America,* the Bland-Lee Lectures Delivered at Clark University (Oxford: Oxford University Press, 1978); W. Andrew Achenbaum, *Old Age in the New Land: The American Experience since 1790* (Baltimore: Johns Hopkins University Press, 1978). Achenbaum's *Shades of Gray: Old Age, American Values, and Federal Policies since 1920* (Boston: Little Brown, 1983), 3-47, repeats this neglect in his application of modernization theory to an understanding of public policy toward the aging.

32. Haber, *Beyond Sixty-Five,* 5.

33. Ibid., 120-24, 174; Dahlin, "From Poorhouse to Pension," 3, 7, 133-35; W. Andrew Achenbaum, "The Obsolescence of Old Age in America, 1865-1914," *Journal of Social History* 8 (1974):48-62.

34. Roebuck, "Grandma." Also useful in showing how attitudes toward the elderly were played out in the transformation of poor laws to pensions is Dahlin's "From Poorhouse to Pension."

35. Frederick Jackson Turner, "The Significance of the Frontier in American

History," in Ray Allen Billington, ed., *Frontier and Section: Selected Essays of Frederick Jackson Turner* (Englewood Cliffs, N.J.: Prentice-Hall, 1961), 37-62. Also see Billington, *America's Frontier Heritage* (Albuquerque: University of New Mexico Press, 1974), where he reviews and evaluates the validity of Turner's thesis. David M. Potter, *People of Plenty: Economic Abundance and the American Character* (Chicago: University of Chicago Press, 1954), in an essay entitled "Abundance and the Frontier Hypothesis," part of this collection of integrated essays, distills from Turner a suggestion of the frontier as a source of economic abundance, critiques the limitations of the thesis, and enlarges the concept showing the critical relevance of abundance in the formation of American character.

36. In Barbara Welter, ed., *The Women Question in American History* (Hinsdale, Ill.: Dryden Press, 1973), 117-32.

37. Some of the notable publications about women in the West to appear in recent years include: John Mack Faragher, *Women and Men on the Overland Trail* (New Haven: Yale University Press, 1979); Joyce D. Goodfriend and Dona K. Flory, "Women in Colorado before the First World War," *Colorado Magazine* 53 (1976):201-28; Julie Roy Jeffrey, *Frontier Women: The Trans-Mississippi West, 1840-1880* (New York: Hill and Wang, 1979); Sandra L. Myres, *Westering Women and the Frontier Experience, 1800-1915* (Albuquerque: University of New Mexico Press, 1982); Glenda A. Riley, "Images of the Frontierswoman: Iowa as a Case Study," *Western Historical Quarterly* 8 (1977):189-202; Lillian Schlissel, *Women's Diaries of the Westward Journey* (New York: Schocken Books, 1982); T. A. Larson, "Women's Role in the American West," *Montana: The Magazine of Western History* 24 (1974):2-11; Beverly J. Stoeltje, "A Helpmate for Man Indeed: The Image of the Frontier Woman," *Journal of American Folklore* 88 (1975):25-41; Paula A. Treckel, "An Historiographical Essay: Women on the American Frontier," *Old Northwest* 1 (1975):339-404. Less has been written about minority women in the West, but a start has been made with Sue Armitage, Theresa Banfield, and Sarah Jacobus, "Black Women and Their Communities in Colorado," *Frontiers* 2 (1977):45-51; Lawrence B. de Graaf, "Race, Sex, and Region: Black Women in the American West, 1850-1920," *Pacific Historical Review* 49 (1980):285-313; Janet Lecompte, "The Independent Women of Hispanic New Mexico, 1821-1846," *Western Historical Quarterly* 12 (1981):17-35; Beverly Trulio, "Anglo-American Attitudes toward New Mexican Women," *Journal of the West* 12 (1973):229-39.

38. Joan M. Jensen and Darlis A. Miller, "The Gentle Tamers Revisited: New Approaches to the History of Women in the American West," *Pacific Historical Review* 49 (1980):173-213.

39. Schlissel, *Women's Diaries,* 15, 42, 153-54.

40. The predominant sources for this collection are drawn from Arizona, New Mexico, Utah, and Colorado, although occasionally primary materials from California are also used. Setting the geographical and political boundaries of "the Southwest" is an invitation to argument; few scholars agree, but the range of

alternatives include Texas, Oklahoma, Nevada, California, and Kansas in addition to the four states in this book. For an interesting discussion of this issue, see John H. Parry, "Plural Society in the Southwest: A Historical Comment," in Spicer and Thompson, eds., *Plural Society in the Southwest,* 299-320.

41. David J. Weber, *The Mexican Frontier, 1821-1846: The American Southwest under Mexico* (Albuquerque: University of New Mexico Press, 1982), xi. Weber's elegant synthesis of "the dark age in the historiography of the Southwest" (xii) examines the history of the borderlands region by viewing events from south, not north, of the border. That American usurpation was "an inevitable phase in the expansion of a virile and superior people" reflects the dominant view in most quarters of the United States at the time of the Mexican War and since, although the war has always held an ambiguous position in the American conscience. See T. Harry Williams, *The History of American Wars: From 1745 to 1918* (New York: Alfred A. Knopf, 1981), 144-85.

42. For a brief summary of these events, see Thomas A. Bailey, *A Diplomatic History of the American People,* 6th ed. (New York: Appleton-Century-Crofts, 1958), 250-66.

43. Howard Roberts Lamar, *The Far Southwest, 1846-1912: A Territorial History* (New Haven: Yale University Press, 1966), 1.

44. Odie B. Faulk, *Land of Many Frontiers: A History of the American Southwest* (New York: Oxford University Press, 1968), 3.

45. Lamar, *Far Southwest,* 2-3.

46. Ibid., 4-5.

47. Gerald D. Nash, *The American West in the Twentieth Century: A Short History of an Urban Oasis* (Albuquerque: University of New Mexico Press, 1977), 18-20.

48. Faulk, *Land of Many Frontiers,* 218. For a useful summary, see David Lavender, *The Southwest* (New York: Harper & Row, 1980), 168-208.

1

Widowhood and Autonomy in the Native-American Southwest

SARAH M. NELSON

Native American widowhood is marked by substantial autonomy for the widow, who makes most of her own choices in the continuation of her life. The contrast with the southwestern settlers is marked in this regard. But it is also interesting to examine the differences among the southwestern Indian groups. This chapter examines the hypothesis that the more autonomy women enjoy in a given society, the fewer economic and social penalties they will encounter upon being widowed.

The argument herein is based on cross-cultural comparisons. Since marriage in some form is practiced in all human societies, the dissolution of marriage by the death of one partner is an event that occurs in all societies. The way a particular culture chooses to deal with this problem—and, indeed, to what extent and to whom it is a problem—is related to other aspects of that culture. Before presenting the methodology of the study, however, it is necessary to discuss the present theoretical understanding of widowhood, to make clear the reasons for my selection of particular variables.

From an anthropological perspective, widowhood is critically in need of both data and theory. In spite of extensive ethnographies, hard data on widowhood in non-Western cultures is difficult to obtain. Until about the last decade anthropologists studied women's roles largely in relation to men—as mothers, wives, and daughters. When women ceased to be wives, they were perceived as peripheral to the social structure and so of little interest. A new focus on women's lives poses new questions from societal and individual perspectives. And widowhood is one problem that requires a solution both for the individual and for the society. The death of one partner in a marriage leaves the survivor with labor deficiencies in the necessary economic activities that are customarily performed by members of that sex. In this sense, men and women are both deprived by the death of a spouse, but not necessarily equally, even if it may be more or less easy to find a stand-in for these activities, for example, a son to plow the field, a daughter to cook the meals or grind the corn.

Loss of consortium is another problem for the individual and for the culture as well. The degree to which individuals of either sex are free to create their own sexual liaisons affects the degree to which the culture is threatened by the possibility of "unlicensed" sexuality. Especially where the paternity of children is important, female sexuality is likely to be closely guarded.

Care of minor children is a concern of the society. If children are defined as belonging to the kin group of the surviving parent, there is little problem, but where the surviving parent is not a natal member of the group to which the children belong, some arrangement for their care is necessary. The extent to which children are seen as "owned" by their kin group affects the kinds of solutions found. For the individual widow, there are the twin problems of obtaining economic support for minor children and keeping them in her household.

Finally, marriage is often seen as a relationship not only between two people, but also between families. When the marriage is broken by death, there may be considerable advantage to the two families, the children of the marriage, and the survivor in customs that allow the links to remain.

In general, the problem of widows per se is greater than the problem of widowers, due to the asymmetrical nature of most cultures. Where women have considerably less economic and social power than men, they are at a greater disadvantage as widows, especially when a woman's position depends on her ability to influence her husband. In societies where a woman may acquire power through influencing her son or her brother, she has fewer personal problems as a widow. Where women's sexuality is seen as dangerous to men, a widow is a particularly potent threat. In general, then, widowhood is different for women than for men, especially when the roles within the marriage and the larger society are different—and unequal—for the two sexes.

A common solution to the problems of widows/widowers is the levirate or the sororate: a same-sex sibling of the deceased is brought in as a replacement. In levirate, a widow is expected to marry one of her deceased husband's brothers, or another man of the same clan, as either a primary or a secondary wife. The man's kinship group recognizes its obligation to provide another husband for the woman and a substitute father for her children. The sororate is the mirror image of the levirate: a man is expected to marry one of his wife's sisters in the event of his wife's death. In both cases the families remain related, and the children continue to be cared for by a relative who has a stake in their upbringing.

Some cultures have found the problem of widows so critical that extreme solutions have been created, which eliminate the status of widowhood (for women) altogether. There are logically only two possible ways to prevent the continuation of widowhood: one is to insist that the widow follow her husband in death, and the other is to require the widow to remarry immediately. Though both solutions for women are known ethnographically, there are no known cultures that make such demands on widowers, demonstrating the inequality of men and women in a most graphic way.

The right to make decisions on one's own behalf has been called "autonomy."[1] In considering women's roles, this term is preferable to concepts of "power" or "dominance," which imply the imposition of one person's choices upon others. The hypothesis here is that in any culture the more autonomy women have, the fewer economic and social penalties will they suffer at widowhood. In cultures around the world an autonomy continuum exists: from societies in which women are considered to be the property of their husbands or their husbands' families (and therefore have no autonomy) to those societies in which women make the major decisions about their own lives while their husbands are alive and expect to continue to do so after his death. Louise Lamphere has suggested that women have their share of authority within the domestic group in societies that do not separate the domestic and political spheres,[2] which is another way of framing the issue but with a different set of variables.

Treating autonomy as a single item that can be ranked along a scale is a convenience for analysis, not a description of reality. A woman's autonomy may vary according to her age and the ages of her children. She may have more autonomy in some subsystems of her culture, and less in others. There is no single trait that defines autonomy, and the complexity of the concept needs to be borne in mind to understand some of the differences among the rather similar groups in the American Southwest.

The selection of a sample or a controlled comparison of several southwestern cultures was made primarily from those that have the largest amount of available data. Of those groups a subset was chosen to provide maximum contrast in economic and social variables. This procedure prevented the formal testing of the hypothesis, but the results nevertheless illuminated interrelationships among several cultural variables as they affect widowhood. These variables are:

1. Social System: A girl's right to select or reject her first husband; a woman's right to select subsequent husbands; the control of a woman over her own sexuality; the possibility of divorce at the wife's instigation; children remaining with the mother in the case of divorce.
2. Economic System: A women's right to inherit property as her own; a woman has and retains control over the means of production, household produce, and her dwelling.
3. Political System: A woman's right to hold extradomestic positions of authority; women's recognition to contribute to selection of others for extradomestic positions of authority.
4. Ideological System: Women's participation in ceremonies (either with men or in groups of women); autonomy for heroines of folk lore; all or some powerful deities are seen as female.

I selected the Navajo, Apache, Papago, and Zuni as having the most pertinent and reliable data for the years 1848 to 1939. These groups, representing differences in social structure, in subsistence systems, and in the size and distribution of housing units, thus provided a living laboratory for examining the effects of these four variables on the nature of widowhood.

By its nature, classic cross-cultural study is ahistorical. Yet some important changes have occurred as cultures have interacted, willingly and unwillingly, with the mainstream American culture. I first describe these cultures in the "ethnographic present," as if they were timeless and continuous. This contrary-to-fact assumption is necessary to hold some variables constant, to see the target variables more clearly. Ethnographic information for each culture is treated as if all cultures had been studied contemporaneously, which, of course, is not the case.

The Southwestern Tribes—A Brief Overview

The ancestors of the southwestern tribes have lived in the region from several centuries to several millennia. Archaeologists date the earliest inhabitants to around 8500 B.C., and their descendants are probably among those still in the Southwest. Following Edward Spicer, I have categorized these groups by living arrangements and subsistence patterns into villagers; the rancheria people; agricultural bands; and nonagricultural bands.[3]

Villagers are characterized mainly by their density of settlement. Closely packed houses arranged around a communal open space is the aboriginal settlement pattern, although a few groups have dispersed dwellings in several settlements. The Spanish gave these people the name Pueblos. The Western Pueblos include the Hopi[4] and Zuni, while those people along the Rio Grande are known as the Eastern Pueblos. I discuss here the Cochiti and Laguna Pueblos. The present homeland of the Pueblo peoples is dotted with prehistoric ruins, the forerunners of the present villages. Irrigation farming, especially the growing of maize as a storable crop, allow these people to live in dense aggregates. Through centuries of experimentation, the Pueblos have adapted to an arid land unpromising for subsistence agriculture.

The Pueblo people are matrilineal (membership in a lineage is acquired through one's mother) and matrilocal (a newly married couple lives in the household or camp of the wife's family), although the extent to which each Pueblo presently engages in these practices is variable. Multigenerational extended families live together in dwellings owned by women. The land also tends to be owned by matrilineages, and the harvested crops are at the disposal of women.

Little political organization exists beyond the village level. Within the villages, men tend to hold the formal political and religious positions. Religious activities center around the kiva, a structure in which unmarried men may sleep, and which may be a gathering place for men's activities. The ideational systems include female deities, and women folk heroes are common. A balance between men and women characterizes these cultures, and women can make decisons about their own lives within the framework of family approval.

The rancheria people (a word meaning dispersed settlements) include the Pima and Papago of southern Arizona as well as some groups who live along the Colorado River. I use the Papago as representative of this type. They may be descended from peoples in the region who had highly developed art forms and irrigated crops as early as 500 A.D. When first encountered by the Spanish, the Papago lived near water sources and planted a few crops; sometimes they moved seasonally to a different location. The dwellings of a few related families were grouped together, and fields were often farmed in common. These people were patrilineal and patrilocal and practiced sororal polygyny—the marriage of two or more sisters to the same husband.

The agricultural bands are represented by the Navajo and Western Apache, branches of the Southern Athapascans who first came to the Southwest more than 500 years ago. When the Spanish entered the area, they recognized the Navajo and Apache as separate but related peoples. These tribes planted crops but left them untended or in the care of a few people, while the women moved elsewhere to gather and the men to hunt. These groups are matrilineal, and polygyny is possible as well. The Navajo have acquired many traits from their neighbors, the Pueblos, while the Apache are believed to be more like their precontact ancestors.

Since no specific information about widows in nonagricultural bands was found, they were omitted from the analysis.

Navajo

The matrilineal and matrilocal Navajos[5] are an excellent example of a culture in which a widow traditionally incurred few economic or social penalties as a consequence of the death of a husband. The social structure is organized around extended family groups that live together in a camp. Although each nuclear family has a separate domicile (a hogan), many of the daily activities take place in the spaces between the hogans, and virtually all economic activities except crafts (weaving and silversmithing) are co-operative enterprises.

The ideal pattern of camp occupants includes a woman and her husband; their daughters and daughters' husbands and children; and their unmarried sons. The system is flexible enough to allow for varied circumstances, however. For instance, if there are no daughters, a son and his wife might join his parents' camp. Separate camps can be set up by a couple as they begin to be economically independent, but the couple continues to be tied to the family group for some economic and ceremonial activities. This larger group is often called the "outfit," a group that acts together in all matters that concern the local group socially (as in the regulation of marriage) or economically (inheritance of property). The focal person of each camp is the woman to whom all other members were related, and the outfit is also composed of matrilineally related kin. A husband's children by a previous marriage have no rights in the camp or the outfit, but any of the woman's children might belong to the outfit and live in her camp, although her sons are more likely to live with their wives' families.

After the death of the woman through whom the camp members are related, the camp composition changes. Siblings tend to split off into separate camps, a process that might have begun earlier but becomes complete at this stage. The surviving widower may live with one of his children or with members of his own matrilineage. Distantly related people can become members of a camp in various ways. Children or the elderly who lost their original household through the death of other members are either taken care of by some group or an older child might be sent to live with grandparents or a childless couple as a helper.

Marriage is a concern of all members of both families, and maternal uncles of both the boy and girl have an especial right to an opinion; but the girl's parents with whom the couple will live are the most influential. Although a girl might be steered in a certain direction, she is never forced to marry against her will. The wealth of the boy's family is certainly of interest: a mother once urged her daughter to ask a certain boy to dance, saying, "His mother has 2,000 sheep."[6]

It often happens that several marriages take place among two unrelated sibling sets, uniting the two groups even more closely than a single marriage does. Plural marriage usually involves sisters married to the same man, and when a woman is widowed, she is expected to find a new husband from the same outfit as the deceased.

The existence of polygyny is often cited as a degradation of women and is used to demonstrate women's low status. The Navajo do not connect polygyny to such concepts. A woman might ask her husband to marry her younger sister: from the point of view of the women, it is a companionable, work-sharing arrangement, and one man is considered sufficient for a household. Alice Schlegel has suggested that sororal polygyny may even enhance female autonomy, since the sisters can present a united front.[7] It is also possible for a man to take his wife's daughter from a previous marriage as a secondary wife. The mother-daughter bond is even stronger than that of sisters, so the same argument for female autonomy could be made in this case as well. According to Louise Lamphere, a Navajo woman's interests never conflict with those of her near female relatives.[8]

Divorce is easy and can be initiated by either party. The children remain with their mother, and the man returns to his maternal kin. Both are likely to remarry. The social structure thus favors women's autonomy to a large degree, although the idea of a "woman's place" is still embedded in the larger family.

The traditional economic system also works to the advantage of women. Women hold property in their own right. They control the agricultural land used by the outfit and in addition may own livestock as personal property. Their assets are never merged with their husbands' as joint property, and cash women earn in any way is considered to be entirely theirs, to dispose of as they wish.

The usual pattern of inheritance of land is from mother to daughters, who inherit equally. Land can go to a son in the absence of daughters, but on his death a dispute regarding the disposition of that land might arise between his children and the members of his matrilineage. The important point is that daughters do not merely have the right to inherit, but the expectation of receiving most if not all of their mother's property. Girls might expect some inheritance of livestock from their maternal uncles as well. Under the same set of rules, on the other hand, a widow has little claim on her husband's livestock, which reverts to his own matrilineage. It appears, however, that far more of the livestock in any camp belongs to the matrilineage than to the in-marrying males.

Although women are clearly socially and economically advantaged, there is some disagreement among ethnographers regarding their place in the political arena. In the traditional society, there was little formal organization above the level of the outfit, thus the part of the culture that might be labeled "political" was restricted to the affairs of the extended family. According to Lamphere, "Navajo parents or a widowed mother [did] not impose their decisions on other households."[9]

Ethnographers' views on the assignment of domestic authority differ, even within the same monograph. Clyde Kluckhohn and Dorothea Leighton inform us that "woman is supreme in the hogan,"[10] but "formally, from the Navajo angle, the 'head of the family' is the husband. Whether he is in fact varies with his personality, intelligence, and prestige. Navajo women are often energetic and shrewish. By vigorous use of their tongues they frequently reverse or nullify decisions made by their men. The Indian Service has made the mistake of dealing too exclusively with men . . . only to wonder or be annoyed when agreements reached with them are not carried out."[11] The pejorative use of the adjective "shrewish" reveals a bias against assertive women on the part of the ethnographers. According to Gary Witherspoon, women conceptually hold the authority, but their husbands exercise it.[12] Yet another view is that the "resource controller," who distributed the male labor in the extended family unit, was usually the oldest male in the outfit.[13] Women are not excluded from this role, although most women resource controllers are widows without grown sons or sons-in-law. Although this is sometimes seen as a form of "real" male dominance in a matrilineal society, it is structurally analogous to the position of mother-in-law in patrilineal extended family households, where there is no suggestion of "female dominance" in the culture.

The symbolic system favors women, especially but not exclusively as mothers. The most revered of the traditional deities is Changing Woman, who is more important than her husband, the Sun. Only girls have puberty rites, although both boys and girls are initiated into the tribe with a special ceremony.

Within the traditional Navajo system, women suffer only minor economic or social penalties when their husbands die. They continue to live in the same place, with their consanguineal kin nearby. Land and livestock that had been theirs are still theirs, although the husband's livestock reverts to his matrilineal relatives. The widow can marry again if she wishes—and is likely to do so unless she is quite old, because a minimum economic unit requires a man and a woman. If adult sons-in-law or sons can fulfill this economic function, she might not remarry. A high degree of autonomy for women among the Navajo correlates well with a lack of social and economic penalties.

Western Apache

The Western Apache[14] are distant relatives of the Navajo, and the traditional cultures of both were similar. The Apache are also matrilineal and matrilocal. Once settled on reservations, the home base became a combination of farmland, which was owned by the matrilineage, and a cluster of houses, each of which belonged to a family unit within the matrilineage.

Girls are free to select their own husbands, but the family, especially the mother, also has a voice in the matter. Like the Navajo, sometimes sisters or other close matrilineal kin might share a husband: "In former times, a man might have more than one wife . . . if he could support them,"[15] but the concept of support appears to be inappropriate here, since both men and women contribute labor to the household and have their appointed tasks. Plural marriage also takes place through the levirate and sororate, if the required substitute mate is already married.

Women own not only the land but also the produce of the land. The stores are theirs to dispose of at will. They also own the dwellings and can ask their husbands to leave. Girls inherit equally with boys, and children can inherit from their father as well as their mother. Land and cattle are the most important part of an estate, while tools, clothing, and adornments are destroyed or buried with their owner.

Western Apache women are more explicitly given scope in the political arena than are Navajo women. The founding couple of a settlement is considered head woman and head man, and each controls the activities of the adults of the same sex. Above this level are women chiefs, whose authority extends beyond their own family group. Although they are usually married to male chiefs, the position is nevertheless an achieved one, in which the incumbent is expected to be wealthy, industrious, and generous as well as possessing the ability to lead. A woman chief has equal rights to speak at chief's councils.

Girls' puberty rites emphasize the importance of women in Apache society. In other ceremonies, too, even those surrounding the usually masculine pursuit of raiding, women play an important role.

A woman's sexuality is not entirely her own. An adulterous wife or a promiscuous widow could have her nose cut by her husband or his family. James L. Haley paints a rather different picture, reporting that young widows and divorcees were called "bizhahn," and at specific ceremonies were expected to "strip almost naked and dance lewdly," which was followed by a "lusty romp."[16]

Widowhood means certain expected behaviors. As signs of respect for her deceased husband's family, a widow is expected to cut her hair, wear old clothes, and eschew social functions. A widow's mourning lasts from one to four years; a widower's, six months to a year.

A widow without children lives with her parents or, in their absence, with other close kin. A widow can live with adult married children. A widow with small children has difficulty without a man to perform customary male tasks, such as preparing land for planting, and needs to remarry or join another household. She is under a strong obligation to marry one of her former husband's brothers or cousins, and only if none of them comes forward within a year is she free to look elsewhere. The children remain with the widow whether or not she remarries into her deceased husband's clan.

The elderly continue to be important and contributing members of the society as long as their health allows. One woman was recorded as gathering and roasting mescal, a somewhat strenuous occupation, until she was past ninety. As the elderly lose their strength, they shift to tasks that can be accomplished within the camp, such as crafts and childcare. Persons in their dotage are housed in a separate but nearby structure. Though they are fed and clothed, they generally receive less desirable food and clothing than other members of the family. Before the Apaches became sedentary, old people unable to walk or ride were abandoned when the camp was moved.

In many ways the Western Apache women have a great deal of autonomy and suffer few penalties as widows. Although they have more scope for political power than the Navajo, their sexuality is more controlled, being perceived as belonging to their husbands and their husbands' matrilineages.

Zuni

The Zuni[17] are also traditionally organized on the matrilineal principle, with extended matrilocal households. It is especially notable that men return to the houses of their mothers or sisters for important religious occasions. Although individual males might own specific fields, the harvested crops belong exclusively to women. A man is not even permitted to enter the storeroom of the household where he lives. The fields are inherited by daughters, even when they are owned by men. Vegetable plots and fruit trees always belong to women, who are responsible for tending them. Sheep, introduced by the Spaniards, are owned by men and inherited in the male line.

Women's ceremonial importance is not as great among the Zuni as among the Navajo and Apaches, but women can become members of the curing societies, which stage many of the ceremonies. The Autumn Harvest Festival, the most important in the ceremonial cycle, is dedicated to the female ancestors, and the "corn maidens" are important deities.

A widowed or divorced woman keeps her children and remains in her residence; the widower or divorced man has to return to his maternal relatives. A woman's new husband acts as father to her children.

The ceremonial mourning period is short—four days. Rituals are the same whether the surviving spouse is male or female. Fasting and purification rituals are required, including scattering black corn meal and taking emetics. The personal property of the deceased is burned or buried, not inherited.

Old people have a high status. The aged help in the education of the children and are especially valued as storytellers, for stories carry morals and folk history important in the education of every child.

Widows in Zuni society generally have few problems. Although the sheep that had belonged to her husband now belong to another household, subsistence is based on agriculture. Her sons, who inherited their father's sheep, see that she does not lack for meat and wool. For the young widow, remarriage is easy and expected. An older widow is free to remarry if she wishes, but if she does not, her place in the famly is secure, with a high status both as a woman and as an older person.

Papago

The Papago[18] are my only example of a patrilineal tradition. Groups of patrilineally related families live in villages, with each domicile inhabited by a nuclear family or another convenient grouping. Each household has its own kitchen and storehouse, but meals are often shared. Either the women cook in rotation for all the local households, or each sends gifts of cooked food daily to the other households. Often these groups of related families consist of a founding pair, their sons, and their sons' families. However, widowed daughters and their children or even kin of the founding wife can also join the group, depending on convenience or necessity.

Land is the major item of inheritance, and before an extensive system of wells was installed on the reservation in the 1930s, land near water was of great importance. Rights to land use are inherited by sons from their fathers, but in the absence of sons, daughters use the land. For example, a small village was reported to have been populated in about 1860 by two sisters and their descendants. The women had no surviving brothers, so they had a right to the land that their father had farmed. One woman's husband was still alive, and he and their five sons worked their share of the land. The other woman was a widow with two sons, each of whom had separate households, and one married daughter, in whose household she lived. Her two sons and son-in-law worked her share. The land was also used by a man not related to the original owner—one of the inheritors' husband's brother's son. In another example, a widow kept the land her husband had inherited even after she remarried. Thus, although the Papago are patrilineal, family arrangements are a matter of convenience.

Women do not have a choice of marriage mates, either for first or subsequent marriages. A father finds his daughter a husband, and if she does not like the man, she can only run away. For this behavior she would probably be beaten by her father or brothers and sent back to her husband. A widow returns to live with her family until they can find her another husband. Small children and daughters go with her, but older sons stay in their father's village.

Plural marriages are common, and a form of the levirate in which a younger brother of the deceased is expected to marry the widow is usually enforced. An informant told of a man in the late nineteenth century who was married to four women. Three of the wives were sisters. The eldest sister was married to the man first, followed by the third sister. The middle sister, when widowed, came to the village to join her mother. The mother, also a widow, was living with her married eldest daughter. The second sister then married the common husband. Each sister lived in her own dwelling with her children. The fourth wife was not related to these women, but as the widow of a classificatory brother of the common husband, she became an obligatory wife. As she was quite old, she remained in her home village. The husband performed his obligations to her by sending gifts of food.

After the father's death, his personal property (including the house) is destroyed or buried. This forces any adult children who had lived in the dwelling to create new households and requires the widow to join another household as a dependent unless or until she can remarry.

Widows are thus thrown into a new situation by the demise of their spouse. This is underlined by the mourning ritual, which demands that the widow cut her hair and wear "nothing but a breechclout and [go] unpainted for a year, after which she might marry again." Members of her husband's family or her own patrilineage are responsible for her care.

Autonomy and Widowhood Penalties

With this background, the "widow problem," from the point of view of the individual and from a societal perspective, can now be examined. That the more autonomy a woman has within a culture, the fewer economic and social penalties she suffers as a widow has been borne out in a general way by the preceding data.

Among the patrilineal Papagos women have little autonomy in contrast with the matrilineal societies where women form the basic kinship tie and can usually participate in all of the major decisions of their lives. In most cases a girl could select her own husband and divorce him if she found she had not chosen wisely. She owned her own dwelling after marriage, and her children stayed with her to adulthood under all circumstances. Her daughters were likely to remain nearby even as adults. In terms of economic autonomy, women were likely to control both the means of production and the produce. In addition to implements and adornments, women could own three kinds of property: land, animals, and dwellings. Ownership of land was always contingent upon use, and land was never sold. Rights in land were usufructuary and dependent on lineage rights. Women owned the land in a matrilineal society—and men in a patrilineal one—but in both cases a good deal of flexibility could accommodate abnormal circumstances. Ownership of dwellings also depended on lineality. Residences could not be sold, and ownership defined the right to continue to occupy the dwelling.

Only animals were seen as individually owned, and in no case was this ownership exclusively female: Papago and Zuni emphasized male ownership of animals; Apache and Navajo allowed for ownership and inheritance by either sex.

Social penalties, while not severe in any of these groups, were greater in the case of the Papago. In that society a woman had to leave her home at her husband's death. Her remarriage was controlled by his kinship group or, in default of this, by males in her natal family. An Apache woman's behavior was monitored by her husband's kin, and they had the right to deface her if they deemed her behavior improper. The form of punishment—nose cutting—may have diffused from other groups of Plains Indians in which the status of women was lower, but that they did not invent it does not explain why it was found acceptable in this matrilineal culture. Among the Navajo and most of the Pueblo a woman's sexuality was largely her own business, although discretion was usually preferred.

In the matrilineal cultures there was often no change in the widow's economic condition at her husband's death, except that his herds would be reclaimed by his matrilineage and his labor might be missed. The household generally continued much as it had. Papago widows, on the other hand, lost their major means of support and had to depend on relatives for sustenance.

From a societal perspective, the problems created by widowhood include (1) the need for another male to perform the male labor roles for the widow; (2) provision for the widow's sexuality—or prohibition of it; (3) continuing care of minor children from the marriage; and (4) continuation of the relationship between the kinship groups established by the marriage.

The first problem was solved by the widow's remarriage, by the widow's father or brothers taking over these roles, by her husband's brothers providing for her, or by her own sons or daughters' husbands undertaking these tasks. The solution selected depended on the social structure of the Indian group and the age of the widow. In large families it was likely that an appropriate male would be available. It must be remembered that the concept of support of women by men is ethnocentric—in most non-Western cultures this support is mutual. Choices that give a widow the most autonomy are either the ability to select a new mate for herself or to rely on her own kin. She had the least autonomy when she was dependent on her husband's family.

A widow's sexuality was either constrained or unconstrained. In matrilineal societies, where all children belong to the mother's family, there was generally little restraint. In patrilineal societies, however, a widow's sexual activity was seen as a slight upon her deceased husband's family, and any resulting children had no secure place in the system.

There were also only two choices for the care of minor children—either they remained with their mother, wherever she was, or they were claimed by the father's kinship group. In matrilineal societies there was no conflict—the children belonged to their mother's lineage. In patrilineal societies small children tended to stay with their mother, although older sons could go with the patrilineage, which was the solution of the Papago. Daughters married out in any case, so their affiliation was less critical, but the loyalty of the sons had to be cultivated.

The breaking of an established relationship between kin groups brought about by the marriage and dissolved by the death of one partner can be a problem in any social structure. Thus both matrilineal and patrilineal societies used levirate and sororate. These constrained individual choices, but provided automatic solutions to other problems.

Changes in Southwestern Cultures

Various changes have occurred within Native-American groups since they were subordinated to a culture organized quite differently. For the southwestern tribes, the impact of Spanish culture was variable, but none was left unchanged. The cultures have been described, in any case, essentially as they were after the reservation system had been established and the federal government had acknowledged some responsibility toward these Indians. By the time anthropologists arrived, they had to use informants who remembered the "old days."

Agents of change in the early reservation times included missionaries, traders, schoolteachers, and Indian agents. Probably the most profound changes, at least for the women, were in the political and economic realms; both, however, had social consequences. One type of political change that affected Indian groups as soon as they had to deal with the American government resulted from the "take-me-to-your-leader" syndrome. The American government always assumed that these groups had a leader and that the leader was male. This expectation created problems when a tradition of coercive male leadership was lacking.

The American government also assumed that males were heads of household and that only males owned land. This would have been merely humorous in the matrilineal Southwest if the result had not been to create a new male status of head of household. For example, a survey of Cochiti

Pueblo[19] in 1922 lists male heads of household in all but five of fifty-two households. The female-headed households included two women said to be living alone and three women who had adult sons living with them. All instances of households containing both wife and husband were listed under the husband's name. The households headed by women can be contrasted to eighteen families with a male head but no wife.[20] Shifting land policies for Indians also affected the traditional matrilineal land ownership. A series of land applications filed at Laguna Pueblo in 1912 show that women's applications had to be as heads of household—and only widows were recognized as heads.[21]

Official Bureau of Indian Affairs policies regarding headship of households, ownership of land, and patrilineal names have inevitably affected the social structure of these tribes, although these policies were not the sole agents of change. It is difficult to be sure of cause and effect, but a documented case of a shift in social structure is that of the Cochiti, which is worth citing even though the final outcome lies outside this time period. A shift from matrilocality to nuclear families was already beginning in the 1920s.[22] By the time of the 1951 census, the nuclear family had become the norm. However, other relatives living with the nuclear family might include "one or two grandparents, paternal or maternal, step-children, grandchildren, siblings of either parent, and children of deceased siblings of either parent."[23] Obviously, the tradition of sharing a home with relatives who lack a complete household has survived the decline of matrilocality.

Attitudes toward ownership had also changed by the 1950s. Although previously both the dwelling and field produce were considered the wife's property, ownership of both was shifting into the hands of the husband. Pensions for widows of veterans, although not common, also affected the attitudes toward old people. For instance, among the Apache, more attention was paid to old women with this income, since the income disappeared with her death.[24]

Official policies also affected social structure. Legal marriages and legitimate children were clearly a concern of the government, as can be seen from the forms that Indians were required to complete (or that were completed on their behalf). Married women applying for lands outside the reservation were required to swear in a separate affidavit that they were married. Several applications indicate that they were married "by Indian custom," which appears to have been acceptable. The records also show clearly that the patrilineal naming system was imposed by the Bureau of Indian Affairs for the purpose of recordkeeping, regardless of local custom.

Attitudes of social workers, teachers, and missionaries reinforced official policies. In documents from a school survey of one Pueblo tribe, these attitudes are made quite clear, as the social worker paraphrases the various opinions of Anglos about Indian families and individuals. Reports of "illegitimate" children and "forced" marriages abound.[25]

Money had no place in the precontact societies, but as the need for manufactured goods grew, cash became a necessity. Both men and women performed temporary work off the reservations, making fields and herds, traditional sources of women's economic strength, less important. A trend toward the nuclear family made women more dependent on men as well. A 1957 study of Navajo women in a border community on the edge of the reservation shows this decline in women's economic status. According to older values, cash was personally owned, so many men could not understand using their wages to provide for their families. Even at that, "the poorest women in Fruitland are generally the middle-aged and old women who have no male providers. They frequently have no economic support except the relatively inadequate welfare aid. Under traditional conditions, these women would be well off; they might be managers of large extended family units, or at least respected female relatives with secure positions within the family group."[26]

As contact with the mainstream American culture has increased, Indian men have acquired some of its prevalent attitudes toward women. One Navajo man acknowledged: "It is very obvious, I think, the infiltration of American mainstream of open discrimination against women is very much alive on the Navajo reservation. There are many isolated cases where you have sexual harassment, open discrimination by denial of equal access and equal opportunity in job competition."[27] Another man said, "The women tend to shy away from issues and their power of concentration is far less than men."[28] Navajo men seem to have acquired and flaunted a disdain for women that is sometimes less overt in the mainstream culture. Despite these changes, one Navajo tribal judge is a woman, and women are described in print as "prominent leaders."[29]

Conclusion

In general, it has been shown that greater autonomy for women in a selection of southwestern Indian cultures was associated with fewer economic and social penalties for widows. The southwestern tribes in this study had traditional ways of caring for widows, although they differed among specific tribes. In no case was a widow without immediate family left to live and cope alone. Where extended families were the basic unit of society, both men and women always had a social group for support. Among southwestern Indians, the worst social penalties for widows included the loss of her children to the spouse's family, an imposed remarriage, and relocation to live with a different group of people. These penalties did not occur in the matrilineal societies in this region, where women's autonomy was greater.

The changes that have occurred since American contact have not improved women's autonomy. What is remarkable is to what extent women still have cultural importance and are unlikely to suffer penalties when widowed. A questionnaire[30] completed by the officials of eight Pueblos indicates that the treatment of widows has not changed in any profound way. A widow still has a place to live, usually in the same house. She keeps her children if they are small, and they look after her if they are adults. Nearly all the groups feel that the widow's sexuality is her own choice, as is her potential remarriage. Thus there are few constraints on the choices a widow may make.

Although the groups described in this study have differing social structures, none is like the dominant American society. In spite of the influence of that society, southwestern Indians have retained much of their ancient heritage in structure as well as in attitudes. Women's place in the social structure determines attitudes toward widows, both as women and as older people, but economic realities also have an effect. Thus the traditional ownership of house and land goes a long way toward explaining the continuing support of widows in the Native-American Southwest. In both the economic and social spheres, women's autonomy is assured, and thus widowhood is less likely to be accompanied by the economic and social penalties that may be found in mainstream American culture.

NOTES

1. Alice Schlegel, *Male Dominance and Female Autonomy: Domestic Authority in Matrilineal Societies* (N.p.: Human Relations Area Files, 1972).

2. Louise Lamphere, "Strategies, Cooperation, and Conflict among Women in Domestic Groups," in M. Rosaldo and L. Lamphere, eds., *Woman, Culture, and Society* (Stanford: Stanford University Press, 1974), 100.

3. Edward H. Spicer, *Cycles of Conquest* (Tucson: University of Arizona Press, 1962).

4. See Alice Schlegel, "Hopi Family Structure and the Experience of Widowhood," herein, for an extended treatment of Hopi widowhood.

5. The information for the Navajo comes from the following sources: Louise Lamphere, *To Run after Them* (Tucson: University of Arizona Press, 1977); David F. Aberle, "Some Sources of Flexibility in Navajo Social Organization," *Southwest Journal of Anthropology* 19 (1963); William Y. Adam and Loraine T. Ruffing, "Shonto Revisited: Measures of Social and Economic Change in a Navajo Community: 1955-1971," *American Anthropologist* 79 (1977):65; Clyde Kluckhohn and Dorothea Leighton, *The Navaho,* rev. ed. (Cambridge, Mass.: Harvard University Press, 1974); Mary Shepardson, "Navaho Inheritance Patterns: Random or Regular?" *Ethnology* 5 (1966):91; Gary Witherspoon, "A New Look at Navajo Social Organization," *American Anthropologist* 72 (1970):63; Witherspoon, *Navajo Kinship and Marriage* (Chicago: University of Chicago Press, 1975); Terry R. Reynolds, Louise Lamphere, and Cecil Cook, Jr., "Time Resources and Authority in a Navajo Community," *American Anthropologist* 69 (1967); Gladys A. Reichard, *Dezba, Woman of the Desert* (Glorietta, N.M.: Rio Grande Press, 1971); Beth Wood and Tom Barry, "The Story of Three Navajo Women," *Integrated Education* 16 (1978):33-34.

6. Kluckhohn and Leighton, *The Navaho,* 229.

7. Schlegel, *Domestic Authority in Matrilineal Societies,* 23.

8. Lamphere, "Strategies, Cooperation, and Conflict," 103.

9. Ibid., 101.

10. Kluckhohn and Leighton, *The Navaho,* 102.

11. Ibid., 101.

12. Witherspoon, "Navajo Social Organization," 63.

13. Reynolds, Lamphere, and Cook, "Time Resources and Authority," 191.

14. The major sources used for the Apache are: Grenville Goodwin, *The Social Organization of the Western Apache,* University of Chicago Publications in Anthropology, Ethnological Series (Chicago: University of Chicago Press, 1942); Goodwin, "The Social Division and Economic Life of the Western Apache," *American Anthropologist* 37 (1935); James L. Haley, *Apaches: A History and Culture Portrait* (Garden City, N.Y.: Doubleday, 1981); Charles R. Kaut, *The Western Apache Clan System: Its Origins and Development,* University of New Mexico Publications in Anthropology, 9 (Albuquerque: University of New Mexico Publications, 1957); Richard J. Perry, "Variations on the Female Referent in Athabaskan Culture," *Journal of Anthropological Research* 33 (1977); Morris Opler, "Cause and Effect in Apachean Agriculture, Division of Labor, Residence Patterns, and Girls' Puberty Rites," *American Anthropologist* 74 (1972).

15. Goodwin, "Social Division and Economic Life of Western Apache," 59.

16. Haley, *Apaches,* 121.

17. The sources for information on the Zuni are: Frank H. Cushing, *Zuni* (Lincoln: University of Nebraska Press, 1979), and An-che Li, "Zuni: Some Observations and Queries," *American Anthropologist* 39 (1937).

18. The sources for information on the Papago are: Ruth M. Underhill, *Papago*

Woman (New York: Holt, Rinehart and Winston, 1979), and Underhill, *Social Organization of the Papago Indians,* Columbia University Contributions in Anthropology, 30 (orig. publ. 1939; New York: AMS Press, 1969).

19. Records of the Bureau of Indian Affairs, Entry #87 in preliminary inventory of the pueblo records created by field offices of the BIA, Northern Pueblos Agency, Report on Individuals in Cochiti Pueblo, 1922, Record Group 75, National Archives and Records Services, Washington, D.C.

20. The sexual imbalance implied here may be a result of faulty counting. Two other enrollment lists are also markedly unbalanced, one in each direction: (1) Enumeration of Jicarilla Apache, Indians belonging to Abiquin Agency, May 12, 1875, entry 24, and (2) List of Enrollment, Nov. 3, 1879, Abiquiu Indian Agency, New Mexico, entry 25, both in records in the Federal Records Center, GSA, Denver, Colo.

21. Indian Allotment Applications, Laguna, New Mexico, 1912, entry 76, records in the Federal Records Center.

22. Esther Schiff Goldfrank, *Social and Ceremonial Organization of the Cochiti* (Menasha, Wis.: Collegiate Press, 1927), 84.

23. Charles H. Lange, *Cochiti: A New Mexico Pueblo, Past and Present* (Austin: University of Texas Press, 1959), 415.

24. Goodwin, *Social Organization of the Western Apache,* 517.

25. A Social Worker's Survey of Laguna Pueblo Indian Families Living in Nine New Mexico Towns, 1933, entry 92, Southern Pueblos Agency, Record Group 75.

26. Laila S. Hamamsy, "The Role of Women in Changing Navaho Society," *American Anthropologist* 59 (1975): 106.

27. Smallcanyon, "Issac Said He 'May Consider' a Women as His Running Mate," *Navajo Times* (July 7, 1982), 1.

28. Smallcanyon, "Women Need to Be Competitive, Says Tso," ibid. (July 21, 1982), 1.

29. "Donald Dodge Criticizes MacDonald Spending Policy," ibid. (July 28, 1982), 1, 3.

30. From questionnaire I prepared and sent to sixteen Pueblo tribes. I am grateful to those who replied: Santa Ana, Zia, Zuni, Cochiti, Jemez, Picuri, Laguna, and San Juan Pueblos.

2

Hopi Family Structure and The Experience of Widowhood

ALICE SCHLEGEL

When one considers that almost half of all adults in the world have experienced or will experience widowhood, it is plain that widowhood is a major social issue that cuts across cultural and national lines. Yet there is little literature on this experience for non-Western peoples, most of our information coming from societies with a European or European type (e.g., American) of marriage and family. Thus, it is impossible to know which of the consequences of loss of spouse are universal human responses to a universal social condition and which are culturally patterned. Since the character of widowhood must be to some degree a function of the character of the marriage that precedes it, and it is known that marriage varies across cultures, it is useful to examine widowhood from a broader, cross-cultural perspective. In this chapter, I discuss widowhood for the Hopi, a Pueblo Indian people of northern Arizona, between the time of first major penetration of the outside world, the 1860s, to World War II, when the Hopi Reservation became open to outside influences much more rapidly and dramatically than it had previously. I describe the traditional pattern and indicate how this pattern began to change as the Hopi began their transformation from a tribal society, based on subsistence horticulture and organized around corporate clans, to a class society, in which sustenance came from wage labor, social benefits, and entrepreneurial activities.[1]

The description and discussion of Hopi family and widowhood shed light on several crucial issues. The first is the question of social continuity versus discontinuity. With the death of a spouse, the widow or widower in our society finds virtually every aspect of personal and social life disrupted. From being a partner in a team that acts as a corporate unit, manages property, and, at some stages in life, socializes children together, the widowed person finds himself or herself forced to make decisions and plan and execute actions alone.

The second is the question of loss or maintenance of status. There is certainly a change in legal and social status in our society from married to widowed person. The overall social effects of this are greater for women than for men, as women in European tradition have derived their status from their husbands, and a woman without a husband is socially incomplete to a greater degree than a man without a wife.

The third concerns the deprivations of widowhood. For both sexes there is loss of companionship and consortium. In the traditional American pattern, the major responsibility for family support rested with the husband, even where wives were employed or did processing tasks, while domestic services were performed by the wife. It is easier for a man to find a woman to cook and clean for him than for a woman to find a man to support her; the potential economic deprivation, therefore, is greater for widowed women than men. One question is whether economic deprivation is a problem of great extent or whether it is found only in capitalist economies, and whether women are universally more affected than men.

In drawing comparisons between Hopi marriage and widowhood and those of the larger society deriving from a European tradition (whether Anglo-Saxon or Hispanic), it must be kept in mind that there were certain similarities.[2] The Hopi were monogamous, and spouses tended to be close in age. Love and respect of each spouse for the other were believed to be essential to a happy relationship. The Hopi disapproved of adultery, because the emotional disturbance it caused would disrupt the harmony of the home and eventually affect the health of its members, physical health being seen as a response to ease of mind. The points of contrast will become clear during the description of Hopi family life.

When we compare the experience of widowhood for Hopi of the late nineteenth century to their contemporaries in the non-Indian world, we see several crucial differences. First, there were fewer widows than widowers. The cessation of warfare with the *pax Americana* put an end to a major cause of early male mortality, yet the benefits of improved sanitation and medical care had not made a dent in the high rate of maternal mortality. Most women, even quite old ones, remarried. Thus, widowhood was more of a problem for men than for women.

Second, the extended kin network, including those kin not residing in the same house as the widowed person, was responsible for economic aid to the widow or widower to a greater degree than was common in the larger society. Specifically, women had claims on brothers, and men had claims on sisters, that carried much greater moral weight than similar claims in the outside society.

Third, the widow's and widower's social position in the community remained unchanged, as it did not depend upon the presence of a spouse. Unlike societies derived from a European cultural base, Hopi women and men conducted most of their daily activities in the company of members of the same sex. Husband and wife were partners, to be sure, but even more important in the organization of society was the partnership of brother and sister, whether biological siblings or simply clan "brothers" and "sisters," i.e., men and women of the same generation who were members of the same clan. Thus, the partnership of Hopi wives and husbands was restricted to clearly delimited areas, and the idea that "the twain shall be one flesh" was foreign. This does not imply that marriage was unimportant; it was unlikely that any normal man, and almost unthinkable that any normal woman, would fail to marry. Nevertheless, once having been married a person held the same status as a married adult regardless of whether the spouse was present, deceased, or had left the marriage. Indeed, there is not even a term for *widow* or *widower*: the terms translated as "man who lives alone" or "woman who lives alone" refer to a once-married person whose spouse is absent from the marriage, whether through death, temporary desertion, or permanent abandonment. These Hopi terms are descriptive and do not place the individual into a socially distinct category with markedly different role expectations and behavior patterns.

Finally, the loss of a spouse was unlikely in most cases to cause, particularly to women, the same degree of despair and feeling that life had ended as it sometimes did in the larger society. Hopi marriages were constrained and closeness of spouses was discouraged in ways unknown to the European-American world, where the unity of the married pair forms the legal, social, and moral basis of the family.

To sum up, Hopi marriage did not carry the same weight of economic dependence, status definition, and emotional bonding that it was designed to do in the larger society. While the loss of a spouse required adjustments in domestic arrangements, and the death of the partner brought on grief and feelings of loss, the Hopi widow or widower was not an incomplete adult, as was often the case for the widowed in the larger population of this time. The character of widowhood derives from the character of marriage, and differences in Hopi marriage from the European-American type of marriage led to differences in the experience of widowhood.

The Cultural Background

The reason for these differences in the character of marriage will become clear if we consider the nature of the Hopi family and kin network and the roles of women and men in household and clan. During the late nineteenth and twentieth centuries the groundwork for a major transformation of Hopi society was being laid; wage work and private enterprise in a developing economy were making inroads into the traditional system of subsistence farming. However, the transformation was only partial by 1939, and the basic pattern of household and kinship support remained intact until the post–World War II period. In these patterns we find the background for understanding the quality of Hopi widowhood and the reason for its difference from widowhood elsewhere. The similarities exist as well, deriving both from traditional Hopi culture, which at certain points was much like European-derived cultures, and from similar responses of both Indian and non-Indian women and men to economic opportunities provided by the developing economy of Arizona during the early years of statehood and the years preceding it.

The Hopi world up to the 1860s was virtually isolated from contact with Anglos and Hispanics. In this, the Hopi were unlike the Pueblo peoples of New Mexico and the Pima and Papago of southern Arizona, who had had intense contact with the Hispanic peoples since the seventeenth century. Sheep herding, a European import, had entered Hopi domestic economy during the 1600s, and some European foodstuffs were imported from the more easterly Pueblos, where they had been introduced by the Spanish, and these latter served to augment rather than replace the native subsistence crops of corn, beans, and squash. When the period under investigation opened, the Hopi relied on a subsistence economy of horticulture, hunting, and some herding, which produced a small surplus, enough for small-scale individual barter with persons of other tribes who brought dried meat, hides, pinon nuts, and other products of the mountains and deserts into the villages.

The 1860s saw the beginnings of major changes in the Hopi economy, with results that affected the organization of the household and the resources of its members. Anglos began entering the region—Mormon missionaries, traders, and scientific investigators—and the nearby towns of Winslow and Holbrook, later important locations of wage labor, were founded. In 1862 the western Navajo were rounded up by Kit Carson and incarcerated at Ft. Sumner, New Mexico Territory, thus putting an end to the raiding that had constantly ravaged the Hopi and reduced contact with neighboring peoples. The Hopi Reservation was established in 1882, and in 1887 the first school was opened. Shortly after, Thomas Keams opened his trading post in Keams Canyon. The construction and maintenance of these facilities utilized Hopi wage labor, with women employed primarily as cooks and matrons in the school. Thus, within a short time, the Hopi took their first steps into the American political, economic, and educational systems, and the transformation of the Hopi from a tribal society into a class-based one had begun.

The appearance of the villages, the pace of daily life, and the seasonal pattern of work and the ceremonial calendar changed slowly and in minor ways from the 1860s to the 1930s. Population on the reservation was small, from about 2,000 to 3,000, with villages ranging in size from roughly 100 to 900. Houses of stone and adobe continued to be built around the plazas, although doors and windows replaced the rooftop hatches, reached by ladders, which had formerly served as entrances and as apertures for daylight. Wagons could be seen parked near the houses, but men continued to walk to nearby fields and most cultivation was still done with hand tools rather than the plow. Homegrown food continued to be the staple of the economy, providing for family subsistence, for ceremonial exchange, and for individual barter with persons of other tribes. Sheep herding was done primarily for home consumption, but cattle herding was introduced by the 1920s and became a source of cash for some. By 1895, judging from photographs, most men and children seemed to be wearing Anglo-style clothing, either purchased or homemade from purchased fabrics or from flour sacking, although older girls and women continued to wear the traditional woolen shift into the early years of this century. Purchased horse tack, metal pans, and Franklin stoves coexisted with homemade pottery and baskets. Coffee, sugar, and bread made from wheat flour were much enjoyed, even though corn, still ground by hand in stone grinding bins, was the staple in Hopi cuisine.

The occupations of most men were farming and some herding, while women's major activities were the grinding of corn and the fetching of water; both sexes supplemented these by some wage labor and commercial craft production. As purchased textiles and leather goods replaced homemade articles, men's burdens were lightened. Women made baskets and pottery for home use, but now the traders, supplying tourists and collectors, provided a market for the commerical production of traditional crafts. With children often away at government boarding school, families were deprived of children's labor, but they were also freed from the responsibility of feeding and clothing them. The rhythms of daily life continued for women and men much as they had in the past, with women spending most of their time in the home, and men, when not out in the fields or pastures or otherwise occupied, passing their waking hours with other men in the kivas, the ceremonial chambers that also served as men's clubhouses. Here the men practiced their weaving, carving, and leather work, done for home consumption or sale to traders, while they discussed village matters; here they planned and conducted much of the ceremonial activity of the community.

A complete description, let alone analysis, of women's and men's roles in Hopi economic, political, domestic, religious, expressive, and other activities is clearly beyond the scope of this essay. Nevertheless, a discussion of household, clan, and village is necessary to support the contention that widowhood did not involve a change in public status for either sex.

The Hopi practiced matrilocal residence, in which sons and brothers left home upon marriage and entered their wives' households. The core group of the house was composed of female kin, mother and daughters and sisters, with husbands and unmarried sons attached to it. During the period under discussion, there was a change from the extended family form, where several married daughters might stay with their mother, toward the stem family form, where only one (often the youngest) remained, the others moving into houses of their own after a time. Authority over the house rested with its female head, although her husband was the manager of the male labor team of sons and sons-in-law. If a separation occurred, a man returned to his mother's house if she were alive, or a sister's house if not, unless he had another woman to go to as consort. In any event, a man usually lived in a house owned and controlled by women; in the rare case when a man lived alone, he at least took his meals with a daughter or other kinswoman.

Female headship and ownership of houses meant that daughters inherited from their mothers. As the founding couple aged, the mother turned authority over to her daughter gradually and slowly retired from active management. The elderly father spent more and more time in the kiva or relaxing in the home as his sons-in-law took over the organization of male domestic labor. An elderly couple or either surviving member of the couple lived with one or more grown daughters. Consequently, daughters were necessary for the continuity of the household, and a couple who did not have one tried to adopt a girl of the wife's clan, if possible the daughter of a biological sister. This is one society in which daughters were desired more than sons and often given more favorable treatment. Families were not necessarily successful in their attempts to adopt.

Most of women's activities took place in the home. The houses of female kin were clustered close together, which provided for constant interaction, and pairs or groups of women friends might go out together to gather grasses for basketmaking or to dig clay for pottery. While men probably interacted with unrelated men (in the kivas) more than women did with unrelated women, there was opportunity for women neighbors to spend time together.

In spite of a high degree of sexual separation in work and recreation, women and men did spend most of their time on activities that benefited the household. In no sense was there formal segregation of sexes. The family ate together as a unit, husband and wife shared the same bed (by no means a universal practice throughout the world), and marriage brought about a partnership, its major goal being to protect and provide for women and children. If the wife held authority in the house, it was mitigated by her economic dependence upon her husband's labor.

The Hopi had a matrilineal system (descent is counted through the female line). The clan, the most important unit of social organization, consisted of men, women, and all children of the women but not of the men. A woman's children belonged to her clan, but a man's belonged to his wife's clan. While girls inherited their clan position and duties from their mothers, boys inherited theirs from their mother's brothers. This put the mother's brother rather than the father in a position of authority over boys and encouraged relations of affection rather than respectful distance between the father and his children.

Clans owned rituals, political offices, and farm land. When all travel was done by foot and transport was by human portage aided by donkeys, most cultivated land was close to the villages. Within the clan, land was allotted to each house for the men of the house to farm. This meant that the critical resources for subsistence were controlled by women, and this economic control was a major factor in the power of women within the house. All produce grown on her clan land, that is, the bulk of her husband's production, belonged to the wife. Most of this was used for food for the family, but the surplus was expended in ceremonial exchange or traded to outsiders.

It has already been indicated that the brother-sister relationship was regarded by Hopi as more critical and central to social organization than that of husband and wife. It was at the core of clan activities, the cooperating pair in many clan rituals being real or clan male and female siblings. When the kachinas, supernatural figures represented by masked dancers, performed, they might be accompanied by "sisters" but never by "wives." A woman's fertility was of great concern to her brothers, for the perpetuation of the clan depended on her, and brothers provided a back-up of economic and moral support should husbands fail in their duties (or so goes the ideal—the reality will be examined later). The brother-sister symbiosis was recognized in the authority structure of the clan, which was headed by a coequal pair that can be called Clan Mother and Clan Uncle. While each member of this pair was principally engaged in organizing activities and making decisions for clan members of the same sex, it was expected that those two would agree on all matters and that neither would act without the approval of the other. This cooperation was expressed in the rituals conducted by the clan, in which each played some role. While men, who were the farmers and knew the quality of the various clan plots, distributed land among clan houses, the final decision over land rested with the Clan Mother. Again, the economic authority of women was expressed at the clan as well as the household level.

In the period under discussion, both clans and factions that cross-cut clan alliances served as the important political interest groups. Villages lost political autonomy under the reservation system and the locus of power shifted to the U.S. government. Nevertheless, the old chief and council system, emasculated though it was, continued to exist. Each village had its own ceremonial cycle of performances and its own chief and council. Even marriage within the village was so strongly preferred as to be almost a rule. The kivas served as the political forums for men, while women's interests were decided among clanswomen or in larger informal groups of women.

Village political structure was masculine: men held the offices of chief and council. However, because of the importance of women in the household and clan, women's concerns and interests were fully expressed in the political process: a man simply could not act in ways disapproved by his clanswomen, and he could not act counter to his wife's approval if he wished peace at home. Women's authority in other areas gave them a powerful, if indirect, voice in village affairs.

Hopi Marriage

In several of its features Hopi marriage seems much like European or American marriage. It was upon marriage that a girl (*mana*) became a woman (*wuhti*). (A boy became a man upon his ceremonial initiation into one of the four fraternities.) It was monogamous, with husband and wife sharing meals and bed. Spouses were near one another in age, and young people had a strong voice in selecting their mates, although the girl's family had to approve her choice before she could bring him into her mother's house. The homilies iterated at the wedding and all the moral maxims about marriage emphasized the need for harmony and cooperation. The ideal character of a woman was to give and sustain life, and her roles as mother and manager of the food supply were imbued with sanctity as the means by which life, the highest value in Hopi ethics, is maintained. The ideal character of a man was to provide and protect, and male nurturance and protection is the principal connotation of the Hopi term for father. Even in this society where a man's children belong to his wife's clan, fatherhood was highly valued and gave a man social dignity.

The ideal picture is one of harmonious partnership, in which the husband cared for his wife and children as the farmer cares for his young corn plants, lovingly and tenderly. Against this were posed the social factors that constrained or militated against the marital bond. The matrilineal kinship system, combined with stem or extended family household form, pulled the woman in the direction of her clan and kin and away from her husband. His time was split among his marital household, where he had ties and duties toward his wife and children, his sister's household, where he had secondary duties toward his sister and important responsibilities in the training of her children, and the kiva, where his ceremonial activities were located and where most of his informal social life took place. It was not easy adjusting one's time and resources between the two houses that had a claim on a man, and there was some ambiguity as to where he really belonged. While he kept most of his personal belongings in his wife's house, most of his ceremonial equipment was kept at his sister's, and it was to the latter that he would invite guests at ceremonial times when it was appropriate to bring visitors home for a meal. This ambiguity is expressed in the expression translated as "the man's place is outside the house," meaning both that he must be outside metaphorically to guard it, and that he does not really belong in this feminine domain. The ambiguity was resolved by his spending relatively little time there.

Another factor that may have had a deadening effect on the marital relationship is the emphasis placed on responsibility in marriage, particularly for men. As boys, Hopis tended to be indulged by their mothers and not always strictly disciplined by their fathers, for upon marriage the family lost the son to another house where he labored under the direction and authority of his father-in-law. There are proverbs that warn men not to feel sorry for their sons-in-law but to make them to get up before dawn and get to work. Following a care-free life as a bachelor, working with greater or lesser diligence in the fields and roaming the village at night with his friends, a boy got a double dose of responsibility within a few years. After his initiation into a fraternity he was expected to give up frivolity and take on the composed and dignified demeanor of one who has assumed social adulthood, with its ritual responsibilities and knowledge. After marriage, he had little time or opportunity for amusement, as he had to prove his worth to his in-laws and the community through hard work. While marriage was desired by women as the means to social adulthood, it seemed to bring little joy to men, at least during the early years. In short, Hopi marriage was weighted in favor of the wife. A husband provided her with food and clothing, children, and adult social status. For men, however, thoughts were rather of duty and responsibility, with virtually all agricultural labor falling on the husband's shoulders and little authority in his home to sweeten it. Young men tended to resist the marriage proposals made by hopeful girls, and even when they had accepted and moved into the wife's household, they might go back home for extended visits. The prospect of finding a husband was, for many Hopi girls, a source of anxiety that bedeviled their late adolescence, and it was common for girls to compete for the favors of the most desirable bachelors.[3] In later years women were vulnerable to the threat that a separated or widowed woman might pose to their own marriages, and it is said that the most common fights among adults were those between women—wife and alleged mistress—over a man.

The husband's position improved as children came along and the young man successfully demonstrated his worth as a father. But it appears that until the partners reached old age, the marital relationship had a certain tense quality, most clearly seen by the warning against teasing the spouse. The Hopi are great teasers. Everyone, even a dignified uncle, is teased with jokes that usually imply laziness, sexual prowess, or misconduct. When they are true, the jokes can have a cutting edge. When they are clearly not, it is the very absurdity of the charges that makes them humorous. The only close relatives who do not tease are husband and wife; husbands, in particular, are warned against teasing wives for fear their feelings will be hurt. Only the old, who have become bound together through long years of partnership and growth of trust, tease each other, and then with gentleness and affection.

One consequence of the unease of the marital relationship, and certainly a contributor to it, was the Hopi concern with adultery and the emotional salience it had, even for those who were faithful spouses. On the one hand, adultery was inveighed against as causing dissension in the home; the direct consequence of a wife's unhappiness, it is still believed, is that she will become ill or that she will be unable in her unhappiness to care for her children and they will become ill. On the other, it is a constant source of gossip and speculation. Both men and women might be accused of having extramarital partners, although it was more common to talk about "private wives" than "private husbands." It was believed that certain women were receptive to men either because their husbands had died or left them or because they simply wanted to be. In the latter case, they were thought to accept men when their husbands were off herding or on other business. It must have been difficult for even a willing woman to entertain another man if she lived with relatives, but the determined seem to have found a way. If she were a widow living alone with her children, as occasionally happened during this time period, or if her husband were the only other adult in the house, it must have been simpler to manage. Even where privacy for adulterous encounters existed, the attention paid to it was probably greater than the facts warranted.

To summarize, then, marriage was considered the normal state for adults, a requirement for female social adulthood, and important although not necessary for men as one proof of their willingness to assume community responsibility. The ideal marriage was one in which husband and wife willingly and cheerfully cooperated for the benefit of the household and the children. Some couples achieved this ideal and were held up as an example to the young. However, the pull of clan responsibilities worked on both wife and husband to weaken the marital bond. It is quite likely that the constant presence of other adults in the house and the lack of privacy prevented spouses from developing intimacy. All people of the house slept in one room, and the couple wishing to have sexual relations had to wait until others were asleep and then conduct themselves with a minimum of noise. Unlike many other tribal or traditional societies, there were no secluded places—no fenced gardens, remote spots, private rooms—where couples could go for sexual activities or simply to discuss matters of concern to the two of them alone.

Exposition of the difficulties in Hopi marriage does not imply that all marriages were troubled all of the time. In every society there are periods of stress in the life cycle, and the life cycle of a marriage has its stress points as well. If Hopi husbands and wives sometimes had difficulty in reaching the ideal of harmony, they had other compensations: young children were a source of delight to both parents, kin were generally loyal, and one spent an uninterrupted life span with close relatives and friends, with whom one could establish relations of intimacy and trust rarely possible among the less deeply rooted occupants of the surrounding world. If the marriage survived into the old age of the partners, the chances were good that they would grow close. It is possible that this happened as a result of greater equality in the relationship. The wife was turning more authority over to the daughter who would replace her as household head, thus reducing her own authority role, while at the same time her husband's position was improving as he became a respected elder, with sons-in-law working under his direction. Whatever the cause, marriage seems to have taken on a different character as the couple aged. Elderly husbands and wives today tease each other gently and with affection, and men spend more time at home in the company of their wives. It is even possible that sexual relations became more gratifying in the later years as couples became emotionally more attached; certainly the Hopi have no notion that sex is inappropriate for the old.

Widowhood

The description of the Hopi family during this time suggests that, ideally, the network of support and obligation for Hopis was quite different from either Anglo and Hispanic kin relations or the Western European pattern from which they stemmed. Brothers had a strong obligation to their sisters and sisters' children and were morally bound to see that they survived. The extended or stem family household would provide a cushion for the widowed person, so that one was never without a home and at least a minimal supply of food. Destitution was not a consequence of widowhood. Nor was a major change in social status: widowed men continued to spend time planting fields for the female head, whether grown daughter or sister, and visiting the kiva; widowed women continued their daily tasks as before and sought companionship with female kin and friends as they had earlier.

Men and women at different stages in the adult life cycle, with and without young children, will be examined to assess the problems and options that faced the widow and widower. Looking at specific cases shows that there is some deviation from the ideal pattern as given by informants. This raises a dilemma that the anthropologist must always face: to what degree does deviancy from the ideal represent the standard deviation, so to speak, found in any culture, and to what degree does it indicate social change?

Given the fact that other critical areas of Hopi life were undergoing transformation, it is probably safe to regard the deviant cases as indicative of change in the structure of the household and the consequent situation of the widow or widower.

Examples of widowed people can be taken from the 1922 Moqui Industrial Survey (*Moqui* being a term formerly used by outsiders for the Hopi).[4] These are not always easy to interpret, since "families," that is, husband, wife, and children, appear to have been the unit surveyed wherever possible, rather than household, the more appropriate unit. It is also difficult to know whether an elderly individual without a family is a widower or someone who never married, a more likely occurrence for men than for women because of the imbalanced sex ratio. I indicate where the marital status of the individual is in doubt.

A childless young widower simply moved back to his mother's or sister's house. If he had young children, he was expected to move back to his natal home, leaving the children in the care of his dead wife's mother or sister and providing meat, clothing, and other necessary items for them. There are some known cases of children going with the father who left because of death or separation, one such mentioned by the Beagleholes in the 1930s,[5] but children generally stayed in their maternal household. It seems plausible that widowed like separated men would seek sexual affairs, but Hopi informants gave no specific cases known to them.

Two young widowers, ages 30 and 32, lived in Hotevilla, Third Mesa, in 1922 in households consisting of themselves and their children. Both appear to have been quite poor, having little or no livestock and growing little corn. It is likely that they ate in the homes of their mothers or sisters. The third case of a young widower is a young man who had married a woman at Shipaulovi, Second Mesa, and left the household after her death to remarry, to a women in the neighboring village of Shongopovi. He left his three children in the care of their maternal grandmother, a widow. Since the grandmother's household was well supplied with food—five wagon loads of corn and fifty pounds of beans—it is likely that he contributed to the support of his children, although male kin of the grandmother may have helped as well.

Without being too specific about age, the older widower was a man with one or more grown children or an elderly man without children. Hopis try to adopt girls if there are none in the family to provide an heiress for the house and a caretaker for the aged parents. Ideally, the widowed father would continue to live in the house with his daughter and her husband, although he might spend more time in the kiva, returning home only to eat and sleep, than would an older man with a living wife.

The Moqui Industrial Survey identifies sixteen men over 50 as being without wives. Of these, nine are listed as widowers and five do not have marital status indicated. The wives of the remaining two had left them. These men will be considered as a group, whether or not they were in fact widowers, because the life conditions of elderly men without wives did not seem to depend much upon the cause of their wifelessness. Much more important than marital status in determining their life circumstances seems to have been whether or not they had close kin to live with, usually a daughter or a sister's daughter. Of these sixteen elderly men, only three lived with a daughter. One lived with a son, whose marital status was not indicated. Four lived alone. Eight lived with kin other than a child.

The economic circumstances of these elderly men do not appear to depend much on whom they lived with. Eleven of the men produced enough corn and beans or had enough livestock to get by without discomfort: three of these lived alone, five lived with kin, one lived with his son, and two lived with their daughters. Of those who had little or no livestock and did little farming, one lived alone and two lived with kin, both of the latter being physically handicapped. Of the two relatively prosperous men, one lived with his daughter, an employee at Polacca Day School. It is possible that his son, a soldier in the army, also contributed to his support. His relative prosperity is indicated by the fact that their house had four rooms whereas most Hopi houses had only one or two. The second prosperous man, age 74, was a bone setter and medicine man much in demand. He and one child (age unspecified, possibly a grandchild) lived with his "niece" (probably a sister's daughter) in a one-room house. His prosperity consisted not so much in his possessions as in the certainty of the food supply. The surveyor states: "No trouble in getting crops grown as he is invaluable as an emergency man in injuries."

A younger widow usually had young children and was without a grown son or son-in-law in the house. Her safety net depended upon the size and composition of the household and the ability of close kin to help her. If she were living with aged parents who had relied upon her husband to farm for them, she and they suffered economic deprivation. If she had a sister and brother-in-law in the house, he simply assumed the total burden of farming and herding for the family. If she lived in a nuclear-family household, her economic well-being depended on whether her father or brothers could assume support.

Of three widows with young children in 1922, one lived with her mother (also a widow) and two lived alone with their children. One of these was supplied with corn by her sister's husband and supplemented her income by making Hopi baskets and plaques "which helps out her income very materially." The other had been left a fair amount of livestock by her husband.

One case reported by an old man, John as we will call him, occurred about 1910.[6] His mother and her husband and children had split off from her parents' house and the husband had built her a house of her own. (This could happen for a number of reasons: the younger couple might wish the privacy of their own house; it could be a means for reducing conflict between the generations; or most commonly, the original house might be too small to house comfortably an expanding set of daughters, sons-in-law, and grandchildren.) When the husband died, he left three girls, the oldest about sixteen, and John, a boy of about twelve or thirteen.

The family continued to live in their own house, but they ate many meals with the widow's parents. Her father also helped her out with produce from his fields. Clothing was more of a problem. The kachinas, masked dancers who give gifts at certain ceremonies, gave them mocassins and buckskin pants. These had been made by the children's maternal uncles and designated as presents for the children. According to another informant, economic coping for a widow meant "a little from here, a little from there" — brothers, grown sons, daughters' husbands all provided something.

John had been away at school, at Sherman Institute in California, when his father died. On his return at about age fourteen, he remained home even though he would have liked to return to school. He helped his uncle and uncle's son herd their sheep, the three of them taking turns. In return he was given six or seven sheep, worth two to three dollars each, as a small herd of his own, which he kept with his uncle's herd. After a few years his oldest sister married a rather prosperous man, who owned a wagon and team that he used for freighting mail and other goods between Holbrook and various places on the Hopi Reservation. They lived with her mother, thus improving the household economy.

At some point during these years the two younger sisters died and the mother remarried. Although John, who at the time of writing was about 86, was vague as to dates and sequence of events, he clearly recalled the addition of the new man to the household. One day a man came to dinner and simply stayed. The children were bewildered at first, as they had not been prepared for this. But the finances of the family improved with an additional male worker, who also had horses and a wagon.

It would have been a rare widow who would have preferred to remain unmarried. The Hopi household relied on adult male workers for its subsistence, and one man's labor would not provide for many people. Other adults in the household would be likely to put pressure on the widow to remarry if at all possible. A brother's help could be grudging, and even if it were not, his wife might resent it as an imposition. In one such case, the widow was able to do her own farming with the help of her children, as the fields she had access to were close to the village. The informant who related this case explained: "She liked to be independent."[7]

One traditional way of obtaining food was to work for it. There is a well-established pattern of either labor exchange—for example, two or more men harvesting each one's fields in turn—or exchange of labor for a meal or for a part of the harvest. A woman who needed corn could help other women who needed labor sort and pile their corn, receiving some in exchange. If a wife were cooking for her husband's harvesting party, other women could offer their help in return for a meal. These are among the devices that constitute "a little from here, a little from there."

The push toward remarriage was the source of another problem the young widow faced: the threat she presented to other women. Since Hopi marriages were rather easily broken and there was little a wife could do to prevent a disgruntled husband from leaving, a young widow eager to remarry was seen as a menace to the security of other marriages. Even if a husband did not leave his wife, he might seek the sexual favors of a widow, giving her gifts in exchange. Thus the young widow had to contend with the likelihood that she aroused suspicion among other women and was the topic of gossip and speculation. Sometimes the suspicions were well founded; the Beagleholes refer to a widow who supplemented her resources with the gifts she received from the men she accepted as sexual partners.[8]

In spite of these various ways of coping, the widow's principal options were remarriage or dependence on brothers or other kin. Beginning about 1890 a third option, wage work, became available, although it was of limited scope. In 1910, for example, sixteen females earning a total of $2,476.66[9] were employed on the reservation compared to 247 men earning $10,674.83. The first school was opened at Keams Canyon in 1887, and this and other schools educated an increasing number of Hopi children. Cooks, matrons, seamstresses, and other female workers were needed. Good information on the marital status of employed women is lacking. An Indian field service report of 1926 indicates that women female employees on or off the reservation at that time were students returning from boarding school (government-supported high school). Presumably these were unmarried. However, three mature women, all widows from First Mesa, are listed as employed: one, age 38, worked as a domestic in Flagstaff; another, age 35, worked as housekeeper for the Hubbels at the trading post in Ganado, Arizona; the third, age not given, was school assistant at Polacca Day School.[10]

A source of supplemental income open to all women with requisite time and skill was production of pottery and baskets that ended up in museums or private collections or for sale to tourists. In 1910, of the 2,122 counted Hopis living on the reservation, there were 40 to 50 female pottery makers and 100 female basket makers who supplied the traders.[11] By 1939 female occupations on the reservation were replicating occupations available to Arizona women generally in the nineteenth century, although a far smaller percentage of Hopi women depended on employment for sustenance. The opening of the Hopi High School in 1939 brought domestic employment as Hopi women cleaned house for Anglo schoolteachers; Polingaysi Qoyawayma (Elizabeth White) was operating a boardinghouse, well known to many anthropologists, artists, and travelers who stayed there over the years. Until fairly recently, Hopi female employment was an extension of women's domestic tasks: cleaning, child care (in the schools), basketry, and pottery making. No one remembers women storekeepers or clerks before the 1950s, although men had been quite successful in these lines.

The older widow with one or more married daughters in the house was more economically secure than her younger counterpart. Her grown sons would also be helpful, providing meat from hunting or herding and cash for flour, fabrics, coffee, cooking pots, or candy from the trading post. But even she might choose to remarry. As one elderly widow stated, "A husband takes care of you better than others."[12] Like the younger widow, the older widow who was not economically secure used labor exchange, wage work, or craft production to supplement what she might receive from her relatives. Cash had not yet replaced the labor of kin as the major economic resource, and the greatest economic security for anyone was to belong to a household with several adults of each sex and livestock or access to good farm land. No one was utterly destitute, but there were variations among households in land and labor resources. The widow in the large family had economic security; the widow in the small family, like its other members, was more vulnerable.

Compared with the large number of elderly men living without wives, there were only four older widows listed in the 1922 industrial survey. One of them, age 51, was the mother-in-law of the widower mentioned earlier who remarried. She lived alone with the three grandchildren. Another, age 49, had four children, two old enough to help. The son did the farm work while the daughter was employed as a school seamstress. Their needs were adequately met, as were the needs of the 78-year-old who lived with her unmarried son and widowed daughter (mentioned above). The only impoverished elderly widow, age 77, also lived with her unmarried son. They lacked livestock and had only five chickens to their name. In relating the crops grown that year, the surveyor dryly states: "Corn ten bushels, no other crop." Considering the number of widowers who would be likely candidates for remarriage, one wonders why at least the younger women remained single.

Changes in Household Structure

During the period under discussion, the Hopi economy moved from an economy of subsistence to one based on cash income. With this major economic shift, the structure of the household changed. As wage labor and commercial stock raising began first to supplement and then to replace subsistence farming, control over family economic resources began to be shared between husband and wife, and in some cases they came under the husband's control. At the same time, the extended family households of the past gave way to stem families. This meant that the daughters who did not inherit moved off, generally to an adjacent house, where they established a nuclear family household that would eventually change to stem family form as their daughters matured and one brought in a husband. However, while the children were young, the married pair had greater privacy than was possible in a household that contained additional adults. While it is difficult to document without written records such as diaries or letters, it appears from remarks of elderly women that marriage became increasingly important as a source of emotional gratification, particularly to women. With new economic opportunities opening off the reservation, grown children and other close kin, who in earlier times had no choice but to remain close at hand, might be living in Winslow, Flagstaff, or even farther away, thus depriving their female relatives of their companionship. This would be a serious deprivation for women, who, much more than men, had looked to close kin for friends and companions, and may have intensified the need for their husbands' companionship. While in no way were reservation wives as economically or emotionally dependent on their husbands as were their Anglo contemporaries, changes in that direction were occurring as consequences of changes in the economy and household structure.

Beginning in the 1920s, some families moved off the reservation for longer or shorter durations while the husband sought employment. This pattern, of course, made the wife virtually totally dependent upon her husband for sustenance and adult companionship. For some couples the distance from family ties and obligations was something of a relief for both partners and allowed them to enjoy a welcome intimacy that was difficult under the traditional household pattern. Many of the oldest couples on the reservation today experienced such a break from the traditional pattern, and it may be that this experience, as much as the natural course of the life cycle of Hopi marriage, accounts for the sweetness and tenderness often seen between them.

As a result of these changes in the character of the household and the nature of marriage from the 1860s to the 1930s, the experience of widowhood began to change also. The obligation of brothers to aid widowed sisters and of adult daughters or sisters to provide a home or at least meals for widowed men persisted and prevented utter destitution as an economic consequence of widowhood throughout this period. The addition of wage labor to the subsistence economy opened up some opportunities for the employment of widowed women, although whether widows disproportionately took advantage of them is unknown. The primary goal of the widowed woman in most cases was to get remarried, in which most seem to have been successful, aided by the sex ratio in which men outnumbered women. As the examples from the 1922 industrial survey indicate, a widowed man was more likely to remain unmarried than a widowed woman.

For those who did not remarry, social status continued unchanged since the marital relationship was confined to the domestic sphere and did not affect the way individuals related to persons outside the home and immediate circle of affinal kin. Under the earlier extended-family household pattern, a widowed woman would simply remain in the household, as would an elderly widowed man. The young widow might suffer from the suspicions of other women, and she would be under some pressure from her family to bring another male worker into the household, but her support would be assured and the possibility of remarriage was favorable. Even elderly women were likely to remarry. Widowers, also, might remarry; if not, their labor was usually a welcome addition to a sister's household. Even the feeble elderly felt compelled to contribute and did so to the best of their ability.

By 1922 the structure of Hopi households had altered. The stem family with its associated nuclear families—the families of daughters who had left the household with their husbands—became the norm. When one member of a nuclear family household died, the remaining partner might choose to continue living there, with children if they were young, without them if they were grown and had established households of their own. In these cases women were likely to be provisioned by male kin, and men usually ate with female relatives. Thus, the closeness of kin ties and economic interdependence were maintained while at the same time the widowed person retained privacy and a large measure of autonomy. This must have been an appealing choice to people who were moving toward a more individualistic way of life: in 1922 only four of sixteen wifeless older men lived alone whereas both of the younger widowers in their early thirties did; all of the elderly widows lived with kin, whereas two of the three younger ones lived alone. While this may simply be an indication of age status, in that older people were more likely to be cared for than younger, more energetic ones, it could also indicate a move toward independence and partial autonomy from the family on the part of younger people who were expressing the individualistic values that accompany the economic behavior of a wage-labor and entrepreneurial economy.

Conclusion

So long as people lived in the traditional three-generation household, discontinuity resulting from the loss of the spouse was mitigated by the presence of other adults. The larger the household, that is, the more able-bodied adult members it contained, the less the loss of one adult was likely to affect the workings of the household as a whole. Discontinuity could occur within the stem family household if a younger adult, on whose labor both the children and the aged parents depended, were to die, and it would certainly be felt in the nuclear family household. Nevertheless, during the time period under discussion, the extension of responsibility to other kin meant that basic household needs would be met and responsibility for decision making distributed among several adults.

The widowed person suffered no loss of status in the public domain. The crucial partnership between woman and man outside the household was that between brother and sister. Since these were defined in clan terms, that is, any member of the same clan of the same generation was considered a sibling, no woman would be without brothers and no man without sisters. These, not husbands and wives, constituted the cross-sex couples that co-operated in political and ceremonial matters. For the most part, though, women and men performed their activities as members of same-sex groups whether married or widowed, and once married, future changes in marital status did not affect the person's relation to others.

The degree to which men and women suffered economic deprivation varied principally along the lines of family resources. The widowed person in a large, productive household was likely to feel little or none, while the person in the smaller family was more vulnerable. The introduction of wage labor into the economy made it possible for widowed people to be less dependent on the support of kin.

Finally, there is the question of the character of bereavement. Without the personal recollections of individuals, such as those contained in letters, diaries, poems, and other archival material from the period, it is impossible to make judgments without strong caveats. Nevertheless, the recognition and encouragement of emotional interdependency that characterized European-American marriages were muted by comparison in Hopi marriages, in which the tie to the spouse was in constant competition with the tie to matrilineal kin. Furthermore, mourning after any death was discouraged, as it was believed that sorrow could disrupt harmony of spirit and ultimately cause physical illness and even death. Thus, even when a personal loss might be deeply felt, it was kept to oneself, and there was no cultural expectation that loss of a spouse would cause one to become despondent or lose interest in life. For these reasons, it seems likely that the experience of loss was somewhat eased. Nevertheless, it must have been keenly felt, particularly by the aged who had become close over many years of partnership.

In summary, the domestic and social life of the Hopi widow and widower was disrupted much less than that of their counterparts in the larger society, even during this period when extended family ties were becoming attenuated and the marital bond was becoming somewhat strengthened. In spite of any economic deprivations the widow might suffer, and the loss of companionship and consortium which in many cases must have caused deep grief, the Hopi widow and widower were cushioned against destitution and did not suffer change of social status. It is ironic but understandable that those factors that put constraints on marriage—close ties to kin, the obligations between brother and sister that competed with marital attachment, and the segregation of the sexes in most occupational and recreational activities—were the very factors mitigating the loss of the spouse and preventing the social disruptions that accompanied widowhood in the larger society.

NOTES

1. Unless otherwise indicated, the data for this chapter come from fieldwork on the Hopi Reservation over a period of sixteen years, during which time I have concentrated on kinship, child socialization, and family relationships. Interviews specific to the subject of widowhood were conducted in 1982. I have discussed the material in this chapter with several Hopis who grew up on the reservation and are fluent speakers of Hopi, although the assertions are my own, based on observations and interviews. Archival material is sparse.

Considerable ethnographic research has been done on Hopi culture, and there are several works that provide background material. The classic ethnography of a Hopi village is Mischa Titiev, *Old Oraibi: A Study of the Hopi Indians of Third Mesa,* Papers of the Peabody Museum of American Archaeology and Ethnology, Harvard University, 22, no. 1 (1944). Illuminating autobiographies of Hopis include Leo W. Simmons, ed., *Sun Chief: The Autobiography of a Hopi Indian* (New Haven: Yale University Press, 1942); Polingaysi Qoyawayma (Elizabeth Q. White), *No Turning Back* (Albuquerque: University of New Mexico Press, 1964); and Louise Udall, *Me and Mine: The Life Story of Helen Sekaquaptewa* (Tucson: University of Arizona Press, 1969). Hopi kinship is described in Fred Eggan, *Social Organization of the Western Pueblos* (Chicago: University of Chicago Press, 1950). Hopi sex roles are discussed in Alice Schlegel, "Male and Female in Hopi Thought and Action," in Alice Schlegel, ed., *Sexual Stratification: A Cross-Culture View* (New York: Columbia University Press, 1977).

2. See Margaret Brainard, "The Hopi Indian Family: A Study of the Changes Represented in Its Present Structure and Functions" (Ph.D. diss., University of Chicago, 1935), 97, 132, 142. Her data come from 1930s, but they corroborate the memories of informants that refer to the 1910s and 1920s.

3. Alice Schlegel, "The Adolescent Socialization of the Hopi Girl," *Ethnology* 12 (1973):449-62.

4. Moqui Industrial Survey, 1922, in Reports of Industrial Surveys 1922-29, Records of Industries Section, Records of the Educational Division, Records of the Bureau of Indian Affairs, National Archives and Records Services, Washington, D.C.

5. Ernest and Pearl Beaglehole, "Hopi of the Second Mesa," American Anthropological Association, *Memoirs* 44 (1935):61.

6. Data collected by the author in 1982.

7. Ibid.

8. Beagleholes, "Hopi of the Second Mesa," 62. One of Brandt's informants from a slightly later period also mentioned that some women received men for cash, stating categorically — and no doubt with much exaggeration — that "the widows all do it" (Richard B. Brandt, *Hopi Ethics* [Chicago: University of Chicago Press, 1954], 201). It should be noted that the old Hopi custom of giving gifts to women other than wives in return for sexual favors began to take on a new character with the introduction of a cash economy. The traditional custom, one of reciprocal exchange, did not denigrate either partner. As Hopi men became aware of sex as a commodity through observations of the Anglo world and visits they paid to prostitutes in Winslow (see *Sun Chief* for specific accounts), some of the pejorative attitude toward prostitution in the larger society began to color the attitude toward sex at home, particularly where promiscuous women were clearly benefiting economically from their activities. It was not extramarital sex per se that was condemned; rather, the traditional disapproval of promiscuity became combined with disapproval of the use of sex for profit.

9. Moqui Agency Statistical Report, 1910, in Superintendent's Annual Narrative and Statistical Reports from Field Jurisdictions of the Bureau of Indian Affairs, 1907-1938, Record Group 75, M-1011, role 88 (on microfilm), National Archives.

10. Indian Field Service Report, Nov. 12, 1926, in Classified Files, Department of the Army, Record Group 94, File 920:34063-1926, National Archives.

11. Moqui Agency Statistical Report, 1910.

12. Data collected by the author in 1982.

3

The Widowed Women of Santa Fe: Assessments on the Lives of an Unmarried Population, 1850-80

DEENA J. GONZÁLEZ

This essay examines the lives of Spanish-Mexican widows living in Santa Fe, New Mexico, between 1850 and 1880. The terms *widow* and *widowhood* can be misleading, however, and require qualification. For some groups of southwestern women a more apt description would be "unmarried," a category that included not only widows but also the far larger community of women who were divorced, separated, or deserted. Placing Santa Fe's widows under the broader category of unmarried women reflects accurately their lives and makes possible the use of material from the censuses that did not enumerate widows separately.

Determining the exact number of widows in Santa Fe is more difficult than for most groups of white westering women. Although the censuses portrayed many women heading households and some elderly unmarried women living within several types of family groups, the number of widows remains undetermined because only the 1880 census specified marital status. Comparisons with earlier Mexican enumerations provide few clues. And the 1845 census for Santa Fe is lost entirely. Still, the task of counting the presence of widows in the population at large or deciphering the patterns of their lives is not impossible. It simply requires applying—and this can be generalized to include all Latin American women—more imaginative criteria to the evidence. Residential habits, income distribution, occupations, and stages in the life cycle thus can embellish the portrait of unmarried women when statistics or other factors cannot.

Unmarried women merit special consideration for another reason: Latin

American societies and communities consistently exhibited higher percentages of unmarried females than those of the United States. Studies on Peru and parts of the Mexican frontier have found that perhaps 7 to 10 percent of the adult population in certain areas could be classified as widows. Moreover, if Latin American societies and communities traditionally included a large number of unmarried women, widowhood would carry different connotations and would be regarded differently. The censuses and some wills provide evidence that this was the case. They also indicate that Spanish-Mexican Santa Fe, like many parts of Latin America, continued its precapitalist economic practices, so that in their families widows as well as other members contributed to the household economy. The censuses, in particular, portray women at work—sewing, laundering, and providing other services for the Euro-American men who poured into town after 1848 when the war with Mexico ended and the United States annexed New Mexico.

Yet another problem confronts any study of Spanish-Mexican women but is used here as a theme for examining their lives. Most white women moving into the southwestern United States after the war participated in the systematic effort to control or acquire property and settle in former Mexican territory. On the other side of that effort stood Native and Spanish-Mexican women, who experienced firsthand the white westering impact. For them, the signing of the Treaty of Guadalupe-Hidalgo, between the United States and Mexico, marked a turning point. Beginning in 1848 even the Spanish-Mexican widow—seemingly protected because she lived among her family and because her community contained so many others in her situation—experienced the effects of conquest.

In this essay I inquire into a woman's widowhood but place it within the postwar period's surrounding turmoil and accompanying economic displacement. I focus on specific characteristics of a widowed population as well as on impinging socioeconomic forces and argue that a widow's life was shaped by the interplay of a changing society and an economy imposed on her by wealthy newcomers, and not solely by her widowhood.

When the United States-Mexican War ended in 1848, all women in Santa Fe faced generally dismal economic circumstances. Only two years earlier, they had heard General Stephen Watts Kearny proclaim peace and promise prosperity. His army, Kearny declared, had come "as friends, to better your condition."[1] When people first watched the soldiers occupy the area peacefully, perhaps they anticipated better times. Since 1820 they had witnessed traders trek to Santa Fe, introduce manufactured items, and alter the town's character.[2] Now they stood on the verge of another conquest, neither military nor economic, but a mixture of both.

The takeover became evident immediately when Kearny and his 200 soldiers commissioned a fort to be built on a site overlooking the community. From its strategic lookout, the army approached storekeepers for supplies and counted on local men to help make adobes. In return, the military exchanged government staples and paid the men wages.[3] U.S. troops soon learned that bargaining for items, including liquor, worked well. Money, though, was scarce among the residents. When haggling proved useless, the soldiers gladly swapped their government salaries. Lieutenant Alexander Dyer recalled asking his lonely soldiers to contribute four dollars toward a well-attended fandango. The sum purchased grapes, candles, whiskey, and mutton; it also paid the musicians.[4] Although skepticism and anger had characterized relations between conquerors and conquered, their growing interdependence gradually drew together the army's village on the hill and the Spanish-speaking town below it.

Across the decades, Santa Fe people had accommodated strangers. Of course, they complained constantly about raucous, drunken soldiers. But trading helped ease the tension in the community. By 1850 a new stream of merchants began pouring in from the East and Europe. They arrived eager to make a quick fortune in a town teeming with visitors. Most retailers barely kept pace with the rising needs of investors, soldiers, and federal agents. One result was a Spanish-Mexican community gradually oriented toward an evolving market economy and increasingly removed from the slower exchange-barter practices of earlier eras.[5]

The economy experienced ups and downs while newcomers tugged at tradition. Politics also changed. Four years after Kearny's successful march into town, New Mexico became a territory of the United States. Legislators then launched a long, optimistic battle for statehood. Ultimately, national acceptance was postponed because of concerns like slavery. Proponents of statehood meanwhile prepared the region by electing a legislature. They housed the lawmakers in a new building, and when they were settled, the English-speaking authorities began the difficult business of working with local politicians.[6]

Newcomers looking for territorial status envisioned an improving, expanding economy. "Our business is with the future," proclaimed the first territorial governor.[7] Still, controversy occurred at every juncture. In contrast to the Spanish-Mexican leaders, most federal appointees in the new government, including military officers, came to Santa Fe without experience.

But they carried one great advantage: like the vendors in town, they brought cash.[8] Charles Blumner, in charge of the first census for the city of Santa Fe, called himself a merchant and was worth $10,000 when he arrived. A decade later he was the tax collector, and his personal worth had risen to $12,000.[9] Other officers or agents listed even larger amounts, while the wealthiest of locals rarely stated assets exceeding $1,000.

The immigrants, whether merchants or appointees, envisioned making over Santa Fe. Previous traders had bemoaned the town's overwhelming insularity and provincialism, while noting its pervasive destitution. "The people were really all in extreme poverty and there were absolutely none who could be classed as wealthy, except by comparison," one recalled.[10]

Earlier ventures had adopted the community's slower tempo; selling was brisk but rested on barter and exchange policies several generations old. During the war changes began. The incentives for improvement, American style, lay everywhere. James Webb, one of several merchants arriving in 1844, remembered that "the houses were nearly all old and delapidated, the streets narrow and filthy, and the people . . . not half dressed."[11] Though he vowed not to continue in the trade, Webb lingered—and profited—for the next eighteen years.

Moreover, Webb's generation invested its cash in such local ventures as mining. In the mountains outside Santa Fe its members staked claims and scoured the hills for copper and silver. They bought up land as rapidly as possible, filing deeds in a court system that was also undergoing Americanization. Retailers quickly built shops and paid for liquor or gambling licenses in a town now bustling with commercial activities. Food carts gave way to stores stocked with the supplies soldiers and miners needed. And merchants constantly stressed advancement. The developing market and its endless possibilities engaged their interests, so much so that before long sellers like Webb were firmly ensconced in town politics as well as in the economy. Politicians and merchants joined voices to declare that New Mexico was indeed approaching better times.[12]

New establishments and a well-equipped fort gave these men reason to celebrate. Santa Fe had been transformed, even in appearance. The old building used for politics and business, the Palace of the Governors, yielded to a capitol of brick.[13] The recently appointed Catholic bishop, Jean Baptiste Lamy, lobbied his parishioners for another cathedral. It soon rose on the dusty ground beyond the plaza—an enormous church made of the stone common in Lamy's native France.

Although he had to import the materials and the masons who could work it, Lamy remained undeterred in his quest for more moral Catholics, a modern-appearing place to worship, and a prosperous parish.[14] He soon reclaimed a chapel that the army had been using. On the same lot, he explained, "stood four stores and one house. The stores yield a rent of [a] hundred dollars a month as everything is extremely dear in this place."[15] The new church leader might have mentioned that the price of mutton, butter, and eggs had risen.[16] Yet Lamy recognized the dollar's power. Through firm, friendly gestures he won over the army and the new merchants. Additionally, Lamy befriended politicians, persevering in a larger plan to link Santa Fe to the rest of the world.[17]

Apparently, the town had taken dramatic turns for the better. Yet despite the appearance of growth and prosperity, fully one-half of the town's population, its Spanish-Mexican women, remained mired in poverty, living under the harshest conditions. They washed and sewed the Euro-Americans' clothes or served them as domestics. For the same work, they received significantly less in wages than others were paid (table 1). In the decades following the peace treaty with Mexico and before the arrival of the railroad in 1880, laboring women found themselves increasingly constrained by political and economic turmoil. Women's circumstances, particularly in the matter of paid employment, became governed by white men and their needs. Such growing dependency insured that the majority of women remained trapped by decisions emanating from church, legislature, and army.

Table 1. Wage Differences, Ethnicity, and Gender in Santa Fe, 1860-80

Occupation	Daily Wage						Percentage of Spanish-Surnamed Female Population over Age 15		
	Americans[a]			Mexicans[b]					
	1860	1870	1880	1860	1870	1880	1860	1870	1880
Day laborer, male	$1.50	$1.60	$1.75	$1.00	$1.10	$1.15	—	—	—
Domestic, female	1.50	1.75	2.00	0.50	0.55	0.85	25	31	48
Laundress, female[b]	0.20	0.25	0.25	0.10	0.15	0.20	30	28	25
Seamstress, female[b]	0.10	0.15	0.15	0.05	0.10	0.10	20	21	15

SOURCES: U.S. Census Bureau, Original Schedules, Social Statistics, Eighth, Ninth, and Tenth Census of Population, for Santa Fe County (microfilm, NMSCR, Santa Fe).

[a] Enumerator's terms.

[b] Per item.

Powerful priests, lawmakers, and soldiers as well as merchants now determined the course of their lives in ways that others had not done before.

Not only jobs and wages detailed the grim contrast between Spanish-Mexican women and prosperous immigrant men. Net worths portrayed another disparity. The 1850, 1860, and 1870 censuses inquired into people's personal income and property. The enumerations showed few non–Spanish-surnamed males with real and personal estates worth below $100 (table 2). Moreover, one-fourth of 400 newcomers in 1860 claimed personal yearly incomes of between $1,000 and $4,000; another twenty-seven individuals listed estates exceeding $5,000. Within a decade, those amounts had risen.[18] Not all of the wealthiest were merchants or retailers, but cash obviously established these men in businesses or helped them launch new projects in mining, agriculture, and merchandising. They formed the body of an investor group that began turning Santa Fe toward a market economy while certain groups became locked in hopeless dependence.

At that end of the spectrum stood Santa Fe's impoverished women. Until 1870, not 1 percent of their number stated net worths surpassing $100. The overwhelming majority in the postwar decades claimed less than fifty-dollar estates. Meanwhile, the price of food and goods rose steadily. When Kearny's soldiers first entered Santa Fe, corn cost $3.50 a bushel. Five years later the soldiers and other newcomers had strained supplies, and the price had risen another dollar per bushel. The cost of eggs doubled, and in less than a decade the value of mules quadrupled.[19] Low and barely rising wages for domestic, laundering, and sewing jobs meant that working women had no

Table 2. Personal Income Index of Non–Spanish-Surnamed Males

	Number of Men	
Dollars	1860	1870
$1-$999	100[a]	50[b]
$1,000-$9,999	28	80
$10,000-$14,999	6	6
$15,000-$19,999	5	5
$20,000-$39,999	11	7
Over $40,000	4	3

SOURCES: U.S. Census Bureau, Original Schedules of the Eighth and Ninth Censuses of Population, for Santa Fe (microfilm, NMSRC).

[a] Includes 34 soldiers at Fort Marcy.

[b] Includes 18 soldiers at Fort Marcy.

protection against such spiraling costs. Even worse, shortages frequently developed. The same amount of crops and number of livestock continued to support the expanding population.[20] The scarcity of commodities led Sister Blandina Segale of the Sisters of Charity to report in the late 1870s that many poor women came into the plaza on Sundays, begging for food while trying to exchange precious possessions like Indian blankets.[21]

Spanish-Mexican women could do little against rising inflation. They had previously supplemented their incomes by raising hens for the eggs but never in sufficient quantity to compete with farmers from the outlying areas in the marketing of chickens. Now women began raising the animals. Local men bought sheep and pastured them on plots outside the urban area. The flocks proved to be a nuisance, in both instances. Sheep devoured good grasses and left the hillsides bare; chickens were noisy and difficult to keep penned. Regardless, the locals could not compete with the newcomers who invested in the more lucrative commodities of cattle and hogs. Such changes had a rippling effect that extended all the way to diet: beef and pork replaced chicken and mutton as delicacies. Cattle and hogs, which the immigrant class purchased as rapidly as possible and leased out to pasture, became unofficial currency worth more than some luxury items. The value of chickens and sheep fell correspondingly.[22]

Postwar Santa Fe was a town turned upside down. Ethnically, it had changed substantially with the arrival of U.S. soldiers and citizens. But the 1870s witnessed unprecedented migration—over 1,300 new men entered Santa Fe (table 3). Their cash flowed in and around the territorial capital lining the pockets of retailers and politicians. Investors used their money to construct new mercantile establishments, a hotel, homes, a hospital, and an orphanage. Yet the economy of the 1870s continued to fluctuate, and its instability affected Spanish-Mexican families. The burgeoning population once more induced food shortages and lowered buying power. The male migrants upset ethnic and sex balances as never before. Men with money in the 1870s increasingly forced locals into menial work. Women in particular struggled under the pressing challenge of changing markets, a new demography, and different occupations. In a matter of decades dual jobs marked their lot.[23]

Social and economic inequalities were most glaring for unmarried women. As used here, the term "unmarried" signifies all adult women who, when enumerated by the census, were living without men. Perhaps 10 percent of adult females had lived or would live with men but were never "legally married." As many as 20 percent outlived their male partners. Placing such

Table 3. Santa Fe's Changing Demography, 1850-80

	1850	1860	1870	1880
Total Population	4,320	4,555	4,847	6,767
Female	2,166 (50%)	2,247 (49%)	2,488 (52%)	2,662 (38%)
Male	2,154 (50%)	2,308 (51%)	2,359 (49%)	4,105 (62%)
Ethnic Background				
Spanish-surnamed females	2,126 (49%)	2,160 (47%)	2,438 (50%)	2,532 (37%)
Spanish-surnamed males	1,915 (44%)	1,995 (44%)	1,803 (37%)	2,178 (32%)
Non-Spanish-surnamed females	40	87	50	130
	(7%)	(9%)	(13%)	(31%)
Non-Spanish-surnamed males	239	313	556	1,927
Female-Headed Households				
Total Households	930	879	1,216	1,461
Unmarried, Spanish-surnamed female heads of households	201 (22%)	253 (29%)	322 (26%)	183 (13%)[a]

SOURCES: U.S. Census Bureau, Original Schedules of the Seventh, Eighth, Ninth, and Tenth Censuses of Population, for Santa Fe (microfilm, NMSRC).

[a] Only those enumerated as widows make up this number.

women in the broadest possible category reflects accurately their common status—women without men.

Among all groups, women over 15 without husbands remained at the bottom of the hierarchy, in income and jobs. From 1850 to 1880, such women made up at least 10 percent of the adult population. Not just work or marital status determined their low position. The majority headed their own households; at least 5 percent lived with women who appeared to be their widowed mothers.[24]

These and other figures were slightly inflated by the number of women whose husbands were away at the mines or, after 1870, laboring for the railroad farther south. The percentage of women "abandoned" will never be known. Additionally, the number legally married and subsequently separated went unrecorded. Nevertheless, other key features of these women's lives coupled with their large number in the population (table 3) suggest that they were the group most adversely affected by the changes in their community.

Despite the renewed growth of the town, single mothers prospered least of all. More headed households in these decades, and their average family size grew by almost one child. Once able to count on relatives or neighbors, such women now found their traditional supporters similarly constrained. The census graphically marked the pattern. On pages enumerating the Spanish-Mexican populace, the euphemistic phrase "at home" rarely described women's work. Rather, the most common occupations were laundress and seamstress, undertaken by mothers and daughters of all ages.[25] Whereas the 1850 census had been peppered with such skilled and semi-skilled trades as "midwife," "confectioner," and "farmer," the next two enumerations (1860, 1870) rarely listed vocations that veered from domestic and cleaning services. The wages paid (table 1) suggest that women did not take these jobs in unprecedented numbers for the extra money but from necessity.

The percentages of single women heading households (table 3) and their deteriorating net worths offer additional insights into women's plight. About 90 percent of all such women had children with their own surname. Across the three decades, their average households grew by one child and an additional adult, almost always a relative, but on occasion, a boarder. These women were not marrying their children's fathers. A randomly selected set of fifty single female heads of household with children of the same surname in 1860 showed not a single male as head of these households a decade later, while the women headed a slightly larger family. Of the fifty, eight listed adopted children in the household.

In 50 percent of the families, children over the age of 15 also worked, thereby aiding the household economy. Mothers heading households with working children appeared slightly better off than either single women listed within a household or women who apparently had no children. But the same random sample yielded the pattern of larger numbers of women per household working as laundresses, seamstresses, and domestics. Few revealed net worths extending beyond $100. Hence, a husbandless or unmarried condition alone did not bind them as a group. Equally pernicious was the growing family and dual, low-paying jobs.

Among these women, age helped determine rank or position. Women between 30 and 80 were most likely to be listed as heads of household. Those between ages 15 and 30 tended to live with their parents, often with sisters or other relatives. The link between age and residence lends credence to the possibility that some who appear to have been unmarried were women whose husbands were away and who had temporarily moved in with relatives. But tracing another group of fifteen mothers in their thirties between the 1860 and 1870 censuses revealed no such pattern and found them still listed without adult men of a different surname. The selection highlighted, however simplistically, the remoteness of temporary separation. It attested to an equally strong possibility that the majority of adult women who appeared to be unmarried lived permanently without male partners and might have been widows.

Within this group of women, widowhood became a distinguishing characteristic. Widowhood also affected how women survived the growing disparities of their time. Unfortunately, because the census did not list familial relationships, age, income, residential arrangement, and ethnicity must also be correlated to marital status to determine how widows and other husbandless women survived inflation and intrusion.[26]

Demographically, Spanish-Mexican Santa Fe had indeed begun to change, but a few patterns remained the same and suggest reasons for the hardy endurance of women without male partners. Few Spanish-Mexican women ever lived alone. Across the four censuses in this period, fewer than twenty resided by themselves. All lived with what appear to have been sons, daughters, or other relatives. A majority of women over 40 headed their households, but some (approximately 30 percent) were counted within a household headed by another woman or an adult man of her surname. Commonly, the husbandless mother, the widow, and other unmarried women lived either with their daughters and sons-in-law, next door to them, or with a married son. Another general pattern, typical of at least half the unmarried women, was that of a single woman heading a household but living in it with an unmarried son, usually in his twenties. Roughly another 10 percent of such mothers made up that group.[27]

Residentially, it could be argued, Santa Fe remained a town of old habits. Women's living arrangments portrayed a community still clustering around neighborhoods, the barrios, with related persons forming the nucleus in most homes. Juxtaposing residence habits, customs, and marital condition depicts a population consistently relying on each other in years of unprecedented growth and change. Women's net worth must thus be evaluated against the specific characteristics of their households. A woman in these decades heading a family sustained it. In a majority of cases she lived without a male partner; in all cases, she labored. Living among relatives, taking several jobs, or remaining unmarried as well as age combined in diverse patterns to insure the household's and the community's survival.

The unmarried Spanish-Mexican woman remained an integral part of her society. She lived and worked with relatives, sons or daughters, married or unmarried. Frequently, she adopted children or cared for children other than her own. These circumstances identify the extent of her incorporation and leadership in family and community life. The widow followed the same pattern. No one thought to place a member of society in a hospital, asylum, or poorhouse; before 1880 Santa Fe had few such institutions.[28]

More important, however, Spanish-Mexican culture either revered its aged or respected their productivity. In one census, about 40 percent of unmarried women over the age of 50 worked as laundresses and seamstresses.[29] Their specific tasks sustained a community under siege. Utilitarian worth undoubtedly joined with cultural mores to secure the position of the elderly and the unmarried. In that regard, the widow of 50 years and older helped households weather the upheaval.

To understand these women of the postwar era only as hard workers or mere survivors or simply to look at their ages when widowed or unmarried is misleading. Santa Fe's women did not pass easily between stages of their lives. Specific profiling—the single mother heading a family, the widow living with her family, the young mother working as a seamstress living with a sister who worked as a laundress—points out how varied, yet universally constrained, each subgroup was.

Marital status obviously influenced survival but also affected the ability to stave off the impact of colonization. Similarly, parenting and grandparenting continued in spite of circumscribing economic and political tumult. Yet a key difference separated these women from the westering woman or Euro-American women generally: Santa Fe's women existed primarily inside the unending, all-embracing pressure of conquest. And it affected every stage of their lives.

Work, disparate property and income distributions, and marital status suggest initially a deepening schism between unmarried women and affluent immigrating men. With so many unmarried women living on the verge of poverty, especially single mothers, widows might have proved most susceptible to the influx of strangers and their cash. In fact, although widows were generally at the bottom of the social and economic ladder in other parts of the Far West, such was not entirely the case in Santa Fe insofar as women's finances can be measured and their status assessed.[30] Widows indeed emerged at the low end of the economy, but, in comparison to all women without male partners, appeared to be slightly more prosperous. And society did not always hold them in low esteem.

These assessments are based on several sources. Few Spanish-Mexican women left written letters or diaries, but they wrote a significant number of wills and testaments. Women comprised about one-third of the authors of 220 wills listed in probate court journals after 1850 and before 1880.[31] Of additional wills located in private family papers, widows wrote about thirty. Furthermore, wills provide exactly the insights missing for other unmarried women. While these wills shed light on the circumstances of all women, that a significant portion were drawn up by widows skews the resulting portrait of unmarried women. But the most prosperous of the unmarried group as a whole, widows looked destitute in comparison with the riches that male immigrants had accumulated and willed.

In addition to will making, another distinguishing feature of widows sets them apart: they had maintained or had held a legally sanctioned relationship with a man, sanctioned by the courts and by the church. Their better financial position might have derived as well from their husbands. But Spanish-Mexican women traditionally held and owned property in their maiden names. They could dispose of it without a husband's signature, and the wills reflected the tendency to retain and pass on inherited property. María de la Sur Ortiz bequeathed her land and another house farther south in San Isidro. She had inherited the property from her father. In 1860 María Josefa Martínez did the same and passed on land, livestock, and furniture to her children and grandchildren.[32] Marriage might have sustained the property for these women or made it unnecessary to sell it, but the land originally belonged to a parent or a wife's family. It was entrusted but not surrendered in marriage.

Many women maintained farms and property apart from their husbands. They rarely drew additional income from it, nor did ownership of farmland indicate general prosperity. New Mexicans had developed a regard for land and concept of ownership that differed markedly from that of the immigrants, even in 1850.[33] Accumulation was relatively unknown because most people inherited land and few bought up acres. One of the most common expressions in wills and testaments is "I leave a plot I bought from ______." Many Santa Fe residents, female and male, continued to own small pastures, but not acreage, outside of town. They used them for grazing or willed them in perpetuity, passing the land to sons and daughters. In some cases the land had been part of an old, divided grant; in others it had been acquired by trade. In *hijuela,* the giving of a share of property, some had received acreage or pasturage. The land did not necessarily carry a peso or dollar value, but it was useful in the exchange market of families or friends.[34]

Moreover, the Productions of Agriculture schedules following each census indicated how little acreage Spanish-Mexicans owned. Few were listed as farmowners in the county. [35] The worth they assigned the land stayed well below its true value on the open market until 1870, when the entry of the railroad was being discussed.

María Josefa Martínez owned twenty acres outside of town; the census found her residing in Santa Fe with her children and claiming a net worth of $50. Her house and furniture alone would have been worth that. Obviously, she did not include her farmland.[36] Unlike inhabitants of other parts of northern New Mexico, Santa Fe's people did manage to hold on to these inherited shares, at least for a time. Land prices, by census indication, had not yet skyrocketed, and much of the pasturage remained in Spanish-Mexican hands. With that in mind, widows who owned land or pastures could hardly be distinguished financially from those who did not.

In another regard, however, a prosperous widow stood alone. She became the woman most subject to the avarice of the greedy politician or the enterprising merchant, something of a pawn in their hands. The widow Chaves, her first name not given, symbolized the extent to which a widow with property might be victimized.[37] By no means poor, the widow Chaves was preyed upon because she had some means and because the immigrant men with whom she dealt carried to Santa Fe prejudices about women's intelligence or wherewithal.[38]

As Territorial Secretary William G. Ritch reported it, the widow Chaves wanted to write her will. In bad health, unable to read or write English, and finding her own attorney absent, the widow asked a law clerk, Edwin Dunn, to draw up the document. Only later, when her son examined the will, did she learn that the stranger had written in donations to the church and the poor. To her horror, she told a friend of Ritch's, it appeared that the law clerk and the priest who was to have received the money had colluded to dupe her.[39]

Several aspects of the tale are important. Each has something to say about the position of Spanish-Mexican widows in Santa Fe after the war and about how outsiders had begun to control women's lives. First, the story was relayed to Ritch by a friend. As a third-hand account, it casts aspersions as much on Ritch as on the conspiring clerk and suspicious priest. Ritch subtitled the document, "How a lawyer and a priest undertook to fix the will of a widow lady in the interest of Truchard [the priest]."[40] That description alone hints at Ritch's anti-Catholicism and his guiding assumption that the U.S. government could relieve Spanish-Mexicans of the ubiquitous Catholic oppression operating in the form of powerful priests. It was a belief uniformly shared by territorial officials.

Ritch twisted his friend's recollections to end on the same note: the widow accused the priest publicly, and in response he began excommunication procedures and would rescind them only if she sought his forgiveness. Of course, she did not ask for it. Smugly, Ritch wound the narrative to its suggestive finale. As a Catholic, Chaves continued to profess her beliefs, fully expecting to be buried in a Catholic rite, but "she had not the supreme confidence in the priesthood that she once had. Nor would she yield to them in matters which appertained to her business and were entirely foreign to the Church."[41] Even women, Ritch seemed to say, were ready for reform. If the wealthier could be converted, perhaps the rest would follow. In any case, the widow Chaves made him hopeful about the Spanish-Mexican willingness to accept change and to embrace it.

Ritch's concerns emerge clearly from his report of the episode. His account also offers insightful commentary into the lives of women in a decade of rising immigration and significant upheaval. Even Ritch could not ignore what motivated the widow Chaves. She was wealthy and thus atypical, a descendant of an affluent family, the Armijos, he said. On a strictly financial level, she reflected the concerns of the wealthiest members of the community. She had married well; her husband, a merchant, Ritch believed, had left a large inheritance to his daughters, giving them each $17,000. One of the daughters was an invalid and incapacitated to the point of being confined to an institution. The daughter intended to leave her brother her share of the estate, but a New Mexico law of that period prevented invalids from bequeathing any one sibling more than one-third of their inheritance. Presumably, this complicated legal situation motivated the widow Chaves to seek assistance from the conniving law clerk.[42]

Despite her wealth, or because of it, Chaves was vulnerable. But her son had uncovered the problem in the will drafted by Dunn and pointed out the way in which women, even wealthier ones, coped with the matters at hand. When institutions like the court or church failed, others stepped in and took over. In this instance, family became the basis upon which to resolve the controversy. Evidently not regarding it as a "private" matter, Chaves had shown the will to her son. After all, it concerned him. Or perhaps Chaves sensed that something was amiss. In any case, her reliance on the son attested to, and identified, the primacy of family. Further, Chaves asked her neighbor, "the widow of Juan Delgado and mother of Juan," to witness her burning the disputed will.[43] Son and neighbor thus rectified the impropriety and helped ease Chaves's situation.

Ritch's efforts to the contrary, the helpers demonstrated the continuing social and cultural tendencies that undermined most attempts at Americanization. At a minimum, the repeated failures of the territorial government and the church illustrated how unpredictable the institutions or their leaders could be. In the final analysis, Chaves had been forced to rely on family and friends, her own kind. They sustained her while new lawyers and a French priest served only to confuse and anger her. The widow Chaves might have been Ritch's champion, but he and his cronies were not hers.

The widow Chaves's experience was repeated throughout the postwar decades, but especially in the 1870s, when the bulk of eastern men arrived and their railroad began approaching Santa Fe. Probate records in that period showed women filing wills as never before (table 4). One book in the court records has been lost, but the remaining materials indicate that the number of women writing their final testaments after 1877 and depositing them before a local magistrate, with two witnesses present, rose dramatically.[44] The rising number owed something to the influx of new people and the havoc they created.

Not all of the women writing wills did so to counter the presence of strangers. Some had even married the newcomers.[45] Some testaments had been framed by widows of mixed marriages.[46] But mixed marriages were complicated by the prevailing social disruptions of the time. In the 1870s, more than ever, such relationships had become primarily a matter of class.

An 1880 sample of non–New Mexico born males married to New Mex-

Table 4. Female Wills and Testaments in Santa Fe County

Wills	Number	Percentage of Composers with Spanish Surnames
Listed in the Index	75	95
Book B, 1856-62	6	99
Book C, 1859-70	6	99
Book D, 1869-77	3	98
Book E, 1877-97	36	95
Missing	24	90

SOURCES: Santa Fe County Records, Wills and Testaments, Index, Books B, C, D, and E, 1856-97, NMSRC, Santa Fe.

ican females bearing Spanish first names implicated economic background in the likelihood of intermarriage. It showed that the majority of such men were craftsmen, semiskilled tradesmen, and, often, of Irish ancestry. An 1870 selection yielded similar results and revealed the male partners of mixed marriages worth less than those who remained unmarried or who brought their wives to Santa Fe.[47] Religion also played a role in the selection of marriage partners and, along with class, encouraged intermarriage between Euro-American Catholics and Spanish-Mexican women.

By the 1870s intermarriage had become a custom with important ramifications for a community experiencing a Euro-American onslaught. It offered Spanish-Mexican women—women with few choices and limited means—a degree of stability. For men without women, entering a new and decidedly different community, marriage afforded opportunities for financial success. Most transplanted easterners left their relatives behind, but the women they married in Santa Fe were privy to an entire network of extended family contacts. A tailor or blacksmith thus had his job virtually secured by his wife's family and friends. Equally important for the woman, the eastern or European-born husband stepped into *her* world. Her contact with people of his race or culture required little of her except by association with him. Even then, she had family or neighbors who spoke her language and who could assist if she found herself lost or confused. Despite imbalances in culture, class, and sense of place, people continued to marry across racial and cultural lines. It remained an important option available to the enterprising woman.[48]

But it was not the only option. The unmarried women who wrote wills pointed to another solution. The majority did not marry the immigrants; women displayed minimal interest in easing men's transition to life in a new society. Instead, they sought stability in their own worlds; they sought to impose order on a world increasingly changed by easterners and their ways. For more and more of these women, the act of writing a will offered a measure of control over their circumstances. Spanish-Mexican women had followed the custom for generations; worldly possessions, however meager, required proper care.[49] The custom took on added significance in the postwar period. Its assumption of stability contrasted sharply with an enveloping sense of disorder; further, it promised children a continuity, a certainty, that their parents lacked.[50]

If more wills attested to a need for order during the turmoil, then their actual composition conveyed another message. Their language, expressed purposes, and stated desires portrayed timeless concerns. "Prometo deberle a nadien nada"—"I am beholden to none"—told the community that the person was leaving the world in good shape. All debts, no matter how small, were recorded with the saying, "I order the following things paid," or, "I ask that the following be collected." Some women listed the debts payable immediately; few exceeded the small amounts of one or five dollars. These women sought to clarify personal and public affairs, to join the two arenas and, by doing so, to preserve harmony in the community.

Within the wills, the arrangement and order of key phrases signaled the extent of women's subordination. "Fui casada y belada"—"I was married to, and watched over by"—usually followed the standard and lengthy proclamations to church and saints.[51] Sometimes a prayer was included, indicating the testator's deep faith as well as her position in the world. God and saints, marriage and husband, and finally children regulated life for women. Next to religious commitment, marriage connoted the second significant phase in a woman's life, and motherhood the third. How the community accounted for the large and growing numbers of unmarried women, given these lifeways, remains a mystery. But one possibility is that a woman who fulfilled even two of the more significant roles was well regarded. As the census recorded, many women who remained unmarried or who had been widowed were also mothers. The majority clustered in their old neighborhoods, and almost every fifth household contained an unmarried woman over the age of 30.[52]

These wills, so often written by unmarried women, starkly expose a community's ideals and mores out of alignment with the realities of many women's lives. "I was watched over by" became a moot point in the wills of at least one-third of these women because they were widowed—some had been widowed longer than they had been married.[53] It might have been more accurate, as with the widow Chaves's friend and neighbor who was widowed, but also a mother, to have brought forward motherhood, after religious commitment, as the next crucial phase in a woman's life. Wills and other documents show that a widowed mother valued both a past marriage and her parenting. In fact, in the neighbor's case, whether widowed or married, the complex middle ground the majority of Spanish-Mexican women occupied was exposed. The short but telling description calling the widow Delgado the wife of Juan and mother of a son by the same name made explicit her dependency, reliance, or regard for her husband and son. Depicting them as widows or as mothers, however, does not define such women's economic circumstances more broadly, especially because they were restricted more than ever by immigrating men with money.

Calling a woman a widow, like terming her wife or mother, conveyed a certain status in Spanish-Mexican Santa Fe. It often did not overlook her reliance on men or children, but told the community that she was a full-fledged member of the society. Not sequestered, rarely living alone, and often heading a family, the widow had to be so included. Yet as a woman without a male partner, she felt increasing pressure from several sides. At home she had fallen victim to the outsider's better economic position. She had few places to turn for support or assistance: even the church, once a traditional sanctuary, was full of new influences and customs.

Yet, as the court documents indicate, the unmarried women and widows writing wills were coping and ordering their lives around people first, institutions second. Some intimately connected to the new church adapted to the changing scene. Sister Dolores Chávez y Gutiérrez, was widowed, entered a convent, and ministered to the poor; for her, the convent was a refuge as well as a life of service.[54]

In the tumultuous decade of the 1870s, will making reflected another alternative to disorder. Women continued to file wills with priests and judges. Perhaps they trusted both; perhaps they should have trusted neither. The widow Chaves had been duped by both church and state. The attorney was as much at fault as the priest, even if the tale exaggerated the influence of one over the other. Yet by 1870 territorial officials had succeeded in passing legislation designed to undermine the power of the church. Bishop Lamy was forced to protect the interests of the church but sometimes that meant helping merchants. He had sold church property to make way for a store. He excommunicated many priests, and this, more than his economic policies, irked Spanish-Mexicans. Factions developed between Lamy's supporters and those upset about his developing collusion with merchants, attorneys, and politicians. Everyone could see that Lamy's immediate goal was to free the church from supposed corruption but that his long-term interest was to advance its economic standing and, if necessary, to try his hand at local and territorial politics.

The melding of both types of institutions, religious and political, predicted other disastrous consequences for the unmarried women, impoverished or not. Bishop Lamy and Territorial Secretrary Ritch occupied different arenas, but they took on the same role—to Americanize. In other parts of the frontier land had changed hands as never before; by some estimates 80 percent of the original Spanish land grants had fallen into newcomers' hands.[55] Lamy himself owned 2,000 acres outside of town. In the resulting confluence, where church, politics, and the economy joined forces, Spanish-

Mexican women recognized a shift that had to be accommodated. The rate at which they filed wills exemplified that recognition.

The world had changed, and women turned to a new court system to make sense of it. Word of mouth, now an unreliable system, did not suffice for dispensing possessions and leaving a mark in life. The witnesses brought into the courtroom were almost always other women, relatives or friends, and reliable. Altogether, a minimum of five people knew what a will contained. If the judges were suspect, at least the community knew a person's final wishes. Never much of a secret, the written document now conveyed a strong public message to residents and newcomers alike; it was an act of faith, but it had its practical side as well.

Among widows, and all women, drawing up a will had become an act demonstrating more than mere orthodoxy or practical commitment. Irrespective of religious meaning or other symbolism, the document laid a life to rest, giving a dying woman (the majority said they were gravely ill) a sense of order and perhaps revivifying her. This final act also bridged life in the present with the hereafter.

The dispersal of worldly possessions, in the Catholic mind, must have connected temporal and spiritual worlds.[56] One was known and measurable—or could be regulated—the other, imagined and unquantifiable. Underneath Catholicism's hierarchy, and over the underlying economic disruptions of the period, wills unveiled a continuing commitment to life's arrangements: religious expressions and devotion remained at the forefront of a dying widow's thoughts, her relationship to her husband, sanctified by church and community, and her relation to a succeeding generation. Not just heirs, but children, marked her existence. Even her final act reflected a spirit and continuity that sustained her.

In the topsy-turvy decades following the war, poverty, death, and general precariousness prevailed. The censuses recorded high death rates among men, which also contributed to the numbers of unmarried women. The conflicts with Natives continued to dominate village life and affected even as large a settlement as Santa Fe.[57] But that alone did not account for the record number of deaths. The newspapers described smallpox and influenza epidemics. Enumerators included at the end of the census other diseases. "The diseases most prevalent have been pleuresy, pneumonia, and fever especially among the poorer class of people."[58] They also noted accidental deaths. "Pablo Lovato, a servant, was killed working a deep acequia [water-ditch] when he was buried by the caving in of one side."[59]

Accidents and illness accounted for some deaths, but when correlated to church burial records, a discrepancy appears. More women than men were buried during this period (table 5). If many unmarried women were being widowed, one would expect to find more adult men than women dying and their burials recorded. Men's burials in almost every year lend some credibility to the point that many unmarried women in the censuses before 1880 were temporarily separated. Or husbands who labored in other towns and died might have been buried in cemeteries away from Santa Fe, and the local parish therefore would not have counted them.

The widows who died were consistently older than the men who died. The 1860 death schedules recorded five such women, all over 40. Only one died of injury, the others of diseases. A 94-year-old developed bladder problems. An 80-year-old did not survive a ten-day illness. Scarlet fever claimed the life of Guadalupe Ortiz, who was 60. María Ortiz, her sister, was 70 and lingered for six months until dropsy killed her.[60]

These women had experienced great changes in their lifetimes. They died before the harshest transformations of the 1870s took hold. Yet in spite of the intrusion that circumscribed their lives, they led a full and rich existence. That should not obscure, however, the number who were impoverished and those who were mothers; of the latter, a larger group per decade headed households. The money entering Santa Fe did little to help them.

Unmarried women had become a fact of life in postwar Santa Fe. They had always been present in Spanish-Mexican communities, but never had their numbers soared as they did after the war. Not all of their troubles could be attributed solely to the military presence or to the politicians who

Table 5. Burial Record: Random Sample for the County of Santa Fe, Archdiocese of Santa Fe

<table>
<tr><th></th><th>1852</th><th>1860</th><th>1870</th><th>1878</th></tr>
<tr><td>Wives</td><td>10 (22%)</td><td>3 (16%)</td><td>12 (13%)</td><td>34 (27%)</td></tr>
<tr><td>Husbands</td><td>9 (20%)</td><td>1 (5%)</td><td>10 (11%)</td><td>19 (15%)</td></tr>
<tr><td>Daughters
Sons</td><td>8
9 (37%)</td><td>3
3 (32%)</td><td>15
16 (35%)</td><td>21
26 (37%)</td></tr>
<tr><td>Total buried</td><td>46</td><td>19</td><td>89</td><td>127</td></tr>
<tr><td>Total uncategorized</td><td>1 (2%)</td><td>2 (11%)</td><td>11 (12%)</td><td>11 (9%)</td></tr>
<tr><td>All others[a]</td><td>9 (20%)</td><td>7 (37%)</td><td>25 (28%)</td><td>16 (13%)</td></tr>
</table>

SOURCES: Archives of the Archdiocese of Santa Fe (microfilm reel 88, NMSRC, Santa Fe).
[a] Infants, for example, are included in this figure.

attempted to bind Santa Fe to the Union. But the circumstances of this period encouraged dependence among unmarried women already exceedingly vulnerable either to politicians or to merchants.

On the other side of the political and economic spectrum were the numerous attorneys and federal appointees arriving in Santa Fe. Although federal appointments were not permanent, the individual wealth of each officer marked the steady march toward higher incomes and richer people. The surveyor general of the 1850s, William Pelham, stated a net worth of $26,500. By 1870 Pelham had been replaced by Thomas Spencer, who claimed an estate of $60,000.[61] Each of the highest government positions and most skilled trades saw escalating improvement—for men.

Meanwhile, unmarried women's finances declined. Their buying power fell, the percentage of those living without a male partner rose, their families grew, and they witnessed a declining net worth during decades of unprecedented transformation. Emphasizing their marital status and ignoring the context in which it occurred would be misleading. They did not live apart or immune from the general dislocations of the period. In that regard, even the widow was not alone. She stood in a very long line of women experiencing conquest in the most fundamental way, as it affected their economy and families.

In Spanish-Mexican communities throughout the Southwest, the role and position of widows and other unmarried women have long been understood but never discussed. Their position may raise many disquieting questions. In this case, however, widows and all unmarried women shed light on the entire frontier. Dislocation and disparity had become facts of life, and yet women subsisted. Barter and exchange practices continued to serve them well, and many probably survived because the old skills had not eroded entirely. Gardening continued in Santa Fe's barrios, and the products were given and traded to relatives and neighbors alike.[62] Extended family networks provided the security needed to raise children, and no matter how difficult reliance on relatives could become, such new institutions as hospitals or orphanages did not yet replace such dependence.

Life for the unmarried woman, the widow included, also exhibited a certain fluidity. Some married, or remarried, the new men in their midst. Others made wills to provide for a future generation. In that manner they might have been like other southwesterners. But they remained Spanish-Mexican women speaking Spanish and not English, practicing Catholicism and not Protestantism, residing in neighborhoods several centuries old, with roots stretching far back. Their story differed fundamentally from the stories of women to whom they might be compared, including Mormon women, city women, or westering women.[63]

To be sure, Santa Fe widows and others who were unmarried shared a language and religion with other Spanish-Mexican women of the Southwest, with Catholic women, and perhaps with the majority of working widows. But I have not been concerned with similarities for two reasons. First, not much information on other unmarried groups exists as yet; and the unifying impulse in such scholarship detracts seriously from the ability to consider these women on their own terms, from the inside out. Second and equally important, further research about the general cultural regard in which widows were held in nineteenth-century Spanish-Mexican communities needs to be done. I have suggested the methods of their survival in this essay, but I have not lost the focus on their financial situation and the general political imbalances pervading their lives. As women of the Spanish-Mexican frontier, they survived the worst decades of turmoil.

At the end of the 1870s, when the railroad tracks had nearly reached Santa Fe, unmarried women stood at another critical juncture. Families and the community were changing; no longer did many groups reside on the periphery, isolated from the government or its institutions. Rather, Spanish-Mexicans were at the center of continuing colonization, their ways irrevocably altered. As immigrants became residents, the unmarried women faced difficult choices. They had persevered, but as the iron horse pushed toward their community, even more pernicious forms of intrusion threatened. They had little choice but to accommodate.

NOTES

1. Ralph Emerson Twitchell, *The Story of the Conquest of Santa Fe: New Mexico and the Building of Old Fort Marcy, A.D. 1846* (Santa Fe: Historical Society of New Mexico, 1921), 30.

2. For evidence of the impact of the Santa Fe trade of the 1820s on residents, see Max Moorhead, *New Mexico's Royal Road: Trade and Travel on the Chihuahua Trail* (Norman: University of Oklahoma Press, 1958); on the nature of conquest in these earlier decades, see David J. Weber, ed., *Foreigners in Their Native Land: Historical Roots of the Mexican-Americans* (Albuquerque: University of New Mexico Press, 1973).

3. On the fort, see L. Bradford Prince, *Old Fort Marcy, Santa Fe, New Mexico: Historical Sketch and Panoramic View of Santa Fe and Its Vicinity* (Santa Fe: New Mexico Historical Publications, 1892). On the army, see Gunther Barth, *Instant Cities: Urbanization and the Rise of San Francisco and Denver* (New

York: Oxford University Press, 1975), 65-67. On wages, see John Taylor Hughes, *Doniphan's Expedition: An Account of the Conquest of New Mexico* (Cincinnati: J. A. & U. P. James, 1848), 52.

4. Dyer War Journal, Oct. 1847, Alexander B. Dyer Papers, Museum of New Mexico, Santa Fe.

5. Alvin Sunseri, *Seeds of Discord: New Mexico in the Aftermath of the American Conquest, 1846-1861* (Chicago: Nelson-Hall, 1979).

6. Howard Roberts Lamar, *The Far Southwest, 1846-1912: A Territorial History* (paper ed., New York: W. W. Norton, 1970), 66-67.

7. Ibid., 83.

8. For an example of the disparities, see U.S. Census Bureau, Original Schedule of the Eighth Census of Population, for Santa Fe, New Mexico (microfilm, New Mexico State Records Center, Santa Fe), 22, 26, 28, 31, hereafter cited as NMSRC.

9. U.S. Census Bureau, Original Schedule of the Seventh Census of Population, for Santa Fe, New Mexico (microfilm, Coronado Collection, University of New Mexico, Albuquerque), 1. See Eighth Census, for Santa Fe, 39.

10. Quoted in James Josiah Webb, Memoirs, July 1844, Museum of New Mexico.

11. Ibid., 44.

12. On the politicians, see Lamar, *Far Southwest,* ch. 4. On the merchants, see Barth, *Instant Cities,* 72, 73.

13. David Meriwether to Building Commissioners, Sept. 1853, William G. Ritch Collection, Box 11, Henry E. Huntington Library, San Marino, Calif.

14. See, for example, Jean Baptiste Lamy to Archbishop Purcell, Sept. 2, 1851, Archives of the Archdiocese of Santa Fe, Loose Diocesan Documents, number 14, 1-3. On the masons, see Sister Blandina Segale, *At the End of the Santa Fe Trail* (reprint ed., Milwaukee: Bruce Publishing, 1948), 81.

15. Lamy to Purcell, Sept. 2, 1851, 2.

16. On the rising costs, see Segale, *End of the Santa Fe Trail,* 105-6; for comparisons, see Sunseri, *Seeds of Discord,* 21-22.

17. Lamar, *Far Southwest,* 103.

18. U.S. Census Bureau, Original Schedules of the Eighth and Ninth Censuses of Population, for Santa Fe, New Mexico (microfilm, NMSRC).

19. On eggs, see Segale, *End of the Santa Fe Trail;* on mules, see Sunseri, *Seeds of Discord,* 30-31.

20. Productions of Agriculture Schedules," in U.S. Census Bureau, Original Schedules of the Seventh and Eighth Censuses of Population, for Santa Fe County (microfilm, NMSRC), 1-7, 1-8.

21. Segale, *End of the Santa Fe Trail,* 104.

22. Sunseri, *Seeds of Discord,* 28, 31.

23. For examples, see U.S. Census Bureau, Original Schedule of the Ninth Census of Population, for Santa Fe (microfilm NMSRC).

24. U.S. Census Bureau, Original Schedules of the Seventh, Eighth, Ninth, and Tenth Censuses of Population, for Santa Fe (microfilm, NMSRC).

25. For examples, see the Seventh Census, 1, 32, 50; Eighth Census, 16, 17, 29; Ninth Census, 12, 23, 25; Tenth Census, 9, 15, 29.

26. For widows in other parts of the Far West, see Joyce D. Goodfriend, "The Struggle for Survival: Widows in Denver, 1880-1912," and Maureen Ursenbach Beecher, Carol Cornwall Madsen, and Lavina Fielding Anderson, "Widowhood among the Mormons: The Personal Accounts," herein.

27. U.S. Census Bureau, Original Schedules of the Seventh, Eighth, Ninth, and Tenth Censuses of Population, for Santa Fe (microfilm, NMSRC).

28. Lamar, *Far Southwest*, 91; on St. Vincent's Hospital, see U.S. Census Bureau, Original Schedule of the Tenth Census of Population, for Santa Fe (microfilm, NMSRC), 17; and the Santa Fe *New Mexican*, Oct. 13, 1865; on the orphanage, see Thomas Richter, ed., "Sister Catherine Mallon's Journal (Part One)," *New Mexico Historical Review* 52 (1977):135-55.

29. U.S. Census Bureau, Original Schedule of the Eighth Census of Population, for Santa Fe (microfilm, NMSRC).

30. On Denver, see Goodfriend, "Struggle for Survival"; on Texas, see Arnoldo de Leon, *The Tejano Community, 1836-1900* (Albuquerque: University of New Mexico Press, 1982), 107, 109, 110, 189; on Los Angeles, see Barbara Laslett, "Household Structure on an American Frontier: Los Angeles, California, in 1850," *American Journal of Sociology* 81 (1975):109-28, and Richard Griswold del Castillo, *The Los Angeles Barrio, 1850-1890: A Social History* (Berkeley: University of California Press, 1979).

31. Santa Fe County Records, Wills and Testaments, 1856-97, Index, Books B, C, D, E (Manuscript Division, NMSRC).

32. Will of Maria de la Sur Ortiz, Apr. 1860, will of María Josefa Martínez, Aug. 1860, Santa Fe County Records, Book B, 1856-62.

33. For a distinction on attitudes and concepts toward land, see Roxanne Dunbar Ortiz, *Roots of Resistance: Land Tenure in New Mexico, 1680-1980* (Los Angeles: Chicano Studies Research Center Publications and the American Indian Center, 1980). For a different assessment, see Victor Westphall, *Mercedes Reales: Hispanic Land Grants of the Upper Rio Grande Region* (Albuquerque: University of New Mexico Press, 1983).

34. On hijuela, see Westphall, *Mercedes Reales*, 225. For examples on the loss of land and hijuelas, see the requests to collect debts for land sold in the will of Dolores Montoya, May 21, 1881, and will of María Josefa Montoya, Aug. 9, 1883, Santa Fe County Records, Wills and Testaments, Book E, 1877-97.

35. "Productions of Agriculture," in U.S. Census Bureau, Original Schedules of the Eighth and Ninth Census of Population, for Santa Fe County (microfilm, NMSRC), 1-8, 1-7.

36. U.S. Census Bureau, Original Schedule of the Ninth Census of Population, for Santa Fe (microfilm, Huntington Library), 22.

37. Official Reports of the Territorial Secretary, Summer 1876, William G. Ritch Collection, RI 1731.

38. See Deena J. González, "The Spanish-Mexican Women of Santa Fe: Patterns of Their Resistance and Accommodation, 1820-1880" (Ph.D. diss., University of California, Berkeley, 1985).

39. On the widow Chaves and who she might have been, see U.S. Census Bureau, Original Schedule of the Eighth Census of Population, for Santa Fe (microfilm, NMSRC), 5; in the same census, "Productions of Agriculture," 1; will of Teresa Chávez, Jan. 1, 1871, Santa Fe County Records, Wills and Testaments, 1856-97, Book D.

40. Official Report, Ritch Collection, RI 1731, 1. For further information on Truchard, see Lamar, *Far Southwest,* 174; Santa Fe *New Mexican,* July 20, 1877; will of María Nieves Chávez, Dec. 1870, Santa Fe County Records, Wills and Testaments, 1856-97, Book D.

41. Official Report, Ritch Collection, RI 1731.

42. Ibid., RI 1731; on the law, see L. Bradford Prince, comp., *General Laws of New Mexico from the "Kearny Code of 1846" to 1880* (Albany: Torch Press, 1880), 52.

43. She may have been the widow Trinidad Delgado; see U.S. Census Bureau, Original Schedule of the Tenth Census of Population, for Santa Fe (microfilm, NMSRC), 27.

44. See Santa Fe County Records, Wills and Testaments, 1856-97, Book E.

45. On intermarriages in an earlier period and a different assessment, see Darlis Miller, "Cross-cultural Marriages in the Southwest: The New Mexico Experience, 1846-1900," *New Mexico Historical Review* 57 (1982):334.

46. See, for example, Santa Fe County Records, Legitimacy and Adoption Records, 1870-82 (Manuscript Division, NMSRC), 5-6.

47. U.S. Census Bureau, Original Schedules of the Ninth and Tenth Censuses of Population, for Santa Fe (microfilm, NMSRC).

48. For an estimate on the number of white men marrying Spanish-Mexican women, see Miller, "Cross-cultural Marriages," 334.

49. For samples of wills in the first half of the nineteenth century, see will of Rafaela Baca, Apr. 26, 1804, will of María Micaela Baca, Apr. 22, 1830, will of Bárbara Baca, Dec. 30, 1838, Twitchell Collection (Manuscript Division, NMSRC).

50. For assistance with these ideas, I thank Helena M. Wall, Pomona College. See her use of court records in her study of British North America, "Private Lives: The Transformation of Family and Community in Early America" (Ph.D. diss., Harvard University, 1983).

51. See, for example, will of Desidéria Otero, Dec. 22, 1870, Santa Fe County Records, Wills and Testaments, 1856-97, Book D; will of Francisca Quirón, Apr.

30, 1857, Santa Fe County Records, Wills and Testaments, 1865-97, Book B; will of Rafaela Baca, Apr. 26, 1804, Twitchell Collection, Wills and Estates, 1.

52. U.S. Census Bureau, Original Schedules of the Seventh, Eighth, and Ninth Census of Population, for Santa Fe (microfilm, NMSRC).

53. For examples, see will of María Miquela Lucero, Feb. 4, 1858, Mariano Chávez Family Papers (Manuscript Division, NMSRC), 1; will of Maria Josefa Martínez, May 23, 1860, Santa Fe County Records, Wills and Testaments, 1856-97, Book B. The two women can be found in the Tenth Census, 31, 62.

54. Segale, *End of the Santa Fe Trail,* 117-22. For a discussion of the convent as a refuge in Latin America, see Asuncion Lavrin, "Values and Meaning of Monastic Life for Nuns in Colonial Mexico," *Catholic Historical Review* 58 (1972):367-87.

55. Ortiz, *Roots of Resistance,* 93. For an analysis that blames Manuel Armijo for selling land to Euro-Americans, see Westphall, *Mercedes Reales,* 147-49; on Lamy, see Lamar, *Far Southwest,* 102-3.

56. For statements reflecting the connection, see the prayers in the will of María Teresa García, Nov. 24, 1879; will of Dolores Montoya, May 12, 1881, Santa Fe County Records, Wills and Testaments, 1856-97, Book E.

57. Lamar, *Far Southwest,* 133; on the general social disquietude and specific incidents of violence, see the Santa Fe *New Mexican,* Jan. 20, 1865, Jan. 12, 1867, Jan. 14, 1868, Aug. 30, 1870.

58. "Death Schedules," in U.S. Census Bureau, Original Schedule of the Eighth Census of Population, for Santa Fe (microfilm, NMSRC), 1. On a smallpox epidemic, see the *Santa Fe New Mexican,* July 20, 1877.

59. U.S. Census Bureau, Original Schedule of the Eighth Census of Population, for Santa Fe (microfilm, NMSRC), 4.

60. "Death Schedules," in U.S. Census Bureau, Original Schedule of the Eighth Census of Population, for Santa Fe County (microfilm, NMSRC), 2-3.

61. On Pelham, see U.S. Census Bureau, Original Schedule of the Eighth Census of Population, for Santa Fe (microfilm, NMSRC), 21; on Spencer, see the Ninth Census, 49.

62. For an observation of the gardens, see the letters of Sarah Wetter, Sept. 14, 1869, to her mother, Henry Wetter Papers, Museum of New Mexico. On the importance of produce, see the will of María Josefa Martínez, May 23, 1860, Santa Fe County Records, Wills and Testaments, 1856-97, Book B; on fruit exchange, see the Santa Fe *New Mexican Review,* Sept. 3, 4, 1883.

63. On the small number of English-speaking women in postwar Santa Fe, see table 1; for a general description, see Miller, "Cross-cultural Marriages," 339.

4

Hispanic Widows and Their Support Systems in the Mesilla Valley of Southern New Mexico, 1910-40

MARTHA OEHMKE LOUSTAUNAU

July 22, 1911
Survivors: one widow (Maria), six children
Assets: personal property value — $60.00
no real property
September 25, 1925
Survivors: one widow (Petra), no children
Assets: no real or personal property
January 19, 1936
Survivors: one widow (Josefina), 10 children
Assets: real and personal property total value — $50.00[1]

Reading probate records can be a curious and disturbing experience. They suggest a lot, including the difficult and sometimes desperate conditions in which widows found themselves. Yet they tell little regarding the personal lives, aspirations, abilities, trials, and responses of these widows. Who were these women? How did Maria manage with no real property? Did Petra have any relatives to help her? What did Josefina do with her inheritance of $50? Although these records do not answer such questions, they do reveal that there were many Marias, many Petras, many Josefinas.

Once widowed, these women, just as other widows, had to learn to cope with the new personal, social, and economic situation in which they found themselves, to deal with their grief and altered status, and to function as women without their husbands. Their degree of success or failure in this endeavor certainly depended somewhat upon individual character and fortitude, but it also related to the various support systems available to them.[2] These support systems were characterized by individual and cultural variations, including background, personal resources such as experience and education, ties with family, friends, and community, economic resources, religiosity, environment, social roles, time, and place. Sociologists indicate that group ties foster abilities to cope and to function as a member of the community. A weakening or absence of ties tends to lead to alienation and decreased ability to cope.[3] It therefore follows that the closer the ties and the stronger the support system, the greater the ability of the widow to cope and adjust to widowhood. This paper examines these support systems and their impact upon Hispanic[4] widows.

Few written accounts were left by Hispanic women who had emigrated to the North, thus limiting resources for historical study.[5] As Joan Jensen and Darlis Miller have noted, studies on western women are needed that utilize various methodologies, such as demographics, cross-cultural comparisons, and description of socioenvironmental conditions. Oral histories, in combination with the above methodologies, can give validity, color, and humanity to western women.[6] I have used these methods to describe the state of widowhood of Hispanic women in the Mesilla Valley of southern New Mexico, from 1910 to 1940, particularly with regard to their various support systems.

I chose this period for several reasons. A number of families from Mexico entered the area around 1910 as a result of the political and economic upheaval of the Mexican Revolution. This period witnessed some growth and development plus an increase in the Hispanic population in the Mesilla Valley. Although some changes were beginning to take place by the 1930s, related to agricultural mechanization, decreased isolation, and the economic difficulties of the Depression, these changes became significantly greater by the 1940s, with the advent of government social programs and World War II. Thus the three decades from 1910 to 1940 form a natural historical period for study.

In addition to defining and describing this Hispanic population, and examining cultural environments and their role in the widows' support systems, I discuss other major elements of the support systems, including religious culture, customs, the family, and the social roles these women played.

The rural, agricultural environment of the valley greatly contributed to physical survival. The culture and religion of the area gave direction and reassurance during a time of psychological pain and stress. However, with little or no outside resources, it was the extended family with its broad network of close relationships that offered the most support. It was also the woman herself who held the family together, and whose strength and resourcefulness were important elements of her own personal support system.

The Population

In 1910 New Mexico still had territorial status; two years later it would become a state. Early Spanish colonization of the area from 1598 to 1831 was located primarily in the northern half of what was to be the state of New Mexico, thus giving it a different cultural tone and character from the southern border areas, which were more influenced by Mexico.[7] Manuel Gamio wrote that in New Mexico, Americans of Mexican origin were a "case apart." In other states the population of Hispanic origin had been "Americanized" to a certain extent, dropping or adapting various Mexican cultural elements and customs. Although the immigrant population of New Mexico had been "Americans" for three-quarters of a century by 1930, it still possessed marked Mexican characteristics. In spite of racial prejudice, these Hispanics had a better economic, social, and cultural position than in other states.[8] An extensive sociological study of Dona Ana County in the late 1930s by Sigurd Johansen bears out this uniqueness and suggests a reason for it. When the area became American territory with the Gadsden Purchase in 1853, the American government recognized and respected the Mexican population, including the old laws, customs, language, and religion. This may easily have been a major reason for cultural continuity in the area.[9]

The average Hispanic woman coming into the Mesilla Valley from the South around 1910 was most likely to be fleeing from the turmoil of the Mexican Revolution or depressed economic conditions. She was fleeing with her family, with her cultural beliefs and values, and with whatever monetary resources could be salvaged. Many women came with their laborer husbands to escape economic and political chaos, lack of food, and unemployment.[10] The Mexican Revolution of 1910, which continued into the 1920s, simply encouraged and gave impetus to the tide of emigration to the North, in progress since the early part of the century.[11] The area already had been settled by a predominantly Hispanic population, rural in character, on land suited to agricultural production. According to 1910 general census statistics, these female immigrants as a group had three to seven children, an estimated life expectancy of approximately 55 years, and about a 20 to 30 percent chance of being widowed. Their average age at widowhood was somewhere between 45 and 55 years of age.[12]

Before 1970 the census did not distinguish Hispanic from Anglo populations and simply counted them as "white" or "non-Indian." However, many of the old Hispanic families that had established themselves in the southern area during and even before territorial days have lived there through the present generation and can be identified through family names.[13] Johansen estimated a high percentage of "Spanish-Americans" by using data from the New Mexico Department of Public Health based on the school census for the 1930s. He estimated that 64.6 percent of the non-Indian population was Hispanic, with the probability of an even higher number since many of these children did not attend school. Counties with the highest percentages of Hispanics were traversed by the Rio Grande.[14]

During the 1920s the U.S. Department of Labor's Bureau of Immigration issued reports indicating numbers of Mexican immigrant aliens admitted to the United States.[15] In 1922, out of 18,246 aliens admitted, 395 gave New Mexico as their intended permanent residence. Five percent of the Mexican immigrants were listed as widows. If one were to assume that New Mexican immigrants were representative of the whole, then twenty of those immigrants destined for New Mexico would be widows. During the period 1922 to 1932, 162 widows would have emigrated to New Mexico.[16] Over that ten-year period, 14,142 immigrants were listed as widowed females. Thus it appears that widows did emigrate, and although ages were not given, it is likely that they were older and came with other family members to establish a new and permanent home.[17]

Other useful demographic data include sex ratios, widowed population, county populations, and age ranges (tables 1 and 2).

Since widows depended heavily upon families, a relatively stable, equal male-to-female ratio would indicate a more family-oriented population. As seen in table 1, male-female sex ratios tended to remain fairly even with only a slight majority of males, thus reflecting a more settled family character in Dona Ana County than in the contiguous border counties of Lea and Grant, where the gender imbalance was much greater.[18] This relatively stable male-female ratio holds even though there were a number of deaths from influenza around 1916, and World War I would have been expected to claim a number of males. This may also be indicative of the large number of families in the area, since males with families and as heads of households were generally exempt from military service. Even with the influenza epidemic and war, however, there was still considerable population growth

Table 1. The Widowed Population of Dona Ana County, New Mexico, 1910-40

Year	Total Population	No. Males	No. Females	Percentage of Widowed[a]	
				Male	Female
1910	12,893	6,717	6,176	5.3	9.1
1920	16,548	8,487	8,061	6.2	10.5
1930	27,455	14,314	13,141	5.6	10.1
				3.8[b]	5.8[b]
1940	30,411	15,486	14,925	4.5	9.7

SOURCE: U.S. Censuses, 1910-40.
[a] Information in these columns is statewide unless otherwise noted.
[b] Dona Ana County only.

Table 2. Age Distribution in the State of New Mexico (percentage)

Age	1910		1920		1930		1940	
	Male	Female	Male	Female	Male	Female	Male	Female
Under 5	12.9	14.9	12.2	13.6	12.3	13.1	11.9	12.2
5-9	11.8	13.3	12.3	13.5	12.7	13.4	11.3	11.7
10-14	10.0	11.1	10.8	11.9	10.6	11.3	10.8	11.2
15-19	9.4	10.5	9.1	10.2	9.8	10.6	9.9	10.5
20-24	9.4	9.6	9.0	9.1	8.7	9.2	8.5	9.1
25-29	8.7	8.4	8.5	8.5	7.4	7.9	8.1	8.6
30-34	7.2	6.8	7.1	6.9	6.5	6.7	7.2	7.3
35-39	7.1	6.4	6.8	6.2	6.8	6.7	6.4	6.6
40-44	5.5	4.9	5.0	4.8	5.6	5.2	5.6	5.4
45-49	4.9	4.0	5.3	4.3	5.0	4.3	5.3	4.7
50-54	4.1	3.4	4.0	3.4	4.0	3.4	4.4	3.7
55-59	2.9	2.4	3.0	2.5	3.3	2.7	3.4	2.8
60-64	2.6	1.9	2.8	2.0	2.7	2.1	2.6	2.2
65-69	1.5	1.1	1.8	1.3	2.0	1.5	2.0	1.8
70-74	1.0	.7	1.1	.8	1.3	.9	1.4	1.1
75+	.9	.7	1.0	.8	1.3	1.0	1.4	1.2

SOURCE: U.S. Censuses, 1910-40.

in the county during this period, some of which, as Johansen pointed out, resulted from immigration as well as natural increase.

The widowed population fluctuated slightly during the period, but shows a majority of widows over widowers. Early parish records of La Mesilla are inconsistent, but tend to reveal a high number of widowers. One possible explanation may be the number of women dying in childbirth. Interviews with local Hispanics, including one early midwife as reported by Shan Nichols and Ella Curry, indicate that in the 1910s this might have been the case.[19] One woman noted that "many men married at least twice. Diseases killed many people and women died giving birth." Census statistics in table 2 show a higher number of males even at older ages.

In 1940, when marital status was broken down by age (figure 1), there was a slightly larger number of males and married males in all categories, but a larger number of widowed females over age 65 and even up to age 75. This tends to indicate that many men did remarry and often chose younger women. Age distribution in New Mexico shows almost half the population to be under 20 years of age. With high marriage rates, the large percentage of younger people may also indicate larger families.

Johansen's study of Dona Ana County[20] in the late 1930s produced some related demographic information. In studying eight of the small communities in the county, he found a very high percentage of Hispanics—up to 100 percent in two locations. He found average size of household to be 4.7 with 224 Hispanic male heads of households, and 41 Hispanic female heads, 19.2 percent of the heads widowed, 8.7 percent male, and 81.4 percent female. Johansen noted that in the majority of cases, when the husband died the wife assumed the headship and had "no marked tendency to remarry." The sex ratio was 106.8 males to 100 females, corresponding to the county as a whole (105.1). Families maintained a great deal of solidarity, although 12.8 percent were "broken families" with the father missing for one reason or another. Over 14 percent of the households had other relatives or even unrelated persons living with them.

Thus demographic data, sketchy as they are, tend to reveal a rural, heavily Hispanic, stable, family-oriented population, most likely to be employed in agriculture. There is a fairly equal male-female ratio, and a predominance of widows over widowers, most likely to be between 45 and 70 years of age, generally with children to support or with family to aid in their support. Although there is obviously population growth during this period, there also appears to be a great deal of continuity in family settlement and in the rural character of the inhabitants.[21]

The Physical and Cultural Environments

The major area of settlement dealt with here is the Mesilla Valley, in southern Dona Ana County of southern New Mexico, a strip of rich

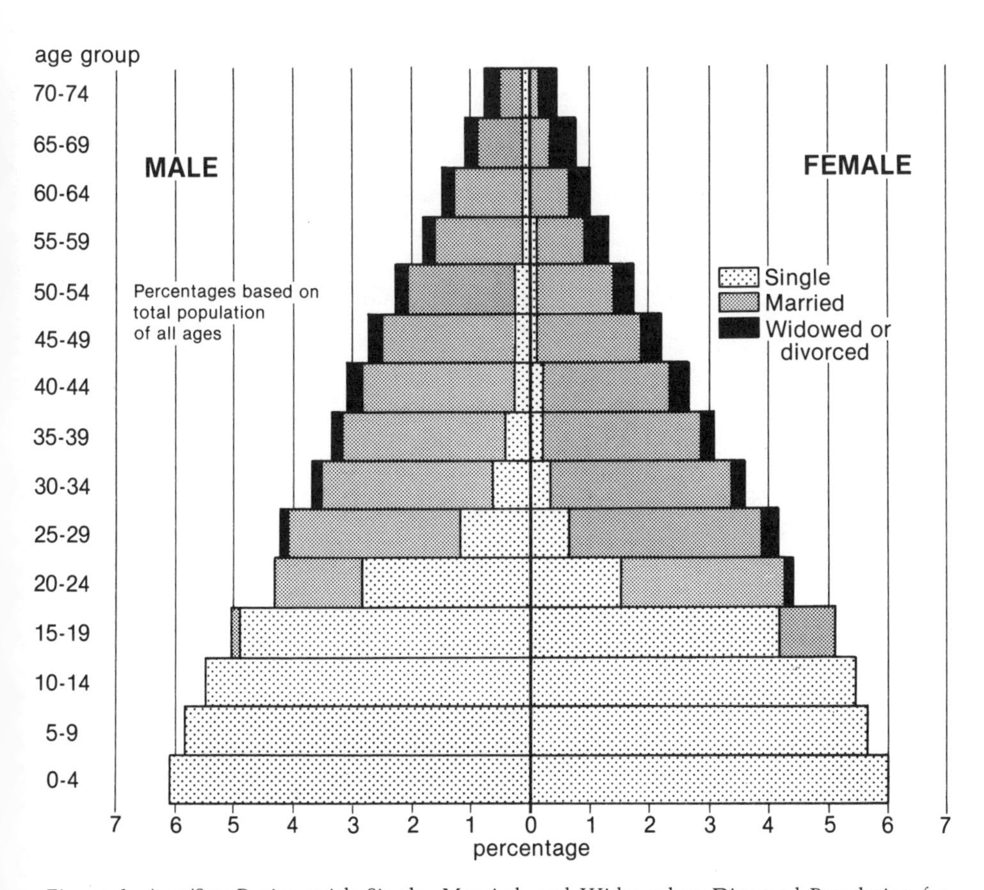

Figure 1. Age/Sex Ratios, with Single, Married, and Widowed or Divorced Population for State of New Mexico, 1940. Source: U.S. Census, 1940.

agricultural land that encompasses the city of Las Cruces, the old territorial capital of La Mesilla, and several small rural villages (figure 2). The valley is approximately forty to fifty miles long and three to ten miles wide, depending upon whether one includes only the irrigable portion or the outer, drier edges as well. The Rio Grande cuts through the area, supplying a fairly constant source of moisture. Major occupations were farming and ranching.[22]

The rurality of the area was one of the most important aspects of the cultural and physical environment. Rural life fostered roles and life-styles not functional or relevant in an urban industrial setting. As David Maldonado has noted, "Agrarian societies produce social structures that are functionally appropriate to them."[23] Characteristic of such social structures were large, extended families, common social and occupational interests, isolation from urban influences, strong religious orientation, and knowledge of and concern for one's neighbor.

Agricultural productivity in the Mesilla Valley was generally high and included a variety of crops. It was described as "an almost unbroken forest of cottonwoods, willow and tornillo, tule swamp and undergrowth, through which meandered the Rio Grande, a raging flood in spring, a trickle in summer."[24] Because these floods left rich silt, the land yielded "great crops" of wheat, corn, beans, and vegetables, so that early settlers referred to the area as "the Nile Valley of New Mexico."[25]

After the construction of the Elephant Butte Dam, sixty miles to the north of Las Cruces, the area became even more productive with a wider variety of crops.[26] Even though more land was gradually devoted to commercial crops and Hispanic land parcels sometimes became smaller, subsistence farming was widely practiced and provided for individual needs. Most subjects interviewed reported that almost everyone had a small "truck garden" and that canning and drying were a way of life. Everyone agreed that this is what helped them through hard times. As long as one had a roof over one's head and something to eat one survived.[27] Since women did most of this work, widowhood did not necessarily change these aspects of their life-style.

The isolation of rural life plus common interests, background, and language of the inhabitants helped keep cultural traditions alive. This cultural continuity was also maintained by various institutions that contributed form, structure, and definition to one's life. The Catholic religion was a major

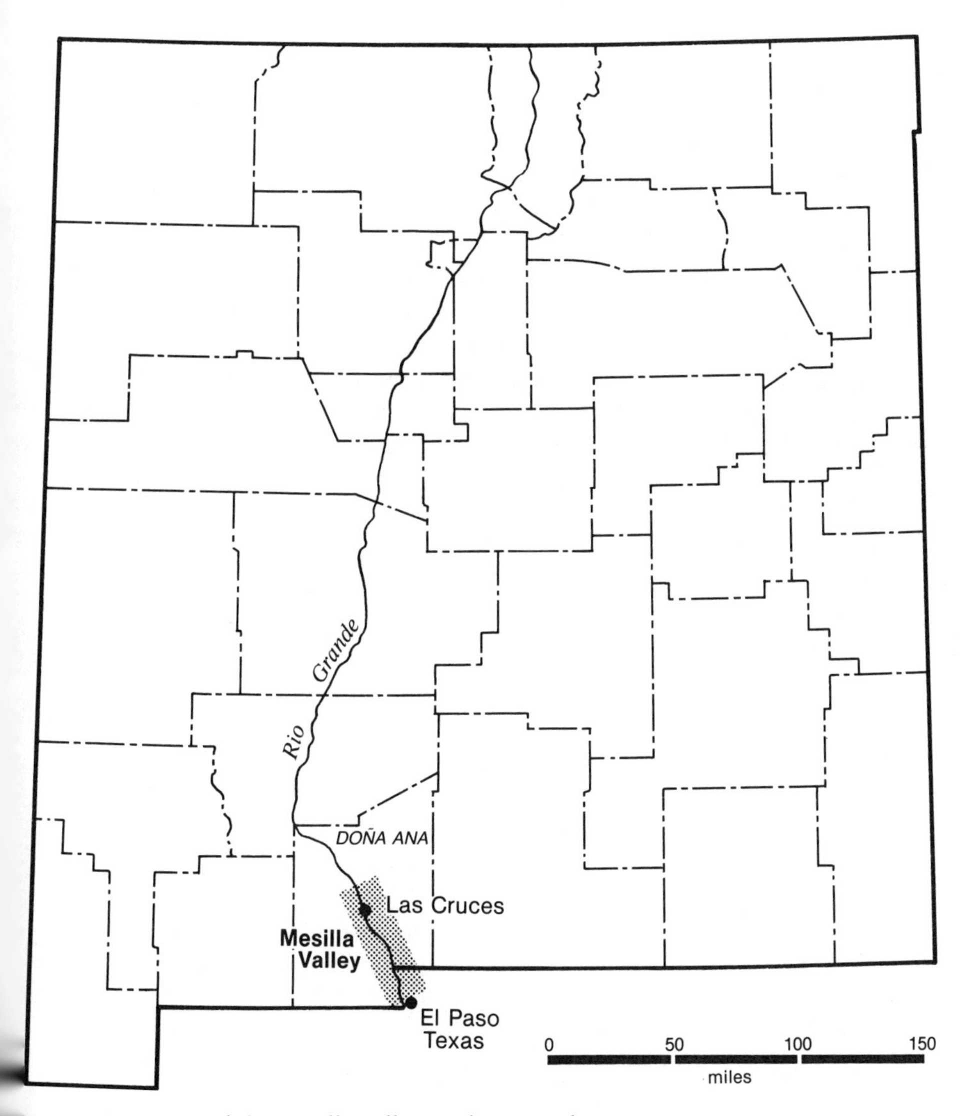

Figure 2. Location of the Mesilla Valley in the State of New Mexico.

element of the Hispanic cultural environment and therefore a major element in the support system of Hispanic widows.

Religion

The religious institution has always been a major force in Hispanic life. As Manuel Gamio stated, "It is precisely in the geographic zones that contribute most largely to immigration that Catholicism is more deeply rooted and intense." He also found that in areas of New Mexico where a large population of Mexican-Americans had been long established, there was a great tendency to remain faithful to the tenets and obligations of the church.[28]

Local priests were instrumental in maintaining faith and custom. One New Mexican priest observed that the majority of inhabitants, especially in small rural towns, were Catholic and perpetuated such customs of old Mexico as paying the priest a peso for each requested mass and bringing offerings like fruit or eggs to the church.[29] Another priest, Dr. C. Gilbert Romero, who taught religion at the University of Texas at El Paso, stated that "coping with various forms of alienation frequently took the form of symbolic expression through the medium of the culture, especially religious faith."[30]

Though priests were not always available and often made only periodic visits to say mass in rural areas, the presence of a community church was a matter of pride and tradition. Women attended mass more regularly than men, but influenced the men to take an active part in building churches and making donations recorded in church ledgers.

As for the church's role in material support of parishioners, a search of its official records indicates no specific material or financial aid from the church for the widowed and destitute. For example, the accounts of one of the area's oldest parishes indicate that expenses included primarily the priest's salary, food, and other necessities, upkeep and maintenance of church and grounds, and gasoline for an automobile. Basic income was derived from special masses, weddings, funerals, and beneficent donations. Rather than providing financial help to the community's needy, the parishes depended upon the populace for economic support.[31]

Various types of material aid were offered to the needy, however, through church-related organizations. The Catholic Daughters of America, for example, founded in 1903 as a national order, had numerous functions, including supplying money, medicine, food, and clothing to needy families and widows. After 1938, a chapter existed in New Mexico, possibly in some measure a response to the ravages of the Depression. Major projects included aid to the needy, as well as disaster relief aid. Altar societies also had specific functions, but these did not necessarily include material aid to widows. They independently chose various projects, such as sewing and providing layettes for new mothers during World War I.

A recent history of the Knights of Columbus in the Las Cruces area indicates that this group occasionally responded with material aid to requests from needy persons, but that official projects were not specifically directed to relief for widows.[32] Founded locally in 1907, the Knights and their Ladies' Auxilliary supported many projects and organizations that aided the poor and needy, including the Good Shepherd Home and the Loretto Convent. Widows were thus aided in indirect ways.

For example, the Good Shepherd Home, founded around 1927 by a group of sisters from Mexico, functioned as a sort of boarding school for wayward girls. Many of the children were from Mexico, but many also came from the surrounding area. Both Anglo and Hispanic children were accepted at the Good Shepherd, and families, including widows who could not care for their children, sometimes brought them to the home.[33] One of the first day-care facilities was operated by the sisters in the 1930s and 1940s for working mothers. They and their pupils did their own gardening, took in laundry, and produced and sold embroidery work. The home was also strongly supported by many Anglos in the area, as well as by such Catholic organizations as the Knights of Columbus.

It thus appears that the major function of the church as a support system of widows was subtle and fundamental. The church offered the support of ritual and spiritual solace, which may be vital in helping the bereaved to deal with the reality of death.[34] Rituals, including funerals, wakes, and various religious observances, served a therapeutic purpose by helping the bereaved to resolve their grief and deal with reality. Saying mass, lighting candles, holding wakes and visitations, funeral services, and wearing black all served to reinforce the reality and acceptance of death for the widow.[35]

Religion offered a strong psychological support in "working through grief." As Bronislaw Malinowski has stated, "Religion steps in, selecting the positive creed, the comforting view, the culturally valuable belief in immortality in the spirit of the body and in the continuance of life after death."[36] Firm religious beliefs do appear to aid people in accepting death. The strong attachment to Catholicism and traditional rituals expressed by the Hispanic population in New Mexico may thus have helped to channel grief and reduce the potential for pathological problems among widows.

Institutionalized Rituals and Customs

There were many rituals and customs to guide and direct the widow. According to New Mexican Hispanic custom, for example, women were required to wear black for a year after the death of a spouse, and they sometimes wore it for shorter periods of time for deaths of other family members as well.[37] Based on information from local interviews, it appears that this custom was widely practiced and continued up until the 1940s. One woman told of a cousin who unfortunately kept losing various relatives at regular intervals. She finally simply began to wear black regularly and despaired of ever leaving a state of continual mourning.[38] Another woman explained that while the custom was still prevalent, her father told her mother that if he were to die, she must not wear black, as he would not like to see her dressed in that manner. He did not like black. Shortly afterward, when he did die, her mother wore gray for mourning, thus breaking with tradition.[39]

There were also social restrictions on the widow's behavior. She could not overtly socialize, attend parties, or dance for a year, although she was permitted to visit friends and neighbors occasionally. Some restrictions applied to the whole family, such as prohibition of music or frivolity in the home. In one home, where the father had been a pianist, the instrument was turned to the wall and draped.[40] In another the crank on the victrola was removed and put away for an entire year.[41] These restrictions tended to reinforce the reality of death and dictated a social response to it. One custom, often burdensome for surviving relatives, particularly widows with few resources, was that of wining and dining friends and relatives who filled the house after a death. This seems strange, since in other times of need, there was considerable sharing of resources. There were, however, many reports of families going into debt to finance the funeral and the *velorio* (wake), apparently an accepted obligation.[42]

The funeral itself, whether conducted at home, at the church, or in a funeral home, was very important. According to Joan Moore, "Uniformly, one meets the flat assertion that the funeral is the most significant family ceremony among Mexican-Americans."[43] In the absence of a professional funeral director, however, since such an establishment first opened its doors in Las Cruces in 1912, bodies were generally laid out at home and prepared for burial by the families themselves. Scholars contend that the ritual of the funeral, in whatever context, must be viewed as psychologically beneficial for survivors of the deceased.[44] This would particularly apply to the widow. For E. T. Eberhart, "The funeral exists within a matrix of human relationships and is not a thing apart, an event unto itself. It is a specialized activity relating to human emotions and belongs to a process which is initiated prior to the funeral's beginning and which will continue long after the funeral is ended."[45] He also argues that the value of the funeral is greatly determined by the quality of the relationships surrounding it. A support network of friends, family, and professionals or clergy, is a key factor in coping with grief and creates a "kinship of sorrow." The widow is not alone, but a part of that "matrix of human relationships." Friends, family, and clergy are especially close and supportive in the Hispanic culture. One woman recalled the charity of neighbors when the family could not afford burial clothes. Her own father gave one of his suits to a family who could not afford one for the deceased head of the household.[46]

Richard Kalish and David Reynolds concluded that Mexican-Americans tend to rely heavily upon this type of network as part of their lives and at death.[47] This feeling was ingrained within the cultural context. The women also play a central role. A spokesman for the Mexican Funeral Directors noted, "Mexican women (including widows) do play an important role in funeralizing the dead. At the family home they serve coffee, soft drinks, and food to those present, and for several months after a death they observe mourning by wearing black clothing and veils, and by keeping to their homes."[48] Women interviewed did recall doing this, and memories of wakes included the serving of drinks, soft and otherwise, with large numbers of people alternately weeping and laughing together.[49] These rituals, which have roots in Mexico, aid in therapeutic adjustment to death. The director of a Mexican-American mortuary interviewed by Kalish and Reynolds in Los Angeles noted an extreme expression of grief among the mourners. "The Mexican-Americans, especially the women, are very emotional, so that sometimes it is necessary to call a physician and to use tranquilizers."[50] Kalish and Reynolds hesitated in generalizing from any of their results but concluded: "Mexican-Americans tackle death and dying head on, while Anglo-Americans try delicately to keep it at arm's length." They cautiously hypothesized, "[The Mexican-American] copes with these distressing thoughts (death and fear of death at a personal level) by mastering death through ritualistic acts, through dwelling on it until the anxiety is worked through, and through integrating it meaningfully into life."[51]

Discussions with funeral directors in Dona Ana County do not completely bear out these contentions on the expression of emotionality. However, interviews with some residents elicited past recollections of excessive demonstrations of grief at funerals and wakes. Social censure, a higher level of education and income, urbanization, and cultural assimilation may have mitigated these demonstrations. William Lamers finds these exaggerated emotional outbursts to be historically "cleansing" and "cathartic," but not peculiar to any group or culture.[52] Thus such demonstrations may also be a result of specific local traditions or socialization processes and therefore not the same in all Hispanic populations.

The problem of finances and paying for burial was another matter. Probate records show that many widows were often left with an average total of $200 to $300, sometimes with real property, sometimes without. After 1912, when the Graham Funeral Home opened in Las Cruces, the average cost of a funeral was approximately $250, and it was often paid for on credit.[53] In addition, parish records from the late 1910s list the average cost of funeral services of the clergy as $8.50. Many widows thus faced immediate financial difficulties in paying for burial. The state paid a funeral fee of $15 if the survivors were classed as "indigent," but the director noted that few of these funerals were held. To decrease costs, some families bought a casket, but not the services of the undertaker.

One arrangement for helping with burial expenses was an organization known as the Unificadora.[54] Founded in El Paso in 1914, it spread through the small communities in the Mesilla Valley, including Anthony, La Mesa, and San Miguel, and finally a branch was organized in La Mesilla in 1924. Dues were 35¢ per month per member. When a death occurred, a member could apply for aid up to $200 for burial expenses. To qualify, dues had to be "paid up," and a legal death certificate was required as proof of demise.[55]

It seems that widows in the Mesilla Valley were often left in difficult circumstances and needed material and financial support. Yet no substantial or uniform governmental aid was available until the late 1930s.[56] Before that time, public aid under "general assistance" was primarily offered at the discretion of state and local governments and was available primarily in the larger, urbanized and industrial areas.

Widows, then, had to rely on their own personal resources and their families. The level of formal education was generally low,[57] and most women learned through experience, "on-the-job." Most of experience came through working with husbands in family businesses, such as neighborhood groceries, farming and truck gardening, selling and trading produce, cattle raising and dairy farming, nursing the family, and domestic labor. This "survival training" took place in the context of a major element of the widow's support system, the family.

The Extended Family

Some sociologists define the extended family as one that includes more than two generations living either in close proximity or under the same roof.[58] The general advantage of the large, extended family is a strong interdependence and support system for the individual members. The widow in such families has a great deal of support and is not likely to be alone. Culturally, Hispanic families have traditionally fit into the close-knit extended pattern. Demographic sources revealed a high marriage rate, an insignificant divorce rate, an average of three to seven children, a high number of households, and established an extended pattern of kinship. Additionally, the custom of *compadrazco* (godparenthood) created a further extension, serving to strengthen rights and obligations among kin.[59] Once chosen, the godparents accepted the obligation of looking after the godchild in the event of need and took an active interest in his or her development and education. The godparents became a part of the family, providing a "comadre and compadre," literally a co-mother and co-father. Thus if a woman with children were widowed, the "co-parents" would be a resource for aid and support of the godchild.

There were other indications of family extensions that would have been beneficial to widows by broadening their support systems. Johansen noted a tendency toward village endogamy, and marriage between cousins was acceptable. This appears to have been the case, particularly in rural areas where population was limited and the area relatively isolated. Many of the families throughout the area today can trace their relationships to other members of the community, even though in urban settings close personal contact was eventually lost in many cases. Rural areas retained closer contact. One woman described her village as a "one-family village."[60]

Another type of practical family extension appeared in some of the smaller rural areas where priests were not always available. Common-law marriages were fairly prevalent, and traveling priests would perform mass marriages, sometimes recorded on or around the same date.[61] Another twist to the common-law marriage seemed quite practical in view of the exigencies of the times: younger widows simply "adopted" a series of male friends who visited occasionally but contributed to the widow's and her children's support. Although this situation was apparently accepted by the community, the liaison was regarded either as a "matter-of-fact" or as a "necessary evil," and these women suffered a loss of status.[62]

Another interesting example of the concept of the extended family of benefit particularly to older widows was the *colonia*.[63] Maldonado has observed that the colonia "is a supportive and flexible structure assuming functions in dealing with the environment and with the emotional and psychological aspects of the family unit and individuals."[64] In such an arrangement a widow at any age is well cared for and the aged are particularly fortunate, since "aging Mexican-Americans within the extended family structure face no threat to their physical survival."[65] A number of families were found to fit the pattern of the colonia, however, only one family appears to have actually been referred to by that name. Located in a small village near Las Cruces, this family started out with only about an acre of land. As the family grew, many of the children received small parcels of the land upon which to build their houses and raise their own families. Although they did not all live under one roof, they lived in extremely close proximity, forming an interdependent colony that shared problems and responsibilities.

This tendency of related family members to remain in close proximity is confirmed by Johansen. An early account of this pattern of extended family living was also found in an Hispanic widow's personal remembrances as related and recorded by a friend. The woman described various events from 1866 to 1917 and particularly recalled that when brothers and sisters were ready to marry and settle down, everyone pitched in building the new homes next to the original family residence.[66] Thus land and homes tended to remain "in the family."

Other colony families existed in such villages as Dona Ana, Tortugas, San Miguel, and La Mesilla. One family group in La Mesilla lived in distinct homes, built around and sharing one central patio. Some of these families still maintain close contact with a number of grown children and their families, who are living on original family property. Thus the colony concept is still observed to some extent today.[67]

Another important benefit derived from the colonia was the maintenance of functional roles for elderly family members, including elderly widows. "Role loss" has been found to be psychologically damaging to the elderly in modern society, when they no longer feel a sense of purpose or that they have something of value to contribute.[68] The interdependence of the extended family thus provided a continued function and role for the elderly widow. Johansen also confirmed that widows found refuge in the family. Younger widows often moved back in with their parents, even adopting their maiden names. Older widows often lived with their children.

Yet the elderly did not always move in with their children. The opposite also occurred, for grown children often lived in the homes of their elderly parents. Hopes of inheritance, inability to purchase land and set up their own households, and the strong tradition of keeping the family together may also have helped to maintain family ties. Many of the rural village families still live on original family property, in modified and expanded homes originally built by grandparents and great-grandparents in the 1800s.[69]

The reliance of women (and widows) upon family was confirmed in a contemporary study of social networks and survival strategies of Mexican-American women in San Jose, California, by Roland Wagner and Diane Schaffer.[70] Although this study did not deal specifically with widows, it did show that Mexican-American women in times of dire need or necessity, as opposed to other ethnic groups, in all situations preferred to turn to relatives and family, and had low frequencies of reliance on friends, commerical organizations, or service agencies. This also points to the strong role of family as a cultural support group.

The Woman's Role

Families were, with all their problems, a major source of support. In keeping them together, however, the Hispanic woman played a central role, which may have given her a distinct advantage in times of crisis such as widowhood. Although the family structure has been recognized as definitely patriarchal or male-dominated, the woman's role within the family was crucial. This structure and role also derive from Mexican roots.

Though subordinate, the woman was extremely important in maintaining stability and promoting integration of the family group. As Robert Staples noted, "The woman's interests, both in theory and in practice, are in producing children and caring for her family and her home."[71] However, she generally had no choice in the "production of children," and "caring for her family and home" meant everything from operating a truck farm to accounting and bookkeeping, and from medical care to teaching.

Living in an extended family thus did not mean that the woman did not "do her part" in providing for the family's survival and well-being. When widowed, the woman's burden simply became greater, particularly for younger women with children to raise. The material resources of even extended families were limited, and the widow often had to seek work or find ways to add to the family income.

Actual occupations were few in number and limited in range, but in addition to teaching, running a store or boardinghouse, or managing a farm, some women delivered medical care or became midwives. One woman's grandmother, a midwife and widow and the only source of medical help in one of the small villages, was known as "La Doctora." Before 1920 some physicians helped to get midwives certified, since care was so badly needed.[72]

Dona Urbana, who was widowed after she became a midwife, practiced around the turn of the century. She learned the art of midwifery from her uncle, who learned it from watching the doctor deliver so many family babies. There was never a lack of clients, and midwifery provided a good living for the family.[73]

Other women were resourceful and innovative when widowhood left them in a financial predicament. Francisca, widowed in the late 1910s, with two small daughters, was fortunate enough to be left with a huge house and a furniture store. Since she did not wish to continue in the furniture business, she sold all the furniture, remodeled the store into a home for herself and her daughters, turned the original large home into profitable apartments and became a landlady. The rental provided them all with a comfortable income.[74]

Eulalia, on the other hand, had problems before she was widowed because her husband was an invalid. When her husband died, a single sister moved in to help her and her two daughters. Eulalia lived in a rural village and owned ten acres on which she raised food for her family. She also took in laundry. Since she had no means of transportation, she used a small hand wagon to collect and deliver laundry to her clients, walking long distances and pulling heavy loads. When the first school was constructed in the village in 1916, Eulalia, with the help of a good friend influential in village affairs and intimately concerned with the school, obtained the position of janitor. Thus, she gardened, took in laundry, and cleaned the schoolhouse. When Eulalia finally retired, she received a small pension from her janitorial position.[75]

Dolores, widowed in 1935, had a limited education and eight children. Although her relatives were immediately helpful, she realized that she would have to find work. She was finally able to secure a position in the employment office in which her husband had worked. Because of political complications, Dolores was eventually forced to seek a job elsewhere, but by then she had made friends and had found jobs for a considerable number of people. When she finally secured a job as clerk in a budget clothing store, she brought many former clients with her as customers, and the business flourished. She also sent her girls to Loretto Academy, and the children worked when they could to help the family and to help pay their own tuition.[76]

The most obvious choice for many widowed women was to obtain domestic employment. The Mesilla Valley was sufficiently settled, with enough families of adequate income, to provide work as cooks, housekeepers, and laundresses. Wages were reported by many women as $2 to $3 per week. Though minimal, this wage often meant the difference between survival and destitution.

Social class, at least in rural areas, did not appear to be a major deterrent to accepting domestic employment, due to the low economic status of most of the inhabitants. Even in Las Cruces, the number of Hispanic families who were quite "well-off" was relatively small, and stores and other businesses offered a bit more variety in choice of employment.[77] There were also often extra benefits in domestic work. One woman, for example, remembered that during the 1920s one older widow who did the washing weekly was given extra food and clothing. Whenever the family gave a party or entertained, the widow would help clean up and was given leftovers in exchange.[78]

In several small villages families of former storeowners told of the closeness and sharing with the needy by extending credit and giving widows produce that had started to spoil.[79] One woman recalled that during the worst of the Depression years, one soup bone was shared by various families.[80]

Thus, women were quite resourceful in acting independently to utilize the various means of support available to them. Although choices were limited, women did what was necessary within their capabilities to keep families together and survive. In the rural area of the Mesilla Valley in New Mexico in the period of 1910 to 1940, Hispanic women seem to have relied primarily on kinship ties, which extended to distant relatives by blood or marriage. Families were large, close, often relatively isolated, and united. Families, friends, and sometimes even strangers provided material aid, particularly in times of great need like the Depression years.[81]

By the 1930s changes in economic conditions, rural isolation, and technological capacity had begun to take place. The impact and effect of these changes on social structure, observed and described by Johansen, tended to undermine to some extent the traditional support systems of Hispanic widows.[82] Modernization of agriculture reduced the need for farm labor, and urbanization brought an influx of Anglo culture and new ideas and helped break down some of the rural isolation. The Depression aggravated economic hardships and insecurity. New government programs of assistance brought some relief, but Johansen felt that this created an "attitude of dependence" and less reliance on family ties. Increased mobility, which threatened the extended family, also became possible.

Further and greater changes would take place in the 1940s, especially with the advent of World War II. Widows in a sense, however, had constructed their own support systems out of their cultural heritage, the need to survive, and whatever resources, material or spiritual, were at hand. They kept their families together for mutual support, abided by and practiced the rituals of their religion, and were highly adaptable in coping with adverse conditions. Although they received both spiritual and material aid, "charity" for these women and their families basically meant sharing with those who had less, rather than receiving from those who had more.

The stability, rural character, and agricultural productivity of the area greatly contributed to the ability to survive and sometimes even prosper. The Catholic religion offered spiritual guidelines and cultural support. Cultural values, customs, experience, and a broad interpretation of socially defined roles provided personal resources, and the extended family played a vital role in the widow's support network. Primarily, however, it was the strength, character, and resourcefulness of the women themselves that were the major support during the crisis created by widowhood.

NOTES

1. Random probate records, Dona Ana County Courthouse, Las Cruces, N.M.

2. Support systems buffer or cushion the individual from physiological or psychological consequences of social disorganization. The most significant are "the nature and strength of available group supports." Research has shown that the coping response is influenced by vicissitudes of the stress and current "ego strength" of the individual, and certainly "by the quality of the emotional support and task-oriented assistance provided by the social network within which that individual grapples with the crisis event." See Gerald Caplan, *Support Systems and Community Mental Health* (New York: Behavioral Publications, 1974).

3. Ibid. For a discussion of importance of group support, see also R. N. Butler and Myrna L. Lewis, *Aging and Mental Health* (St. Louis: C. V. Mosby, 1973).

4. Although the women I discuss in this paper include many born in Mexico (Mexican) and many born in the United States of Mexican parentage (Mexican-American), many claim Spanish heritage and ancestry and identify themselves as "Spanish-American." Racial designation may in some cases involve personal biases and preference. The term "Hispanic" is therefore used (except for quoted reference) to designate residents of Spanish or Mexican origin or roots. For a discussion of

problems of racial designation, see Carey McWilliams, *North from Mexico* (New York: Greenwood Press, 1968), 42-43.

5. Joan M. Jensen and Darlis A. Miller, "The Gentle Tamers Revisited: New Approaches to the History of Women in the American West," *Pacific Historical Review* 49 (1980):176, 182. Reports of subjects interviewed indicate that there may still exist a number of diaries, personal letters, and accounts kept by families who either do not perceive their historical value or relevance or who are protective of personal privacy and do not wish to make these family possessions public. Uncovering these resources and gaining the confidence of their owners will take time, persistence, tact, care, sensitivity, and good bilingual ability. A number of letters and accounts of deceased area residents, including some Hispanic women, are available in the collections of the Rio Grande Historical Society, New Mexico State University Library, Las Cruces. Examples are the correspondence of Julieta Juana and Maria Amador.

6. Ibid. Jensen and Miller argue that traditional historical studies "characterize" women as invisible, few in number, and "not important in the process of taming a wilderness." They also note that racial stereotypes of New Mexican women were very pronounced in the writings of Euro-American men. As apparently faceless, domestic bearers of children, women were seldom seen as individual characters with unique or shared problems. One problem was widowhood.

7. These differences have been noted with regard to linguistic forms, particularly use of Spanish archaic forms in the North and border slang or Mexicanized terms in the South for holidays, festivals, cultural character, among other items. With regard to support systems of church and kinship ties for widows, however, there may have been more similarities than differences.

8. Manuel Gamio, *Mexican Immigration to the United States* (Chicago: University of Chicago Press, 1930), 130.

9. Arthur Sigurd Johansen, *Rural Social Organization in a Spanish-American Culture Area* (Albuquerque: University of New Mexico Press, 1948).

10. Lawrence A. Cardoso, *Mexican Emigration to the United States, 1897-1931* (Tucson: University of Arizona Press, 1980), 4. Another reason for emigration from Mexico into the Mesilla Valley, as noted by many interviewed subjects, was political. Many had to leave Mexico due to political alignments, support, or sympathies that endangered their lives when the opposition became locally threatening.

11. Mark Reisner, *By the Sweat of Their Brow: Mexican Immigrant Labor in the United States, 1900-1940* (Westport, Conn.: Greenwood Press, 1976), 15.

12. These figures are estimated from the U.S. Census of 1910 for the Territory of New Mexico; U.S. Bureau of the Census, *Historical Statistics of the United States* (Washington, D.C.: Government Printing Office, 1961), 29; and the *Statistical Abstract of the United States* (Washington, D.C.: Government Printing Office, 1975), 59. They do not reflect specific county data, which are not available.

13. *1910 Federal Population Census,* microfilm publication T1224, film no. 914 (Washington, D.C.: National Archives Trust Fund Board, 1982). The manuscript census for 1910 contains a wealth of information on families and their descendents in the area, verifying the predominant and settled Hispanic population by family names, as well as relationships among various families.

14. Johansen, *Social Organization,* 17-19.

15. Migrants, or "temporary immigrants," are not designated in population reports and are very difficult to estimate. Gamio questions accepting official U.S. statistics in estimating the number of Mexican immigrants in the United States. The decennial census is taken at a time of year when the greatest number of temporary immigrants are in the country, and many immigrants do not register at all.

16. U.S. Department of Labor, Bureau of Immigration, *Annual Reports of the Commissioner General of Immigration to the Secretary of Labor,* June 1922 through June 1932 (Washington, D.C.: Government Printing Office, 1922-32).

17. Widows were not likely to emigrate alone with children unless they already had family established in the United States. Families who emigrated together would be unlikely to leave older widowed family members behind.

18. Johansen, *Social Organization.*

19. Shan Nichols and Ella Banegas Curry, *Our Heritage, Our People* (El Paso, Tex.: Nichols and Curry, 1974).

20. Johansen, *Social Organization.*

21. Ibid. Johansen's study also reflected the changing conditions brought about by the economic ravages of the Depression. He theorized that the cultural values and supports that had served this population in the past, i.e., family interdependence, orientation to manual labor rather than formal education, and small farms and agricultural pursuits, were actually hindrances in coping with and adjusting to modern society and the influx of Anglo culture.

22. Jerry T. Williams and Paul McAllister, eds., *New Mexico in Maps* (Albuquerque: University of New Mexico, Technology Application Center, 1979), 44-47. Census statistics also show farming and farm labor to be major occupations for males in the state from 1910 to 1940; females were primarily employed in domestic and personal services (servants, laundresses, and boardinghouse and hotel managers). By 1940, however, the number of occupations had greatly multiplied, and the percentage of the population employed in agriculture had decreased by more than 35 percent. Although it is clear that agricultural pursuits were still major occupations, it is difficult to measure actual decline, since classifications change somewhat, and urban areas had begun to grow with a proliferation of new occupations. Data are also statewide. By 1940 female occupations were still heavily domestic, but clerical jobs and professional occupations of teaching and nursing, for example, had grown to equal or surpass domestic employment.

23. David Maldonado, Jr., "The Chicano Aged," *Social Work* 20 (1975):213-16.

This can also be seen in Okah L. Jones, Jr., *Los Paisanos* (Norman: University of Oklahoma Press, 1979). Jones bases observation of early settlers on the census of 1790 and notes that families were large and marriage came early. Widows, widowers, and orphans, although also listed separately, were often integrated into extended family listings. "Of particular interest is the fact that where financially and socially possible, whole families of Indians, widows and orphans were freely accepted into the families of the paisanos." Ibid., 133.

24. Edward Hernandez, ed., *Spanish-Mexican Influence in U.S. History* (Las Cruces: New Mexico State University, 1976), 169.

25. Ibid.

26. Although there was a consequent influx of Anglos and a move toward larger commerical farming, there was still land to be developed under the Homestead Act and the smaller Hispanic subsistence farms did not suffer to the extent that occurred during the Depression years of the 1930s. In 1910, in Dona Ana County, 1,923,176 acres of public land were open to entry under U.S. laws. None was irrigable from the Rio Grande, but they could be — and were — made productive by pumping. See Elephant Butte Water Users' Association, *Agricultural Opportunities in Connection with the Rio Grande Project* (Las Cruces, N.M.: El Paso Printing, 1910). Also see Joan Jensen, "New Mexico Farm Women, 1900-40," in Robert Kern, ed., *Labor in New Mexico: Strikes, Unions, and Social History since 1881* (Albuquerque: University of New Mexico Press, 1983). Also see Johansen, *Social Organization.*

27. Personal interviews, June 27, July 2, 14, Aug. 14, Sept. 4, 1982. The emphasis on small subsistence farming is also noted in Jensen, "New Mexico Farm Women," and Johansen, *Social Organization,* 28.

28. Gamio, *Mexican Immigration,* 116.

29. Ibid.

30. Interview with Dr. C. Gilbert Romero, appearing in the El Paso *Times,* Feb. 27, 1983.

31. Mesilla, New Mexico, parish accounts, 1916-19.

32. Robert Medina, *Diamond Jubilee* (Las Cruces, N.M.: Knights of Columbus, 1982).

33. Interview with Sister Laura Tejada, Good Shepherd Home, El Paso, Sept. 20, 1982.

34. See G. R. Krupp, "The Bereavement Reaction: A Special Case of Separation Anxiety—Sociocultural Considerations," *Psychoanalytic Study of Society* 2 (1962):42; L. Siggins, "Mourning: A Critical Survey of the Literature," *International Journal of Psychoanalysis* 47 (1966):14; and C. M. Parkes, "Effects of Bereavement on Physical and Mental Health — A Study of the Medical Records of Widows," *British Medical Journal* 2 (1974):274.

35. Willadean W. Turner, "Grief Therapy for the Bereaved," in Otto S. Margolis

et al., eds., *Grief and the Meaning of the Funeral* (New York: MSS Information Corp., 1975), 75.

36. Bronislaw Malinowski, *Magic, Science, and Religion and Other Essays* (Glencoe, Ill.: Free Press, 1948).

37. No one interviewed really knew where this custom originated, but most felt it had nothing to do with religion. They termed it "tradition." Margaret M. Coffin, *Death in Early America* (Nashville: Thomas Nelson, 1976), traces the custom to the Middle Ages, when evil spirits were thought to linger about the deceased. Mourners wore black to make themselves "inconspicuous," so that the evil spirits would take no notice of them.

38. Personal interview, Aug. 14, 1982. Because of the desire for anonymity expressed by many of the subjects, most names have been changed with reference to interviews.

39. Personal interview, Sept. 4, 1982.

40. Personal interview, June 27, 1982.

41. Personal interview, June 25, 1982.

42. Personal interviews, June 27, July 17, and Sept. 4, 20, 1982.

43. Joan Moore, "The Death Culture of Mexico and Mexican-Americans," *Omega* 1 (1970a):277.

44. See Turner, "Grief Therapy," 75-78, and Linda Colvin, "The Creative Funeral" (105-10), and Patricia Hannaford, "The Social Meaning of the Funeral to the Elderly" (71-74), both in Margolis et al., eds., *Grief.*

45. E. T. Eberhart, "The Kinship of Sorrow," in Margolis et al., eds., *Grief,* 15.

46. Personal interview, June 27, 1982.

47. Richard A. Kalish and David K. Reynolds, *Death and Ethnicity: A Psychocultural Study* (Los Angeles: Ethel Percy Andrus Center, University of Southern California, 1976), 168.

48. Robert Habenstein and William M. Lamers, *Funeral Customs the World Over* (Milwaukee: Bulfin Printers, 1974), 583.

49. Personal interviews, Aug. 14, Sept. 4, 20, 1982.

50. Kalish and Reynolds, *Death and Ethnicity,* 180.

51. Ibid., 182-83.

52. William M. Lamers, "Grief and Its Katharsis," in Margolis et al., eds., *Grief.*

53. Interview with Las Cruces funeral home director, July 20, 1982.

54. Literally, a "unifying entity." This organization is actually quite typical of other Hispanic self-help organizations throughout the country. See a discussion of similar organizations in Nancie L. Gonzalez, *The Spanish-Americans of New Mexico: A Heritage of Pride* (Albuquerque: University of New Mexico Press, 1967), 86-115.

55. Interview with present treasurer of the Unificadora, which now lists 104 members, only seven of whom reside in La Mesilla. Other members reside in El

Paso, Anthony, and several small towns in the area. Dues have risen to 70¢ per month, but the functions and purposes remain basically the same.

56. See Blanche D. Coll, *Perspectives in Public Welfare,* 3d ed. (Washington, D.C.: U.S. Department of Health, Education and Welfare, 1973), and Donald Brieland et al., *Contemporary Social Work,* 2d ed. (New York: McGraw-Hill, 1980), 168-69.

57. Johansen, *Social Organization,* 118.

58. Richard T. Schaefer, *Sociology* (New York: McGraw-Hill, 1983), 297.

59. Gonzalez, *Spanish-Americans of New Mexico,* 41.

60. Personal interview, Sept. 4, 1982.

61. One can only speculate as to when and where these marriages took place.

62. Children born from these liaisons were often given the last names of their various fathers and yet lived within the same family. Parish records of births and deaths regularly recorded the children as "l" for "legitimo," or legitimate or as "natural" or with no designation at all, which indicated illegitimacy. The designation was made at the priest's discretion, but most of them were consistent in their registration, one way or the other. One woman had seven "natural" children, all with different last names. Another indication that women were supported by and bore children of various men was found in the records of public welfare and aid to dependent children programs. In the late 1930s numerous women having several children but no husbands for one reason or another quickly applied for aid, most probably due to the hardship of the Depression. These liaisons were seen as a reflection of and adaptation to social and economic conditions of the times and did not constitute any cultural characteristic.

63. Literally, "colony." This is descriptive of cluster housing, also noted by Johansen, and does not indicate any subcultural uniqueness.

64. See Marta Sotomayor, "Mexican-American Interaction with Social Systems," *Social Casework* 5 (1971): 32, quoted in Maldonado, *The Chicano Aged.*

65. Maldonado, *Chicano Aged,* 214.

66. Personal document of experiences related to and recorded by Mrs. Sophie Waldrip, San Miguel, N.M.

67. Maldonado, *The Chicano Aged,* 213.

68. For a discussion of "role loss" and its implications, see Zena S. Blau and Helena Z. Lopata, "Role Change in Widowhood: A World Perspective," in Donald O. Cowgill et al., eds., *Aging and Modernization* (New York: Meredith, 1972), 299-308.

69. A number of subjects interviewed confirmed this. In some of the older homes, one can note where additional rooms and wings have been added; also see Johansen, *Social Organization.*

70. Roland M. Wagner and Diane M. Schaffer, "Social Networks and Survival Strategies," in Margarita B. Melville, ed., *Twice a Minority* (St. Louis: C. V. Mosby, 1980), 174.

71. Robert Staples, "The Mexican-American Family: Its Modification over Time and Space," *Phylon* 32 (1971):180.

72. Personal interview, Sept. 4, 1982.

73. Personal interview with former midwife, Aug. 5, 1982.

74. Personal interview with family friend of subject, Sept. 4, 1982.

75. Personal interview with family friend of subject, Sept. 15, 1982.

76. Personal interview with daughter of subject, Sept. 12, 1982.

77. Johansen, *Social Organization.* Johansen noted a generally low economic status, particularly for the rural areas, that undoubtedly was aggravated by the Depression. However, Okah L. Jones's description of very early settlers around 1790 noted that "there was no single race or class employed exclusively as servants. Voluntary and involuntary servitude existed, mostly in the form of domestic servants for families who could afford to employ them." Manual labor was an accepted way of life for Spanish settlers. In Jones, *Los Paisanos,* 134.

78. Personal interview with family member, July 2, 1982.

79. Interview with granddaughter of storeowner, July 2, 1982.

80. Personal interview, Aug. 18, 1982.

81. In these situations the "kinship" network may expand to include all those who have a common need to survive. In addition to blood ties, the networks then include racial and cultural ties, and finally, simply human ties.

82. Johansen, *Social Organization,* 140.

5

Widowhood among the Mormons: The Personal Accounts

MAUREEN URSENBACH BEECHER, CAROL CORNWALL MADSEN, and LAVINA FIELDING ANDERSON

The social interaction of the Mormons ameliorated the circumstances of the widowed. From their beginnings as a distinct religious group in New York, through their communities in Ohio, Missouri, and Illinois in the 1830s, and eventually in their settlements throughout the western United States after 1847, the Mormons adopted social and ecclesiastical practices that potentially, at least, could lessen the burden of the "poor and the widowed."

Through the colonizing efforts of Brigham Young, "Mormon Country" reached far beyond its center in Salt Lake City, near the Great Salt Lake, the low point of the Great Basin. Mormon settlement extended to southern Utah and thence along what has been called the "Mormon Corridor" through northern Arizona and Nevada to San Bernardino, California. Westward from Salt Lake City Mormons colonized parts of Nevada and established clusters of communities in California. Mormons moved north into Idaho, east into Colorado, and south into the Little Colorado region of Arizona. The 1880s found Latter-day Saints establishing towns in Wyoming, in southern Alberta, and in the states of Sonora and Chihuahua, Mexico. By 1900, half a century after the first settlement of Mormons in Utah, their cities and villages dotted the map in a strip of western North America 1,500 miles long and, at its widest, 500 miles wide.

Although individual families pioneered, more frequently Mormons settled as communities consisting of several families, often related. From its first census, Utah, the core of the region and the most heavily populated Mormon state, has shown an almost equal balance of male to female population. As communities were established by ecclesiastical dictum, whole families would be "called" to venture into the new territories to settle. Once there, they would plat their towns in a pattern dictated originally by their founder, Joseph Smith. The "City of Zion" model differed from the usual ranch-style frontier settlement in that all the dwellings were built in compact blocks around a church house–dominated central square, with the farming and large cattle pastures on the outskirts of town. The Mormons' strong sense of mutuality was thus reinforced and lubricated by geographical proximity, and whether or not they were at a given time practicing "consecration" or the "United Order" forms of property ownership, the Latter-day Saints were strongly committed to their material interdependence.[1]

This study of widowhood among the Latter-day Saints is based on the personal writings of as many women as we could find who recorded their lives after the death of their spouses. These have been culled from the three hundred-odd collections of diaries, reminiscences, and letters in the Church Archives of the Church of Jesus Christ of Latter-day Saints in Salt Lake City, augmented by those in other repositories, as listed in Davis Bitton's *Guide to Mormon Diaries.* Some are published in the collected lessons provided by Daughters of Utah Pioneers, and others are printed in isolated family histories. The availability of such sources embodies a selective process that builds a bias into this study, a limitation balanced in part by the demographic study of Geraldine Mineau. The women reflected here were essentially an elite, with particular characteristics: they were literate; they were confident that their lives were worth recording; they had descendents who shared that view enough to preserve their writings and to donate them to mostly Mormon institutions. A disproportionately large number of the diarists lived in polygamy, a fact related most likely to the need the women felt to defend the practice and their lives within the practice. Within the framework of the information conveyed by the diaries, however, they offer a significant resource in appraising the personal response of a select group of women to the trauma of widowhood. Any conclusions are at best impressionistic, but since the women do represent a limited variety of communities, reflect a fairly wide economic range, and fit the spectrum from very private to prominently public, their accounts can be instructive, if not conclusive.

Obviously, these firsthand, written accounts, ranging over nearly a century—many of them little more than brief comments—can be neither fully representative nor comprehensive. Few, for example, mention any probate proceedings. Where they do, the account is usually brief, such as that of Lovenia N. Sylvester Berry. Her husband, serving as a missionary, was killed by an anti-Mormon mob in Tennessee. He left no will, but, she writes, "the property was prorated and fairly divided." She did not remarry, and "through careful management" the money left her by her husband was "the means of raising their children."[2] Do we infer, therefore, that there was not a large enough estate in most instances to be probated? Or that such proceedings, if they did occur, were not significant enough to mention? Or that family and/or ecclesiastical leaders guided the disposition of property? Most of the women in the sample were within the purview of legal jurisdiction, but, as reflected from their diaries, widowhood did not entail extensive legal formalities. References to financial matters were almost exclusively about their own efforts to support themselves and their families.

Mormons living in rural towns in the first stages of settlement or in urban communities in a more established industrial mode were divided into ecclesiastical wards or smaller branches, like a parish. Their presiding ecclesiastical officer, a bishop or president, carried responsibility for the temporal as well as the ecclesiastical well-being of the Saints under his charge, following the injunction of Brigham Young that the temporal and spiritual could not be separated. Theological considerations governed all aspects of life among the Mormons.

In few cases are the interworkings of doctrine and practice more clearly seen than in the situation of widows at the time of and in the years following the loss of their spouses. Two doctrines concerning marriage particularly impacted on practices surrounding widowhood: the faith that mortal life is a part of an eternal continuum in which birth and death are alike merely portals, and its concurrent practice of marriage "for time and for all eternity"; and the acceptance of the practice of polygyny, plural marriage, or polygamy in contemporary writings, as a practice not only approved by God, but also required of the faithful.[3] The ramifications of both of these are extensive.

The theology of pre- and post-mortal life was preached so ardently at Mormon funerals and believed so literally by the faithful that there was little reason for a bereaved wife to doubt the celestial happiness of the lost spouse or her eventual reunion with him. Eliza R. Snow, who from 1867 presided over the women's organizations of the church, interpreted the doctrine for her contemporaries in the many poems she wrote on the occasions of the deaths of friends and leaders. One such, on the death of church leader Heber C. Kimball, reads, in part:

> Be cheered, O Zion!—cease to weep:
> Heber we deeply loved:

He is not dead — he does not sleep —
He lives with those above.

. . . .

His mighty spirit, pure and free
From every bond of earth
In realms of bright Eternity,
Is crowned with spotless worth.[4]

There was then, however, and still is in contemporary Mormonism, the concept that such doctrine should be so consoling to the widow that the parting should be not a time of mourning but of rejoicing. But in the comment of one contemporary woman, long since widowed, is the suggestion of paradox. Asked how long she grieved for her husband, the woman replied, "Oh, it was a year before I could say my prayers without crying." Faith in the doctrine did not necessarily eliminate the trauma of a spouse's death. In fact, that it was at times of personal devotion that the pain was most severe suggests deep-seated dissonance: if I believe him to be living happily in God's heaven, why do I mourn so long? That for Mormon widows mourning still occurred, however inappropriate it might be doctrinally, is also suggested in the concluding quatrain of Eliza Snow's poem:

Let wives and children humbly kiss
The deep afflictive rod:
A "father to the fatherless,"
God is "the widow's God."[5]

Accompanying whatever grief Mormon women might experience at separation from a spouse, then, was also a gnawing awareness that in mourning they were either somehow guilty of denying their faith in Mormonism's promises of a hereafter or selfish in begrudging the departed his right "to partake with the martyrs a banquet of love."

However ambivalent the widow's response to the loss of her spouse might have been, there was a longer-lasting assurance provided in the Mormon belief that the marriage was contracted, not "until death do us part," but "for time and all eternity." This sealing of the partners to one another, ordained to the faithful in one of several endowment houses or temples, assured the wife of eternal union not only with her husband but also with their children on condition of enduring faithfulness to the covenants of the church. Moreover, the highest rewards in mortal life, as in life beyond the grave, were reserved for those thus sealed.[6]

For such coupling to be binding, the husband promised to honor his priesthood obligations as his wife honored her temple covenants. Lucinda Lee Dalton, widowed in 1883, considered her husband lax in those obligations and after his death petitioned church leaders to "cancel the sealing," in effect divorcing him posthumously.[7] The literalness with which the doctrine was, and is, adhered to required an equitable reward for those who, despite their personal faithfulness, remained single, or, as in the case of Lucinda Dalton, became single again. Such explanation is provided in a doctrine of a millennial reign in which all things necessary for full salvation will be provided for, or restored to, the faithful. A faithful widow bereft of her worthy spouse could rest assured that her husband had "gone on ahead" and was actively preparing a place for her in the heavenly kingdom. For Mormon women the tendency, observed by Murray Parkes, of widows in the first six weeks after the husband's death to think of him as though he were still alive was doctrinally extended, for good or ill, to last indefinitely.[8] And for a woman not so well married, there was the millennial promise of a worthy mate hereafter. There was much in Mormon doctrine to console a widow and assist her psychologically through the first phases of bereavement, if she chose to accept such affirmations.

Belief in a literal life beyond death was no more varied in its effect on bereaved Mormon women than was the practice of plural marriage on those who lived it. One unnamed woman, after a long and unhappy marriage in polygamy, is reported to have said of her deceased spouse, "The happiest day I spent for twenty years was the day I saw him laid in the grave."[9] Another plural wife, after a similarly long polygynous marriage, experienced her husband's death thus: "All was quiet. His head lay on or against my bosom. Good angels had come to receive his precious spirit. . . . But he was gone, my light, my sun, my life, my joy, my Lord, yea almost my God."[10] Emmeline Wells, a prominent Mormon woman, remembered at her husband's death the emotional roller coasting of marriage with a shared husband, whose death became a poignant loss. She reflected on her life with him, now "only memories, only the coming and going and parting at the door. The joy when he came the sorrow when he went as though all the light died out of my life."[11] Such responses, of course, said more about a woman's marriage experience itself than about her theological position or institutional circumstances. Polygamous marriages were as individually distinctive as monogamous ones.

As a practice, however, polygyny created a unique set of marital experiences and expectations among Mormon women. The most successful plural families were established on the basis of caring and concern of the wives not only for their shared husband and their own children, but also for each other and the other children in the family. That such mutual concern could exist is more readily understandable to twentieth-century observers in the light of the observations of Carroll Smith-Rosenberg in her "Female World of Love and Ritual," a seminal study of relations among nineteenth-century women.[12] There she observes that the most essential affective support came to women, not from their husbands, but from their female relatives and friends. The bonding that was observed among several wives of one Mormon man follows to a point the patterns demonstrated among American women generally, reinforcing those patterns with the permanence of marriage and parenthood. That the whole practice was perceived by those who entered it as obedience to a higher divine law explains the phenomenon of someone as capable as Martha Cragun disdaining marriage to a more personable contemporary and choosing instead to become a plural wife to Isaiah Cox, "the poorest man in Washington county."

Plural marriages, most studies suggest, comprised approximately 20 percent of the total in Utah, even at the peaks of the practice, around 1855 and the early 1880s. After 1890 when, because of federal sanctions, continuation of the practice was officially abandoned, few more such marriages were contracted, and existing ones died out.[13]

Some observations, however, should make more meaningful the following examples of widows in Mormon communities coping with their circumstances. Taking a particular segment of Mormon population—the wives of as many bishops as he could identify—D. Gene Pace summarized his observations about these women as they became widows.[14] His findings relate predictably well to those of Geraldine Mineau, herein, of the more general Mormon population and add the extra dimension of distinguishing between monogamous and polygynous marriages. About six in ten of his set of 835 women outlived their husbands; and of the 180 identified polygamist bishops, 143, or nearly four-fifths, left at least one widow, and more than two-fifths left two. Only 4 percent left four or more widows. Bishops and other ranking Mormon leaders were more likely than lay members to practice plural marriage, however, so to suggest how several widows of one man, living and working together, might care and provide for each other, although there are such cases, would be to deal with a very small minority of Mormon women.

The two larger groups in Pace's study are more significant: those who, when widowed, were one of two wives, and those who had been married monogamously. Polygamy affected both groups. Statistically, the first wife in a polygamous marriage was about the same age as her husband, having married him while both were in their early to mid-twenties. In Pace's study, these first wives of bishops remained widows about twelve years until their own deaths. The second wives, however, entering the marriage later when they as brides were likewise in their mid-twenties, faced an average of fifteen years of widowhood.

Mormon communities were replete with women living more or less alone. Plural wives whose husbands had other wives in separate houses, or even in other communities, not only provided models for widows, but also paved the way for their acceptance as contributing members of the community. The support systems established among women who were alone made the widow's path less lonely, provided she accept the mores and morals of the prevailing Mormon culture.

Each community, as noted, had its ward or wards, an organization of between 100 and 300 families. Mormon women had their own organization, the Relief Society, which, however closely it cooperated with the male ecclesiastical hierarchy, enjoyed an essential autonomy in its dealing with community problems. Besides the benevolent purposes of the society, it had as a mandate to watch over the morals of the community and, as an ongoing purpose, the spiritual education of its members. By 1868-69, when nearly every ward had a fully functioning Relief Society, women's roles in the rituals of community life were established, and further institutionalizing merely gave order and assigned responsibility to functions already being met informally.

The merging into one of secular and ecclesiastical functions served the emotional as well as temporal advantage of the Mormon widow. At the husband's death it was the Relief Society sisters who came to lay out the corpse, who sewed the burial clothes and the cloth linings for the coffin, who sat up with the widow, and who provided food for the bereaved family. The immediacy of their ministrations gave them reason to be there for emotional support and to provide continuity of concern after relatives had returned to distant homes. And it was most often the bishop of the widow's ward who, after delivering the funeral sermon, then had official responsibility for her well-being, although in the personal writings of Mormon women on which this study is based no woman reflected the view that her continuing sustenance did or should come from the church or the community coffers.[15]

Similarly almost none of the diaries refer to the obviously accessible charitable help available through the Relief Society, although the minutes of both bishops' meetings and Relief Societies record such support being given to "the poor and the widow." Did they prefer not to record even the offer of such help, or was assistance so universally expected and accepted that it was not noteworthy?

Nor do the later diaries reflect the impact of a growing professionalization in the area of human welfare, especially in the early decades of the twentieth century, including funeral and burial service and community agencies for social services.

Apart from the psychological advantages of their faith that in varying degrees offered a particular kind of solace and assurance during times of bereavement, Mormon women, like the majority of their counterparts everywhere, found the economic dislocation of widowhood the most impelling factor of the experience to record. Some inherited from husbands, some learned to sustain themselves (many had been self-sufficient in marriage as well), some turned to their grown children, some remarried, and some depended, if only partially, on the church or community for sustenance. Most made use of a combination of these resources.

Utah had a legal history that made the inheritance rights of widows at best inconsistent. Neither on the forefront nor backward in its concern for the rights of women, the territory/state legislature found federal injunctions against polygamy a burr under the saddle of its own attempts at equity, so that in the courts it was the interplay between the two levels of government that determined how much of her husband's estate, and with what control, a wife, or wives, might receive.

The Organic Act, which established the Territory of Utah in 1852, included a provision allowing the heirs of a father who died intestate to share equally in his estate. In order to provide for the subsequent wives of polygamists and their children, lest federal courts disallow the plural marriages, the law guaranteed similar rights to "illegitimate" offspring and their mothers (an unfortunate euphemism for children and wives of polygamous marriages), a clause that won many injunctions for second and later families.[16]

The pain this practice inflicted on at least one widow is apparent in the diary entry of Mary Ann Weston Maughan, widowed in Cache Valley in 1872. After thirty years as wife of Peter Maughan, she protested that since it was ruled "best for all to share alike" the two-year-old son of her sister wife Libby "was awarded just as much as I was."[17] Another widow, Emily Dow Partridge Young, was more explicit in her outrage. The estate of her deceased husband, Brigham Young, was particularly complex, and had in fact not yet been fully probated when she lamented: "A paid servant had more liberty and feels more independence than a married woman. A wife has nothing but her board and clothing (and that grudgingly) while her husband lives; and after his death, she has no right to any of his property; although she has worked for his interest and shared his poverty all her married life."[18] Neither Brigham Young nor his wives lived in poverty; Emily was prone toward dark and gloomy images. Nevertheless, what she wrote next is basically true of her legal status and that of her contemporaries: "[The widow] is left to the mercy of his children. They are given preeminence, while the wife and mother is ignored. This is true as the case stands today; at least this is my experience; even my home that I hold the deed of is given to my children and I am not allowed the right to own anything but am fed with a spoon like a baby."

In 1887 the Edmunds-Tucker Act, prohibiting polygamy and providing numerous sanctions against the church, repealed the existing law regarding the heirs of intestate husbands and formally established the right of dower, by which a widow inherited one-third of her husband's estate. Dower, though understood in common law, had not been explicitly provided for in the Organic Act of 1852 and had been expressly abolished by the Utah territorial legislature in 1872. In 1898, two years after Utah received statehood, the provision relating to dower was enlarged. Widows were given control over their inherited property, this time in *fee simple,* that is, with full legal right to use or dispose of it. This and other provisions of the 1898 statute marked generous extensions of the provisions of dower right.[19]

Problems still remained, however, for existing plural families. When in 1912 David Eccles, a polygamist and Utah's first millionaire, died, his estate was initially divided among his first wife and his twenty-two children. The second wife received nothing, nor did a third woman who claimed wifehood, though she satisfied the court that her son was offspring of the deceased and won a settlement for him.[20] One astute daughter of another polygynist, Anne Leishman, understanding the law, encouraged her father to provide for his second wife, "Aunt Betsy," before his death. "Aunt Betsy would only be treated as a child [actually, not as well as a child]," Anne explained to her father. "She can't write a check, she can't sign a deed, she can't do anything." The subsequent will gave Betsy title to her home and a share in her husband's property.[21] A clause was added to Utah's succession law in 1907 allowing heirs of plural marriages to make claims against the estate of the deceased husband and father.

All this, however, was moot to the wives of men who died owning little more than the lot their house stood on, which, in continually urbanizing Utah, became increasingly the case as the nineteenth century moved toward the twentieth. In such cases, widows whose personal records exist seem more frequently to depend on their own resources than any other single source of support.

By far the majority of Mormon widows who left first-person accounts accepted the responsibility for their own sustenance from the time of their husbands' deaths. The young widowed, especially those with small children, reflect, or their children report, the hours of dreary labor to keep bread on the table by whatever means. One daughter remembered how "every night [mother] would spin and how in the daytime I would split fine splinters off from the pichy [pitchy] wood and at night I would sit with her and tend the baby and keep holding and lighting these pitchy sticks for her to see to spin by, and how I would cry when I went to bed to think my sweet little mother had to work so hard."[22] However tinged with sentimentality the account might be, the reality it reflects is not to be doubted.

In the early agrarian economics of Mormon settlement in the West, the traditional women's tasks were the chief means of their support whether as single women or as co-providers with husbands. Ellen Bradshaw Fowler is typical. When her husband died in 1865 of tuberculosis, she was left with five children and, in the words of her daughter, "had to work very hard at sewing, gleaning wheat, and teaching school three months of the school year. Still we suffered for want of food and with the cold."[23] Other accounts reflect similar ventures, along with the usual provisioning activities of the kitchen garden, the chickens, and the cow.

As Mormon community economics improved and women were freed from the necessity of agrarian subsistence-level economy, they found a wider variety of options for supporting themselves and their children. Hannah Smith Dalton, at the time of her husband's death in the Mormon community of Manassa, Colorado, found herself saddled with his debt of "thousands of dollars." John Dalton had been bishop at Manassa and in that capacity had often hosted visitors in their home. Unwillingly, since "to think of charging for meals seemed awful to me," his widow turned that experience to good account to provide for her children's education by establishing her home as a hotel. She wrote: "I remember well the first traveling man that ever came to stay with us. He stayed all night and for dinner the next day. We were sitting at the table and he asked what his bill was. I told him I did not know for that was the first meal I had ever sold in my life. He said this was his first trip as a traveling man and he did not know the prices. He was lonesome and I was heart sick and we both sat there and cried. When we got control of ourselves we decided that $2.00 a day would be about right and we kept that price always."[24]

Alice Parker Isom recounts the variety of the enterprises by which she sustained her family when her husband died in 1885. Like several other storekeepers' wives, she maintained her husband's mercantile establishment after his death: "I had done most of the buying from the first and understood the business quite well," she wrote. Later, moving her family from their home in the Virgin River valley to Provo so her son could attend the academy there, she took in boarders, a frequent recourse among widows. Her former neighbors in Virgin appealed to Alice to return and open for business again, which she did. Among other activities, she invested in cattle land, ran a hotel, kept boarders, built a sawmill, served as a midwife, and organized a shipping company. At age 70 she retired in a "neat little house," where she lived for another fifteen years.[25] Alice Isom's daring and diversity, however exceptional, have elements in common with the resources available to many of her female head-of-household sisters: the business that gave her her start had been her husband's; the property on which her cottage sat belonged to her son; her boardinghouse was an obvious opportunity; her services as midwife kept her in contact with the female networks and were valued in the community. But the ingenuity with which she marshalled her resources was her own and not unknown to other women widowed young. A generation later the pattern could still be seen in the life of Hilda Andersson Erickson who, by the time she was widowed, had been running the general store in Grantsville, near Salt Lake City, as "manager, buyer, and clerk." She, too, was a midwife, often the area's chief medical practitioner.[26] For such entrepreneurial women, the financial aspect of widowhood was hardly a change from the work they had done while their husbands were alive.

Similarly, for polygynous wives, the change was less than profound when they found themselves permanently rather than sporadically without husbands. In the experience of Martha Cragun Cox of St. George, Utah, are elements repeated many times over in the lives of other such plural wives who learned before widowhood to deal with the difficulties that single parenthood would present. She had begun her teaching career simultaneously with her marriage as third wife of Isaiah Cox, a poor man many years her senior. In addition to bearing eight children, Martha taught school at least part of every year but three from her marriage to her retirement. Isaiah's death seems to have made little change in either her family life or her financial status. After her retirement from teaching, she pondered, "Is it wrong to wish for money?"—a revelation of the unrelenting poverty in which she lived. When she retired at age sixty-eight, however, with her savings and the financial help of her children she was able to live out her life doing volunteer church work in comparative ease.[27]

Plural marriage had also prepared Annie Clark Tanner, a generation younger than Martha Cox, for the same sort of enforced autonomy. Married in 1883 as his second wife to her professor at Brigham Young Academy, Annie bore eight children during occasional periods of living with her educator husband. Her marriage, in fact, ended before the husband's death—he left her and moved to Canada, where he invested in sheep ranching and eventually died. She sums up how her life in polygyny had prepared her for eventual widowhood: "I established my first little home in Franklin, unaided, and I broke it up alone. I supervised the building of our big home. I moved to Provo with four young children while my husband was in Canada, and I moved from there alone. Naturally, these experiences give one a confidence in their own judgment and a certain independence in attitude."[28]

Though basically trusting their own resources, many widows, both those with young families and those with grown children, turned also to close relatives for support. Annie Tanner, for example, living in a rural community, discovered when her husband's support ceased that "in the country there were many advantages for a large family who were short of money. There were thriving farms all about us owned by my brothers who gave my boys employment any time they wanted to work. It did not cost us much for fruit which we bottled in abundance. A few sacks of potatoes, for which the boys worked, were always stored away for the winter."[29] The brothers actually provided even more substantive help, especially in emergencies. But it was her own children who proved Annie Tanner's mainstay. Her oldest son Kneland quickly became "the family financier," a role he continued to play even after he married and moved from the family home. The years of familial self-sufficiency before and after their father's death molded this family into an interdependent unit that enabled them to provide well for their mother once the children entered their professional careers.

Annie Tanner's life before and after her husband's departure suggests that her primary bonding, in the absence of strong marital ties, was primarily to her children. Such mother-children closeness was more the rule than the exception, and Mormon widows frequently turned to their sons for financial as well as social and emotional sustenance in the absence of their husbands.

When Emma Jeffs Gunnell, her husband's second wife, was widowed in 1890, she "wept . . . for now she would have to stay in a little one-room log cabin with her five children," wrote her granddaughter. "She had to borrow clothes . . . for her children to wear to the funeral." She and her oldest daughter "would take turns going out to do house work and scrubbing on the board, doing washings for 50 cents a day and a pound of butter." One of her sons, who would walk home with her from work, pained at "seeing how worn and tired she looked," promised that "she would never work again when he got big enough to help." Some five years later, Emma Gunnell's son-in-law purchased the property her sons had inherited, and with the proceeds they all built a four-room frame home for Emma. "They fixed it up beautifully for those times, with wall to wall carpeting of red roses, an organ, and a blonde bedroom set. . . . They had her charge her groceries and clothes and every Fall they would go in together and pay her bills."[30]

While most of the recorded personal accounts suggest the hard economic necessities of widowhood, some women were left in relative comfort. Serena Knudson Staaleson was converted to Mormonism in Stavanger, Norway, and left a widow with four children in 1862. She sold her own property at "a ridiculously low price out of prejudice on account of her being a Mormon" and paid for the passage of her family and seventeen other Mormon converts leaving Stavanger at the same time. Before setting out across the plains from Florence, Nebraska, Serena bought "two yoke of oxen, three cows, one wagon, one tent, a stove, boiler, cooking utensils, etc." to supplement an extensive set of copperware that she had brought with her from home. "She also brought many pieces of valuable silverware, silk, and other dress materials; also shoes and clothes enough to last the family two years." Though apparently financially comfortable, she married again in Florence.[31]

Elizabeth Brook Scarbrough Fox was widowed in England and emigrated to America with her two children in 1861. The next year she married Charles Fox and moved to Franklin, Idaho. She brought from England "dishes, cashmere and silk shawls, two black silk taffeta dresses, one silk poplin, two small silk hats, two silk parasols, a gold neck chain, a gold brooch, two gold rings, a Brussels carpet bag full of pieces of cloth, thread, needles, thimbles, baruches and other necessities." Her husband built her a large six-room stone house. At his death in 1880 she boarded railroad surveyors "for company," paid for the emigration of two converts from

England, and traveled extensively until her own death. Widowhood imposed no financial difficulties on her.[32]

Another church convert, Mary Lee Bland Ewell, a southerner, was widowed in Florence, Nebraska, on the way to Salt Lake City. She was left with five children and "Mammy Chloe," a black servant and gift from her mother at her marriage. Mammy Chloe helped take the family to Utah, took care of the children, taught Mary Lee to card wool, quilt, and weave "darky-style" straw hats that Mary Lee elaborated into a fancy style that Mammy Chloe peddled to the stores "until my sons were old enough to earn and make a home for us."[33]

There was always the possibility of remarriage for widows in Mormon communities, a possibility enhanced, one would expect, by the practice of polygyny that, doctrinally at least, made any man, married or single, a potential husband. That it did not prove to be a realistic option for most women is suggested in Gene Pace's conclusion that "widowed polygamous wives generally did not remarry." Pace's data on the 243 widows represented shows that only between 7 and 9 percent married again.[34] Geraldine Mineau's statistical breakdown of a much larger group indicates that of even the youngest widows, only about 37 percent remarried, though that figure could reach 50 percent. Of older widows, between 4 and 6.7 percent remarried. The primary urgency in remarriage, according to the diaries, was, predictably, financial security but other motives were compelling. Leora Margyanna Talmadge married at sixteen, gave birth to "the first white child born in Ogden Valley," bore six others, and was left a widow in 1875. Her oldest child was fifteen, the youngest nine days old, and, by her account, the family did not have "a thing to live on." Her reminiscence does not explain how she managed for the next nine years, but in 1884 she married Franklin Green Clifford "because I needed help to raise my family." Her honest admission comes into focus later when she summarizes her marital history: "I didn't love either of my husbands when I married them. . . . I learned to love them both. I shut my eyes and grabbed and got two good men."[35] Her experience, shared by many, is encapsulated in the words of Patty Sessions who, fully capable of providing for herself by dint of her midwifery, her orchards, and her real estate investments, was pleased to remarry because "at last I have someone to chop my wood for me."[36] Practical considerations remove sentiment from many accounts, but close readings reveal that in many cases an emotional bonding followed the marriage.

Except for immediate, short-term help, church and community resources (usually the same during most of Utah's territorial period) were a last recourse for either total or permanent assistance. While the church assiduously collected "fast offerings" for the poor (so-called because they were donated on a monthly day of fasting) and established the Relief Society for the avowed purpose of succoring "the poor and the widow," its aid appears to have been only piecemeal in the lives of destitute women. Though church records consistently report aid to indigent or bereaved families,[37] none of the personal accounts shows a Mormon widow receiving or acknowledging the expectation of receiving her whole support from the church or the community.[38] The discrepancy between the institutional records and the private accounts may arise from the fact that the women who wrote were ashamed to admit the extent of their reliance on charitable support or that those who were forced to rely on such support did not write. In any case, Pace's allegation that "the largest burden for the care of widows probably fell most heavily on the community bishops"[39] is not confirmed by these personal accounts.

Perhaps more noteworthy at the transitional juncture of widowhood was the availability of informal support systems. The ordinary amenities of female friendship—gifts of food, welcoming households, sewing circles and quilting bees, and visiting—replenished larders, mitigated travel expenses for visits to friends and family, helped provide clothing and household needs, and offered company and solace. Moreover, a widow who remained attached to the Mormon church found herself provided not only with an on-going sisterhood, both informally through friendships and formally through the Relief Society, but also with a place and purpose in the community, a status dependent more upon her personal adherence to the values of the community than upon material status props. The experience of Eunice Stewart Harris is suggestive. Widowed in 1912 in the Mormon colonies of Canada, she moved her family to Provo, Utah, for the sake of the children's education. Inclined to withdraw into the family circle, she nevertheless found herself conscripted into service in the Relief Society. "Although I felt weak and incompetent," she wrote, "I accepted the call, and it proved a great blessing to me. It brought me in contact with a wonderful group of women. Their friendship helped me to rise above my great trial." Moving again, she found herself "a stranger," but again received companionship in church service. "With each handclasp I felt that I had met a true friend, who would give me her support, her confidence, and her love, and that feeling has always existed between them and me." The Relief Society was then involved with the Red Cross, and of her contribution there, Eunice Harris wrote: "I wonder if we appreciate the blessedness of work. . . . In times like these work is the best panacea."[40] The value of such esteem-producing functions to a woman alone is obvious.

The pervasiveness of the after-life consciousness in Mormon life and thought, the concomitant anticipation of a life in eternity that would fully compensate for the hardships of mortality, and the assurances to the bereaved that their loved ones were better off where they were mitigated in varying degrees the pain of loss. The tenets of belief that would assure a widow of her husband's continued existence and the temple sealing that would give her the promise of a continued relationship were operative, of course, only to the extent that she believed in their truthfulness and found psychological shelter in the image of the next world. To this believing widow, the confidence in eternal relationships frequently ignited a determination to live worthily enough to meet the deceased in an eternal setting. Thus, there was motivation to take charge of one's life, to meet the circumstances of widowhood, and to rear the children successfully enough to prove one's worthiness to be reunited with the deceased husband. Eunice Harris keenly felt the responsibility of rearing children "without a father's counsel." If they failed in life, "then I, as a mother, had failed," she wrote. In remembering the thirty years of marriage to her husband, she counted the "prospect of our union being eternal as the greatest privilege God ever granted unto me."[41] While none of these religious/psychological supports eliminated the necessity for a Mormon widow, like any other, to pass through the steps toward functional rehabilitation endemic to widowhood, they did facilitate the process.

The practices of Mormonism, like its theology, aided the rehabilitation process in varying degrees. In nearly every case, the Mormon widow had to deal with temporal needs that pressed more urgently for attention than did the abstractions of theology. With children to provide for, in most instances, and the lack of training or experience of many women to make decisions, allocate labor outside of the house, plan for long-term sustenance, hire or trade farm work, or market or barter her own services, a widow came up against the realities of making her way alone almost immediately upon the death of her husband. Such demands precluded extended mourning. The church, through the bishop and the Relief Society, provided a surcease of financial worry. Never meant to be permanent sources of financial assistance, they met interim material needs until a woman was able to establish a dependable means of livelihood, either through family members or her own efforts. The effect of this welfare insurance was to provide every Mormon woman with the assurance that she would never need to find herself destitute at the death of her husband. While the extent to which the system functioned depended primarily upon the claims a woman made on it, that these limited resources were available ameliorated some of the anxieties experienced by the new widow while providing her time to make long-range plans for her own sustenance. The absence of references to church assistance could well suggest, in addition to reasons already discussed, that most women did not attempt to exploit the system but met the exigencies of widowhood as independently as their varing circumstances permitted.[42] The relatively low remarriage rate, even in a polygamous society, meant for most women that the death of a spouse irrevocably altered their financial and domestic circumstances.

For those few women who had been plural wives, widowhood presented a different set of circumstances. Financially disadvantaged by fluctuating legal interpretations of their status, they were generally more self-reliant than monogamous wives, many of them having had virtual sole financial and parenting responsibility even before the death of their shared husband.[43] Losing their right to claim a legal inheritance by the Edmunds Act of 1882 if their husband died intestate—and most husbands did—plural wives and their offspring did not recover that right for twenty-five years. This legal disability in many cases, however, made little difference since the division of an estate among many wives and children naturally yielded a diminished individual share. The absence of legal status, for most women, was probably more of a psychological than a financial disability.

The records show that widows who inherited their husband's businesses or had skills such as teaching, midwifery, nursing, and doctoring, or who had training in telegraphy, bookkeeping, and accounting, all of which Brigham Young encouraged for women, were best able to cope financially.[44] Untrained women found remuneration in performing household tasks for neighbors. Few married women or widows sought employment in the woolen or cotton factories that developed in Utah during the latter part of the century. Young single women, usually between 16 and 24, were the primary workers in these small factories.[45]

Emotional support systems were inherent in the structure of the church. Each ward varied in population, depending on location, but aside from the populous wards of Salt Lake and Utah counties, the average ward comprised about sixty-five families. These geographical clusters of Mormons functioned like micro-Mormon villages, particularly in rural areas, and naturally induced a communal spirit. The women of these wards routinely met together in a variety of church-based activities. Relief Society meetings along with meetings of the church-sponsored children's and young women's associations, all staffed by adult women, brought women together on a weekly basis as did Sunday church services. Moreover, the ward was traditionally the source of cultural and social activities, again providing opportunity for building close ties. Thus a typical neighborhood pattern of association was reinforced by shared religious and social programs.[46] In such a setting, death, illness, or other familial problems easily shifted from a private to a community concern. The bonding fostered by this kind of interaction was expressed by a Salt Lake City widow who, though a prominent public woman who entertained national and even foreign visitors frequently in her home, nevertheless savored best "the beautiful little meetings which the sisters often held in my house." Most of those sisters were widows like herself who, despite large families of their own, valued the companionship of women who shared with each other the common experiences of their generation and circumstances.

Whatever the varied circumstances in which they found themselves when widowed, the writers of these personal accounts either dramatically stated or cautiously implied that the loss of their husband was a wound from which they never fully recovered. The sturdy independence of a polygyny-trained Martha Cragun Cox or the zestful entrepreneuring of an Alice Parker Isom are invigorating exceptions. Typically, a woman's account of her own life concluded with the death of her husband, like that of one widow who summarized her twenty-nine years of widowhood with the sentence, "I have lived with my children." The harsh implication of such statements is that the only event of importance a woman could expect after her husband's decease was her own death.

This pattern, visible in autobiography after autobiography, may have come about partially because the widow's audience was presumably her children who would know what she had done since their father's death. It may have also developed from a vital statistics approach to autobiography that included dates and places of births, marriages, and deaths along with changes in residence as the only events worth remembering. Or it may have genuinely reflected a widespread attitude that a woman separated from her man was not a whole person and therefore unable to assume a natural place in the social order. At a time when, and in a culture where, marriage and maternity were the primal experiences of a woman's life, interruption or variation in either of these female rituals struck at her identity as a woman. That some women could transcend the debilitating effects of widowhood speaks more for the individuality of the woman than for the enlightenment of society.

NOTES

1. The history of communitarian thought and practice among the Mormons is discussed in Leonard J. Arrington, Frank Y. Fox, and Dean L. May, *Building the City of God: Community and Cooperation among the Mormons* (Salt Lake City: Deseret Book, 1976).

2. "Lovenia Nicholson Sylvester Berry," in Kate B. Carter, comp., *Our Pioneer Heritage,* 20 vols. (Salt Lake City: Daughters of Utah Pioneers, 1963), 6:399-403. The series, hereafter cited as *Pioneer Heritage,* reprinted many such autobiographical sketches or personal histories for use in chapter meetings.

3. The present doctrines of the Church of Jesus Christ of Latter-day Saints, or Mormons, are summarized in Bruce R. McConkie, *Mormon Doctrine* (Salt Lake City: Bookcraft, 1966), s.v. "eternal life." That particular doctrine has not measurably altered in the over 150-year history of the movement; if anything, the nineteenth-century Mormons believed even more literally in the continuity of life before, during, and after mortality. Early sermons on the subject are found in *Journal of Discourses,* 26 vols. (Liverpool: F. D. and S. W. Richards, 1854-86). While no single comprehensive investigation of plural marriage among the Mormons is yet available, many scholarly articles and monographs have been published. Davis Bitton, "Mormon Polygamy: A Review Article," *Journal of Mormon History* 4 (1977):101-18, provides an annotated bibliography to the best of these to that date.

4. Eliza Roxcy Snow [Smith], "Lines Written for the Occasion and Sung at the Funeral of Heber C. Kimball, Counselor to President Brigham Young," in *Poems, Religious, Historical, and Political,* 2 vols. (Salt Lake City: LDS Printing and Publishing Establishment, 1877), 2:165-66.

5. Ibid., 166. Further discussion of Mormon beliefs and practices concerning death is in Mary Ann Meyers, "Gates Ajar: Death in Mormon Thought and Practice," in David E. Stannard, ed., *Death in America* (Philadelphia: University of Pennsylvania Press, 1975), 112-33.

6. McConkie, *Mormon Doctrine,* s.v. "celestial marriage," "sealings."

7. Lavina Fielding Anderson, "Lucinda Lee Dalton: A Tough Kind of Testimony," in Vicky Burgess-Olson, ed., *Sister Saints* (Provo, Utah: Brigham Young University Press, 1978), 163.

8. Murray Parkes, as quoted in Helena Z. Lopata, *Widowhood in an American City* (Cambridge, Mass.: Schenckman, 1973), 51-52.

9. Jennie Anderson Froiseth, ed., *The Women of Mormonism: or the Story of Polygamy* (Detroit: CGG Paine, 1882), 37.

10. Bathsheba B. Smith, Reminiscence, typescript, Church Archives, Historical

Department, the Church of Jesus Christ of Latter-day Saints, Salt Lake City, Utah, hereafter cited as LDS Church Archives.

11. Emmeline B. Wells, Dairy, holograph, Special Collections, Harold B. Lee Library, Brigham Young University, Provo, Utah.

12. Carroll Smith-Rosenberg, "The Female World of Love and Ritual: Relations between Women in Nineteenth-Century America," *Signs* 1 (1975):1-29.

13. James E. Smith and Phillip R. Kunz, "Polygyny and Fertility in Nineteenth-Century America," *Population Studies* 30 (1976):465-80; also see Lowell C. Bennion and Ellen Bennion Stone, "What Percent of Which Population?" paper delivered at the annual meeting of the Mormon History Association, Ogden, Utah, May 6-9, 1982. Further studies under the direction of Dean L. May at the University of Utah, tracing individual families longitudinally rather than laterally, in time may raise the percentage estimates markedly.

14. D. Gene Pace, "Wives of Nineteenth-Century Mormon Bishops: A Quantitative Analysis," *Journal of the West* 21 (1983):52-53.

15. It is difficult to assess the real value of church welfare support to the families of widows in the nineteenth century. Records of the Relief Society suggest the intent of supporting the poor and list donations in the form of goods and labor, but the total annual collection of any one ward's Relief Society would not have provided necessary food and clothing for that ward's poor on a continuing basis. The account of the founding, in 1869, of the St. George Relief Society, comprising the women of four wards in that southern Utah town, suggests the scope and intent of the leaders there. Bishop Henry Eyring, one of the four bishops involved, said that "the Sisters can do more good among the people than the Brethren, for the needy would sooner make their wants known to them, than to the Brethren." His statement is put more completely in context by the comment of his fellow bishop, Robert Gardner, that "we are all poor here." St. George Relief Society Minutes, June 8, 1869, and May 28, 1872, LDS Church Archives. See also Relief Society reports on the *Woman's Exponent,* 1872-1914, 42 vols.; Leonard J. Arrington, *Great Basin Kingdom: An Economic History of the Latter-day Saints, 1830-1900* (Cambridge, Mass.: Harvard University Press, 1958); minutes of Ward Relief Societies, Bishops Meetings, LDS Church Archives.

16. "Act in Relation to the Estates of Decendents," section 24, *Laws of Utah,* 1852-70, 45. Also *Utah Code Annotated, 1953,* 8:61. These considerations are part of a larger work, "The Legal Status of Women in Utah Territory," in process by Carol Cornwall Madsen.

17. "Mary Ann Weston Maughan," in *Pioneer Heritage,* 2 (1959):396.

18. Emily Dow Partridge Young, autobiography and diary, typescript, Feb. 28, 1880, LDS Church Archives.

19. *Compiled Laws of Utah* 1876, 273-4; 1898, 1:119; Section 2826, 626.

20. Leonard J. Arrington, *David Eccles: Pioneer Western Industrialist* (Logan: Utah State University Press, 1975), 183-88.

21. Anne W. Leishman Oral History, interview by John Stewart, 1973, typescript, 37-38, in Utah State University Voice Library Interview, Utah State University Archives, Logan.

22. Hannah Daphne Smith Dalton, *Pretty Is as Pretty Does* (Privately printed, n.d.), 11.

23. Sketch of Florence Ellen Fowler Adair, in *Pioneer Heritage* 7 (1964): 269-71.

24. Dalton, *Pretty Is as Pretty Does,* 11.

25. Alice Parker Isom, "Memoirs," *Utah Historical Quarterly* 10 (1942):55-81.

26. Hilda Andersson Erickson, diary, 1830-85, *Pioneer Heritage* 6 (1963):82-95, 98-100.

27. Martha Cragun Cox, Autobiographical sketch, holograph, LDS Church Archives; typescript by Kathy Stephens in possession of Lavina Fielding Anderson, 117-18, 128-29, 196-97, 276, 283.

28. *A Mormon Mother: An Autobiography of Annie Clark Tanner,* ed. by Obert C. Tanner (Salt Lake City: Tanner Trust Fund, University of Utah Library, 1969), 271.

29. Ibid., 250.

30. Ruth Victor, "Emma Jeffs Gunnell," photocopy of typescript in possession of Carol Cornwall Madsen, unpaginated.

31. In a sketch of "Ann Maria Staaleson Dorius," *Pioneer Heritage* 7 (1964):53-55.

32. "Elizabeth Brook Scarbrough Fox," biographical sketch, in S. George Ellsworth, "An Inventory of Historical Resource Materials for Cache Valley, Utah-Idaho" (Logan, Utah, 1957), microfilm, reel 5, item 4, Utah State University Archives.

33. "Mary Lee Bland Ewell," *Pioneer Heritage,* 8 (1965):532-35.

34. Pace, "Wives of Mormon Bishops," 53.

35. "Leora Margyanna Talmadge Campbell Clifford," *Pioneer Heritage* 4 (1961):54-56.

36. Patty Sessions, diary, Dec. 14, 1851, holograph, LDS Church Archives. At the time Patty, who had crossed the plains driving her own wagon, had been widowed of David Sessions less than eighteen months.

37. Relief Society financial reports were frequently printed in the *Woman's Exponent,* a Mormon woman's paper published from 1872-1914. These indicate donations and expenditures in both cash and kind for the individual ward societies. Expenditure columns always included substantial disbursements to needy individuals and families. The continued request for members to pay their donations and fast offerings further indicate that the charitable resources were constantly drained. See also note 15.

38. The personal record of one prominent Mormon woman gives some insight. The widow of a former mayor of the city and counselor to Brigham Young,

Emmeline B. Wells, an officer in the General Relief Society, suffragist, and editor of the *Woman's Exponent*, relied solely on her own financial resources. Dependent on subscriptions to the *Exponent* for her livelihood and frequently in debt, a worry she often recounts in her diary, she never refers to any financial assistance from either her family or the church. Though an officer in both the National Suffrage Association and National Council of Women, she attended their conventions only when her expenses were voluntarily paid by the Relief Society, which affiliated with both organizations.

39. Pace, "Wives of Mormon Bishops," 53.

40. Eunice Stewart Harris, "Autobiographical Sketch, 1932," carbon copy of typescript, 61-73, 78-80, LDS Church Archives.

41. Ibid., 90.

42. When burial procedures became commercialized in Utah around the turn of the century, the Relief Society gradually relinquished this essential social function, thereby placing the costs of burial primarily on the family of the deceased. In 1914 the Relief Society offered a program of burial insurance for its members, setting premiums at marginal costs through a local insurance agency. This popular insurance program served a transitional need until burial insurance became subsumed under broader coverage, though a separate policy could still be obtained. The Relief Society continued the program for just a brief period.

43. One plural wife lost a child by fearing to act decisively in the absence of her husband and learned from that experience to be self-reliant. "Always after that cruel experience," she wrote, "I decided for myself and acted if possible." "Ellen Elvira Nash Parkinson," *Pioneer Heritage*, 8 (1965):202-18. In the absence of their shared husband, sisters Emma and Margaret Smith had to support themselves. See also Hannah Daphne Smith Dalton, 11. Vicky Burgess-Olson, in her doctoral dissertation, "Family Structure and Dynamics in Early Utah Mormon Families, 1847-1885" (Northwestern University, 1975), 112, indicates that 96 percent of plural wives either fully or partially supported themselves and their children.

44. Harriet Cook Young, a widow of Brigham Young, worked as a bookkeeper for ZCMI, a large department store. She financed her son's mission to Europe and extensive traveling afterward from her own earnings. A visitor to Salt Lake City, Elizabeth Wood Kane, noted in her account of her travels throughout the territory, that "in some ways these people [are] the most forward children of the age. They close no career on a woman in Utah by which she can earn a living." Elizabeth Wood Kane, *Twelve Mormon Homes Visited in Succession on a Journey through Utah to Arizona* (rpt. ed., Salt Lake City: University of Utah Library, 1974), 5.

45. See Occupational Statistics, 15th Census.

46. Occasionally widows were overlooked. In a community in southern Utah, Eva Harrison and three other widows were upset when the old folks' outing

excluded them. They, therefore, according to Eva's account, "collected food, dishes, and silverware, and with the help of our older daughters, served a dinner in the two north rooms of my home" to the bishopric, her brother, and sixty-five widows, all of whom were thereafter invited to the old folks' outing. "Eva Christine Beck Zimmerman Harrison," *Pioneer Heritage,* 8:48-51.

6

Utah Widowhood: A Demographic Profile

GERALDINE P. MINEAU

Studies of widows in historical demography have generally been of three types: computations of the incidence of widowhood; studies of remarriage; or studies of the households in which widows reside. In this essay I touch on selected aspects of these issues by analyzing women in their family contexts and following women from their first marriages through widowhood and possible remarriage until death. I have used a large set of family genealogies to study individuals residing in Utah from the mid-nineteenth century through the early twentieth century. My emphasis is the variations among widows that derive from the age of the wife and children when the husband dies, whether she remarries, and the number of years she is a widow. The process of family adaptation and change differs according to the timing, arrangement, and duration of events in the life course of these women.[1]

Widowhood appears to have been a common state for older women throughout American history, although the proportions were somewhat less than today. Mathilda Riley and Anne Foner calculate the chance that a wife will eventually become widowed and show that it has increased from 1890, when the wife was the surviving spouse in 56 percent of all marriages, through 1930, when the figure was 60 percent, to 1964, when it was 70 percent. Noreen Goldman and Graham Lord's recent calculations basically agree with these figures: 57 percent of women outlived their spouses in 1890 and 69 percent in 1977.[2] Howard Chudacoff and Tamara Hareven studied census data from 1865 through 1900 for Providence, Rhode Island, and indicate that "widowhood was one of the most characteristic experiences of old age in the lives of the population . . . although it was chiefly restricted to women."[3] They find that widows made up nearly a third of all women ages 55 to 64 and 60 percent or higher for women in their late sixties and early seventies. Among men the proportion of widowers seldom rose above 15 percent under the age of 70. Utah census data on marital status for 1890 and 1900 supports the results of Chudacoff and Hareven. About one-third of women age 55 to 64 were widows; and for ages 64 and older, it was 55 percent and 58 percent in 1890 and 1900, respectively. For men in these ages, the rates ranged from 7 to 10 percent (ages 55 to 64) and from 17 to 21 percent (age 65 and older).

Studies of remarriage, utilizing mainly family reconstitutions, have as their primary focus the effect on fertility of different levels of mortality and varying cultural norms regarding remarriage. Recently they have emphasized the need to analyze the age at termination of the first marriage, the duration of widowhood, the number of dependent children, and the marital status of the second spouse.[4] Susan Grigg's work includes the spouse's valuation in the last year of life to determine the relationship between wealth and remarriage.[5] Both Dupaquier et al. and Grigg, in their separate reviews of European and American studies covering the sixteenth to early nineteenth centuries, indicate that remarriage was more common for men than women and occurred more often among the young than the elderly. John Knodel and Katherine Lynch, studying German villages during the eighteenth and nineteenth centuries, confirm these results and analyze the decline in remarriage generally observed in Europe during this period.[6]

Chudacoff and Hareven, in their studies of the nineteenth-century household structure,[7] find an increase in the proportions of older people, especially in cities, and note that women constituted a majority of old people in the cities. This was partly due to longer life expectancies among women, but it may have also reflected in-migration among adult females of all ages. Their analysis indicates that older women had more varied living situations than older men; and the loss of independence, that is, the loss of being household head, was experienced predominantly by older women. These data also suggest that in cities a widow could share her household space with boarders or other family members more easily than in rural areas and that families might have more interdependent relationships. European data also support this; for example, David Herlihy's study of Florence in the fifteenth century finds about 25 percent of adult women were widows and suggests that "the widow could live alone, successfully and comfortably, within the city, and she did not need a male to help her with heavy agricultural labor."[8]

All of these studies, however, have limitations. For example, marital status at the time of a census does not indicate the proportion of people who have experienced the death of a spouse; it only gives an indication of those presently in that marital status. Knowing the current marital status is necessary for studying household composition, but it does not tell us about the life course of individuals and their families. Widowed individuals who remarry are simply classified as married. In addition, women who are widowed at young ages and then die young are typically lost in census or survey data. For those individuals classified as widowed, one does not know the length of time they have survived their spouses nor their family structures at the time of the spouses' deaths. Additionally migration from one community to another is difficult to study with either census data or family reconstitutions. To overcome these limitations in studying the experience of losing a spouse, I present a different approach for the demographic analysis of widowhood by combining the methodology of cohort analysis[9] with the theoretical orientation of life course. I focus on (1) the life cycle of cohorts of married women specifying which spouse survived, (2) profiles of women within each cohort widowed at different ages, and (3) the residential location of widows at their death.

An innovative concept, suggested by recent scholarship in family history, is the life-course approach.[10] According to Glen Elder, the life-course approach to the family views an individual in three dimensions: the individual's aging process, the social timing and structure of her life, and the historical context in which she lives. "Life-course analysis keeps in view the collective aspects of family and household, the actions and lives of members, and their interplay, placing all of this in relation to macro trends and their local expressions."[11] Hareven states that the life-course approach focuses on individual development and the collective development of the family unit. She emphasizes "the synchronizations of individual with family transitions; the interaction between life-course transitions and historical change; and ultimately, the cumulative impact of earlier life-course transitions on subsequent ones."[12] These authors believe that the family life cycle,[13] which employs a discrete classification of a few fixed stages, is too limiting because "families with an identical history as defined by a sequence of stages, vary markedly in their respective life course. Much of this variation is due to the differential timing and arrangement of events."[14]

Norman Ryder's classic discussion on cohort analysis suggests that "social change occurs to the extent that successive cohorts do something other than merely repeat the patterns of behavior of the predecessors."[15] However, Elder believes that emphasis should be on variations within successive cohorts rather than the aggregate level of the whole cohort. Peter Uhlenberg extends the use of cohorts by suggesting that "social diversity between groups in a population occurs to the extent that collateral cohorts in different groups vary in behavioral patterns. Thus by tracing the behavior of successive cohorts through time we can observe patterns of social change, while by examining collateral cohorts across groups we can measure intergroup diversity."[16] Thus Elder and Hareven are building on this research tradition and adding a developmental view of the family and a perspective of family behavior as it is influenced by the social context of the time.

Susan Watkins points out in her methodological critique of the life-course approach that the unit of analysis can be both the individual and the family simultaneously.[17] Any possible confusion is avoided in my study because the main issue or turning point is widowhood, which requires, as the unit of analysis, married women. Thus, I focus on a specific individual within a family structure, examining five ten-year cohorts of women born between 1830 and 1879 from their marriages through their entire lives. Since genealogical data rather than census data are utilized, analysis begins with a woman's first marriage; how and when this marriage terminates; and for those who survive their husbands, their subsequent demographic experiences (e.g., remarriage, length of widowhood, residential change, and life expectancy). Thus I can study the timing, arrangement, and duration of events in the life course of women who became widows from approximately 1850 through the first half of the twentieth century.

The data I have utilized are derived from a set of approximately 180,000 computerized Utah genealogies. Initially this project, part of a larger medical genetics research effort, selected family group sheets if they met the criterion of least one individual in the family having experienced a birth or death on the Mormon (Church of Jesus Christ of Latter-day Saints [LDS]) pioneer trail or in Utah. Thus, the data base includes individuals born from about 1800 through the present. The recorded data include birth date and place, marriage date and place, and death date and place for each spouse along with the names of the parents of each spouse. In addition, space is provided for recording other marriages for both the husband and wife. The sheets also include the birth date and place, marriage date, spouse's name, and death date for each child of the family (see figure 1). The data repository from which the family group sheets were selected, the nature of the data

FAMILY GROUP RECORD 1972 The Genealogical Department of The Church of Jesus Christ of Latter-day Saints PFGS0029 2/78 100M Printed in the United States of America

HUSBAND JONES, Robert

	Date	Place
Born	4 Feb 1838	Bolton Lanes, Lncshr, Engl
Chr.		
Mar	6 May 1863	Salt Lake City, S-Lk, Utah
Died	13 Aug 1921	
Bur.		

HUSBAND'S FATHER JONES, George — HUSBAND'S MOTHER WHEELER, Jane

HUSBAND'S OTHER WIVES JOHNSON, Elizabeth

WIFE DOTY, Harriet

	Date	Place
Born	3 Sep 1842	Blowich, Lncshr, Engl
Chr.		
Died	2 June 1923	Salt Lake City, S-Lk, Utah
Bur.		

WIFE'S FATHER DOTY, Raymond — WIFE'S MOTHER WEBB, Nancy

WIFE'S OTHER HUSBANDS

Husband JONES, Robert 1838
Wife DOTY, Harriet
Ward Examiners: 1. (18th)C.T.R. 2. N.C.
Stake or Mission Ensign

NAME & ADDRESS OF PERSON SUBMITTING SHEET
Blanchard, Sylvia W.
428 I Avenue
Salt Lake City, Utah

RELATION OF ABOVE TO HUSBAND: g dau — RELATION OF ABOVE TO WIFE: g dau

FOUR GENERATION SHEET FOR FILING ONLY: YES [X] NO [ ]

DATE SUBMITTED TO GENEALOGICAL SOCIETY: 6 Apr 1978

LDS ORDINANCE DATA

	BAPTIZED (Date)	ENDOWED (Date)	SEALED (Date and Temple) WIFE TO HUSBAND
HUSBAND	3 Nov 1853	3 Feb 1866	3 Feb 1866
WIFE	1852	Feb 1866	

SEX M F	CHILDREN List each child (whether living or dead) in order of birth. Given Names SURNAME	WHEN BORN DAY MONTH YEAR	WHERE BORN TOWN	COUNTY	STATE OR COUNTRY	DATE OF FIRST MARRIAGE / TO WHOM	WHEN DIED DAY MONTH YEAR	BAPTIZED (Date)	ENDOWED (Date)	SEALED (Date and Temple) CHILDREN TO PARENTS
1	JONES, Katherine Anne	1 Apr 1865	Nephi	Juab	Utah		2 Sep 1871	Child	Child	1 Jun 1950
2	JONES, David Wheeler	29 Dec 1866	Moroni	Snpt	Utah	24 Apr 1895 Bricker, Mary Ann	20 Feb 1931	31 Jan 1877	24 Apr 1895	BIC
3	JONES, Charlotte	29 Sep 1869	"	"	"	21 Apr 1890 Denton, Richard	27 May 1949	Reb. 1 Apr 1890	21 Apr 1890	BIC
4	JONES, Arlene Marie	20 Aug 1871	Salt Lake City	S-Lk	"		25 Sep 1872	Child	Child	BIC
5	JONES, Louise Nancy	18 Nov 1873	" " "	"	"	2 Nov 1896 Taylor, John	31 May 1929	7 Jun 1883	2 Nov 1896	BIC
6	JONES, Marilyn	31 Aug 1876	" " "	"	"	31 Jan 1906 McNeil, Joseph	23 Dec 1926	30 Mar 1886	27 Aug 1902	BIC
7	JONES, James Lowell	8 Aug 1878	North Point	S-Lk	"		8 Aug 1878	Child	Child	BIC
8	JONES, John Lawrence	24 Aug 1879	" "	"	"		15 Apr 1880	Child	Child	BIC
9	JONES, Isabel	6 Aug 1881	" "	"	"		13 Nov 1904	1 Apr 1890	31 Jan 1906	BIC
10	JONES, Elliot George	6 Nov 1883	Salt Lake City	"	"	30 Aug 1911 Creighton, Cynthia		29 Mar 1893	8 Mar 1905	BIC
11	JONES, Sarah Jane	2 Jul 1886	" " "	"	"	22 June 1910 Anderson, Thomas A.		2 Jul 1894	22 Jun 1910	BIC

SOURCES OF INFORMATION
Personal diary and family records of Robert Jones

OTHER MARRIAGES

NECESSARY EXPLANATIONS

Figure 1. Sample Family Group Sheet. Fictitious names have been substituted in place of real names.

set, and its utilization, strengths, and weaknesses have been described in a number of other publications and are not repeated here except as they apply to this study.[18]

Genealogies underrepresent certain kinds of people and so may introduce biases. In connection with this research, at least two possible instances occur: those married individuals with a long life span may be overrepresented and those who remarry may be underrepresented. First, by their nature, genealogies are more likely to contain information on people who marry, have large families, and live to an old age. Families that die out and have no surviving descendants are underreported in genealogical records. Second, to study accurately remarriage requires at least two marriages with the date of marriage or the birth date of children recorded, so that the researcher can distinguish between first and second marriages. Individuals who remarry and do not have children (some because they are too old at their second marriage) are less likely to have full genealogical records created for that second marriage. Also, if different descendants submitted records for these marriages and different spellings of a name or different birth dates were given, as happens in historical records, it is unlikely that the computer could match the individual and link their sequential marriages properly. Thus, there is a recognized bias that causes incomplete recording and underidentification of individuals who have more than one marriage. The proportionate number of women who were widowed and then remarried is thus slightly low.

Comparing this genealogical data to the Utah census of 1890, I find that widows generally are slightly underreported (overall probably less than 5 percent) and specifically it is the younger widows who are underrepresented while those over age 60 are more fully represented. Using total U.S. census data, Riley and Foner followed the 1865-74 cohort over time and found 55.6 percent were widows at age 65 and older while 9.3 percent never married and 34.3 percent were currently married.[19] Using the 1865-74 cohort in this data set, one finds that for exact ages 65, 70, and 75 the percent of widows was 37.1, 50.6, and 64.5, respectively. In Utah the percentage of single women (never married) after age 45 is consistently low, 2.6 in the 1910 census;[20] thus, they have only minor effects on the figures. In comparing the Utah genealogy figures to the total U.S. census figures, one finds that the patterns of change are similar and that the levels of widows at given ages are in the same range. While one can argue that the figures derived from genealogical records are not exact, they present the correct magnitude and trend.

A final comment on the population represented by these computerized

Utah genealogies will aid in the evaluation of this study. The work being undertaken by the Mormon Historical Demography Project includes linking the 1880 manuscript census for the Territory of Utah to the individuals in the genealogical data base. This project applied computer record-linking techniques to 142,754 enumerated individuals. Currently 63.4 percent of the records have been linked and the final linking rate is expected to be about 70 percent. The communities of several counties have been studied in detail; the level of linking varies with the economic base of the community. In agricultural communities 78 to 90 percent of individuals link to genealogical records while mining communities (mainly consisting of adult males) link at very low levels. In general, the genealogies provide good coverage of families and excellent coverage of families in agricultural communities.[21]

Several restrictions have been placed upon the data, so that they conform to a study of the life course of widows. Those females selected for study have survived their childhood and youth and married from one to four times, as evidenced by the creation of one or more family group sheets for these women. Using birth and death places for the woman and the birth places for her children, it has been determined that the family did reside in Utah for all or a portion of the woman's life. And as mentioned earlier the women were born in the fifty years from 1830 to 1879. Our computerized files contain records for 44,862 women with these criteria. Further specifications eliminated 13.0 percent of these.[22] Fortunately, our data set is of sufficient size that even with a number of necessary constraints, the remaining cases are adequate for a detailed study. Thus, this research reports on 39,040 women who were born between 1830 and 1879, first married between the ages of 10 and 49, resided in Utah, and had a family group sheet filled out and placed at the Genealogical Society of Utah.

The study of the life cycle of these women begins by focusing on the outcome of their first marriage. Note that the first marriage of the wife may be the husband's first marriage, but it may also be his second, third, or higher order. The husband may be a polygamist[23] at the time of this marriage or may eventually become one. There are three possible outcomes for women in marriage defined by this data set:[24] divorce, their own deaths, or their husbands' deaths. The incidence of a husband dying first occurs in 57 percent[25] of families and is fairly close to Riley and Foner's figures for 1890, in which the wife was the surviving spouse in 56 percent of all marriages.[26] The proportion of divorces (1.4 percent) is probably low; some of the marriages in the other categories ended in divorce, but there was no remarriage and no divorce recorded on the genealogical sheets. In the 1890 Utah census only 1.23 percent of ever-married women were currently divorced, and in the 1910 census it was 1.19. Since the divorce rate was fairly low in the 1800s and early 1900s, one can assume that this would not be too great an error. However, there is a slightly higher incidence of divorce among the earlier cohorts and this is probably related to the practice of polygamy and lax divorce laws that existed in Utah Territory.[27]

If earlier experiences in life affect later experience, then previous demographic experience should be considered in addition to the way in which the marriage is terminated. In table 1 the family life cycle is specified by marriages ending in divorce, the wife's death, or the husband's death. The first major difference observed is in those families that end in divorce. The wife married at a younger age and divorce occurred during her early reproductive years resulting in fewer children in this marriage. The second observation is the lack of any great difference in family life ending in the death of the wife or the death of the husband. Families ending with the death of the wife/mother show a very slightly older age at marriage and a slightly younger age when the last child was born; these factors combine to produce a slightly lower number of children. But the largest difference observed relates to when and how the marriage terminates; the wife is on average in her mid-fifties if her death terminates the marriage and about age 59 to 60 if her husband's death terminates the marriage. The marriage union lasts two to four years longer if the wife is the surviving spouse.

The age at death for the women varies considerably, as one would expect. As mentioned earlier, the study is based on a group of women who survived infancy and childhood and married on average at age 20 to 21. They experienced an average age at death of 69.5 with a slight improvement over time.[28] About 95 percent of widows live to be age 60 or older, but only 25 percent of the women who die before their husbands live past this age. Divorced women fall between these groups in life expectancy but are more similar to widows.

The timing of the death of a spouse or parent should also be considered from the standpoint of the surviving spouse and children. When one looks only at mean age, it appears that the death of a parent does not affect a large number of children at a very young age. If we use the 1850-59 cohort as an example and subtract the mother's age at last birth from her age when the family terminated, we observe that in one family type there is a surviving father with the youngest child at age 17.8 and in the other

Table 1. Family Life Cycle by Termination of First Marriage and Woman's Birth Cohort

Birth Cohort	Mean Age at Marriage	Mean Number of Children	Mean Age at Last Birth	Mean Age at Termination[a]	Mean Age at Death
			All Women		
1830-39	21.86	7.59	38.67		69.53
1840-49	20.54	8.05	38.32		68.58
1850-59	20.21	8.02	38.22		68.99
1860-69	20.67	7.48	37.94		69.69
1870-79	21.48	6.72	37.46		70.22
	20.93	7.45	37.98		69.54
			Marriage Terminated by Divorce		
1830-39	20.44	3.25	26.70		70.17
1840-49	19.07	4.00	28.08		71.00
1850-59	19.21	4.13	27.93		73.07
1860-69	18.93	4.33	27.80		74.11
1870-79	19.89	4.06	28.84		73.52
	19.52	3.97	27.92		72.42
			Marriage Terminated by Wife's Death[b]		
1830-39	22.07	7.46	38.52	57.17	57.17
1840-49	20.66	7.79	37.74	54.85	54.85
1850-59	20.26	7.88	37.77	55.62	55.62
1860-69	20.76	7.28	37.36	56.82	56.82
1870-79	21.55	6.60	37.06	57.28	57.28
	21.02	7.28	37.52	56.51	56.51
			Marriage Terminated by Husband's Death		
1830-39	21.66	7.85	39.29	59.32	77.98
1840-49	20.39	8.34	39.02	58.61	77.52
1850-59	20.14	8.21	38.80	59.45	78.04
1860-69	20.63	7.67	38.56	61.40	79.08
1870-79	21.46	6.85	37.93	61.25	79.48
	20.85	7.65	38.56	60.10	78.65

[a] Age at termination of first marriage. For marriages that ended in the death of a spouse, this age is the wife's age at death or the age at which she becomes a widow. For those marriages that ended in divorce, this age is not calculated because family group sheets do not consistently record the date at which divorce occurred.

[b] Includes cases where the wife died before the husband and where the wife and husband have the same death date.

there is a surviving mother with the youngest child at age 20.6. It is probable that given the large family sizes the older children are no longer at home and are least likely to have life course disruptions as a result of a parent's death. But using the mean for a cohort obscures the diversity experienced by families as Uhlenberg and Elder suggest. Thus the next section provides a more detailed profile of different groups of widows.

If one views the death of a spouse as an involuntary and intervening event in one's life, then the timing of this event will have significant consequences. In table 2 the mean age of widowhood is reported along with a breakdown of proportions widowed at specific ages. About 10 percent are widowed by age 40, 34 percent between 40 and 59, and 56 percent at age 60 or older. There is a slight change in the trend over time, with the later two cohorts experiencing fewer husbands dying when the wife is young and more when the wife is age 60 or older. As indicated above, the proportions for young widows is slightly low by several percent but not greatly in error.

The mean age at death of husbands (table 3) is remarkably consistent over time.[29] Husbands who die before their wives tend to be about age 66 to 67; over 70 percent die at age 60 and above.

Both wife's age at widowhood and husband's age at death have been specified by wife's age at marriage and are presented across the bottom of

Table 2. Proportions of Women Widowed at Specific Ages by Woman's Birth Cohort and Age of Marriage

Birth Cohort	Mean Age	Under Age 40 (%)	Age 40-59 (%)	Age 60 and over (%)
1830-39	59.32	11.93	34.29	53.77
1840-49	58.61	11.66	35.61	52.72
1850-59	59.45	11.18	34.93	53.90
1860-69	60.40	10.06	33.32	56.62
1870-79	61.26	8.97	32.48	58.55
	60.10	10.39	33.82	55.79
Age at Marriage				
<20	59.23	11.49	34.37	54.14
20-24	61.29	9.34	31.74	58.91
≥25	62.06	6.18	34.80	59.02

Table 3. Husband's Age at Death (for Women in Table 2) by Woman's Birth Cohort and Age of Marriage

Birth Cohort	Husband's Mean Death Age	Under Age 40 (%)	Age 40-59 (%)	Age 60 and over (%)
1830-39	67.11	5.87	19.95	74.19
1840-49	67.64	5.52	18.92	75.56
1850-59	66.94	5.51	20.72	73.77
1860-69	66.41	5.75	22.30	71.95
1870-79	66.52	5.69	22.59	71.72
	66.79	5.66	21.34	72.99
Wife's Age at Marriage				
<20	67.37	5.64	19.67	74.69
20-24	66.62	5.55	22.01	72.44
≥25	67.17	4.22	22.45	73.33

tables 2 and 3. There is a positive association between age at marriage and age at widowhood. Wives who marry at a younger age do tend to be younger at widowhood (specifically more are widowed under age 40), and women who marry at older ages are older when widowed. But husband's age at death again remains fairly stable. If wife's age at widowhood is substracted from husband's age at death for these three age-at-marriage groups, the age difference is 8.1 years for women married before age 20, 5.3 for women married at age 20-24, and 5.1 for women married at age 25 or older.[30] Thus the positive association between age at marriage and age at widowhood should be attributed to the age difference between husbands and wives. In other words, women who marry under age 20 are widowed at age 59 because their husbands are on average eight years older than themselves while women who marry at age 25 or older are not widowed until age 62 and have husbands only five years older than themselves. Alan Bideau in a study of several French villages "emphasizes that it is women married young to older men who most risk becoming widows."[31] That the age difference between a husband and wife is one obvious factor related to widowhood and that women who marry young in this population are more likely to have husbands relatively older than themselves support Bideau's findings that they have also increased the likelihood of widowhood at younger ages. A profile of women widowed at different ages is presented in table 4 and discussed below.

Table 4. Profiles of Widows by Woman's Birth Cohort and Age at Widowhood

			Those Who Remarry		Do Not Remarry	
Birth Cohort	Mean Dependent Children[a]	% with One or More Children	% Who Remarry	Mean Age at Remarriage	Mean Years of Widowhood	Mean Age at Death
			All Widows			
1830-39	1.10	36.76	6.01	34.96	17.34	78.36
1840-49	1.20	37.03	4.99	35.85	17.83	77.87
1850-59	1.13	34.23	4.94	39.25	17.49	78.26
1860-69	1.02	32.46	5.17	42.64	17.52	79.26
1870-79	0.86	29.02	6.44	46.38	16.95	79.70
	1.03	32.91	5.56	41.57	17.37	78.90
			Widowed under Age 40			
1830-39	3.70	98.26	41.87	31.35	36.68	71.63
1840-49	4.17	98.31	36.31	31.97	35.91	69.81
1850-59	4.18	98.01	31.94	32.75	38.53	72.25
1860-69	4.16	97.78	35.70	34.97	37.32	71.37
1870-79	3.69	98.46	39.73	35.80	37.84	71.81
	3.99	98.14	36.76	33.81	37.43	71.47
			Widowed Age 40-59			
1830-39	1.88	69.80	1.93	53.61	23.61	75.54
1840-49	1.98	68.56	1.56	52.91	23.80	75.11
1850-59	1.85	64.28	3.30	55.13	23.05	74.80
1860-69	1.79	66.16	3.53	57.30	24.16	75.96
1870-79	1.61	60.43	6.95	57.12	24.00	76.01
	1.79	64.91	3.98	56.39	23.77	75.56
			Widowed Age 60 and over			
1830-39	0.03	2.15	0.31	69.32	10.89	81.03
1840-49	0.03	2.29	0.37	71.80	11.31	80.87
1850-59	0.02	1.48	0.29	70.82	11.03	81.31
1860-69	0.02	1.11	0.69	69.03	11.47	82.07
1870-79	0.01	0.94	0.94	70.77	11.33	82.37
	0.02	1.39	0.61	70.25	11.26	81.75

[a] The number of children alive and under age 16 at the time of the father's death.

Widowed under Age 40. Over 98 percent of these widows have one or more children under age 16; in fact, on average a widow has four dependent children. For this widow and her children the death of the husband/father is a major disruption in their life course.

A large portion, at least 37 percent but probably more, of these women remarry. One might speculate that if most of the cases omitted because of incomplete remarriage information (see note 22) were valid instances of remarriage, then the proportion of widows under age 40 who remarry could increase to between 50 and 65 percent. For the existing cases, the cohort of 1830-39 has the highest incidence of remarriage, mostly attributable to remarriage involving polygamy. It was certainly not uncommon for a polygamist to take a widow as one of his wives. The two cohorts that follow (1840-49, 1850-59) experience a decrease in remarriage as polygamy was first persecuted by the federal authorities in the 1880s and then became forbidden by church manifesto in 1890. The last two cohorts (1860-69, 1870-79) experience an increase in remarriage, which for the most part was monogamous.

Age at remarriage is on average 34. This age increases across all cohorts from 31 for the 1830-39 cohort to 36 for the 1870-79 cohort. The interval to remarriage also consistently increases over time, from 3.4 years to 6.6 years (not shown in table 4). Widows who remarry have 2.6 dependent children at the time of their remarriage.[32]

The young widows who do not remarry have as their next demographic event death at about age 71. They experience a very long period—approximately 37 years or over half of their lives—as widows. While their early years of widowhood may revolve around raising children, there is still a considerable time period when they are not in a nuclear family.

Widowed Age 40 to 59. Over 64 percent of these women have at least one dependent child at widowhood and average 1.8 dependent children per widow. The fairly consistent decline across cohorts in being a widowed mother and in the mean number of dependent children reflects the general decline in marital fertility experienced in the population.[33] Since these women were widowed after age 40, their fertility experience and number of dependent children are likely to be similar to that of all families that remain intact until the wife is over age 40. Given the high fertility level and fairly young age at marriage of Utah women (table 1), one can speculate that the majority of widows also have several children over age 15 who would be in residence with their mothers.

A fairly small portion of these widows remarry, from a low of 4 percent to an estimated high of 7 percent. The proportion remarrying does increase over time, as does the age at remarriage. But the majority of these women experience twenty-four years as widows—about one-third of their lives—and die at age 75 to 76.

Widowed Age 60 and Older. These women make up the majority of all widows. For the 1830-39 cohort, 29 percent of widows experience their husbands' deaths while in their sixties and 25 percent at age 70 or older; by the 1870-79 cohort the split is about even, 29 percent in the sixties and 30 percent at 70 or older. The most significant demographic information for these women is that they survive their husbands for about eleven years and die at age 81 to 82. Very few have dependent children and very few remarry. It is more likely that they rely on the assistance of their grown children or others. Thus this early western society, not unlike society today, included a large number of older women who were widows.

Comparisons by Age at Widowhood. A widow is apt to survive for years and even decades following the death of her husband. One of two experiences end the state of widowhood for a woman: remarriage or death. Remarriage is almost completely concentrated among the small portion of women widowed before age 40. After this age and certainly after age 60, widowhood is a lifelong state. This finding for Utah reinforces findings of other researchers among American and European populations.

Children as a liability or a source of support vary greatly when considering the age of the widow. Those women widowed at young ages have young children to support while those widowed at much older ages have large families and, potentially, many adult children to aid them.

For the majority of Utah widows who do not remarry, a considerable amount of time in life is spent in this status. Almost half (47 percent) will survive their husbands for more than fifteen years, and 36 percent will live twenty or more years without a husband. Among those women who are widowed young, 85 percent can expect to live for twenty or more years, while for women widowed at age 60 or older, about half will live less than ten years. Whether it is for twenty years or ten years, what experiences do these women have? Without census or household data one cannot determine whether they are living alone or with others, but genealogical data do allow us to observe at least one possibility: migration after becoming a widow.

Based upon the studies of Essex County, Massachusetts, and Providence, Rhode Island by Chudacoff and Hareven, one might expect to find that some widows in Utah migrated into urban areas, either to live with adult children or to live independently. Any movement on the part of widows, whether into an urban area, a change of rural location, or a household move in the same community, could indicate an inability or lack of desire to maintain the household in which the widow lived at the time of her husband's death. Without comparing the household structure before and after the move, one can only speculate on reasons underlying migration: inability to maintain a household economically, inability to maintain a household physically, physical demands of the rural farm, or reciprocal aid to other family members. Thus a widow might migrate to maintain or gain independence, to attain an interdependent relationship in another household, or to become dependent.

The data available in the genealogy give full place of death of husband and wife—city, county, and state. A comparison of these places produces a classification of four residential types: (1) same city; (2) different city but same county, an intracounty move; (3) different county but same state, an intercounty move; (4) different state, an interstate move. Movement within a community is not discernible with these data. In previous research we have described the counties of Salt Lake, Utah, and Weber as composing the central Mormon settlement area of Utah.[34] These cannot be identified as purely urban because they contain some concentration of agricultural activities, especially in the earlier cohorts, but they do form an area becoming increasingly urbanized in this region.[35] Thus a second classification is used to determine if the places of death occur in a central settlement or noncentral settlement.

Results for the first classification are presented in table 5 and figure 2. Families in which either wife or husband were missing both city and county information were eliminated; this was 13.6 percent of widows who never remarried. The following results are based on approximately 18,243 families. In the 1830-39 cohort, 60 percent of widows remained in some household arrangement in the community in which they were living at the time of their husbands' deaths. This proportion steadily declines to 48 percent for the 1870-79 cohort. As widows in later cohorts become more mobile, both city and county moves increase while moves to a different state change little; if anything, they become less likely.

To understand the residence pattern one can focus both on who is more likely to be migrant or stable and where they are moving or staying. Two groups of women can be used to identify those stable and migratory. First, one might assume that women of different ages have different needs and abilities and thus a classification of age at death is necessary. When this cross-tabulation is analyzed (second panel of table 5), no major variations occur in the residential pattern. Stable widows and migrant widows are

Table 5. Comparison of Place of Death of Husbands and Wives by Woman's Birth Cohort, Age at Death, and Length of Widowhood

Birth Cohort	Same City (%)	Intra-county (%)	Inter-county (%)	Inter-state (%)	Missing Place (%)
1830-39	60.42	8.94	12.90	14.21	3.53
1840-49	59.30	9.16	14.92	13.26	3.36
1850-59	56.80	10.53	14.96	12.76	4.95
1860-69	52.65	11.07	18.73	12.79	4.76
1870-79	48.04	14.04	22.33	12.53	3.07
	54.00	11.29	17.79	12.94	3.98
Widow's Age at Death					
<50[a]	52.71	8.87	16.75	14.29	7.39
50-64	54.68	10.91	15.62	14.43	4.36
≥65	53.96	11.35	17.99	12.79	3.91
Length of Widowhood					
<10 yrs.	63.74	9.72	13.74	9.08	3.72
10-19	55.30	11.34	17.33	12.26	3.76
≥20	43.67	12.74	22.02	17.15	4.41

[a] There were only 203 cases in this row, and some cell sizes are below 50. Thus, the data may be erratic due to a small number of cases.

similar for women who die before age 50, age 50-64, and age 65 and older. A second analysis deals with the length of widowhood; those with a long period as a widow would have more possible exposure to the need for migration. When residential types are specified by the number of years of widowhood (third panel of table 5), a definite pattern emerges: the shorter the period of widowhood, the more stable the individual. Just over half of widows of 10 to 19 years die in the same community as their husbands; however, for widows of 20 or more years, over half are migrant. They are most likely to move between counties, next between states, and finally between cities in the same county. In attempting to understand this phenomenon one must remember that younger adults are in general more mobile than older adults. Additionally, some widows may be moving to maintain independence as well as to become dependent.

The four categories in table 5 are classified by central or noncentral residence to answer the second question: in what area do widows choose to reside? The death place of both the husband and wife is determined to be either a central settlement area or noncentral settlement area, and the

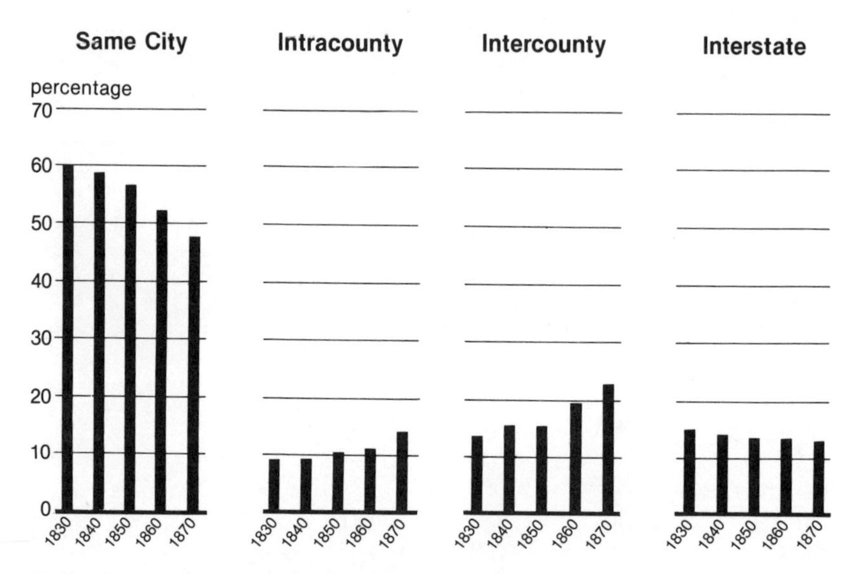

Figure 2. Comparison of Place of Death of Husband and Wife.

four possible combinations are: (1) both are in a central area; (2) the husband's death place is noncentral while the wife's is central, indicating a move into the central area; (3) the husband's death place is central and the wife's is noncentral, indicating a move out of the central area; and (4) both are noncentral places. Noncentral places include counties other than Utah, Salt Lake, and Weber as well as settlements in Idaho, Nevada, Arizona, and Mexico, among others.

First, over time the likelihood of a widow's place of death being in the same city as her husband declines (figure 3). There is a consistency of stable residence in the central area, and all the decline in stability (figure 2) results from a decline in stability in the noncentral area. By the time the later cohorts die, say 1925 to 1945, urbanization has had a definite effect on the pattern observed here.

The specification of three types of migration are shown in figures 4, 5, and 6, and there are three major conclusions. Almost all intracounty moves are in the noncentral area; these would be short moves in which the widow changes the place of residence but not the county of residence. Next, the increase in intercounty moves mainly involves the increase in movement

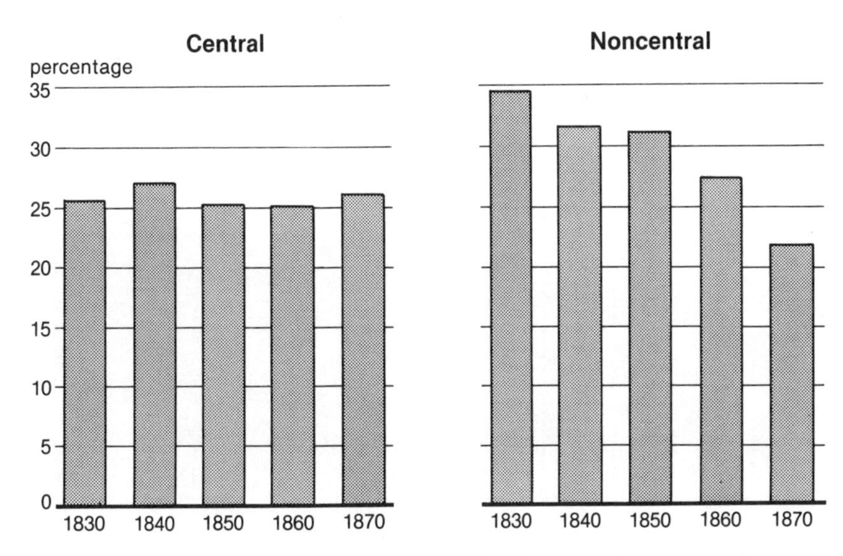

Figure 3. Stable Residency (Same City) Specified by Central/Noncentral Location.

into the central area by widows after the deaths of their husbands. Finally, there is a decrease in interstate migration within the noncentral area, and this relates to less movement between Utah, Idaho, and Mexico, among other places. Two possible reasons for this decline are a general end to the era of Mormon development of new areas and a decline in the disruption of families as a result of federal persecution of polygamists. The year 1890 not only marked the end of the practice of polygamy but also the end of major colonization. Wayne Wahlquist states, "Although Mormon colonization continued on a minor scale throughout the 90's and even into the twentieth century, it was definitely on the decline after 1890."[36]

If one looks at just the dichotomy of central and noncentral areas, the majority of both husbands (64 percent) and wives (60 percent) died in the noncentral area for the 1830-39 cohort. However, when the 1870-79 cohort of women and their husbands dies, this figure has decreased to 57 percent and 52 percent, respectively. Thus an increase in the proportion of widows in the central area results from a slight increase in population in the central area, which remains stable, and a greater movement into the central area than out of the area by widows.

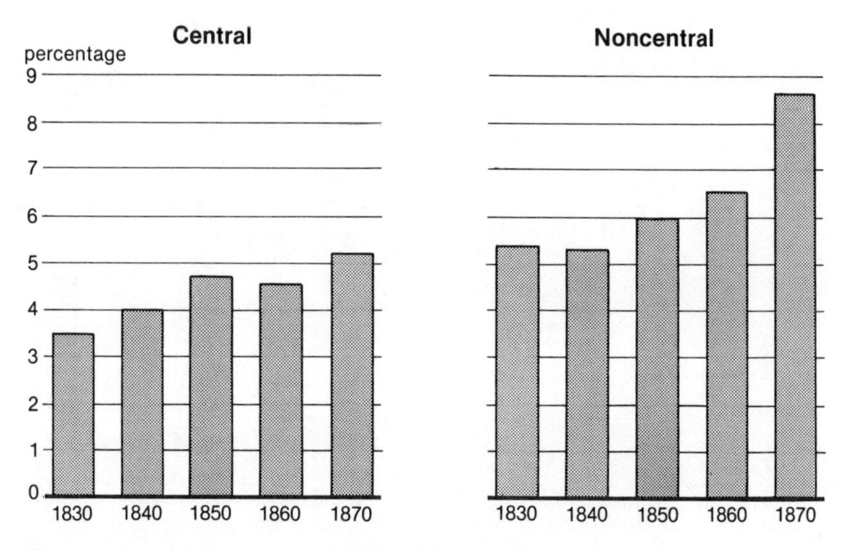

Figure 4. Intracounty Moves by Central/Noncentral Residency.

Summarizing the data for these cohorts, one finds that among Utah women who married, about 57 percent survived their husbands. The majority of these (56 percent) women were at least age 60 when the husband's death occurred; 10 percent were under age 40. The death of a spouse, viewed as an intervening and involuntary event, is more disruptive and has a more dramatic impact if it occurs earlier in life. The age of the surviving spouse and the number of dependent children are two indicators of how disruptive this event can be on family members.

A profile of women based on their ages at widowhood confirms that they experience very different life courses. Almost all (98 percent) widows under age 40 have dependent children at the time of their husbands' deaths; for those age 40 to 59, over half (64 percent) do, and for those age 60 or older, only 1 percent have dependent children. Remarriage appears to be an option almost exclusively for younger widows, but those young widows who do not remarry can plan on approximately half of their lifetimes in this status. On the other hand, the women widowed at older ages have experienced what Uhlenberg calls a "preferred form of family," in other words, a long married life disrupted by neither divorce nor early death.[37]

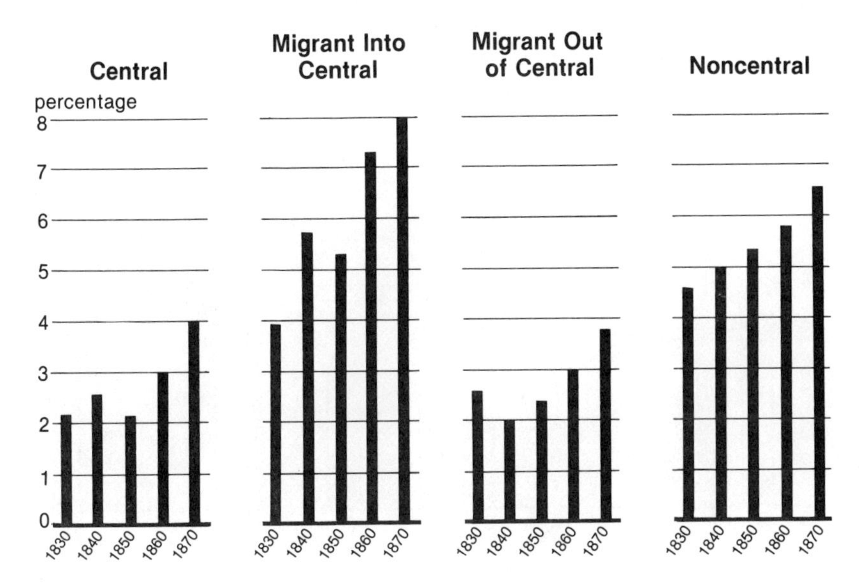

Figure 5. Intercounty Moves by Residency.

The length of widowhood appears to be another key variable in understanding the needs of these women and their families. Widows who die within ten years of their husbands are likely to have resided in the same community since their husbands' deaths. These women are, on average, older and, one might suppose, have developed strong family and community networks of support. Widows who survive their spouses by 20 or more years and do not remarry are most likely to have moved at least once since the deaths of their husbands; 44 percent remain in the same community, 13 percent make short moves, and 39 percent make a major move to another county or state.

In several ways these results indicate that the Utah population followed the same general trends as historical populations in Europe and the eastern United States. For example, women were likely to outlive their husbands and many lived to older ages. These women must have utilized customs and practices to meet their needs similar to widows in other areas. On the other hand, the people of Utah did have unique characteristics. First, the religious atmosphere included a forty- to fifty-year period where the practice of polygamy provided a greater opportunity for young widows to remarry;

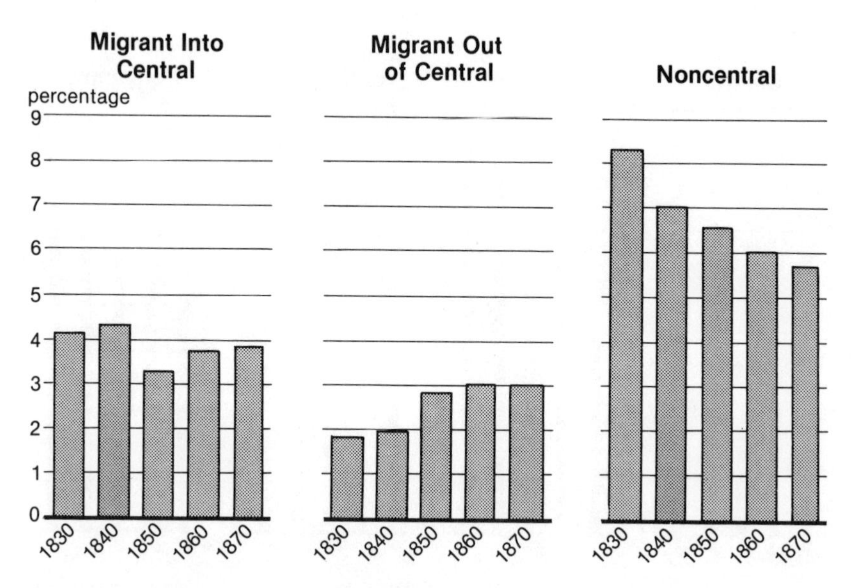

Figure 6. Interstate Moves by Residency.

this atmosphere undoubtedly also provided strong social and family networks for widows. Second, the early Mormons were involved in the settling and colonization of an agricultural society while the later generations experienced increased urbanization. Thus, migration was a familiar experience to many of these families and is reflected in the movement of widows who do not remarry: 40 percent in the 1830-39 cohort and 52 percent in the 1870-79 cohort moved from the community in which they had been living at the time of their husbands' deaths.

While this early Utah population may not be representative of the entire western frontier area, it should be fairly typical of those agricultural areas that involved family migration. Other areas originally settled by miners and prospectors had very different social and demographic characteristics and, surely, women had different life experiences there.

NOTES

My research was supported by grants from the National Institute of Aging and the National Institutes of Health (HD-15455).

1. Glen H. Elder, "Family History and the Life Course," in Tamara K. Hareven, ed., *Transitions: The Family and the Life Course in Historical Perspective* (New York: Academic Press, 1978), 56.

2. Mathilda White Riley and Anne Foner, *Aging and Society. 1: An Inventory of Research Findings* (New York: Russell Sage Foundation, 1968), 166; Noreen Goldman and Graham Lord, "Sex Differences in Life Cycle Measures of Widowhood," *Demography* 20 (1983):185.

3. Howard P. Chudacoff and Tamara Hareven, "From the Empty Nest to Family Dissolution: Life Course Transitions into Old Age," *Journal of Family History* 4 (1979):73.

4. J. Dupaquier et al., eds., *Marriage and Remarriage in Populations of the Past* (New York: Academic Press, 1981); Alan Bideau, "A Demographic and Social Analysis of Widowhood and Remarriage: The Example of the Castellany of Thoissey-in-Dombes, 1670-1840," *Journal of Family History* 5 (1980):28-43.

5. Susan Grigg, "Toward a Theory of Remarriage: A Case Study of Newburyport at the Beginning of the Nineteenth Century," *Journal of Interdisciplinary History* 8 (1977):183-220.

6. John Knodel and Katherine A. Lynch, "The Decline of Remarriage: Evidence from German Village Populations in the Eighteenth and Nineteenth Centuries," *Journal of Family History* 10 (1985):34-59.

7. Howard P. Chudacoff and Tamara K. Hareven, "Family Transitions into Old Age," in Hareven, ed., *Transitions,* 217-43; Chudacoff and Hareven, "From Empty Nest."

8. David Herlihy, "Deaths, Marriages, Births and the Tuscan Economy (ca. 1300-1550)," in Ronald Demos Lee, ed., *Population Patterns in the Past* (New York: Academic Press, 1977), 135-64.

9. Cohort refers to a specific age group with a common experience. In this discussion I study birth cohorts.

10. For a discussion of the life course approach, see: Tamara K. Hareven, "Introduction: The Historical Study of Life Course," in Hareven, ed., *Transitions,* 1-16; John Demos and Sarane Spence Boocock, *Turning Points: Historical and Sociological Essays on the Family* (Chicago: University of Chicago Press, 1978); and Glen H. Elder, "History and the Family: The Discovery of Complexity," *Journal of Marriage and the Family* 43 (1981):489-519.

11. Elder, "History and the Family," 509.

12. Hareven, "Historical Study of Life Course," 5.

13. H. S. Shryock and J. S. Siegel have described the family life cycle and its treatment by demographers as follows: "The social and economic characteristics of families vary widely from family formation through family building to the launching of the younger generation into their marriages and on through the 'post-children' stage to the ultimate dissolution of the family. Because of this highly dynamic nature of the family, the conceptual framework provided by the

idea of a 'life cycle of the family' has been used extensively by many demographers, sociologists, and economists to add meaning and order to their analyses of family behaviour." Shryock and Siegel, *The Methods and Materials of Demography,* 1 (Washington, D.C.: Department of Commerce, 1973), 310.

14. Elder, "Family History and the Life Course," 56.

15. N. B. Ryder, "Notes on the Concept of a Population," *American Journal of Sociology* 69 (1964):461.

16. Peter Uhlenberg, "Cohort Variations in Family Life Cycle Experiences in U.S. Females," *Journal of Marriage and the Family* 36 (1974):284-92.

17. Susan Cotts Watkins, "On Measuring Transitions and Turning Points," *Historical Methods* 13 (1980):181-87.

18. See L. L. Bean, D. L. May, and M. H. Skolnick, "The Mormon Historical Demography Project," *Historical Methods* 11 (1978):45-53; M. H. Skolnick et al., "A Computerized Family History Database System," *Sociology and Social Research* 63 (1979):506-23; G. P. Mineau, L. L. Bean, and M. Skolnick, "Mormon Demography History II: The Family Life Cycle and Natural Fertility," *Population Studies* 3 (1979):429-46; and Geraldine Page Mineau, "Fertility on the Frontier: An Analysis of the Nineteenth-Century Utah Population" (Ph.D. diss., University of Utah, 1980).

19. Riley and Foner, *Aging and Society,* 160. These percentages do not add to 100 percent but are taken directly from Riley and Foner.

20. The low percentage of never-married women in the 1910 census is the result of at least two factors: (1) a social-religious emphasis on marriage and family life, and (2) an excess of males in all age groups below age 60. The sex ratio for individuals age 15 and older was 131, and for individuals age 45 and older it was 103.

21. Lee L. Bean and Geraldine P. Mineau, "Linking the 1880 Manuscript Census to Family Genealogies: Methodological Techniques and Problems," paper presented at Social Science History Association Meeting in Toronto, Oct. 26, 1984.

22. The data were omitted as follows: (1) 1.4 percent had no genealogical information on their first marriages other than husbands' names and marriage dates; (2) 5.8 percent had two marriages but lacked marriage dates or childrens' birth dates for at least one marriage; this made it impossible to classify which was first and which second; (3) in 5.0 percent the woman or her husband lacked a death date; (4) in 0.4 percent the woman was less than age 10 or greater than age 49 at first marriage or had some input or recording error causing an illogical age at marriage; (5) in 0.3 percent other input or recording errors existed; and (6) 0.07 percent had a marriage recorded but no marriage date and no children.

23. Polygamy is commonly used in this culture to indicate the practice of plural marriage; more properly this practice should be referred to as polygyny. The Mormon church recognized the legitimacy of multiple marriage for men from

1842 through 1890, although from 1842 to 1852 it was not practiced openly or widely.

24. Use of these data provides no way of indicating the "separation" of a couple, and it is not discussed.

25. We are aware of a slight underrecording of women who die with the birth of their first child. See J. P. Barder et al., "La Mortalité Maternelle Autrefois: Une Etude Comparée (de la France de l'ouest a l'Utah)," *Annales de Démographie Historique* (1981):32-48. However, adjusting for this would increase the figures for a wife dying only from 40.61 to 40.66 percent. Taking into account a reclassification of some marriages for divorce and an underrecording of wives dying very young, one still finds that about 57 percent of first marriages end with the death of the husband.

26. Riley and Foner, *Aging and Society.*

27. The Utah divorce rate was higher than the total U.S. divorce rate between 1870 and 1900 as shown by the number of divorces per 100,000 population.

	1870	1880	1890	1900
United States	29	38	53	73
Utah	62	114	74	92

For 1870 and 1880 the Utah rate was two to three times higher than the U.S. rate; by 1890 and 1900 the difference had greatly decreased. From U.S. Department of Commerce and Labor, Bureau of Census, *Special Reports. Marriage and Divorce, 1876-1909. Part 1* (Washington, D.C.: Government Printing Office, 1909), 72. "The [divorce] legislation of Utah begins in 1852 with an act so faulty that its consequences have become notorious in the divorce annals of the United States." It combined generous grounds for divorce with no proof of residence, providing lawyers in eastern cities with the opportunity to promote clandestine divorce on a large scale. George Elliott Howard, *A History of Matrimonial Institutions,* 3 (Chicago: University of Chicago Press, 1904), 131-32.

28. To give the reader some comparison of life expectancy, I give here some information on Swedish birth cohorts. Swedish females who were 0 to 4 years of age in 1830 and lived to be age 20 could expect to live to approximately 65.85. For 1850 it was age 66.99, and for 1870 it was age 68.09. See Nathan Keyfitz and Wilhelm Flieger, *World Population: An Analysis of Vital Data* (Chicago: University of Chicago Press, 1968), 616, 621-26. These figures are based on all women in the population. Since married individuals have longer life expectancies than unmarried or divorced individuals, the life span would be longer for married individuals. Therefore, the age at death for these Utah cohorts is approximately correct and probably only slightly high due to the bias produced by the use of genealogical data.

29. Men who survived to their mid-twenties and married did not experience

much change in life expectancy. The improvement in married women's life expectancies may be related to a decrease in maternal mortality.

30. An analysis of once-married couples (husband and wife married only once) showed smaller age differences between husbands and wives for these same cohorts. For example, the 1840-59 cohort of women who married from age 15-19, 20-24, and 25-29 were on average 5.89 years, 3.22 years, and 1.45 years, respectively, younger than their husbands. See Geraldine P. Mineau and James Trussell, "A Specification of Marital Fertility by Parents' Age, Age at Marriage, and Marital Duration," *Demography* 9 (1982):335-50.

31. Bideau, "Demographic and Social Analysis," 36.

32. For widows under age 40 who remarried the following table shows the mean age widowed, the mean age at remarriage, the mean interval to remarriage, and the mean number of children under age 16 at remarriage:

Cohort	Widowed	Married	Interval	Children
1830-39	27.97	31.35	3.38	2.58
1840-49	27.99	31.97	3.98	2.94
1850-59	28.00	32.75	4.75	2.65
1860-69	28.74	34.97	6.23	2.75
1870-79	29.23	35.80	6.57	2.56
Total	28.51	33.81	5.30	2.60

Some preliminary results indicate that for all widows the mean interval to remarriage was shorter if the widow had less than four children under age 16 and longer with four or more dependent children. For the 1850-59 cohort the interval was 4.58 years with one to three children and 6.45 years with four or more.

33. D. L. Anderton et al., "A Macrosimulation Approach to the Investigation of the Fertility Transition," *Social Biology* 3 (1985):140-59; Lee L. Bean, Geraldine Mineau, and Douglas Anderton, "Residence and Religious Effects on Declining Family Size: An Historical Analysis of the Utah Population," *Review of Religious Research* 24 (1984):91-101.

34. G. P. Mineau et al., "Evolution Differentielle de la Fecondite et Groupes Sociaux Religieux: L'Exemple de l'Utah au XIXe Siecle," *Annales de Démographie Historique* (1984):219-36.

35. Wahlquist indicates that during the 1880s there was an unprecedented urban growth in the core. "Salt Lake City more than doubled its population, increasing from 20,768 in 1880 to 44,843 in 1890 (a 116% increase), while Ogden jumped from 5,264 to 14,889 (a 184% increase), and Provo grew from 3,432 to 5,159 (a 50% increase)." Wayne L. Wahlquist, "Settlement Processes in the Mormon Core Area 1847-1890" (Ph.D. diss., University of Nebraska, 1974), 174, 178. The 1900 census shows 67 percent of the population in Salt Lake, Utah, and Weber

counties lived in towns with populations of 2,500 or larger; by 1910 this had increased to 72 percent. Comparable figures for the state of Utah were 38 and 46 percent.

36. Ibid., 173.

37. Uhlenberg, "Cohort Variations in Family Life Cycle," 285.

7

The Struggle for Survival: Widows in Denver, 1880-1912

JOYCE D. GOODFRIEND

In 1882, stirred to action by the assassination of James Garfield, the U.S. Congress passed a law providing for an annual pension of $5,000 to the four surviving widows of former presidents of the United States.[1] In enacting this legislation, Congress implicitly recognized the economic vulnerability of American widows in the late nineteenth century. Whether middle class or working class, a family that lost its male breadwinner was soon likely to find itself in precarious financial condition. Prior good fortune was no guarantee of future economic security in an era when savings, life insurance, and private pensions were rare or nonexistent.[2] Only a minority of widows inherited sufficient property to shield them completely from financial worries. With few exceptions, being widowed around the turn of the century meant, at the minimum, economic dislocation, and in countless instances, outright hardship.

Widows living in Denver, Colorado, between 1880 and 1912 were not immune to the economic problems attendant on the loss of a husband. Even though Colorado boosterism had implanted a roseate image of "the Queen City" in the late nineteenth-century popular mind, Denver had its share of the economic and social ills that plagued the nation's older cities. Moreover, its widely touted climate created a distinctive set of problems that affected widows adversely.

Established in 1858 as a supply point for the miners flooding into the Pikes Peak country, Denver was transformed by a period of rapid urbanization from a frontier settlement to a major city.[3] Denver's economic importance was rooted in its role as a marketing center. Its commercial enterprises, cattle ranchers, and miners in the surrounding territory and formed the underpinning of the fortunes of many of its residents. By 1876, the year that Colorado entered the Union, with Denver as its capital, the city had become the metropolis for the entire Rocky Mountain region. In the following decades, as its population expanded, Denver consolidated its preeminent position in the area and achieved a national reputation as a desirable place to live.

Although Denver was neither an industrial giant nor a haven for European immigrants, its social structure exhibited the extremes of wealth and poverty characteristic of other cities in the late nineteenth and early twentieth centuries. Nor was Denver, despite its strong economic base, impervious to cyclical depressions. Indeed, Denver was particularly hard hit by the depression of 1893. Consequently, ordinary families living in Denver enjoyed no greater opportunities than families in other cities to accumulate reserves that would enable them to surmount crises. In addition, Denver's reputation as a mecca for health seekers undoubtedly multiplied the number of widows in the city who faced severe economic problems.[4] Desperate male tuberculosis sufferers, hopeful of a cure in Denver's salubrious climate, poured into the city in the late nineteenth and early twentieth centuries, many having expended their savings on the trip west. Not surprisingly, some succumbed to their disease and their widows found themselves stranded without recourse.

No less vulnerable to the economic impact of widowhood than women in other cities, Denver's widows were also subject to the imperatives of the reigning philosophy of voluntarism regarding the minimal part government should play in aiding victims of misfortune.[5] Like their counterparts throughout the nation, Denver widows could not depend on the federal or state government for assistance. Not until 1912, when Colorado passed a Mothers' Compensation Act, modeled after the pioneer legislation enacted in Illinois a year earlier, did a widow in Denver have any hope of governmental aid targeted specifically for women in her condition.[6]

Moreover, there was general agreement among the city's privileged citizens that it was the task of private charity to relieve the distress of the needy. The allotment of charitable funds, however, was linked to a moralistic screening process that imposed stringent behavioral standards on potential beneficiaries.[7]

Denver's widows were aware that society viewed them with sympathy but assumed no responsibility for their plight. The burden of support rested squarely on the individual widow. Yet women were rarely prepared to assume the role of breadwinner in late nineteenth-century America. Indoctrinated with the belief that women belonged in the home, those women whose altered conditions necessitated that they support their families found that not only did they have to overcome these deeply ingrained prejudices against holding a job but also that they had to vie for employment in an economic system that discriminated against women workers. Employers, operating on the premise that women were never the sole supports of their families, consistently paid female workers less than males and confined them to a few singularly unrewarding jobs, where advancement was virtually impossible. Widows could foresee a life spent struggling to maintain their families and their dignity.

I explore here the ways in which widows living in Denver between 1880, when the federal census firmly established Denver's position as an urban center, and 1912, when the Mothers' Compensation Act inaugurated a new era in the history of widowhood, coped with their predicament. The focus is not on well-to-do Denver widows, who were cushioned from financial anxieties by sizeable inheritances, but on the great majority of women for whom widowhood was clouded by economic concerns. No longer able to take for granted the promise of lifelong security implicit in the marriage contract, they faced the prospect of an uncertain future taken up with devising strategies for producing income. Compelled to make hard choices respecting employment, child care, and living arrangements, many widows demonstrated their resilience and learned to meet the challenges of their new circumstances. Others floundered amid the mounting pressures of unfamiliar responsibilities. Although the gravity of their situations varied, as did their responses, all confronted the bedrock problem of economic survival in a hostile social climate.

The spectacular growth of the city of Denver in the decades following 1880 is well known. That the number of widows in the city increased tenfold between 1880 and 1910 is less familiar.[8] The proportion of widows in the female population of Denver also increased substantially, from 6.7 percent in 1880 to 9.7 percent in 1910. Denver's widows, like the city's inhabitants in general, were overwhelmingly white and predominantly native-born. In 1880 only 5.4 percent of the city's widows were black and 31.4 percent were foreign-born. Immigrants and blacks, however, were more numerous among the city's widows than among the population at large.[9] By far the largest group of foreign-born widows was the Irish; widows of German and English origin ranked second and third.

Denver's widows were also relatively young. The median age in 1880 was 44.5. In 1890 the national figure was closer to 55, and in 1975 it was 68.[10] Looked at in another way, merely 11 percent of Denver's widows were 65 or over in 1880, and as late as 1900 only 21 percent fell into this category. By contrast, 32 percent of the nation's widows in 1890 were 65 or over, and 63 percent fell into this category in 1970.[11]

The most plausible explanation for the youthful age structure of Denver's widowed female population in this era would be that Denver boasted a higher than average mortality rate for men in their prime. The presence of an unusually large number of men with tuberculosis, a disease known to strike down young adults primarily, coupled with the fact that tuberculosis caused a major portion of deaths in Denver in these years, bolsters the hypothesis that the abundance of young widows in Denver is inextricably linked to the large-scale migration of tuberculars to the city in the late nineteenth and early twentieth centuries.[12] An additional contributing factor might be that young widows from other sections of the country moved to Denver in search of opportunity after the loss of their husbands.

That the majority of Denver's widows in this era were relatively young has a bearing on the question of the size of their inheritances. As a rule, men who die early in life are less likely to have amassed substantial amounts of property than those whose deaths occur at an advanced age. Thus, one can speculate that the concentration of Denver's widows in the young age brackets may have made them particularly vulnerable to economic difficulties. However, data on the age structure of Denver's widowed female population must be assessed in light of broader patterns of wealth distribution in Denver during this era.

Although the existence of both wealthy and poor families in late nineteenth- and early twentieth-century Denver is well documented, precise figures on the size and property holdings of the city's social classes are lacking. One study of late nineteenth-century Denver's social structure, based on analysis of occupations recorded in city directories, concludes that "the vast majority of the persons listed were workers and employees of one kind or another, with only a small minority of the entries categorized as businessmen or professionals."[13] Another overview of Denver in this period, which relies mainly on impressionistic evidence, states that "most citizens were never touched by the social extremes in the booming city. They lived comfortably in the middle class."[14]

Until a definitive study of the distribution of wealth is completed, it is not possible to designate accurately that portion of Denver's population that was effectively insulated against the occurrence of catastrophic events. Nonetheless, given the available evidence on Denver and findings of national investigations that estimate that 40 percent of Americans in 1900 can be classified as poor, it is probable that only a minority of Denver's gainfully employed males in this era were able to put aside significant reserves of money for use in emergencies.[15]

Blue-collar workers, who in one estimate comprised roughly 37 percent of the city's population in the final years of the nineteenth century, lived close to the margin of existence.[16] Their wages, although presumably higher than those in eastern cities prior to the 1890s, were not ordinarily great enough to allow them to accumulate any substantial savings.[17] Expenditures for daily living consumed the bulk of their income. The massive unemployment that occurred in Denver during the depression of 1893 graphically illustrates the precarious financial position of laboring people in times of crisis.[18] Members of the middle class, particularly small businessmen, were equally vulnerable to the fluctuations of the economy. Moreover, family crises frequently exposed the insecurity of the middle class in the late nineteenth century.[19] Although some middle-class families in Denver were undoubtedly able to weather personal and social crises, the weight of the evidence leads us to conclude that the majority of Denver families in this era were not prepared financially for the death of the breadwinner.

The inability of ordinary men to provide a sufficient nest egg for their families does not mean that these men were unconcerned about protecting their loved ones in emergencies. Death or incapacitation due to disease or industrial accidents was common in late nineteenth- and early twentieth-century America, and working men endeavored to shield their families against these occurrences as best they could, knowing that voluntary effort constituted the sole means of guaranteeing security. Although deficient by today's standards, the mechanisms developed to safeguard family welfare in the period prior to the emergence of social insurance merit close scrutiny because they alone stood between widows and total devastation.[20]

Cognizant that they could depend only on each other for assistance in times of crisis, middle-class and working-class American men shaped the associations they participated in to serve a perceived need by specifically instituting death benefits for the widows and orphans of members. Fraternal organizations such as the Masons, the Odd Fellows, the Knights of Pythias, and the Knights of Columbus were extremely popular in the decades preceding World War I, and most of these groups offered some form of insurance program to members.[21] Denver possessed a representative spectrum of fraternal organizations during these years, thus enabling its male citizens to take advantage of the benefits available to members.

The composition of Denver's fraternal organizations reflected prevailing notions of religious and ethnic separation. The dominant group of white Protestants created and filled the local branches of major national societies. Benefit programs were maintained as a matter of course. A Masonic Board of Relief was established in Denver in 1879. The Grand Lodge of the Odd Fellows distributed benefits to eighteen widowed families in 1894, and in the same year the Woodmen of the World recorded the payment of death benefits of $3,000 and $1,000 for two deceased Denver members.[22]

Denver's sizeable Catholic population supported a number of fraternal associations that aided the survivors of deceased members. The Knights of Columbus, an organization with a primary interest in aiding the widows and children of members, established a council in Denver in 1900. By 1913 the Denver Knights of Columbus was reported to have 750 members.[23] Other Catholic fraternal organizations with branches in Denver by the early twentieth century included the Knights of St. John and the Catholic Knights of America. These groups also assisted the widows of members.[24]

B'nai Brith, a fraternal and benevolent association of Jewish men, was established in Denver in 1872, and followed in the tradition of the national organization by providing aid to the dependents of members.[25] Denver's small black community supported a Masonic lodge and a chapter of the Odd Fellows.[26]

Ethnic associations constituted another layer of group life in turn-of-the-century Denver, and many of these organizations operated mutual aid funds. For example, the lodge associated with the Czech-Slavic Benefit Society was established in Denver in 1892, and another lodge associated with the Western Bohemian Fraternal Association was founded in 1897. These lodges merged shortly thereafter.[27]

For laboring men, affiliation with a labor union was an additional source of potential assistance to their widows. In most cases, this amounted to a small death benefit. Members of the Colorado State Conference of the Bricklayers and Masons Union, which was headquartered in Denver, were entitled to a $100 death benefit that was instituted in 1902.[28] The Cigar Makers' Local Union No. 29 of Denver reported in 1912 that "sick benefits, private loans, death benefits and donations are paid to the 380 members."[29] Other Denver unions, like locals across the country in this period, undoubtedly also maintained benefit funds.[30]

Although the actual sum of money made available to the widows of members of fraternal associations and labor unions was small in most cases, the value of a husband's membership in such a group may have transcended the stipulated death benefit. Lodges and unions were of vital importance in the lives of American men in this era, natives as well as immigrants. Men bonded together in fellowship would most likely be inclined to assume more of the burden of support for the widow and children of a deceased brother than formally required, especially if the circumstances of his death were tragic.[31] Taking too narrow a view of the functions of fraternal associations and labor unions may impede understanding of the actual role they played in helping widows adapt to their altered conditions.

A man's occupation might entitle his survivors to a pension. Denver policemen and firemen, for example, were able to guarantee a measure of security to their widows and children due to the establishment of the Firemen's Pension Fund in 1903 and the Police Department Relief Fund in 1904. The widow of a fireman or a policeman received $30 per month until she remarried and each child under 14 received $6 per month. In addition, there was a promise of $100 for funeral expenses.[32] Methodist ministers living in Denver could ensure that their widows and children would receive some aid after their death by joining the Methodist Episcopal Colorado Annual Conference Preachers' Aid Society, which was incorporated in 1899 "for the benefit of its members, and the widows and minor orphans of its deceased members."[33]

To a considerable extent, a widow's access to benefit programs depended on her husband's social and occupational history. A husband's participation in the Union army during the Civil War was even more significant. Widows of Union veterans were entitled to a federal pension, the amount of which was increased periodically and the eligibility requirements for which were loosened during the course of the nineteenth century. As a result, a sizeable number of widows in Denver (238 in 1890) were assured of a regular income for the remainder of their lives.[34] In an era when the federal government scrupulously avoided involvement in any form of public welfare program, one favored category of citizens—veterans and widows of veterans—was singled out for special treatment.

Widows who did not qualify for these benefits or whose benefits lasted only for a short period of time often turned to family members or close friends for help.[35] Material aid from relatives and friends in small amounts tided many widows over temporarily. But more fundamental rearrangements in family life predictably followed on the heels of widowhood. The case of elderly widows is instructive in this connection.[36]

For many older widows, the death of the breadwinner signaled the end of the independent household. Unable to support herself because of age or infirmity, the elderly widow moved into the household of a married son or daughter. In 1880, 139 widows in Denver were listed in the census as either the mother or mother-in-law of the head of the household. It is important to note, however, that widows who became partially or even totally dependent on their married children for support ordinarily made contributions to their new households in the form of labor or items of furniture or clothing that they brought with them.[37] Occasionally, widows went to live with other family members such as brothers or sisters or parents.[38]

Older widows without kinfolk sometimes chose to enter an institution. The Old Ladies' Home of Denver, operated by the Ladies' Relief Society, admitted women over 65, some of whom paid for themselves while others received charity.[39] The Visiting Society for the Aged, incorporated in 1909, provided assistance to elderly people in their homes.[40]

Younger widows with unmarried children usually continued to head their own households. Yet the pattern of their family life also changed considerably as a result of the death of the breadwinner. In numerous cases, the widow remained at home while one or more of her unmarried children, ranging in age from 12 through the twenties, assumed the role of breadwinner. Although the earnings of young children were small, they contributed much needed income for family support.[41]

The experiences of the McCune family of Denver provide an illuminating perspective on how one middle-class family adapted to the death of the breadwinner. Alvin McCune was the proprietor of a shop at 334 Larimer Street that specialized in house, sign, and ornamental painting. When he died in 1881 of heart disease, he left a 44-year-old widow, Elmira, a 21-year-old daughter Florence (Flora), and two younger children, one a baby. The McCune family's rapid downward mobility is vividly chronicled in Florence's diary.[42] On May 9, 1881, Florence wrote: "Mamma's 45th Birthday. could only give her a book oh to be rich once more I wonder if we must always be so poor and count where every nickle goes."

Further testimony of the McCune family's economic decline in the aftermath of Alvin's death was that they had to move to less pretentious quarters. On May 10, 1881, Florence noted: "Papa's friends have given us a beautiful little house six rooms a bath room two lots and hot and cold water. Carrie stayed with us all during the month of June and helped us move." Despite the welcome gift of the new house, the family's financial security was still in jeopardy. Unable to keep the family business running successfully, the family soon realized that a regular means of support had to be found. By 1882 Florence had taken a job as a clerk in the office of the county treasurer. Mrs. McCune stayed at home to care for her two other children. The McCune family had resolved the problem of family support by placing the eldest child in the role of breadwinner.

Not all widows, however, could rely on the labor of their offspring. Some had no children living in Denver. Others had children too young to find employment. Consequently, widows themselves frequently had to compete in the marketplace. Examining the experiences of Denver widows as they confronted the problem of earning a living in the years between 1880 and 1912 reveals the anomalous position of the widow in American society.

Since the great majority of Denver's widows in these years were of working age, it is surprising to learn that only a minority of them held jobs. Fewer than three out of ten Denver widows (28.6 percent) were employed in 1880, and the proportion of the city's widows with jobs increased only moderately to 32.8 percent in 1890 and 34.6 percent in 1900 (statistics are not available for 1910). When the age structure of the widowed population is taken into account, the results are even more striking. In 1880 only 38 percent of Denver's widows under the age of 50 were employed. Nationally, approximately half of the widows under 55 were in the labor force in 1890.[43] In recent years "a substantial majority of widows in the main working ages are found to be working at paying jobs."[44] The salient fact is that widows of working age in the three decades before any governmental benefits for widows were instituted were less likely to hold jobs than their present-day counterparts, many of whom have recourse to other means of support. How do we explain this puzzling fact? What forces were in play at the turn of the century that kept so many widows out of the labor force?

Widows in this era were reluctant to seek employment because they identified with the role of wife. A widow understandably continued to think of herself as a married woman, and married women in the nineteenth century were highly conscious of the standards of ladylike behavior set forth in the ideology of domesticity. A wife was advised to spend her days in the domestic arena, keeping house, raising children, and serving as a source of spiritual comfort to her husband, who was required to enter the marketplace and earn a sufficient income for his family. Although both wife and husband were conceived to be making indispensable contributions to the well-being of the family, their roles were rigidly demarcated. Thus, holding a job was, by definition, off limits to married women. And, in fact, fewer than 5 percent of the country's married women were in the labor force in 1890.[45]

However powerful these conventional notions regarding a woman's place, they did not deter all widows. In numerous instances considerations of propriety were overshadowed by the immediate need for money. When the breadwinner died, cultural ideals began to crumble in the face of economic realities and starvation. Many widows were compelled to make the difficult transition to the role of family breadwinner.

If it was economic necessity that forced widows into the marketplace, it was a combination of economic and cultural factors that determined precisely what kinds of work they undertook. Employment opportunities for women in Denver were limited at the outset of this period, but improved with time as white-collar jobs opened to women.[46] Female workers comprised just 11 percent of Denver's labor force in 1880 and 15 percent in 1890, but 22 percent in 1900 and 24 percent in 1910. Yet it was single women like Florence McCune who benefited most from the expansion of white-collar jobs. Throughout these decades, widows were clustered in the traditionally low-paying, demanding, and demeaning female occupations: domestic servant, laundress, and seamstress. Struggling to make ends meet under adverse conditions, many of Denver's widowed workers could identify with the anonymous woman interviewed in the late 1880s: "I work hard at dress-making and make by the piece and by hard work from $4.00 to $6.00 per week. Am a widow with five children dependent on me, and I lose considerable time attending to my children. They are all boys from five to twelve years of age. The oldest is a cash boy, earning $2.00 per week. He is young and intelligent and ought to be in school, but circumstances compel me to have him work until one of the other boys is old enough to take his place."[47] Another young widow, Elinore Stewart, who later achieved fame as the author of *Letters of a Woman Homesteader,* found few job opportunities in Denver when she arrived from Kansas at the turn of the century with her two-year-old daughter to support. Despite her literary talent, she was forced to earn her livelihood as a laundress and housecleaner.[48]

The experiences of Elinore Stewart and the anonymous dressmaker illustrate the point made impersonally in census statistics: Denver widows who had no choice but to work had few choices with respect to the kind of work they performed. The limited availability of factory jobs for women in Denver blocked one avenue of employment commonly pursued by widows in other cities.[49] Given the narrow range of occupational possibilities, then, and the undesirable nature of the jobs that were available, it is likely that many of the city's widowed job holders were drawn from the groups in society that historically have lived closest to the edge of poverty. And, indeed, analysis of data from the 1880 census has shown that blacks and immigrants constituted a disproportionate share of Denver's working widows in that year.

What happened, then, to widows of middle-class background and sensibility, whose search for work was hindered by considerations of respectability?[50] Some undoubtedly succumbed to the pressures of the marketplace and accepted menial jobs. Others, however, aspired to the small but growing category of occupations deemed suitable for "ladies." Unfortunately, employers preferred single women for these jobs. In 1900, 88 percent of Denver's female teachers were single and only 7 percent were widows. Among female stenographers and typists, 90 percent were single and 4 percent widowed; for saleswomen, the proportions were 85 percent single and 7 percent widowed.

Because the jobs thought to be commensurate with middle-class status were monopolized by single women, a significant number of Denver widows may have resorted to a form of work with deep roots in the past. Homework enabled widows to earn money while remaining at home to fulfill family responsibilities. The most common method was taking in boarders.[51] The extent to which widows (and other women) practiced this occupation was consistently underestimated by the census, but it still ranked as the fourth largest occupation of Denver widows in 1880 and the third largest in 1890 and 1900.[52]

Other kinds of homework, although invisible to census takers, were of vital importance in the economic calculus of widows in modest circumstances. The Woman's Exchange, established in Denver in the late 1880s by the Woman's Christian Temperance Union, constitutes tangible proof of the magnitude of handicraft production in the confines of women's homes. Situated at 1648 California Street, the Woman's Exchange and Lunch Room advertised its object as "to provide a place where woman's work of every kind that is purchasable, may be placed for sale, and where orders for such work may be taken, and in this way aid those who are trying to help themselves." Among the items listed for sale were "Doylies and Embroidered Toilet Sets, Crocheted Hoods, Skirts and Slippers. Infants' Hoods, Socks, Shirts and Sacques. Dinner Cards, Placques, Banners." Thus, handmade goods produced by widows could be sold on consignment at the Woman's Exchange and the profits returned to them as much needed income. That the Woman's Exchange filled a pressing need is suggested by the report that in 1892 the "Denver Woman's Exchange furnished work to 125 consigners and have paid them $17,850, thus enabling them to support themselves and their families." Clearly modeled after Woman's Exchanges in cities such as Boston and Buffalo, the Denver exchange combined charity and self-help in a form familiar to the Progressive Era.[53]

It is clear from statistical evidence that many Denver widows could not bring themselves to compete in a labor market that discriminated against women by restricting them to the least desirable jobs. Nevertheless, hundreds of poor widows with no viable alternatives did cross the boundary into the male world of work to support their families. Being able to secure a job that paid low wages for long hours of service, or required as a condition of employment that a woman live in the home of her employer, however, created a new problem of major proportions for the many Denver widows with young children.[54] These working widows were confronted with the dilemma of providing care for their children while they were working to support them.

For obvious reasons, widows preferred to have a family member supervise their young children. In some instances neighbors functioned as substitutes for relatives.[55] But working widows possessed another option in the form of the day nursery, designed specifically to tend the children of working mothers. The Denver Central Union of the Woman's Christian Temperance Union established a Day Nursery in 1888 and by 1890 reported that "once this year they have been forced to move into larger quarters, and are again on the outlook for a still larger home. The children cared for number from 350 to 400 per month."[56] By the first decade of the twentieth century, a number of other day nurseries were operating in Denver, including the Day Nursery, the West Side Day Nursery, the nurseries run by the Globeville Social Service Club and the West Side House, and the Social Center and Day Nursery begun by the Denver Woman's Club.[57] The fees charged were nominal and in some cases not always collected. The Day Nursery operated by the Woman's Christian Temperance Union reported that mothers were required to pay "ten cents a day for one child, and five cents a day for every additional child." The Globeville Day Nursery charged five cents for each child.[58]

To what extent considerations of cost, hours, age requirements, or availability deterred widows from leaving their children at day nurseries cannot be determined. That day nurseries aroused the suspicion of working mothers is made clear in other studies. Katharine Anthony, in her 1914 investigation of working mothers in New York City, reported that "the women regard the day nursery as a type of institution, and, as such, distrust it."[59] Historian Sheila Rothman, who describes day nurseries as mixing moral uplift with caretaker services, states bluntly that "the nurseries generally received children from the woman who had no other option; they were in every sense a last resort."[60] Nonetheless, it seems reasonable to suggest that the drawbacks of the day nurseries were often compensated for by the conveniences they offered. The moralistic attitude of the people who ran them could be overlooked when it was recognized that the valuable service they performed enabled widowed mothers to hold jobs and still keep their children. Widows who arranged to keep their children at day nurseries while they were at work seem fortunate in comparison to those who were compelled to institutionalize their children.

Widows did not willingly surrender their children, but at times their circumstances were so desperate that the children had to be given up. The children of widows were placed in orphanages for a number of reasons, including the illness of the mother or the fact that she had been deemed an unfit parent by community authorities. Nevertheless, the most important explanation for institutionalization was economic. Widows who could find no other jobs than as live-in servants, or whose wages were inadequate to support their children, found it necessary to place their youngsters in an orphanage. Most children were put in orphanages only temporarily, but some were given up for adoption. That widows were reluctant to institutionalize their children is indisputable. After noting that only 45 out of 1,232 children of a group of New York City wage-earning mothers were in institutions, Anthony suggested that the reason "so small a number of children had been 'put away' is mainly due to the ever lively and active prejudice against institutions on the mother's part. This prejudice, combined with fear and suspicion, furnished indeed the chief spur to their efforts. What were they working for if not to keep the home together?"[61]

The proliferation of orphanages in Denver in this era underlines the difficulties that widowed parents without means encountered in keeping their families intact. "Half-orphans," as the children of widowed parents were called in this period, comprised a significant proportion of the children found in turn-of-the-century orphanages.[62] Among the private institutions found in the city were the Denver Orphans' Home, the E. M. Byers Home for Boys, the Clifton-Hughes Training School for Girls, St. Vincent's Home, St. Clara's Orphanage, the House of the Good Shepherd, the Queen of Heaven Orphanage, the Denver Sheltering Home for Jewish Children, the Home League Orphanage, and the Colored Orphans' and Old Ladies' Home.

In addition, the state of Colorado operated the Colorado State Home for Dependent and Neglected Children.[63]

The detailed records of the Denver Orphans' Home for the period 1882-97 enable us to glimpse the stark realities of the lives of poor widows who committed their children to the institution.[64] The notation of admissions to the home in February 1895 provides insight into the causes of distress in widows' families: "Bert Carpenter aged 9 years—his father dead, his mother a servant. James and Annie Lodge aged respectively 11 and 9 years—Father dead and the Mother works in the Troy Laundry. Elder Michelmoore & Thomas Michelmoore aged 6 & 4 years—the Father dead and the Mother a clerk. Elmer Burgess six years old, Father killed on the Railroad and the Mother trying to get work but too sick."

Many of the widows who placed their children in the Denver Orphans' Home agreed to pay as much as they could for the board of the children. For example, the minutes of September 1886 noted that "one little boy Chas. Evans, aged 5 years, received into the Home, his Mother a widow able to get work if her boy could be cared for. She will pay something each month for him." Since these payments rarely covered the entire cost of keeping the child, it is clear that these widows were forced to accept charity. More significant, however, is that impoverished widowed mothers, instead of abandoning their children, did everything in their power to assure that their offspring enjoyed a decent life. When it was possible, working widows removed their children from the institution. "Eleanor Ellwood was removed by her Mother who has a place to work where the child can help" (June 5, 1895). Sometimes widows moved to other cities in search of better opportunities. "Mrs. Martinovich took her 3 boys to Omaha" (November 4, 1891). Occasionally, children were sent to relatives in other localities. "Lillian and James Furr were sent to their grandparents in St. Joe, Mo." (July 7, 1897). A few widows remarried and took their children back to live with them. "The mother of Ernest Metcalf having lately remarried, again assumes the care of her boy" (May 6, 1896).

The widowed mothers who placed their children in the Denver Orphans' Home had few choices. Although the majority eventually retrieved their children, one cannot ignore the trauma associated with even the temporary disruption of normal family life. Accounts of half-orphans forced to live in child-care institutions at the turn of the century typically concentrate on the fate of the children, a perspective that mirrors that of the reformers of that generation. Yet it is essential that this phenomenon be examined from the point of view of the widowed mother. Locked into a job that paid wages insufficient to support her children, the desperate widow was forced to turn over her children to the care of an institution, not knowing what sort of life awaited them. The loss of her children was the ultimate consequence of the loss of her husband.

Steady employment was unusual in the years between 1880 and 1910, and widowed female workers were continually subject to the vagaries of the marketplace. Crises such as the depression of 1893 exacerbated the already uncertain employment picture for working widows and undoubtedly left many destitute and dependent on charity. In addition, advanced age, chronic illness, or other disabilities made some widows perennial candidates for charity. These penniless widows sought aid from Denver's charitable agencies to survive.

Private charity in Denver, originally centered in the Ladies' Relief Society and a few religiously oriented groups, was rationalized in the late 1880s with the creation of an umbrella organization subsequently known as the Charity Organization Society. The groups that comprised this society assisted needy persons in Denver in a variety of ways. Moreover, there was a central relief department that dispensed aid in cases of emergency. Numerous widows were given assistance by the central relief department over the years.[65]

The well-to-do Denverites who shaped the city's charitable enterprises envisioned their work through the prism of voluntarist values. Convinced that individuals should learn to help themselves, they defined charity as the provision of stopgap aid rather than a continuing stipend. Only truly disabled people merited more than a limited amount of aid. Moreover, recipients of charity were expected to exhibit gratitude for the token aid allotted. An example of the demeanor deemed appropriate by the dispensers of charity emerges in an 1884 newspaper account of a poor widow living in the Bottoms. "Near the residence of Mrs. Woodhave there lives a bright young woman with 2 children, whose husband died about a year ago of pneumonia. She does washing & works when she can get it, and when she is not ill. She has had many misfortunes, but always appears cheerful, smiling, neat and happy. The society are in love with the little woman, whose face is always sunshiny & who brightens everybody with whom she comes in contact."[66] Most charitable organizations in Denver in this era exacted a price for their help in the form of behavioral conformity. However, there were exceptions such as Sunshine Rescue Mission run by James Goodheart and the charitable enterprises of "Parson Tom" Uzzell.[67]

Charitable groups serving particularized constituencies also played a part in assisting poor widows in Denver. As a rule, individual churches looked out for widowed members of their congregations who had fallen on hard times.[68] Organized groups, such as the Colorado and Wyoming Department of the Women's Relief Corps of the Grand Army of the Republic, provided help to needy widows who met narrowly defined eligibility requirements. This organization doled out small amounts of money to widows of soldiers who had fought in the Union army during the Civil War. The "Report of the Department Relief Committee" dated May 1, 1899, noted a series of disbursements to soldiers' widows.[69]

Nov. 19, 1898	Gave soldier's widow (coal)	2.00
	. . . . . .	
Nov. 22, 1898	Gave soldier's widow (rent)	2.00
	. . . . . .	
Nov. 30, 1898	Gave soldier's widow (groceries)	2.00
	. . . . . .	
Feb. 9, 1899	On ticket for soldier's widow (Neb.)	2.00
	. . . . . .	
May 1, 1899	Bed for soldier's widow (sick)	.50

Widows who asked for assistance from the Pioneer Ladies Aid Society had to fulfill even more stringent qualifications. The group's constitution stated that the society would "extend aid and relief to all persons who arrived in what is now the state of Colorado, prior to the first day of January 1861—after investigation shall warrant such action, and relief may be extended to families of such persons in the discretion of the Society, considering the age, condition and circumstance of each case. No aid shall be given to persons who have children able to support them, without a two-thirds vote of the members present."[70] A 1908 report reveals the nature of the screening process implemented by the ladies of the society:

> Called as requested on Mrs. Marie Pelham of 2506—15th St. to investigate her case. I ascertained that her husband came here in '58.' She suffers a great deal with rheumatism. She makes a Hair Tonic—which she tries to sell when able to get out. She has a son living in California who helps her some, but he has a large family of his own, and it is all he can do to support them. She is very neat—has what little household goods she has in "spick-span" shape. She is a woman who used to have plenty before she met with misfortune. . . .
>
> Called on Mrs. Pelham, and after consulting with our president, left her two dollars, as she was in very straitened circumstances. I would recommend that she be given at least five dollars a month.[71]

Poor but respectable widows like Mrs. Pelham were clearly the favored candidates for assistance from private charitable groups like the Pioneer

Ladies Aid Society. Yet there were scores of needy widows who could not meet the criterion of middle-class respectability insisted upon by the wealthy ladies who furnished the aid. As a last resort, impoverished widows applied to the county for assistance. Because of the stigma attached to poor relief in this era, it is unlikely that the widows who requested funds from the public authorities had any other recourse.

Although a few widows were inmates of the Arapahoe County Poor House in the late nineteenth century, most needy widows received aid in the form of outdoor relief or small stipends given over a short period of time. Beginning in the 1860s poor relief for Denver residents was dispensed exclusively by Arapahoe County. For the year ending December 1, 1901, it was reported 2,676 outdoor—noninstitutional—poor were aided in that county.[72] After 1904 widows living in the city received aid from newly created Denver County. Analysis of information contained in the Denver County Poor Report of 1910 enables us to delineate the characteristics of widows receiving relief in that year.[73]

Persons identified as widows constituted 95 (14 percent) of the 699 cases that received funds from Denver County in 1910. Because of the way in which the data are presented, this figure is probably an underestimate.[74] The majority of widows were young or middle-aged mothers. The median age of the 95 widows listed on the Denver County relief rolls in 1910 was 41 and the mean age was 42. Eighty-one (85 percent) of the widows had children in their households, and 37 had at least one child under five years of age. Although no precise information on the relationships between household members is given, it is clear that the households of some poor widows contained other dependents, such as an elderly relative. Data on the nativity of relief recipients discloses that 45 (47 percent) of these widows were from the United States, and nine each were from Ireland, Russia, and Sweden. Seven were from Germany, six from Italy, and five from England. The remainder came from other countries.

Investigators specified the "Cause of Poverty or Distress" in each case where the county granted aid. Although the designation "widow" was sufficient in the majority of cases, sometimes the investigator elaborated on the precise reason: "widow unable to work," "widow with family to support," "widow with large family," "widow—destitute," and "widow—sick."

Outdoor relief was conceived as an emergency measure by public authorities, and the record of funds dispensed to poor widows in 1910 bolsters this contention. The amount of aid given to widows was minimal, usually no more than a few dollars a month, although it varied in each case, presumably because of the size of the household. The duration of aid for widows ranged from one to twelve months.

In a society in which both charity and public assistance were niggardly, it was predictable that some women, deprived of the normal source of support—a husband—and unable to maintain themselves satisfactorily because of the poor wages paid women workers, would turn to prostitution. Since most women became prostitutes as a result of economic need, it is not surprising to find that poor widows joined the ranks of their single sisters in this occupation.[75] Documenting the number of Denver widows involved in prostitution is not possible for obvious reasons, but it is fair to speculate that more than a few of the 700 prostitutes in Denver in 1913 were widows.[76] The two widows who actually identified themselves as whores to the census-taker in 1880 were exceptional. An accurate tabulation of the number of prostitutes in Denver during this period and their marital status is unattainable. Despite the lack of evidence, it is unrealistic to assume that the desperate circumstances of some widows were not enough to drive them into prostitution or possibly other forms of criminal activity.

When the irreducible goal became survival, widows could not afford to look askance at any activity designed to bring in food or money. A story printed in the *Rocky Mountain News* in 1884 entitled "Bread Beggars" reveals the lengths to which families headed by poor widows had to go to keep from starving. After discovering that poor children in Denver made the rounds of restaurants and hotels seeking discarded food scraps to feed their families, a reporter followed a group of these children home to meet their mother.

> Well, I found the mother and an almost grown daughter, a grandmother and a handsome shepherd dog. They were devilish poor, having but a little common furniture in the room. The widow told me that her husband used to be a bricklayer and supported the family very well, but was unable to lay up any money. He died about two years ago. The mother was sickly, the grandmother unable to work and the biggest girl unable to support the family on her wages as a servant girl. She is working out yet. I suppose the children got into the habit of taking home cold chuck from the restaurants and hotels, where they went to sell water cresses.[77]

Throughout the period 1880-1912, widows in Denver, as elsewhere, had to shift for themselves. The misguided belief of authorities that families and friends would fill the gap left by the loss of the breadwinner proved erroneous in countless cases, as charity workers and local government administrators learned. Nevertheless, it was only in the early twentieth century, when reformers were successful in conveying the idea that individual effort was insufficient to solve the complex human problems fostered by a growing urban industrial society, that social values and government policy began to alter. Increasingly, people in power were willing to acknowledge that there were circumstances under which the state should step in to aid people unable to support themselves. Revealingly, it was one segment of the widowed population—widowed mothers of young children—that first captured the attention of legislators.

It is mistaken, however, to conclude that it was widows who were singled out for special treatment in the Mothers' (or Widows') Compensation Acts passed in rapid succession in a number of states after 1911. In reality, it was dependent or neglected children who were the object of concern. Mothers' compensation legislation was not directed at widows per se, but at widowed mothers of young children. These acts, in essence, were child welfare measures, not widows' welfare measures. The idea was that the state should pay the natural mother a sum of money to provide proper home care for her children, since keeping a child in the home—and the family intact—was preferable to institutionalizing the child. In the words of Denver Judge Benjamin Lindsey, the key figure in securing the passage of the Mothers' Compensation Act in Colorado in 1912, "It is a recognition by the state that the aid is rendered, not as a charity, but as a right—as justice due mothers whose work in rearing their children is a work for the state as much as that of the soldier who is paid by the state for his services on the battlefield."[78]

The Colorado Mothers' Compensation Act did very little to ameliorate the condition of poor widows in Denver. The small appropriation, administered in Denver under the aegis of the juvenile court, was apportioned not only among needy widows but also among deserted wives and wives of men who were invalids or in jail. Problems of funding, eligibility, and administration marred its operation in the years following its passage. The women who received aid under its provisions were critical of the close scrutiny of government investigators and complained that the funds allotted were insufficient.[79] Nevertheless, this act was a watershed in the history of Denver widows.

Few American women at the turn of the century would have disputed the notion that widowhood was an unenviable condition. Despite sympathetic portrayals of widows in contemporary literature, it was common knowledge that the typical widow was hard-pressed financially and that the government took no responsibility for her welfare. It was also widely recognized that women were not brought up to function as the primary support of their families, nor was the labor market structured to accommodate this possibility. Under these circumstances, widows could anticipate a bumpy road ahead.

This study of widows living in Denver between 1880 and 1912 has documented the responses of women in a growing urban center to the economic difficulties that confronted them after the deaths of their spouses. Accustomed to depending on her husband for support, a widow at first relied on the resources he had accumulated. For the majority of widows, personal savings were exhausted rapidly, and the benefits accruing from their husbands' membership in unions, fraternal, or professional associations proved inadequate. Kinfolk traditionally formed a bulwark in times of crisis, and widows initially turned to relatives for assistance. If a widow was in a position to become the dependent of a family member, be it a married child, a sibling, or a parent, then her maintenance was assured.

When a surrogate breadwinner was not available, the widow had to explore other avenues for support. Because the jobs open to widows in Denver were concentrated in the service sector, they tended to be filled by widows whose background and prior experience had inured them to menial work. Widows whose cultural standards precluded their entry into the labor force on these terms attempted to earn a living by means of homework, a form of labor whose importance in this era is consistently underestimated. Undoubtedly, many widows combined a variety of economic strategies to survive. A small pension, taking in boarders, and occasional contributions from adult children, for example, might have enabled a widow to get by. Nevertheless, the grinding struggle for daily existence probably disposed most widows to view remarriage favorably.

Widows who were incapable of working or whose labors produced insufficient income sought assistance from community agencies. In this age of voluntarism the normal recourse was to private charity. Women who resided in Denver during their widowhood had an advantage over their counterparts in the countryside, since urban centers boasted a far broader range of charities than rural areas. However, rigid eligibility standards left some destitute widows with no choice but to apply for poor relief from the county. For those widows who were unable or unwilling to secure private or public aid, extralegal activities such as prostitution offered an alternative means of self-support.

The measures taken by Denver widows to deal with their economic problems often had a negative impact on their family lives. At the minimum, the loss of the breadwinner meant a lower standard of living for the survivors, as economies previously deemed unnecessary were now implemented as a matter of prudence. Living frugally was not enough in many cases, and the price of keeping the household intact was the substitution of an older child for the deceased father as the family's primary earner. As a consequence, that child's opportunities for additional education, a particular career, or even marriage might be sacrificed to ensure continual support for the widowed mother and younger siblings. Even more severe disruptions of family life occurred when a widow was forced to break up her household and move in with relatives or to a boardinghouse and, in some instances, place her children in an orphanage.

The specter of poverty and family collapse loomed as a possibility for widows in Denver long after the enactment of Colorado's Mothers' Compensation Act in 1912. Nevertheless, the state's recognition of the rights of one subgroup of the widowed population paved the way for expanded coverage of widows in future decades. Although some widows still do not qualify for survivor's benefits under existing federal legislation, there is no doubt that today's Denver widows are more fortunate than their predecessors, who had to rely for aid exclusively on family, friends, and charity.[80]

NOTES

1. Robert Seager II, *And Tyler too: A Biography of John and Julia Gardiner Tyler* (New York: McGraw-Hill, 1963), 549.

2. Sheila M. Rothman, *Woman's Proper Place: A History of Changing Ideals and Practices, 1870 to the Present* (New York: Basic Books, 1978), 85; Leslie Woodcock Tentler, *Wage-Earning Women: Industrial Work and Family Life in the United States, 1900-1930* (New York: Oxford University Press, 1979), 166.

3. The most recent history of the city of Denver is Lyle W. Dorsett's *The Queen City: A History of Denver* (Boulder: Pruett Publishing, 1977). See also Carl Abbott, "Boom State and Boom City: Stages in Denver's Growth," *Colorado Magazine* 50 (1973):207-30; and Bernard Rosen, "Social Welfare in the History of Denver" (Ph.D. diss., University of Colorado, 1976).

4. Billy M. Jones, *Health Seekers in the Southwest, 1817-1900* (Norman: University of Oklahoma Press, 1967), 157-59; James Richard Giese, "Tuberculosis and the Growth of Denver's Eastern European Jewish Community: The Accommodation of an Immigrant Group to a Medium-Sized Western City, 1900-1920" (Ph.D. diss., University of Colorado, 1979).

5. Roy Lubove, *The Struggle for Social Security, 1900-1935* (Cambridge, Mass.: Harvard University Press, 1968); Hace Sorel Tishler, *Self-Reliance and Social*

Security, 1870-1917 (Port Washington, N.Y.: Kennikat Press, 1971); Robert Bremner, *From the Depths: The Discovery of Poverty in the United States* (New York: New York University Press, 1954).

6. Ben B. Lindsey, "The Mothers' Compensation Law of Colorado," *The Survey* 29 (Feb. 15, 1913):714-16; Mark H. Leff, "Consensus for Reform: The Mothers' Pension Movement in the Progressive Era," in Frank R. Breul and Steven J. Diner, eds., *Compassion and Responsibility: Readings in the History of Social Welfare Policy in the United States* (Chicago: University of Chicago Press, 1980), 244-64.

7. Rosen, "Social Welfare in the History of Denver"; Milton Lawrence Kephart, "Charities and Corrections in Colorado" (M.A. thesis, University of Colorado, 1903).

8. Unless otherwise indicated, the statistics herein are derived from the published volumes of the U.S. census for 1880, 1890, 1900, and 1910, and from computer analysis of data recorded on Denver widows in the manuscript schedules of the 1880 census.

9. For background on Denver's immigrant population, see Stephen J. Leonard, "The Irish, English, and Germans in Denver, 1860-1890," *Colorado Magazine* 54 (1977):126-53; and "The People of Colorado, 1876-1916," in Carl Abbott, Stephen J. Leonard, and David McComb, *Colorado: A History of the Centennial State,* rev. ed. (Boulder: Colorado Associated University Press, 1982).

10. Robert W. Smuts, *Women and Work in America* (New York: Schocken Books, 1971), 52; Helena Z. Lopata, *Women as Widows: Support Systems* (New York: Elsevier, 1979), 35.

11. Hugh Carter and Paul C. Glick, *Marriage and Divorce: A Social and Economic Study,* rev. ed. (Cambridge, Mass.: Harvard University Press, 1976), 439.

12. *Report on the Mortality and Vital Statistics of the United States as Returned at the Tenth Census* (June 1, 1880), part I. (Washington, D.C.: Government Printing Office, 1885), 549-52; *Fourth Report of the State Board of Health of Colorado, including the Reports for the Years 1892, 1893, and 1894* (Denver: Smith-Brooks Printing, 1894), 254-69; Denver Tuberculosis Society, *Seventh Annual Report,* Dec. 1, 1922–Dec. 1, 1923, 2; *Tuberculosis in Denver: A Survey Conducted by the Health Committee of the City Club,* pamphlet 6 (Denver: City Club, 1925); Giese, "Tuberculosis and Denver."

13. Rosen, "Social Welfare in the History of Denver," 83. See also Robert M. Tank, "Mobility and Occupational Structure on the Late Nineteenth-Century Urban Frontier: The Case of Denver, Colorado," *Pacific Historical Review* 47 (1978):189-216.

14. Dorsett, *Queen City,* 110.

15. James T. Patterson, *America's Struggle against Poverty, 1900-1980* (Cambridge, Mass.: Harvard University Press, 1981), 13.

16. Rosen, "Social Welfare in the History of Denver," 83.

17. Abbott, Leonard, and McComb, *Colorado,* 201.

18. William Alexander Platt, "The Destitute in Denver," *Harper's Weekly,* Aug. 19, 1893, 787-88; Leah Hannah Feder, *Unemployment Relief in Periods of Depression: A Study of Measures Adopted in Certain American Cities, 1857 through 1922* (New York: Russell Sage Foundation, 1936), 72-73; 80; Rosen, "Social Welfare in the History of Denver," 169-71.

19. Cindy S. Aron, " 'To Barter Their Souls for Gold': Female Clerks in Federal Government Offices, 1862-1890," *Journal of American History* 67 (1981):838-41.

20. Lubove, *Struggle for Social Security;* Tishler, *Self-Reliance and Social Security.*

21. Charles W. Ferguson, *Fifty Million Brothers: A Panorama of American Lodges and Clubs* (New York: Farrar & Rinehart, 1937); Alvin J. Schmidt, *Fraternal Organizations* (Westport, Conn.: Greenwood Press, 1980).

22. George B. Clark, comp., *History of Union Lodge No. 7 A.F. & A.M. Denver, Colorado, 1863-1938* (Denver: R. J. Williams, 1938), 54-55; *The Book of Odd Fellowship in Colorado* (Denver: Canfield & Haviland, 1895), 124; *Proceedings of the Head Camp Woodmen of the World* (Pacific Jurisdiction, Aug. 1890–Aug. 1897), 206.

23. Christopher J. Kauffman, *Faith and Fraternalism: The History of the Knights of Columbus, 1882-1982* (New York: Harper & Row, 1982), 111; *Denver Directory of Agencies for Community Welfare* (Denver: City Federation, 1913), 43.

24. *Denver Directory of Agencies for Community Welfare,* 42-43.

25. Allen duPont Breck, *The Centennial History of the Jews of Colorado, 1859-1959* (Denver: Hirschfield Press, 1960), 29-31; Ida Libert Uchill, *Pioneers, Peddlers, and Tsadikim* (Denver: Sage Books, 1957), 133-34. See also Schmidt, *Fraternal Organizations,* 52-54.

26. Rosen, "Social Welfare in the History of Denver," 196.

27. M. James Kedro, "Czechs and Slovaks in Colorado, 1860-1920," *Colorado Magazine* 54 (1977):110.

28. "Workmen's Insurance and Benefit Funds in the United States," *Twenty-Third Annual Report of the Commissioner of Labor* (Washington, D.C.: Government Printing Office, 1909), 59-60.

29. *Denver Directory of Agencies for Community Welfare,* 24.

30. On unions in Denver, see Harold V. Knight, *Working in Colorado: A Brief History of the Colorado Labor Movement* (Boulder: University of Colorado, Center for Labor Education and Research, 1971).

31. Numerous instances of widows being aided by the fellow workers of their deceased husbands are cited in Mary E. Richmond and Fred S. Hall, *A Study of Nine Hundred and Eighty-Five Widows Known to Certain Charity Organization Societies in 1910* (orig. publ. 1913; New York: Arno Press, 1974). See, for example, the case of a thirty-four-year-old man who died in 1908: "There was no insurance when Mr. G died in January 1908, but the Cutters' Union to which he belonged

paid the funeral expenses, fellow workmen collected $65, and the church contributed $20." Ibid., 75.

32. *Denver Municipal Facts,* Apr. 3, 1909, 14. Prior to the establishment of the Police Department Relief Fund, other means were used to assist the widows and children of Denver policemen. A police ball was held on December 20, 1900, "for the purpose of raising money to aid sick and disabled policemen and the families of officers killed while performing their duties." Eugene Frank Rider, "The Denver Police Department: An Administrative, Organizational, and Operational History, 1858-1905" (Ph.D. diss., University of Denver, 1971), 500.

33. According to the constitution of this society, "The net income of the society . . . may be distributed annually among the most necessitous members, widows, and minor children, and shall be appropriated among them according to the best judgment of the Board of Managers, . . . considering their cases in the order of widows and children first, and then superannuated and supernumerary members of the Conference, before those who hold an 'effective' relation." *Journal of the Thirty-seventh Session of the Colorado Annual Conference of the Methodist Episcopal Church held at Denver, Colorado, August 30 to September 5, 1899* (Denver: Dove Printer, 1899), 1-6, at back of pamphlet.

34. "Soldiers and Widows," *Compendium of the Eleventh Census* (Washington, D.C.: Government Printing Office, 1892), 583. There were also twelve widows of Confederate soldiers living in Denver in 1890. Ibid., 585. On federal pensions for widows of Civil War veterans, see William Henry Glasson, *History of Military Pension Legislation in the United States* (New York: Columbia University Press, 1900); and William H: Glasson, *Federal Military Pensions in the United States* (New York: Oxford University Press, 1918). See also an advertisement addressed to "Soldiers and their Widows believing themselves entitled to pension and increase or increase," *Denver Times,* July 20, 1899, 7.

35. For the role of family members in aiding a widow in St. Louis during the Civil War, see the case of Bethiah Pyatt McKown in Joyce D. Goodfriend and Claudia M. Christie, *Lives of American Women: A History with Documents* (Boston: Little Brown, 1981), 329-38.

36. On older widows, see Michel Dahlin, "Perspectives on the Family Life of the Elderly in 1900," *The Gerontologist* 20 (1980):99-107; and Daniel Scott Smith, "Life Course, Norms, and the Family System of Older Americans in 1900," *Journal of Family History* 4 (1979):285-98.

37. See Howard P. Chudacoff and Tamara K. Hareven, "Family Transitions into Old Age," In Tamara K. Hareven, ed., *Transitions: The Family and the Life Course in Historical Perspective* (New York: Academic Press, 1978), 238-39. See also Howard P. Chudacoff and Tamara K. Hareven, "From the Empty Nest to Family Dissolution: Life Course Transitions into Old Age," *Journal of Family History* 4 (1979):69-83.

38. In the 1880 Denver census thirteen widows were listed as sister of the head

of household, nine widows were listed as sister-in-law of the head of household, and twenty-six widows were listed as daughter of the head of household.

39. Rosen, "Social Welfare in the History of Denver," 176, 195-96.

40. *Twelfth Biennial Report of the State Board of Charities and Corrections of Colorado for the Biennial Period Ending November 30, 1914* (Denver: Smith-Brooks Printing, 1914), 102-3.

41. See p. 175 above.

42. Florence McCune Diary, 1881, State Historical Society of Colorado, Denver. See also Joyce D. Goodfriend and Dona K. Flory, "Women in Colorado before the First World War," *Colorado Magazine* 53 (1976):205-6.

43. Smuts, *Women and Work in America,* 52.

44. Carter and Glick, *Marriage and Divorce,* 291. In 1970, 67 percent of widows between 45 and 54 were working for pay. Lopata, *Women as Widows,* 39. See also Carol J. Barrett, "Women in Widowhood: A Review Essay," *Signs* 2 (1977):859-60.

45. Smuts, *Women and Work in America,* 23. Alice Kessler-Harris, *Out to Work: A History of Wage-Earning Women in the United States* (New York: Oxford University Press, 1982), 122. By the late nineteenth century it had become increasingly legitimate for single women to hold jobs.

46. For background on women's work in Denver during the years 1880-1910, see Goodfriend and Flory, "Women in Colorado before the First World War," 219-29; Helen L. Sumner [Woodbury], *Equal Suffrage: The Results of an Investigation in Colorado Made for the Collegiate Equal Suffrage League of New York State* (orig. publ. 1909; New York: Arno Press, 1972), 150-79, 275-76; and Dorsett, *Queen City,* 107-8. For an overview of the work of women in the West, see Joan M. Jensen and Darlis A. Miller, "The Gentle Tamers Revisited: New Approaches to the History of Women in the American West," *Pacific Historical Review* 49 (1980):173-213.

47. *First Biennial Report of the Bureau of Labor Statistics of the State of Colorado, 1887-1888* (Denver: Collier & Cleaveland Lith., 1888), 339. Section VIII of this report, "Female Wage Workers," contains scattered information on the wages and expenses of widowed workers in Denver.

48. Elinore Pruitt Stewart, *Letters of a Woman Homesteader* (orig. Publ. 1914; Lincoln: University of Nebraska Press, 1961).

49. See Daniel J. Walkowitz, "Working-Class Women in the Gilded Age: Factory, Community, and Family Life among Cohoes, New York, Cotton Workers," *Journal of Social History* 5 (Summer 1972):464-90; Thomas Dublin, *Women at Work: The Transformation of Work and Community in Lowell, Massachusetts, 1826-1860* (New York: Columbia University Press, 1979), 170; and Susan J. Kleinberg, "The Systematic Study of Urban Women," in Milton Cantor and Bruce Laurie, eds., *Class, Sex, and the Woman Worker* (Westport, Conn.: Greenwood Press, 1977), 24-26.

50. The ideology of domesticity provided some guidelines regarding appropriate occupations for women. If a woman had to take a job, she should pursue only those lines of work that were seen as an extension of her natural functions—domestic servant, laundress, dressmaker, and teacher. But the definitions of "women's work" were further refined in accordance with conceptions of social class. Middle-class women were enjoined from performing household labor or factory work, which were regarded as too demeaning for respectable women. Only certain occupations, the best example being teacher, were viewed as suitable for ladies.

51. See John Modell and Tamara K. Hareven, "Urbanization and the Malleable Household: An Examination of Boarding and Lodging in American Families," *Journal of Marriage and the Family* 35 (1973):467-79.

52. In 1880 the census listed only thirty-five widows as boardinghouse keepers in Denver, but 150 widowed female heads of household had boarders listed in their households. See also Clyde and Sally Griffen, *Natives and Newcomers: The Ordering of Opportunity in Mid-Nineteenth Century Poughkeepsie* (Cambridge, Mass.: Harvard University Press, 1978), 230-31.

53. See *Annual Report of the Colorado Woman's Christian Temperance Union, 1892,* 41, and *Annual Report of the Colorado Woman's Temperance Union, 1888,* advertisement, both in Western Historical Collections of the University of Colorado, Boulder. See also the report of Mrs. Henry Goodridge, superintendent of the Woman's Exchange in the *Rocky Mountain News,* June 3, 1887. Sheila Rothman (*Woman's Proper Place,* 86) states that there were Woman's Exchanges in approximately seventy-five cities by the 1890s. There is an account of the Woman's Exchanges sponsored by the Women's Educational and Industrial Union in Boston and Buffalo in Karen J. Blair's *The Clubwomen as Feminist: True Womanhood Redefined, 1868-1914* (New York: Holmes & Meier, 1980), 80, 86.

54. In 1880, 441 Denver widows had at least one unmarried child residing with them in the same household, and seventy had at least one child 5 or under in their household.

55. Among the families of sixty-one widows whose cases were studied intensively by Mary E. Richmond and Fred S. Hall, the grandmother cared for the children in six cases and other relatives in five cases. In one case, a neighbor took care of the widow's children; in three cases, a woman was paid for this service (Richmond and Hall, *A Study of Nine Hundred and Eighty-Five Widows,* 45). Katharine Anthony, in her study of 370 wage-earning mothers in a West Side neighborhood of New York City, 125 of whom were widows, found that of 221 children below school age living at home, "181 . . . were looked after by relatives or neighbors in haphazard fashion." Anthony, *Mothers Who Must Earn* (New York: Survey Associates, 1914), 19, 151-52.

56. *Annual Report of the Colorado Woman's Christian Temperance Union, 1890.* See also Rosen, "Social Welfare in the History of Denver," 181, 183.

57. U.S. Bureau of the Census, Special Reports, *Benevolent Institutions, 1904*

(Washington, D.C.: Government Printing Office, 1905), 58-61; *Denver Directory of Agencies for Community Welfare,* 29-30; W. H. Slingerland, *Child Welfare Work in Colorado: A Study of Public and Private Agencies and Institutions and Conditions of Service, in the Care of Dependent, Delinquent and Defective Children,* University of Colorado Bulletin 20, no. 10, Gen. Series no. 161 (1920); Mary Louise Sinton, "A History of the Woman's Club of Denver: 1894-1915" (M.A. thesis, University of Denver, 1980).

58. *Annual Report of the Colorado Woman's Christian Temperance Union, 1889; Denver Directory of Agencies for Community Welfare,* 29.

59. Anthony, *Mothers Who Must Earn,* 152. Anthony found that only forty of 221 children of working mothers who lived at home "were cared for in day nurseries." Richmond and Hall noted that twelve of sixty-one widows' families with young children placed the younger children in day nurseries. Richmond and Hall, *A Study of Nine Hundred Eighty-Five Widows,* 45.

60. Rothman, *Woman's Proper Place,* 89, 90.

61. Anthony, *Mothers Who Must Earn,* 153. Anthony continues: "Most of those who had put their children away were widows with more children than they could possibly support. They had kept at home the younger children, spreading a small income out thin to make it nourish as many as possible, and had put the older ones in institutions." Richmond and Hall reported that seven of the sixty-one widows' families under study had committed their children. Richmond and Hall, *A Study of Nine Hundred Eighty-Five Widows,* 45.

62. Statistics from the New York State Board of Charities in 1910 disclosed that almost 50 percent of the children admitted to local institutions were half-orphans; only 17 percent were full orphans or foundlings. Susan Tiffin, *In Whose Best Interest? Child Welfare Reform in the Progressive Era* (Westport, Conn.: Greenwood Press, 1982), 42.

63. U.S. Bureau of the Census, *Benevolent Institutions, 1904,* 58-61; U.S. Bureau of the Census, *Benevolent Institutions, 1910* (Washington, D.C.: Government Printing Office, 1913), 90-91; Slingerland, *Child Welfare Work in Colorado,* 7-62; Rosen, "Social Welfare in the History of Denver," 146, 165, 167, 178-91, 197.

64. Records of the Denver Orphans' Home, State Historical Society of Colorado. See also Vera Bussett, "A Study of Denver Orphans' Home" (M.A. thesis, University of Denver, 1937).

65. See *Annual Reports of the Denver Charity Organization Society* for 1894, 1895, 1898, 1903, 1904, 1906, 1910, and 1912 for statistics regarding the "social state" of recipients of relief from the Central Office.

66. "Poverty's Portion," *Rocky Mountain News,* Feb. 1, 1884, 8.

67. Dorsett, *Queen City,* 115-16, 145. See also Rachel Wild Peterson, *The Long-Lost Rachel Wild, or Seeking Diamonds in the Rough. Her Experiences in the Slums of Denver* (Denver: Reed Publishing, 1905).

68. Richmond and Hall in *A Study of Nine Hundred and Eighty-Five Widows*

cite a number of cases in which widows were aided by their churches. See note 31 above for an example.

69. *Journal of Proceedings of the Fifteenth Annual Convention of the Department of Colorado and Wyoming Woman's Relief Corps Auxiliary to the G.A.R., 1899*, 46-47.

70. "Constitution and By-Laws of the Pioneer Ladies' Aid Society, State of Colorado" (Denver, 1907), in Mary Butler Brown Collection, State Historical Society of Colorado.

71. Report of relief work, Jan. 30, 1908, Pioneer Ladies' Aid Society Collection, State Historical Society of Colorado.

72. *Sixth Biennial Report of the State Board of Charities and Corrections for the Biennial Period Ending November 30, 1902* (Denver: Smith-Brooks Printing, 1903), 105. On public welfare in Denver, see also Rosen, "Social Welfare in the History of Denver," 102-33, 156-75.

73. Poor Report Filings, Secretary of State Papers, Colorado State Archives, Denver. See also Alan K. Lathrop, "Office of the Secretary of State: 'Poor Report' Filings," unpublished paper, 1970.

74. Cases are presented without names and in terms of family or household groupings. The identification of widows is derived from the portion of the report that specifies the "causes of poverty or distress." Therefore, it is likely that only widows who were heads of household are accounted for in the number ninety-five. A widow who was a dependent in the household of another aid recipient would not be identifiable.

75. Ruth Rosen, *The Lost Sisterhood: Prostitution in America, 1900-1918* (Baltimore: Johns Hopkins University Press, 1982), 139, 149-50.

76. Abbott, Leonard, and McComb, *Colorado*, 187; Roland L. DeLorme, "Turn-of-the-Century Denver: An Invitation to Reform," *Colorado Magazine* 45 (1968):5; Lawrence H. Larsen, *The Urban West at the End of the Frontier* (Lawrence: The Regents Press of Kansas, 1978), 86-88. There were 275 houses of prostitution in Denver in December 1883. Rider, "The Denver Police Department," 255*n*52.

77. "Bread Beggars," *Rocky Mountain News*, Aug. 11, 1884. See also the story of "The Gifted Widow" in Caroline Nichols Churchill, *Active Footsteps* (orig. publ. 1909; New York: Arno Press, 1980), 94-97.

78. Lindsey, "Mothers' Compensation Law of Colorado," 716; Benjamin Barr Lindsey, *A Pamphlet Containing Arguments in Favor of the Mothers' Compensation Act, Being an Act to Amend an Act, Concerning Dependent and Neglected Children and Permitting Keeping Such Children in Family Homes, and for Workhouses for Men Convicted of Non-Support.* To be submitted to the legal voters of the State of Colorado for their approval or rejection at the regular general election to be held on the fifth day of November, 1912 (N.p., 1912).

79. Gertrude Vaile, "Administering Mothers' Pensions in Denver," *The Survey*, Feb. 28, 1914, 673-75; Mary Bickford Howe, "A Study of the Later Histories of

Families Receiving Mothers' Compensation in Denver before 1922" (M.A. thesis, University of Denver, 1932).

80. Margaret Gates, "Homemakers into Widows and Divorcées: Can the Law Provide Economic Protection?" in Jane Roberts Chapman and Margaret Gates, eds., *Women into Wives: The Legal and Economic Impact of Marriage* (Beverly Hills: Sage Publications, 1977), 221.

8

The Economics of Widowhood in Arizona, 1880-1940

DONNA J. GUY

Throughout the transition from territory to statehood, women accompanied their families in their trek to Arizona forts and towns, although men always greatly outnumbered women in the early years of settlement. The arrival of the railroad in 1880 marked a period of increased migration to Arizona as well as increased economic activity. From then until the Depression of the 1930s widows formed a significant sector among working women in Arizona. These working widows, as well as nonworking widows who relied on private and public aid, formed an important but rarely studied component of Arizona population during the transitional years from 1880 to 1940.

By 1912, when Arizona had sufficient population to be granted statehood, one writer had already begun to notice the contribution of women, particularly widows, to the settlement of the area.[1]

> The widow, too, is here. Some who came as widows, some left as widows after coming. The woman with small means and children . . . has looked to the West. . . . Others have come with invalid husbands, seeking our climate with hopes of recovery. Often within a few months the wife had been left alone to finish the struggle of deeding a homestead. Generally they are brave and out of their desolation give that influence which only a woman can give for the establishment of the best in family life.[2]

To this group of homesteading widows, one must add those without property and those who lost their husbands to mining or railroad accidents, to gunfights, and to the general violence of the frontier, as well as to ill health and old age.

The number of widows grew steadily as Arizona's general population increased. Consequently, the tremendous demographic imbalance of 1880, when there were only 12,238 women compared to 28,202 men, had disappeared by 1940, when the total state population of 499,261 was nearly evenly divided by sex.[3] During this time the number of widows increased along with the general female population; between 1900 and 1930 the total number of widows grew from 3,971 to 14,650, representing between 10.5 and 12 percent of all females.[4]

The death of the husband forced most widows to confront major changes in their economic security. Many went to work to support their families or turned to their families for support. Sometimes they had to resort to public aid to survive. What happened to widows in Arizona reflects much about the social and economic conditions of frontier areas at this time, and I propose here to describe how widowed women, their families, and the state dealt with the economic problems associated with widowhood.

First, the impact of widowhood was influenced by many factors. In general one can group widows according to age: young, middle-aged, and old; by presence of children: dependent, adult, or none; and whether they were living with family, alone, or with nonrelatives. Material inheritance in the form of real estate, livestock, commercial wealth, stocks, insurance policies, or the right to collect on a husband's pension also helped predict how well or in what way a woman might be able to support herself or her family. The emotional response of the grieving woman and her children, if she had any, was also critical.[5] In the final analysis, the widow's or children's economic management skills during this time of crisis determined how wealth would sustain the family.

Second, widows, especially the poor, ill, and elderly, were considered to be a public responsibility in Arizona. The capability and willingness of state government to aid these women and their dependent children can be viewed as an index of societal well-being and communal spirit. From territorial days in the 1860s until statehood in 1912 and into the present, Arizona's legal tradition has provided for widows, but the protection of the law was constrained by insufficient state revenues. Furthermore, until the Depression years, the state relegated much of the burden and responsibility for indigent and welfare care to counties and rarely supervised their disbursement and allocations policies. Consequently, as the population grew and the economy of given counties varied considerably, so did the provision of aid.

Third, all women, including widows, had to deal with a new kind of frontier society, which had the primitive conditions of all newly settled communities as well as access to the rapidly changing technology, social mores, and educational opportunities available in other parts of the United States. Thus electricity and automobiles coexisted with adobe huts and horses; the typewriter came into use just as copper was discovered in the southern part of the state; and women arrived in Arizona with degrees in higher education as a primary school system was being developed there. Arizona women had opportunities unimagined in earlier frontier societies while they still had to struggle to form new towns and cities. There was also greater legal freedom for married and widowed women than there had been in earlier frontier areas. While this situation enabled some widows to support themselves by taking advantage of new skills and jobs, others still had to struggle with more traditional and often difficult methods of coping with widowhood.

Fourth, widows were affected by Arizona's growth. Between 1880 and 1940 Arizona evolved from a sparsely populated frontier area to an economically complex state characterized by densely settled mining towns, commercial centers, and the state capital of Phoenix surrounded by a hinterland sustaining ranching and commercial agriculture. The construction of railroads to service these ranches, farms, and towns served as an important catalyst in the process of economic development. And as people continued to migrate to Arizona, the rapid influx of new ethnic and racial groups often altered the family and living patterns of longstanding inhabitants. Furthermore, many towns sprang up overnight, only to disappear after a mine played out or farming proved to be more difficult than anticipated. All of these changes affected widows. Hence, the residential patterns and occupations of widows should reveal the extent of that dislocation. I examine here Bisbee, Tucson, Phoenix, and to a lesser extent, Prescott, which represent respectively a mining town, a commercial center, the state capital and administrative center, and the former capital that served as a center for ranching and agriculture. A brief review of the history of these cities and towns reveals the diverse challenges faced by pioneer groups in early Arizona.

Located in the southeastern corner of the territory, Bisbee was one of the most important late nineteenth-century state mining communities, although the town was not incorporated until 1900. Copper was discovered as early as 1875, but it was ignored in the search for silver. The second discovery of copper two years later by a group of army scouts led to several mining claims. By 1880 a number of important copper companies such as Phelps Dodge had bought property in the area, and battles had begun for control over mining claims.

Founded originally by Anglos, the rapidly growing town and its suburb of Warren eventually had a large number of Mexican and Slavic families residing there, although Mexicans were discouraged from working underground in the mines due to prejudice-based superstition. Located where there were few trees and everything had to be shipped in, Bisbee always had a short supply of housing until the mining boom declined after World War I. And although the city was first listed in a national census in 1910 with a population of 9,010, by 1940 the number had decreased to 5,853. Nevertheless, unlike many other mining towns that fell on hard times and disappeared, the social fabric had been strong enough and work opportunities sufficient for a reduced population to remain rather than move on.[6]

Tucson, located to the northwest, was a much older city whose first population boom did not occur until some one hundred years after its authorized settlement by the Spanish government. Tucson was ordered occupied by the Spanish in 1769, an often formidable task as it was subject to Indian attacks. After an initial population boom during the Civil War, by the 1880s the city had more than 7,000 inhabitants protected by the U.S. cavalry and had become an important commercial center served by the railroads. The growth of the mining economy to the south as well as expanded ranching and farming activities around the edge of the city enabled Tucson to maintain a population larger than the territorial capital of Phoenix. Its second spurt of population occurred between 1900 and 1920, when the number of people residing in Tucson rose from 7,531 to 20,292. By 1940 the city boasted 36,818 inhabitants.[7]

One reason that Tucson became so attractive to new settlers was its reputation for a dry and healthful climate, believed to be ideal for patients suffering from tuberculosis. Arriving first by railroads and later by airplanes, health seekers continued to move to places like Tucson and Denver long after 1900, when it was discovered that a bacillus, not climate, caused the disease. As late as 1928, when doctors no longer recommended desert life as a cure, local journalists were still lauding the extensive medical and nursing facilities that equaled approximately 1,000 beds and were mostly owned and staffed by women.[8]

Phoenix, about one hundred miles northwest of Tucson, was less important as a health resort but more significant as an administrative center and capital city. Its location in the Salt River Valley also placed it in the center of what became Arizona's principal farming area. Founded in the late 1860s by Anglo settlers, the future city was renamed Phoenix in 1870 to replace the more humble Pumpkinville. In 1889 the town of 3,000 was selected to be the territorial capital over the larger city of Tucson, thereby creating a source of extensive employment that allowed Phoenix to grow steadily. In 1910 it counted 11,134 residents, and by 1940 it had surpassed Tucson with a population exceeding 65,000.[9]

Prescott was also a territorial capital of Arizona. Located in the central part of the state near a mining area, Prescott from its founding in 1864 was the territorial capital of Arizona until 1867 and again from 1877 to 1889, when that privilege was permanently transferred to Phoenix. Because it had been settled for the specific purpose of hosting the territorial government, Prescott immediately took on the appearance of an important town by having such amenities as a theater and restaurants, even though the first buildings were constructed of logs. Its growth, however, never equaled that of Tucson and Phoenix, and even in 1900 it had only 3,559 inhabitants. By 1940 it had increased only modestly to 6,018 residents as the mining towns nearby had faded into obscurity and were replaced by ranch and farming activities.[10]

The unequal development of these four urban areas was intimately affected by the vagaries of the Arizona economy. Other towns as well as the rural hinterlands settled by Indians, Hispanics (people of Mexican nationality or parentage), and Anglos were also attuned to the shifting rhythms of traditional and new forms of endeavor. Similarly widows, too, were affected by the need to devise old and new strategies of survival and sometimes felt the necessity to migrate from one place to another to find help or work.

There are a number of ways to investigate the place of widows in Arizona society and economy between 1880 and 1940. In the public sector, state and local agencies intended to aid the indigent, elderly, and young mothers all developed from the early days of the territory until the advent of social security legislation in 1939, which specifically included widows and assumed much of the financial burden for public assistance. In the private sector, the role of family and friends, the occupational income of widows and their children, and the widows' age, housing, and ethnicity were all factors in how, and how well, the widow coped.

The Public Sector

Like other territories and states, Arizona recognized the special vulnerability of widows. Upon her spouse's death a widow automatically inherited one-half of the community property, and their homestead was exempt from seizure and $1,000 of its value was free of state taxes. These laws dated from the 1864 Howell Code and subsequent revisions enacted in December 1865.[11]

Since no record was kept of debates concerning this body of law and others created during Arizona's formative years, it is difficult to account for the high degree of liberality toward married women and widows. One might assume, however, that the demands of the traditional frontier made it imperative that women be able to take care of themselves financially. It is also likely that reforms of more restrictive legislation elsewhere in the United States, which had been achieved by some feminists, served as a model. That the territorial legislature in 1912 wanted Arizona to become a state with female suffrage supports this hypothesis. Even though political conditions made this goal unattainable at the time, shortly thereafter Arizona legislators did give women the vote.[12]

Regardless of the cause, the consequence of the modified Howell Code allowed some fortunate widows to live more prosperously after the death of a spouse than before. This often related to wise investments in business, land, or insurance. Folly could easily dissipate such wealth, too, but the important factor was the legal ability of married women and widows to control either their own or their community property after their husbands' demise.[13]

In addition to the state legal codes, Arizona recognized other duties to divert scarce resources to poor, elderly, and ill groups residing in the state. Aid was usually disbursed indirectly, through the petition of neighbors or a physician who would testify to the extreme need and worthiness of the women. In the 1860s and 1870s the local justice of the peace or the sheriff handled these matters, but by the 1880s this function had been turned over to the county board of supervisors. Only the neediest and most desperate received help in this way, and there seemed to be little discrimination against poor Hispanics at that time, particularly in Pima County where most towns like Tucson had been settled initially by people of Mexican origin. If funds were available and the supervisors approved the petition, goods could be purchased and the infirm were sent to specified hospitals or to doctors who had bid for the county indigent business.[14] Other doctors or hospitals participated in the system by submitting bids that offered health care at a fixed daily fee.[15]

Counties also controlled admissions to the state mental hospital that operated from the 1890s. Widows comprised a minority of the women admitted and often were placed there for senility. No details are available on ethnicity. After 1911 a state old-age home provided for the few elderly who could prove their long-established pioneer origins and demonstrable contribution to the state. Women were admitted with the construction of a new wing in 1916. From the time of the home's establishment the term *pioneer* for both men and women was a code word for the Anglo population; no Indians and few Hispanics ever gained admittance during the years before 1940.[16]

In 1914 the state of Arizona attempted to rationalize its public welfare system through the closing of state and county institutions. The proceeds from their sale were to be used to finance a statewide pension law:

> This law proposed to abolish all the almshouses in the State, sell the grounds and buildings, and devote the proceeds towards caring for aged people and people incapable of earning a livelihood, and widows and wives whose husbands are in penal institutions or insane asylums, they being mothers of children who are under the age of sixteen years. . . . each man and woman sixty years of age, resident of the State for five years without visible means of support, was to receive Fifteen Dollars per month. All widows who were mothers of dependent children . . . were entitled to Fifteen Dollars per month, and Six Dollars additional for each child.[17]

This law established a right to a state subsidy for all indigent and elderly people as well as for widows with dependent children. This was supposed to sustain them without the need for institutionalizing their children or themselves at the expense of the state. Its impact was not at all equal to its intent. Counties refused to enforce the law because they did not want to sell their property, and the Arizona State Supreme Court declared the statute unconstitutional in July 1916. Thus the first old-age pension and widowed mothers' law in the United States had almost no impact on the community it was designed to aid.

From 1916 until the passage of national social security legislation in 1939, Arizona continued to rely on county-based welfare for the aged and infirm while the state legislature enacted new guidelines for aid to widows and poor women with dependent children. In 1917 Arizona passed a new widowed mothers' pension law that charged county boards of child welfare to provide stipends for poor women with dependent children in order to keep such youngsters out of foster homes. According to a report by Mary Kidder Rak on the availability of social services in Arizona, published in 1921, just after the enactment of yet more legislation, several county superior court judges did not believe in the law and therefore had refused to authorize the formation of local boards or to release funds for such services. The arbitrary and inconsistent actions of county boards of supervisors were an even more serious problem: "The local Board of Child Welfare may grant aid to suitable women who can meet the . . . requirements 'Provided such allowance be approved by the Board of Supervisors of said county.' Since the supervisors have it in their power to refuse the allowance there might be in the State fourteen policies in regard to mothers, ranging from extreme liberality to niggardliness."[18]

This observation was confirmed in a 1921 report of the state board of child welfare. In March of that year an act supplementing the mothers' pension mandated that the state of Arizona provide $30,000 yearly to support dependent children. It was still the individual county's responsibility to disburse the funds. By the end of the year all fourteen counties had released funds, but in Mohave County this amounted to only one case involving four children, whereas in Cochise County sixty-two children in eighteen cases were aided. According to Rak, stipends could be as much as "twenty dollars for one child, fifteen additional for the second, ten additional for the remaining children, but no family pension may exceed sixty dollars a month."[19] Yet the average amounts granted ranged from $2.91 in Apache County to $13.75 in Greenlee County, with a state average of $8.48. Thus the aid a widowed mother might receive depended entirely upon the county in which she resided, and the sums received were to be used to sustain her children, not herself.

Only ninety-nine children benefited from the widowed mothers' pension in 1921. At least sixty-one of these children had no living father. Of the mothers, fifty-six were widowed, all by law were U.S. citizens who had lived in Arizona for at least one year, and more than one-third were employed but did not make enough money to support their children. The most common occupation listed was that of laundress. One-third of the mothers owned their own homes or other property, but an even larger portion, including some who owned homes, were indebted.[20]

The $30,000 annual subsidy authorized by the Arizona legislature for the care of dependent children did not increase during the 1920s, and by 1930 the report of the state board of child welfare noted that the law was "wide in scope but limited in application; noble in aim but beggardly in its attempted generosity. . . . With $30,000 as the yearly limit many a little waif and orphan must go unmothered and many a child surrounded by criminal influences of all sorts."[21] By that time 373 orphans or dependent children were being cared for with the same amount that had sustained ninety-nine, and once again the number of children and the average subsidy varied drastically from county to county.[22] It is unknown how many children were turned away from this program because of such defects.

Yet the need to increase allocations for dependent children became at once more desperately necessary and more difficult with the onset of the Depression, especially after national publicity led to clamoring for special programs for relief and pensions. Maricopa County had the ability and resources to provide for dependent children, and in 1938, 651 cases were awarded $23,074.10 with a case average of $35.44. Others were less fortunate. Yavapai County, for example, made no mention of child welfare.[23] And, given the direction of state relief during this time period, unless the individual counties mandated otherwise, attention shifted from the widowed mother with dependent children to the elderly widow.

Unlike the counties, individual cities and towns had no specific obligation under state law to supply welfare. Nevertheless, city welfare boards were established at different times for a variety of purposes. With larger populations to deal with, as well as a greater concentration of widows, who tended to live in urban areas with somewhat greater frequency than rural ones, county and private charity were not always sufficient. But only the wealthier communities, or those with private charities such as church groups or benevolent associations, could afford such largess. In the capital city of Phoenix, no board to coordinate and publicly supplement private charity existed until July 18, 1923, when the board of charity was created by public ordinance. Before that time, complaints had been made by a Phoenix public school nurse about the lack of aid for indigents:

> One of the worst problems we have to solve is the old, old fundamental one. What is the use of finding trouble if no remedy can be applied? There . . . is no provision made by County, State or School District to take care of the defects or diseases of indigents. When parents are poor some society, some doctor or some individual must be charitable. . . . 'Twould seem as if, for only mercenary reasons, the State should guard the health of its citizens for 'tis an economic measure in the long run. A municipal medical charity under the supervision of the school should make it a business to provide for the maladies of the needy.[24]

The system of school nurses tending the school-age poor gave way to the Phoenix board of charity, which provided aid to the whole city of Phoenix, young and old. It was run by society women and clergy, who were given an annual appropriation of $15,000 per year from the city as well as other donations from the Community Chest. Even though that amount was one-half the sum supplied to all counties by the state for the widowed mothers' program, it was insufficient for the needs of Phoenix. In a letter to the city manager on June 29, 1928, the board of charity noted that its medical department had cared for 3,882 cases, while the relief department had dealt with 7,383 in the previous five months. The board estimated that such services cost the city $5,825 or an average of "about seventy-eight cents each," mostly for hospitalization of eighty-one persons. "That, however, is only a part of the story: We have cared for all that we could do within our appropriation, but there have been a large number of persons who ought to have been aided, but for whom we could do nothing as we had not more money. Phoenix is growing . . . and we have our responsibility as well as our privileges."[25] The board requested an increased allocation, but it was refused.

By 1936 the city was in the midst of the Depression and even less able to cope with relief measures than earlier. Funds had been increased to more than $40,000 for the board of charity, but its chairman, the Reverend Bertrand Cocks, wanted $60,000 at the least. In another letter, this time to the mayor, he listed services provided as well as those insufficiently funded. He aired his concern over the intrusion of ethnic discrimination in the allocation of funds, a development he believed stemmed from too many complaints about relief offered to transients, particularly Mexicans. Such criticisms, he believed, ignored the fact that these needy people were indeed residents of Phoenix.[26]

Other cities set up committees and organizations to provide aid, but fewer details are known of their activities. In Tucson the Associated Charities was formed after 1908, a group that after 1918 became known as the Organized Charities of Tucson. It was created to care for the poor and needy, most of whom suffered from tuberculosis. In 1919 it provided $9,000 worth of aid. At a similar time in Warren, a suburb of Bisbee, the Warren District Relief Association was organized but in 1918 had only $3,788.89 to spend on all its activities. Among the eighty-two families aided in the Bisbee area, thirty were widowed families and thirty-nine were of Mexican origin. Prescott also had an organized charity group, but no information is available about its accomplishments.[27]

Although Arizona enacted its first but ill-fated old-age pension in 1914, no new legislation addressed the problem of indigent elderly until the passage of a law in 1933. And, given the increased population of Arizona as well as its dwindling resources because of the economic crisis gripping its main industry, copper, the new law, like the widowed mothers' pension plan, was designed to distribute money to the few rather than to all. Modeled after the requirements for entry into the state old-age home, pensioners had to prove thirty-five previous years of Arizona residence with only a five-year absence allowed. Adopting age requirements even more stringent than those for the home, the old-age pension was limited to those over 70 instead of 60.[28] Using a population base of Arizona citizens in 1898 over the age of 35 years, the new law excluded Mexicans who had migrated northward later in search of work in the mines and in agriculture, especially those who had never acquired citizenship. Such requirements tended to exclude many elderly widows who had come to Arizona more recently, as well as those who might have left the state for periods of time yet who still considered Arizona to be their home state. A plaintive letter from one woman was received by Governor Benjamin Moeur in 1934:

> As a pioneer and widow I am appealing to you personally concerning the Pioneer Pension. I know that it is hard to make a law that will fit every person's needs. . . . I came to Arizona in 1880. . . . The cattle business took us out of the State for the best part of eleven years, but DURING THE WHOLE OF THIS PERIOD OUR HOME AND INTERESTS WERE IN ARIZONA. . . .
>
> My appeal to you is as a pioneer, a widow 76 years of age, and always a continual taxpayer in Arizona . . . to my knowledge there are people who get this pension that have lived less years in this state . . . yet receive a pension. . . . They could not even begin to equal the frontier life and homebuilding that others of us can.[29]

Although no answer to this petition remains, it is presumed that this elderly widow was eligible neither for a pension nor for entry into the state old-age home because she had followed her husband as he conducted his cattle business. It may, however, have covered poor women such as the black nurse, 86 years old, crippled and sick, who had been nursing since she was 18. As she put it, "I think I have nursed long enough to take a rest." Based upon records found in Prescott, newspaper articles about the old-age pension, and records of county pension contributions, enough old people qualified to strain both county and state resources to their limits, often causing reductions in other services for the nonelderly ill and needy. There is no way, unfortunately, to determine with accuracy the ethnic and racial composition of recipients and those denied pensions, although advanced age became the most important criterion for acceptance into the old-age home.[30]

After 1935 the U.S. government began to enact old-age pensions through the Social Security Administration, but each state could decide whether or not to accept the plan. Until 1939 Arizona remained outside the system, unable to support its own program, yet unwilling to relinquish control. In

1937 a new old-age law was passed in the state, which lowered the age requirement to 65 and reduced the residency requirements to five years out of the previous nine, but changed the law from a pension to an assistance act, thereby forcing individuals to prove need more rigorously than before.[31] At the same time the state legislature initiated a campaign to return old-age assistance obligations to the counties, many of which could not afford to assume them.[32] By June 1938 the implications of the legislative move became evident when Pima and Yuma counties eliminated aliens from their welfare roles unless they had dependents born in the United States. This brought forth a storm of protest from the Spanish-American Democratic Club.[33] Yet even had the counties chosen to be less exclusionary, they still could not have afforded to provide welfare benefits for all needy residents and thus would have had to find other ways to declare large numbers of people ineligible.

The role of the state, counties, and cities in the provision of aid for widows both young and old in Arizona became critical as families and widows themselves, through misfortune or economic crisis, became less able to provide alternative forms of sustenance. When the history of state aid to these women is coupled with occupational statistics for widows and married women, it becomes clear that by 1940 vulnerable groups of widows and their offspring had increased in Arizona and were in an even more precarious position than during the frontier days of the late nineteenth century. But now the rules had changed and groups that might have found succor in earlier years found themselves automatically excluded. The assumption by the federal government of programs such as aid to dependent children and old-age pensions became the only way that the state of Arizona could live up to the expectations it had established by law.

The Private Sector

The distance between private and public aid was often very small. In addition to state aid to widows and their dependent children, private community and church assistance constituted another way to provide help. Often strong community ties were forged through religion and ethnicity, and these not only helped widows but also created mechanisms by which needy widows could be identified.

The ethnic and racial background of the widow proved to be an important factor in how she coped. Indian, European, native-born, black, and Hispanic widows all faced somewhat distinctive socioeconomic conditions during these years. Some, like rural Hispanic widows in the late nineteenth century, had lived in their communities for extended periods of time and could rely on family for help. Others, like miners' widows of European birth, found themselves in foreign communities without parents and other relatives. Still others, Anglo and Hispanic city dwellers, were also sometimes without deeply rooted family ties. Although it is impossible to generalize about such situations, the evidence suggests that women lacking extended family ties turned to community and church.

The census of 1880, discussed below, provides substantial evidence that Hispanic widows far outnumbered Anglo widows in Tucson and that urbanization and changing conditions there had left many widows both young and old without family assistance. As early as 1872 Hispanic and Anglo women in Tucson had founded a Woman's Association for Mutual Benevolence to help impoverished Hispanic women. The St. Vincent de Paul Society, a Catholic charity group, also worked diligently in Tucson in the 1890s to provide care for many sick and lonely elderly people, including Hispanics. The Alianza Hispano-Americana was founded in Tucson in 1894, originally to combat local discrimination. Its leaders then decided to organize its male members into a mutual aid society to assist widows of members as well. Widows would receive a death benefit twice as large as a widower would obtain. Eventually the society expanded its membership to include women and offered death benefits based upon actuarial statistics. The inexpensive policies provided the Hispanic families critical financial protection in Arizona, Colorado, New Mexico, California, Texas, Wyoming, and Mexico. These policies were very popular in mining communities where Hispanics often had no other form of death benefit insurance.[34]

Small towns as well as large cities could devise community strategies to help widows within specific ethnic or religious groups. Some churches had relief or aid societies specifically for that purpose. Among the most organized was the Mormon church. Its relief societies were run by women to help impoverished members of the community and to assist in burying the dead of any faith. The Relief Society of the St. Joseph Stake, as it was called in Arizona, was established in 1878, and in 1919 it claimed to have 970 volunteer workers. Relief groups would be able to detect the needy through a system of visitation by church members, which helped monitor the feeble and infirm. In addition, the group would also sponsor activities such as an annual old folks' day to honor its elderly.[35]

In the early 1920s Jewish groups in Phoenix and Tucson also offered welfare activities for members of their synagogues. The Council of Jewish

Women of Phoenix was a local branch of a national group committed to religious, philanthropic, and educational goals. Although much smaller than the Mormon organization, it, too, served an important function.[36]

Pensions, especially those derived from work, military service, or mutual aid societies, formed another link between the public and the private sectors. As in Colorado, a number of national organizations had local chapters in Arizona that offered men fraternal sociability and their widows pensions or death benefits. Despite such planning, however, there were many reported cases of widows being cheated out of pensions or compensation, from inadvertent errors made in filing forms to obvious attempts to limit benefits through fraudulent means.[37]

The onset of the Depression in 1929 also caused groups such as these community and religious-based ones to redouble their efforts to help their own. The Mormon church, for example, decried the intrusion of government into what it considered a community responsibility. Its members were determined to keep all Mormons off relief rolls by using their community farms to donate food they would otherwise have consumed. The Catholic church, which often had provided aid to widows and poor people on an informal level through parish churches, also rationalized its charity efforts by creating a Catholic Relief Agency in 1933. And, as in the past, individual efforts to help the needy complemented community projects.[38]

Widows' Personal Resources

Despite all the sources of outside aid for widows in these early years, the most sustained help for widows came from their families and their ability to eke out an existence in their own communities. Thus, the most common way of coping with the economic demands of widowhood was to depend almost entirely on personal resources, no matter how meager. Some widows had private means, some were too old to work, and some got jobs or sent their children out to find work. From this perspective, a widow's resources included many intangibles. The invitation to live with a relative, typically an adult child, might have meant the difference between economic security and homelessness and the need to turn to public authorities. Even young children could help out by working at odd jobs.

Although not all the manuscript censuses for Arizona are available for the period between 1880 and 1940, the early censuses such as the one for 1880 indicate that the present-day U.S. pattern of young widows living with children was common in Arizona, especially among Hispanic families who also took in their elderly parents. Many widows in the state who were living with adult children were listed as "keeping house" while other adult female relatives had no such "occupation."[39] This probably indicated that the widow had assumed the role of housekeeper in exchange for food and lodging. That situation seemed to be less frequent in the 1900 census in which many elderly widows listed themselves as head of the household, but not the housekeeper. One explanation for such a change could have been that the mother owned the house and her children had come to live with her. Sometimes boarders also resided with the family, yet the woman still claimed no gainful occupation. Such an omission often led to distorted statistics about the number of females working in Arizona. Hispanic widows, who along with Indians constituted the largest number of widows in the state before 1900, were rarely found living alone or with groups of nonrelated adults in the countryside, but such patterns could be found in urban areas. In either case, if these women did not hold full-time jobs outside the home, or if they did not consider their part-time work as a basic source of income, their work patterns were ignored.

Cities posed other problems for widows. New groups came in and changed the tempo and customs of the place. This was especially true in Tucson. In 1880, 195 of Tucson's 225 widows were Hispanic. Most resided with members of their families, but some lived with nonrelatives or banded together with other widows and their children to form a household. In contrast, there were fifteen Anglo native-born and two European-born widows in the entire city, as well as fourteen widows of indeterminate national origin. These non-Hispanic women also lived with children and relatives when possible, but some lived alone with no family in town.[40]

Only twenty-three widows lived in Prescott in 1880. Twenty-one were Anglo, either native-born or European, and fifteen of them lived with nonrelatives, often boarders. The other two widows were Hispanic. Significantly, one-quarter of the Anglo widows and one Hispanic woman openly admitted to being prostitutes, while only one Anglo widow in Tucson made such admission. Even more surprising were their ages: only three prostitutes could be considered young, while the rest were in their forties and fifties.[41] The living arrangements of these widowed women in two frontier towns revealed the extent of the safety net provided by relatives, particularly older children, who could sometimes help them financially or offer shelter. Prostitution could be engaged in by widowed and single women if family, public charity, and the demand for female labor left no other choices.[42]

Many widows may have tried to avoid seeking full-time employment by maintaining a marginal existence financed by a scant inheritance, family aid, and performing odd jobs for neighbors. Some were sustained by their own vegetable gardens. Taking in boarders, doing sewing or laundry for others, trading labor for school tuition expenses for children, and other part-time employment have all been reported in accounts about Arizona widows.[43] Often these women had no alternative but to carry on in this fashion, since the dominant economic industries—mining and ranching—did not hire women except as domestic or clerical workers, and agriculture only required part-time harvesters. Furthermore, in the early years few positions existed for schoolteachers and clerks; demand for administrators only developed in the second decade of the twentieth century. After 1900 store clerking was an important job open to all women. Before then it was a position for a family member, as was postmistress.[44] Equally important, by supporting oneself even by odd jobs, the widow could postpone becoming a burden to her family.

In the early years widowhood forced women to make many decisions about their future economic activities. Less cushioned by the prospects of state aid, they tended to rely on themselves and their families. If they decided to work, they often had to create their own employment in activities ancillary to the dominant, male-focused ones, and often their efforts to provide domestic services for bachelor miners, soldiers, and ranchers helped make frontier existence more comfortable for all.

That most Arizona women, like others in nonindustrial regions, widowed or not, performed many part-time tasks makes quantification of their numbers and occupations difficult. Census statistics in the United States and elsewhere are designed to show one full-time occupation of each individual, and the instructions given to national census-takers recognized that women often did not fit into this labor pattern. They were told not to count some part-time occupations, as seen by this excerpt from the 1910 instructions:

> KEEPING BOARDERS—Keeping boarders or lodgers should be returned as an occupation if the person engaged in it relies upon it as his (or her) principal means of support or principal source of income. . . . If, however, a family keeps a few boarders or roomers *merely as a means of supplementing or eking out the earnings or income obtained from other occupations or from other sources, no one in the family should be returned as boarding or lodging house keeper.*[45] (Italics added.)

The invisibility of many forms of part-time employment to census-takers accounted for serious under counting of working women in Arizona and reinforced the stereotype that depicted men but not women contributing their labor to build the West. Yet there is abundant evidence that even part-time labor was constructive and that it often prepared widows for entry into full-time work. Biographies of minority widows demonstrate that some widows could make a successful transition from precarious part-time work to formal employment, but it is difficult to assess whether these experiences were typical.[46]

Despite the dearth of information about part-time labor, some figures provide striking revelations about the role of widowed women in Arizona's female labor force. Published statistics on full-time jobs in Arizona reveal that both widowed and married women were more prominent components of the female labor force than was true elsewhere in the United States where single women predominated (table 1).

Although Arizona reported a smaller percentage of adult women working than the national average, in 1890 widows formed about 32 percent of the female labor force and married women represented about 20 percent. After 1900 married women were proportionately more important than widows. By 1930 married women in Arizona had surpassed widows by claiming more than 40 percent of the jobs while widows represented less than 23 percent.[47]

In the rest of the nation single women traditionally comprised the largest group of working females. The difference between national and local female labor statistics (table 1) meant that Arizona widows initially worked more

Table 1. Female Employment by Marital Status, 1890-1930

Year	Arizona	Mountain States	Nation
1890	19.6 married 32.0 widowed	15.7 married	13.9 married
1900	42.8 married 40.0 widowed	20.8 married	15.4 married
1910	40.2 married	26.1 married	24.7 married
1920	34.9 married	24.6 married	23.0 married
1930	41.4 married 22.7 widowed[a] 35.9 single	34.3 married 22.0 widowed[a] 43.6 single	28.9 married 17.2 widowed[a] 53.9 single

SOURCE: *Fifteenth Census of the United States: 1930, Population,* 4:75-76.
NOTE. All data are given in percentages; women are defined as females over age 15.
[a] Widowed and divorced.

frequently than other women in the area and more than widows did in other parts of the country. Gradually married women replaced widows as the most numerous working women in Arizona, far exceeding their counterparts elsewhere, as had widows in the earlier years. The reason that so few single women were hired in Arizona compared to the rest of the United States was the tendency of Arizona women to marry at an early age, so there were few single women available to work.

Furthermore, as seen in table 2, all Arizona women were hired less frequently than their counterparts in the rest of the United States. Initially there were few establishments looking for female employees in the territorial years. Commercial firms, which tended to offer more employment to women, as did schools and other offices, were established gradually. Similarly, the shortage of qualified teachers and stenographers afforded married women, who had often migrated to Arizona with impressive educational credentials, access to work often restricted to unmarried women in the East and Midwest. Finally, the decline in widowed workers could be explained either by improved material conditions or increased competition from married and single women for employment until 1929. Thereafter, the hardships caused by the Depression, plus the continued decrease in employment for widows, meant that widows were not as well off as before.

In general jobs were scarce for all women in frontier Arizona in 1880, when only 471 females claimed employment and no Indians were counted (table 3). By 1900, when Indians were counted and marital status was more carefully recorded, the occupational niches of widows and ethnic groups became clearer. In that year census-takers noted that 6,788 women over age 10 were employed in Arizona; 40 percent were widowed. Most Indian widows engaged in agricultural pursuits or in the manufacturing of blankets

Table 2. Percentage of Employed Females, Age 10 and Over, 1880-1930

Year	Arizona	Mountain States	Nation
1880	5.4	7.4	14.7
1890	9.6	11.6	17.4
1900	18.3	13.2	18.8
1910	16.8	15.8	23.4
1920	16.4	15.0	21.1
1930	22.2	19.5	24.8

SOURCES: *Thirteenth Census of the United States: 1910,* 4:37; *Fourteenth Census of the United States: 1920,* 4:442; *Fifteenth Census of the United States: 1930, Population,* 4:75.

Table 3. Gainfully Employed Women in Arizona, 1880-1940

Occupation	Year	Total Number	Number of Widows
Total	1880	471	
	1890	1,538	490
	1900	6,876	2,654
	1910	10,589	
	1920	18,386	
	1930	29,653	6,729[a]
	1940	36,931	7,794[a]
Agriculture	1880	12	
	1890	100	
	1900	2,270	686
	1910	816	
	1920	3,282	
	1930	1,666	588[a]
	1940	1,695	634[a]
Manufacture	1880	337	
	1890	591	
	1900	1,329	
	1910	3,233	
	1920	2,215	
	1930	4,197	800[a]
	1940	7,927	1,215[a]
Trade	1880	12	
	1890	76	
	1900	241	28
	1910	501	
	1920	1,516	
	1930	3,305	629[a]
	1940	2,106	664[a]
Professions	1880	39	
	1890	167	
	1900	505	44
	1910	1,208	
	1920	2,976	
	1930	5,571	646[a]
	1940	5,529	852[a]

Table 3. Gainfully Employed Women in Arizona, 1880-1940 (continued)

Occupation	Year	Total Number	Number of Widows
Clerical	1880		
Occupations	1890		
	1900	133	9
	1910		
	1920	2,256	
	1930	4,071	532[a]
	1940	7,927	1,215[a]
Domestic	1880		
Service	1890	951	
	1900	1,780	600
	1910	885	
	1920	5,600	
	1930	10,357	3,403[a]
	1940	10,752	2,712[a]

SOURCES: Census of the United States: *Tenth, 1880,* 1:712-13; *Eleventh, 1890,* 16:cx; *Twelfth, 1900, Special Report on Occupations,* 226; *Thirteenth, 1910,* 4:96-108; *Fourteenth, 1920, Population,* 4:878-79; *Fifteenth, 1930, Population,* 4:74-75, 145-46; *Sixteenth, 1940, Population,* 3, part 2, 120-21.

[a] Includes widowed and divorced.

and baskets. Native-born and foreign-born white women, including Hispanics, held positions primarily in domestic service, professional careers, and such occupations as boardinghouse keepers, teachers, nurses, shopkeepers, and saleswomen. A few black and Indian widows worked as domestics.[48]

An examination of household arrangements and occupations of widows in the cities of Arizona in 1900 offers yet another glimpse of how women coped with the economic pressures of widowhood. The number of widows in Tucson had increased from 225 in 1880 to 315 in 1900, 87 percent of whom were Hispanic. More than 23 percent of all the widows were aged 60 or above, and 67 percent listed themselves as heads of households. More than 10 percent lived alone, although most lived with relatives. In terms of their employment, of the 25 percent who stated occupations, only three claimed to operate a boardinghouse, but twenty-seven others took in boarders, some of whom were widows themselves. When occupations were listed, the most frequent categories were laundress (24), dressmaker (11), cook (7), and servant or housekeeper (7). There were no nurses and only two teachers, indicating that the growth of professional groups among widows proceeded slowly in Tucson. No one declared herself a prostitute, but given the lack of work opportunities for widows, one might assume that prostitution was an occupation for at least some.

Until 1920 Phoenix had a smaller population than Tucson, but offered different opportunities for women's work. In 1900 there were only 192 widows in the capital city. Of these only thirty, or 16 percent, were Hispanic, and 21 percent of the widows were older than 60. Although there were fewer widows in Phoenix, more of them lived as boarders, and fewer lived alone than in Tucson. As in Tucson, many more women took in boarders than claimed it as an occupation.

As a rapidly growing administrative center, Phoenix provided more job opportunities than Tucson. In contrast to the 75 percent unemployment rate for widows there, in Phoenix widows had a rate of only 44 percent. The most common occupation was that of housekeeper (27), followed by that of dressmaker (19). There were also eight widowed nurses, five teachers, and two clerks, occupations not found among Tucson's widows.[49]

In 1900 Bisbee also revealed how women's work, including that of widows, was conditioned by economic and demographic forces. Of the eighty-six widows in a town with large numbers of foreign-born women, many engaged in economic activities that complemented the mining industry and in that way sustained their families. One-tenth of all the widows operated boardinghouses as a full-time occupation, making it the most common job for widows. Since there was an extreme housing shortage, anyone with a home could make money catering to miners. Still others had jobs such as laundresses (10) and nurses (7) and thereby reaffirmed the relationship of widows' work to mining.[50]

During the first two decades of the twentieth century, alterations in the composition of the female work force also reflected changes in the economy and society of Arizona. Possibilities for urban employment were more numerous, and professional opportunities developed in teaching, nursing, and public service. In contrast, whereas one-third of the female labor force had been employed in the agricultural sector in 1900, only 18 percent worked at rural pursuits in 1920.[51] Urbanization, immigration of new groups into the state, and the emergence of new agricultural crops and techniques generated the shift in female occupations away from steady work. New groups diluted the earlier prominence of Indian women as rural female workers, and they lived in the countryside with less frequency and tended to work at part-time harvesting rather than operate farms themselves.[52]

No discussion of changing patterns of women's work in Arizona, particularly that of widows, would be complete without considering age. Access to formal education and training, particularly after 1900, might have been greater for older women, who brought such skills with them, than for younger women growing up in a frontier area. Yet this advantage would disappear rapidly as Arizona established a state university in Tucson and a normal school in Tempe. Commercial schools were also established. Gradually younger women had the advantage of the new education in clerical skills, and they filled the ranks of stenographers, typists, and clerks. Nevertheless older women, including widows, figured significantly in the few administrative positions available in teaching and state bureaucracy, especially after 1920. For other older widows, work continued, but usually in less sophisticated employment.

Agricultural workers, especially Indian women, worked into old age without much change, in accordance with longstanding traditions. Women still wove blankets and baskets and as a matter of course planted crops or tended animals. This can be seen in the breakdown of female occupation by age. In 1920, for example, of 332 women, mostly Indian, over 65 who still worked, 28.6 percent tended farms or livestock, and 27 percent, again mostly Indian, worked at what was called manufacturing—mostly weaving textiles. In contrast only ten women, mostly Anglo, still taught school, but 33.4 percent of the elderly women of all races worked at service occupations, principally as domestics. For a few (23) operating boardinghouses meant the possibility of perhaps delegating work to others, but for most elderly women who had to work, a job meant menial drudgery.[53]

Within a decade the number of elderly female workers had increased to 664, but the proportion of agricultural laborers had decreased to 15.5 percent, while 26.2 percent still manufactured textiles. The number of elderly professional women had increased to sixty-six (10 percent), as did sales clerks and real estate agents (6.5 percent). The greatest increase came in the number of older women in domestic and personal service (40.8 percent). In Arizona as elsewhere older women lagged behind the younger workers in seeking new types of employment.[54]

Widows and the Depression

When the work of elderly women was categorized by race and ethnicity, other interesting data emerge from the 1930 census. The small proportion (2-5 percent) of black female workers among women workers in Arizona reflects the low number of blacks in the population. Nevertheless, in 1910,

50.3 percent of all black Arizona women claimed employment, but in 1930 only 39.8 percent still made the same assertion. Even though black women worked more frequently than women of other races in the state, examinations of city directories reveal that most labored as domestic servants, while a few were schoolteachers. Among the elderly, however, few black women over 65 worked—2.1 percent—while foreign-born elderly women, principally Hispanic, had the highest employment rate—6 percent of employed Mexican women were over age 60.[55]

Analyses of 1930 employment statistics by marital status show widows in similar occupations to elderly women. Of 6,729 widowed or divorced women, 588 or 8.7 percent worked in agriculture, whereas only 5.6 percent of the total female labor force engaged in this activity. Similarly, 3,403 widows (50.6 percent), worked in domestic service, compared to the 34.9 percent of the total female labor force that claimed such employment. In contrast, widows were underrepresented in the professional, commerical, and clerical categories.[56]

The 1930 census was taken at the outset of the Great Depression. By the time the crisis was fully affecting Arizona, the private ways in which widows had coped with the economic realities of their lives began to fail, and more and more turned to public assistance. Most did not want to: in the correspondence files of the state old-age home, for example, one finds women applying for a room only to withdraw the application or leave the home when they thought they could survive outside. Others relied on family and friends until they became too much of a burden. By the time relatives petitioned for help, many elderly women were unaware of how much of a burden they had become. No letters were found in a foreign language, indicating that such petitions, at least to state officials, were most frequently written by native-born English-speaking people or those who had learned the language.[57] As long as women could help themselves or be helped by family, they chose to do so. Usually the loss of jobs, the cancellation or nonpayment of pensions, or the onset of illness or incapacity finally caused them to apply for child relief, old-age pension, or admission to an old-age home.

Until the federal government assumed most of the burden of public welfare, married women and widows had limited prospects for outside aid. Academics and politicians promoted the idea that married women should relinquish jobs to unemployed men, while women widowed at this time found that family savings for such eventualities had disappeared with bank closings and property foreclosures. The proportion of widows in the Arizona work force declined from almost 23 to 21 percent between 1930 and 1940. The decline in the mainstay of the economy—mining—was partly to blame. During these years its work force decreased from 18,900 to 10,400. Thousands of agricultural laborers in the Salt River Valley found themselves in the same predicament, and thus Phoenix was filled with the unemployed. The loss of jobs compounded the economic woes of women as fewer men could support families, purchase goods, or contract for services. This caused other businesses to fail and unemployment to soar.[58] Almost 50 percent of the boardinghouses closed, and in 1940 there were one-third fewer housekeepers than in 1930. Similar or greater job losses for widows occurred among laundresses, servants, or untrained nurses.[59] Among experienced workers seeking employment in 1940 were 2,634 women. Of these 1,000 sought work in domestic services, 514 in wholesale and retail trade (mostly as waitresses and clerks), 229 in professional jobs, and 300 in agriculture.[60] All areas of the economy that employed women had been affected.

The situation for Mexican aliens was particularly difficult. Many found that their lack of citizenship papers and knowledge of English were obstacles to public assistance, even though they had lived in Arizona for years. The collapse of commercial agriculture had led to high unemployment for Mexican farm workers and public criticism about the provision of relief for them. At the same time a national campaign had begun to encourage the repatriation of Mexicans to their homeland, mostly on a voluntary basis. In Arizona 18,520 Mexicans were repatriated between 1930 and 1932.[61] It is not known how many women were part of this migration, but since many left as family groups, married women and widows were probably included. In this way some Mexican women had the additional worry of following their families back home, while others saw friends and relatives depart.

Conclusions

From its beginning, the widow has participated in the development of Arizona, and the state recognized her rights to property in some of its first laws. For financial assistance, widows with young children and indigent or ill widows had some access to help through county facilities and state institutions, but the disbursement of such privileges was increasingly arbitrary, capricious, and discriminatory. When children were involved, the help was for them rather than the mother. State aid was for its pioneers—a code word for Anglo. Thus aliens were excluded from many state facilities, and counties adopted this tactic as well. Black residents encountered similar obstacles. For those who did not receive help from the state, towns, cities, and religious groups partially filled the gaps, but it was evident long before 1929 that such efforts were inadequate.

During the early years, widows often had the potential to create their own sources of employment and thereby fend for themselves. The opportunities existed because the economy was expanding and in need of services. Gradually widows lost this early advantage due to competition from other women, especially younger married women or single females whose training and skills were even more valuable than those of older widows. By 1940, after a decade of economic contraction and disappearance of earlier opportunities for self-employment, neither widows nor their families could rely on the demand for full-time labor to sustain themselves. After 1935 even the frontier closed, as homesteading was no longer permitted.[62] Prostitution, a final resort for poor women, was also restricted. In 1938 Tucson prostitutes were mugged by the police, and female vagrants were rounded up to prevent crime.[63]

From this perspective it appears that the position of the widow, especially if she were Hispanic, black, or elderly, had deteriorated considerably from the early years. By 1930 both public and private solutions to her dilemmas had been narrowed by the economic conditions, changing demands for female labor, and different attitudes toward the allocation of public assistance. The widow had become much more a victim than a participant in the state's history and development.

Forced by necessity to make the best of private resources, widows in Arizona showed similar coping strategies, regardless of race or ethnicity. In rural areas families continued to be the main source of support, offering companionship and shared material resources. In urban areas, however, families were not always available or capable of taking in relatives. Under such circumstances, Anglo, black, and Hispanic widows lived with strangers or took in boarders.

The age of the widow often had an impact on the ability of family and friends to offer assistance. Young widows with children offered the prospect of additional income-earners who could supplement group income. Elderly widows, in contrast, often only had their wealth in the form of real estate or inheritance capital to contribute, and the possibility of physical or mental infirmity meant that they might become burdens to those who took them in.

The changing nature of women's work in Arizona paralleled the growth and diversification of the state economy and social structure. Even non-working women, including widows, could not have remained unaffected by the state's rapid population growth unless they remained in isolated rural communities. Consequently aid emanating from state, local, and religious institutions became inextricably related to the fate of vulnerable individuals such as widows. Under these circumstances, the increased population of Arizona made it imperative to assure adequate and equitable distribution of aid to such individuals. Without adequate funds and assurances of fairness, states like Arizona were simply unable to fulfill social welfare commitments at a time when families could not sustain the burden by themselves.

NOTES

I thank C. Niethammer, G. Hearn, J. Garcia, S. Deeds, A. Scadron, E. Countryman, and K. Anderson for comments on earlier drafts and G. Hearn, D. Larson, and C. Dargel for their research skills.

1. Odie B. Faulk, *Arizona: A Short History* (Norman: University of Oklahoma Press, 1970), part 2.
2. M. Margaret Shaw, "The Homestead Women," *Arizona, the New State Magazine* (Feb. 1912), transcribed in Louise M. Mulligan, "Pioneer Women of Arizona," 1937 ms., Special Collections, University of Arizona, Tucson.
3. U.S. Bureau of the Census, *Sixteenth Census of the United States: 1940, Population,* vol. 3, part 1, p. 149.
4. U.S. Bureau of the Census, *Fourteenth Census of the United States: 1920, Population,* vol. 2, 398; *Fifteenth Census of the United States: 1930, Population,* vol. 3, part 1, 149.
5. See Arlene Scadron, "Letting Go: Bereavement among Selected Southwestern Anglo Widows," 243-70 herein, for a discussion of grieving.
6. U.S. Bureau of the Census, *Thirteenth Census of the United States: 1910,* Abstract with Supplement for Arizona, 568; *Sixteenth Census, 1940, Population,* vol. 2, part 1, 381; Arizona WPA Writers' Program, *Arizona: A State Guide* (New York: Hastings House, 1940), 174-75.
7. Faulk, *Arizona,* 41-46, 112; *Thirteenth Census: 1910; Sixteenth Census: 1940, Population,* vol. 2, part 1, 382.
8. Billy M. Jones, *Health Seekers of the Southwest, 1817-1900* (Norman: University of Oklahoma Press, 1967), 120; Joyce D. Goodfriend, "The Struggle for Survival: Widows in Denver, 1880-1912," 167; *Tucson* 1 (Nov. 1928):15.
9. Faulk, *Arizona,* 127-68; *Thirteenth Census: 1910; Sixteenth Census: 1940.*
10. Faulk, *Arizona,* 121-22; *Thirteenth Census: 1910; Sixteenth Census, 1940, Population,* vol. 2, part 1, 381.

11. The specific parts of the Howell Code can be found in Bashford Coles, comp., *The Compiled Laws of the Territory of Arizona, including the Howell Code and the Session Laws from 1864 to 1871, Inclusive* (Albany, N.Y.: Weed Parsons, 1871), ch. 32, sec. 11, 307; ch. 33, sec. 4, 312; and ch. 37, sec. 1, 9, 340-41.

12. This aspect of statehood is ignored in Faulk, *Arizona;* see Sandra L. Myres, *Westering Women and the Frontier Experience, 1800-1915* (Albuquerque: University of New Mexico Press, 1982), 213, and for a general discussion of western suffrage see the entire chapter therein.

13. See the example of Helen Ivancovich in Scadron, "Letting Go," 253-54.

14. Dr. P. B. Purcell to M. Samaniego, Jan. 15, 1898, Pima County, Territorial Records 1864-1923, AZ 83, vol. 19, 1898 Letters, Special Collections, University of Arizona.

15. Examples of health care bids can be found for St. Mary's Hospital, Tucson, where acceptable bids declined from $20 per month or $1.25 per day in 1888 to $18 per month or $1.15 per day, including medical and surgical attendance. AZ 83, vol. 17, 1888 Letters, and vol. 19, 1902 Letters, Special Collections, University of Arizona.

16. See State of Arizona, *Annual Reports of the Commission of State Institutions* (Phoenix, 1917-18).

17. Arizona State Child Welfare Board, *First Annual Report* (Phoenix, 1922), 5.

18. Mary Kidder Rak, *A Social Survey of Arizona* (Tucson: N.p., 1921), 38. The author was a noted writer and rancher.

19. Ibid.

20. Arizona State Child Welfare Board, *First Annual Report,* 10-12.

21. Arizona State Child Welfare Board, *A Report of the Activities of the State Child Welfare Board* (Phoenix, 1930), 3.

22. Ibid., 6.

23. Maricopa County Welfare Board, State Audit No. 1, Dec. 1936 to Oct. 17, 1938, TA 9791 FA 912A, Box 2, Special Collections, University of Arizona. Yavapai County records can also be found there.

24. Arizona State Board of Health, *Bulletin* 10 (Oct. 1922):14.

25. Letter dated June 28, 1928, Phoenix Board of Public Charities, Arizona State Archives, Phoenix.

26. Letter dated Sept. 17, 1936, Phoenix Board of Public Charities.

27. Rak, *Social Survey,* 54-57.

28. Governors' Files, Pioneers Home Admission Requirements, Section 2941, R.C.A., 1928, Microdex 17.5.2, Arizona State Archives, hereafter cited as Governors' Files.

29. To Governor Moeur, Aug. 15, 1934, Governors' Files.

30. Letter dated Feb. 17, 1933, Governors' Files. The number of years in residence

is illegible. The number of female applicants to the Pioneer Home as well as pensions increased greatly in the 1930s. As the governor wrote on March 23, 1931, "There are 115 applications waiting to be passed on, among which there is quite a representation of women, so we will be forced to admit those according to the gross need of the applicant. In this connection age will be almost the controlling factor." Governors' Files.

31. *Arizona Daily Star,* June 4, 1937, 6.

32. Ibid., Aug. 5, 1937, 1. This move had been initiated by the State Board of Social Security and Public Welfare; ibid., Mar. 17, 1937.

33. The action was taken by individual counties; ibid., Jan. 6, 1938, 16.

34. Alburn Martin Gustafson, ed., *John Springer's Arizona* (Tucson: University of Arizona Press, 1966), 268; St. Vincent de Paul Society to Pima County Board of Supervisors, Mar. 1, 1894, lists names of indigents under the care of the society. See Pima County, AZ 83, Vol. 18, 1894 Letters. For information on the Alianza, see Kaye Lynn Briegel, "Alianza Hispano-Americana, 1894-1965: A Mexican-American Fraternal Insurance Society" Ph.D. diss., University of Southern California, 1974), 41-82; Alianza Hispano-Americana, *Estatutos de la Sociedad Hispano-Americana de Tucson, Arizona, Aprobados el 18 de Febrero de 1894 y Reformados el 10 de Marzo 1895* (Tucson: N.p., 1913), 1-5.

35. WPA Federal Writers' Project, Arizona: Harry L. Payne, "Annual Old Folks Day," Biographical Sketches, Box 5, Arizona State Archives; Rak, *Social Survey,* 57.

36. Rak, *Social Survey,* 57.

37. Goodfriend, "Struggle for Survival"; an example of pension collection problems can be seen in *Arizona Daily Star,* Mar. 10, 1937, 2.

38. "Catholic Community Services of Southern Arizona, Friends for Fifty Years, 1933-1983," ibid., Jan. 24, 1983.

39. Technically, keeping house was not a designated occupation. For information on family structure, see Mark Friedberger and Janice Rieff Webster, "Social Structure and State and Local History," *Western Historical Quarterly* 9 (1978):297-314.

40. *1880 Census Population Schedules,* Rolls 36-37, microfilm copy no. T9, National Archives and Records Service, Washington, D.C.

41. Ibid.

42. Ibid.

43. Guy Weech, ed., *Pioneer Town: Pima Centennial History* (Pima: Eastern Arizona Museum and Historical Society of Graham County, 1979), 104-33, 155-71; Robert C. Stevens, ed., *Echoes of the Past: Tales of the Old Yavapai,* 2 (Prescott: Yavapai Cowbelles, 1964), 210-22, 228-32.

44. This observation is based upon the interview with Mary Price, Tucson, Oct. 13, 1981, as well as information based upon city directories in Arizona.

45. *Thirteenth Census: 1910,* 4:88.

46. File W948d, Arizona Heritage Society, Tucson; clipping file, *Arizona Daily Star*, June 9, 1974; *Phoenix Gazette*, June 1, 1976.

47. *Fifteenth Census: 1930, Population*, 4:75-76.

48. U.S. Bureau of the Census, *Tenth Census: 1880*, 1:712-13; *Twelfth Census: 1900, Special Report on Occupations*, 225.

49. 1900 Population Schedules, Rolls 1-4, microcopy 4668, National Archives and Records Service.

50. Ibid.

51. See table 3.

52. Joan M. Jensen and Darlis A. Miller, "The Gentle Tamers Revisited: New Approaches to the History of Women in the American West," *Pacific Historical Review* 49 (1980):209.

53. *Fourteenth Census: 1920, Population*, 4:878-79. For the accomplishments of widowed educators and administrators after 1920, see Gertrude Bryan Leeper and Maud Morris House, *Who's Who in Arizona Business, Professions and Arts. Authentic Biographies of Distinguished Men and Women of Arizona*, vol. 1, 1938-40 (Phoenix: Arizona Survey Publishing, 1938).

54. *Fifteenth Census: 1930, Population*, 4:143; W. Andrew Achenbaum, *Old Age in the New Land: The American Experience since 1790* (Baltimore: Johns Hopkins University Press, 1978), 66-67.

55. *Thirteenth Census: 1910*, 4:67; *Fifteenth Census: 1930, Population*, 4:78, 140.

56. *Fifteenth Census: 1930, Population*, 4:145.

57. These conclusions are based upon an examination of all extant correspondence in the Arizona State Archives regarding the old-age home and pension system. Governors' Files.

58. Nat de Gennaro, ed., *Arizona Statistical Abstract: A 1979 Data Handbook* (Flagstaff: Northland Press, 1979), 357; Abraham Hoffman, *Unwanted Mexican-Americans in the Great Depression: Repatriation Pressures, 1929-1939* (Tucson: University of Arizona Press, 1974), 122-23.

59. *Sixteenth Census: 1940, Population*, vol. 8, part 2, 121.

60. Ibid., vol. 3, part 2, 130.

61. Hoffman, *Unwanted Mexican-Americans*, 122-23.

62. *Arizona Daily Star*, Oct. 11, 1935, 4.

63. Ibid., May 13, 1938. See also ibid., July 1, 1939, 2.

9

A Successful Search for Security: Arizona Pioneer Society Widows

DEBORAH J. BALDWIN

Widowhood is an experience shared by women of varied backgrounds who cope with their changed families in a multitude of ways. The family's cultural heritage, social status, and economic position largely determine the security and well-being of the widow. In this essay I explain how the widows of the Arizona Pioneer Society successfully secured an economically comfortable widowhood through familial involvement in multiple businesses, investment in urban property, provisions for clear inheritance, and the creation of kinship arrangements often based on Hispanic traditions.

The Arizona Pioneer Society (APS) was primarily composed of middle-class families in the Tucson area headed by American males of European descent who married Mexican-American women. Despite its homogeneous appearance in this respect, the APS did not formally exclude ethnic or socioeconomic groups. It only required that individuals (males before 1915) were to have lived in Arizona fourteen years before the creation of the society in 1884. This provision allowed me to focus my research on a settled population that was intimately involved in the region's development. In addition, the APS espoused an interest in the support of widows and orphans, although its records indicate little direct assistance was given or requested through a fund established for this purpose. Why the widows' and orphans' fund was not extensively used is explored in later sections of this essay. Further, Hispanic traditions and kindred networks insulated many Arizona widows before 1930 from the isolation and hardship reported in other areas of the country. The economic strategies and landholding choices of families greatly determined the possibility for continual income after the husband's death.

Probate records provide the bulk of the data for the description and analysis of the APS. The husbands' records—financial statements, personal and real property listings, and wills that inventory the material accumulation of the family—re-create the financial predicament of women on the eve of widowhood. Widows' probate records contain the same material and yield an understanding of how well, materially, widows lived until their deaths. These data were organized and coded into forty-two separate variables describing the Pioneers and their wives. These were entered onto a computer file to generate the statistics presented herein. Probate records made the computerized method particularly useful, since numerous discrete facts were incorporated into the lengthy probate files. The other major document collections analyzed and coded were APS records, census records, city directories, the Carl Hayden papers and the Ben Sacks collection, the latter two at Arizona State University, Tempe, as well as many Arizona newspapers.

Few states in the United States display a greater variety of terrain than does Arizona. The landforms vary from broad, flat valleys and mesas to rugged mountains. The climate is arid and the temperature range dramatic. Nowhere in Arizona is rainfall the minimum necessary for nonirrigated farming, and severe droughts are not uncommon, although irrigation facilitates a long growing season.

The potential for farming, however, did not stimulate the original interest of easterners in Arizona. Engineering expeditions following the United States–Mexican War of 1846 explored the area of western New Mexico (later Arizona) and stimulated an interest in this territory as a railroad route to California. The next twenty years saw innumerable railroad schemes designed to capture the market created by the newly completed wagon road and southern mail routes.

The first American pioneers of European heritage who moved into southern Arizona aligned themselves with the Mexican settlements at Tucson and Tubac, using them as staging points from which to trade with the thirteen army forts that had been established in the region by 1869. Indian conflicts forced the populations to concentrate into defendable locations, like Tucson, and isolated one settlement from another until 1874 when Indian wars lessened. The 1864 census reported 4,187 white persons living in Arizona; the clear majority were Mexican-Americans from Sonora.[1]

Arizona remained remote and underpopulated until its mineral wealth was widely publicized. The discoveries of copper and silver generated the founding of mining towns like Tombstone in the decade of the 1870s. Amid the flurry of mining growth and its accompanying developments came the organization of a territorial government and the creation of the Arizona Pioneer Society. Pioneer Society members C. R. Tully, Soloman Warner, Estevan Ochoa, and C. H. Lord established freight lines and general stores. Hiram Stevens, Samuel Hughes, and M. G. Samaniego were successful miners, ranchers, and merchants. Aaron Zeckendorf, the Goldwaters, Goldbergs, and Goldbawms invested in commercial ventures. These men and their families were among the economic and political organizers of the territory, and they established the APS to preserve this heritage. Over half of the society's members held public office, and it eventually boasted three governors, eight mayors, and twenty-two legislators at various times before 1904.[2]

These political leaders were also strategically positioned to take advantage of the economic benefits generated by developments in mining and later the railroad. People like A. P. K. Safford, governor in 1869 and a Pioneer, opened several mining operations and a banking firm after the railroad began to operate.[3] By 1890 the Arizona territory had 1,000 miles of railroad, 700 miles of canals, and cattle, wool, timber, copper, and silver industries all connected to the world market. In 1912, when Arizona attained statehood, it may have been perceived by easterners as the "wild west," but its social and political institutions, of which APS was an example, were well established.

The APS was incorporated on March 5, 1884, after an initial meeting on January 31, 1884. Qualifications for membership specified that propsective members "must have arrived in Arizona before January 1, 1870, or have been on their way here before that date, and [included] all male offspring of such men."[4] Several hundred people attended the first meeting, and by December 1884 the society counted 108 members. Consideration of women members received attention with the first meeting, but resulted in their exclusion. It was suggested, however, that women create their own society. According to one newspaper account this idea was not popular: "It appears that no ladies responded to the invitation to meet . . . and organize a branch of female pioneers. As one of the sex laughingly remarked . . . the colonel [Poston] must confess he lacks a thorough appreciation of a women's character. Do you think . . . that any daughter of Eve wishes to be considered a pioneer?"[5]

Women were eventually organized into a women's auxiliary in 1902. The purpose of this group was "to aid the pioneers in making memorable the annual election . . . by some pleasantry."[6] Membership in the auxiliary was restricted to persons connected by law to a pioneer. Eighty-one women signed the membership books in 1902. This remained the only direct role for women until 1915 when membership in the APS became possible. A woman first served as president of the APS in 1937, and in 1947 the Arizona legislature removed the term "male" from membership requirements.

Prior to the 1930s women played a relatively passive role in the society. Even still, as a fraternal order the APS was potentially important for women, since it provided certain safeguards for members and their families. Burials, announcements of death, preservation of family records, and protection for widows and orphans were among the benefits of membership.

In 1885 the APS passed a motion to allow 20 percent of the treasury and 20 percent of all funds thereafter received to be set apart and designated the widows' and orphans' fund.[7] The fund began with $75 but had increased to $325 in 1888 when Mrs. Oury, widow of deceased APS president Granville Oury, requested a pension. In 1891 the APS decided to invest the fund with bidders offering the highest interest. During the years before 1930 the society made one-time grants to widows and sustained several on-going pensions from $5 to $25 per month.[8]

Despite its availability, the widows' and orphans' fund was used infrequently by the Society's members. Requests for funds were few relative to the number of eligible women. Instead, the money was used to pay medical expenses of pioneers and operating expenses of the APS. Even through the Depression years, the widows' and orphans' fund maintained a modest balance.

The APS was created to preserve the local history of its members, to secure decent burials for pioneers, and to provide for widows and orphans. Because of this preoccupation with life after death, the APS carefully collected information on the families of Arizona pioneers. Much of the information in the following section helps to characterize the APS widows and their familial arrangements and to explain the paucity of demands on the widows' and orphans' fund.

The APS membership lists recorded the names of 195 men (and a few male children) before 1904, the year in which the Arizona legislature proclaimed the organization the Arizona Historical Society. The majority of these men and their families lived in the Tucson area, although a number of them had ranches or businesses in Nogales and Tombstone, and several had moved to Phoenix when it became a county seat in 1871. APS members and their wives comprised about 1 percent of the total Tucson population of 1870, but as high as possibly 20 percent of the adult population.[9] More important, they represented a stable population base for the city's development during a period of significant population shifts in the West.

The composition of the APS was primarily Anglo rather than from the old Tucson Mexican families. Ninety-six percent of the pioneers were Americans of European descent. A quarter of these men were, in fact, born in Europe, and the remainder were born in the eastern United States. Fewer than 10 percent were Mexican-Americans.[10] Pioneer wives, however, were often of Mexican descent (50 percent), and it was they who brought the two cultures together.

In addition to representing both major ethnic groups in Tucson, the individual lives of pioneers and their wives spanned enough time—1804 through 1964—to illustrate various changes in this society. Despite the fact that 75 percent of the Pioneers had died, at an average age of sixty-seven, by the time of statehood in 1912, 57 percent of their widows survived to see statehood and slightly more than 25 percent lived through the Depression.

In 1870 the population of the West consisted of 384,898 men over the age of 21 and 172,145 women, a ratio of approximately 2:1. In Arizona, however, the ratio of men to women was nearly 4:1.[11] Thus, the possibility of marriage for many Arizona men was not a foregone conclusion; yet nearly 75 percent of the Pioneers married. The majority married only once, but at least 14 percent married twice, and a few third marriages have been detected. Why such a large proportion of the Pioneers married may never be definitively learned, but the character of this population may have been decisive. They were a stable, legalistic, and generally ambitious group interested in the preservation of these qualities. These same characteristics would dictate, in part, the positions their wives would retain in society after their husbands' deaths.

In their first marriages Pioneers married women with a mean age of 22. The mean marriage age of their second wives was 27. These figures vary slightly over time, so that marriage at 19 was common before 1870 for first marriages, and marriages of women in their mid-twenties were most common after that date. The marriage age for women did not tend to be particularly young despite the relative shortage of women. In fact, the figure of 22 years for first marriages is similar to findings elsewhere in the West.[12] It appears, from the data gathered, that the child-bride of the West is more myth than reality in certain regions.

Large families also seem to be a false stereotype for APS members, although large numbers of children were encountered (the largest number being fifteen). But overall, large families were not the norm. The average number of children for APS families was four, although the mode was two, and ten couples were known to have had no children. Over time the mean figure for children decreased further, from 5.5 before 1860 to 3.6 after 1900. This decline may be indicative of the increasingly urban character of the Tucson area. The number of children per family is an especially valuable variable when studying widows, since minor children are a heavy responsibility for the widow, and adult children can relieve some of the burdens of widowhood. Unfortunately, information on the age of children at the death of their father is very difficult to ascertain.

Exactly 50 percent of the known Pioneer first marriages resulted in widowhood and 78 percent of the second marriages ended in widowhood. Too little information on third wives was available to be statistically important. The widowhood of Arizona women was generally quite long, which probably greatly affected its quality. Women of first APS marriages were widowed at a mean age of 55 and remained widowed for an average of 23 years. Women of second APS marriages were widowed at a younger age—49—and remained widows somewhat longer, twenty-five years. Arizona widows represented 10.5 to 12 percent of the female population during the period 1900 to 1930. Widowers, on the other hand, made up 4 to 5 percent of the population during the same period.[13]

The issue of remarriage is always relevant for research on widows because remarriage indicates, theoretically, a return to a secure environment for the women. In past decades the prevailing literature indicated that remarriage was frequent and speedy for both sexes. Recent research questions this remarriage pattern, particularly for women.[14] Information on remarriage is especially difficult to detect in American culture because of the subsequent name change with a second marriage, but marriage records in Arizona, organized by male and female names, were examined for the entire period of this study. Only one Pioneer woman was found to have formally remarried in Arizona, although two others are known to have remarried in another state. This evidence appears to reaffirm recent research, but the evidence is inadequate. Women could have engaged in informal wedding ceremonies that were not registered with the county, or they could have remarried outside of the counties studied. More research on remarriage must be conducted before definite conclusions can be drawn on its frequency and consequences.

The kind of economic support available to widows was generally determined by several key factors: the type of occupation of the major family supporter, the amount of family savings, debts, insurance, or old-age benefits, the type of property owned, and the availability of female employment. In this section, all variables except the last are discussed.[15]

In frontier Arizona, wealth rarely appears to have been connected with specialization, but with diversification. Several Pioneers were engaged in four or more occupations and nearly 30 percent participated in at least two occupations. Mining was the most frequently noted occupation, reflecting the original interest of easterners in the territory. Slightly fewer Pioneers were engaged in either agriculture, transportation, or trade (16.7 percent each). Twelve percent were professionals (e.g., doctors or lawyers), and several were employed in, or owned, service-oriented businesses such as hotels or bathhouses.[16] The wealthiest families and those who left the largest estates to widows were Pioneers who engaged in multiple businesses. The most profitable combinations tended to be either mining and transportation or trade and transportation. Some financially successful individuals won lucrative government contracts to provide transportation to support forts in the territory. This stable source of income for the ambitious few also provided opportunities to bring in goods for their own retail stores or to haul out minerals. The public contracts and private businesses, therefore, worked hand in hand. It was not unusual to find the wealthiest families engaged in all three of these endeavors while also owning a considerable amount of urban and rural property.

There were those few like Anthony Hubbard who found the million-dollar mine.[17] Most gains were more modest, however. Samuel and Jennie Drachman represent one economically successful couple. They were either partners or individual owners of several retail stores in Tucson and owners of other rural and urban property. Atanacia and Samuel Hughes were also involved in trade and government contract businesses in and around Tucson. The estates of both men were worth $15,000 when they died, Drachman in 1911 and Hughes in 1917.[18] Although the estates appear to be equal in value, when the cash value of each is adjusted using 1970 constant dollars the Drachman estate was worth approximately 38 percent more, $62,292, compared to $45,427 for the Hughes estate.[19] Patrick and Pauline Holland's businesses were more diversified than the Drachman or Hughes enterprises. The Hollands were involved in mining, transportation, and ranching. The cash value of this estate was $24,000 in 1888 ($103,359 in 1970 constant dollars); the larger value of this estate reflected the Hollands' more complex economic activity. The important question about these various familial economic activities is the extent to which they benefited the widow. Can we differentiate among activities that helped widows only at the time of the spouses' death and those that had more long-term effects? Were these estate values sufficient for long-term support? Were women sufficiently skilled in managing these estates to support their families?

Probate records for APS members indicate a median Pioneer estate with a cash value of $19,300 in 1970 constant dollars. However, three men had estates over $100,000 (current dollars) and nine others had estates under $1,000 (current dollars). The current-dollar median estate was $4,500.[20] The debts on these estates were relatively few; most resulted from legal fees or taxes. Only when a retail business was appraised with the estate were debts high, but then assets were also high, thus balancing the impression of indebtedness.

The cash value of Pioneer estates did not increase at a constant rate throughout the 1870-1930 period. Instead, when Pioneer estate values are aggregated by decade, their fluctuations appear to follow national trends. By 1889 the median estate value was already $3,850 dollars or $16,580 in constant dollars. Pioneer financial success reflected the development of the region by that date with copper and silver discoveries, the advent of the railroad, and an end to Indian wars. The 1890s, however, saw the median estate value dip to $1,900 or $8,191 in constant dollars. This downward movement can be partially explained by the panic of 1893, which had a severe impact on Arizona. This already difficult economic period was aggravated by the silver campaign of 1896 and subsequent depression. The downward trend reversed from 1900 to 1910, and the median estate value reached $7,700 or $35,424 constant dollars. This upward trend followed a general worldwide movement, due in part to an outpouring of gold and improvements in mining techniques.[21]

Although it is difficult to gauge the practical worth of these Pioneer estates, some relevant comparisons can be made, based on early records of consumer income and expenses. For example, the census reports that the average net income to farmers from agricultural activities in 1910 was $650 per farm (current dollars). During the entire decade of the 1910s the ten-year average of net income was $850 per farm.[22] Therefore, the median Pioneer estate of $4,500 (current dollars) could translate into more than five years of average farm income. Most APS widows lived longer than five years beyond the death of their spouse; therefore, to continue this level of income, widows had to manage and invest their inheritances.

In the cities, housing prices and the cost of consumer goods are probably a more relevant comparison. Although no direct records of the median price of housing are available for the West, estimates can be drawn from other regions. For example, according to census data the median asking price for existing housing in Washington, D.C., in 1920 was $6,296 (single-family housing).[23] The relevant ratio of per capita income in 1920 for the Washington region (mid-Atlantic states) to the Arizona region (mountain states) was 1.34:1 (the earliest year for which records are available).[24] Therefore, a first estimate for housing prices in Arizona cities like Tucson in 1920 was approximately $4,700 (current dollars), which approximately equals the average APS estate.

Retail prices for common food items in U.S. cities increased only moderately from 1890 to 1905, according to the Bureau of Labor Statistics.[25] For example, the price in 1890 for five pounds of flour was 14 cents while the price of bacon per pound was 12.5 cents and the price of eggs per dozen was 12.5 cents. The period 1905 to 1929 saw the price of flour advance by 59 percent, bacon prices rise 143 percent, and the price of eggs increase by 94 percent. Most APS widows would have had no trouble purchasing these items.

Estate values tend to be higher than individual net worth values recorded on census records because more wealth is generally accumulated with age, and because the information elicited by census-takers is not always accurate.[26] In addition, it should be recognized that a widow did not necessarily have the cash value of the estate for her own or her family's immediate use. The actual extent of economic security for APS widows, therefore, might be misleading if it is not considered along with additional factors like property types and other investments.

The value of the husband's estate does not by itself provide the clearest picture possible of the widow's circumstances. Instructions of the probate court to estate appraisers charged them to record, among other items, all cash, real estate and improvements thereon, personal property, bonds, notes, securities.[27] Historians have called these documents "the pots and pans" of history for good reason. Probate and family archives record more than kitchen utensils; they also list a wide range of property types. One-third of the properties held by the Pioneer families were ranches, another third urban lots, some with houses and others without. The final third was divided between mining and commercial properties.

The division of property appears to have been a significant variable for indicating the long-term support of the widow. The inheritance of a ranch by an elderly woman in an underpopulated area meant little for long-term support. This was particularly the case when an extended family or kinship network was absent, as in the case of many of the Anglos living in Arizona. Even if family members were present, the widow often lost direct control of the property. In the case of M. G. Samaniego, for example, the ranch he and his wife owned was incorporated into the extended family's estate after his death. Dolores Samaniego, the widow, sold her property to her brothers during the probate proceedings.[28] In fact, the probate records are full of requests by widows or their families to sell this type of property to pay for the immediate needs of the family.

Urban property, on the other hand, proved to be a source of continual support through its rents. Many of the Pioneer wills specified that the rents of urban holdings were to go directly to the widow. The advantages of urban property ownership for the elderly appears to have been recognized by the Pioneer families because urban property became a larger proportion of the properties owned as Pioneer buyers invested in more and more properties.

The value of Pioneer estates and the strategy of selective property ownership helped widows survive a sometimes lengthy widowhood. The presumption that many of these widows were inexperienced in the areas of world finance neglects the fact that these women usually managed their estates very well. That other family members helped does not detract from the outcome, since a shared-management decision may reflect sound judgment. The median estate value for APS widows was $5,000, $500 above the males' median value. The adjusted value of the APS widow's estate is $19,070 (1970 constant dollars), only $230 less than the adjusted male estate.[29]

Individual widows, of course, lost as well as gained on the value of their husbands' estates in equal proportions among APS widows. Fifty percent of the widows increased the value of their estates by an average value of $2,700 annually (1970 constant dollars); 50 percent decreased the average value of the estate by $3,600 annually. It is not possible to present a clear explanation for the changing value of widows' estates here. However, it is probable that ethnicity was not a factor in determining the direction of fluctuating estate values, since Anglos and Hispanics both increased and decreased the value of estates.

This analysis of APS widow estates indicates that widows had moderate to substantial sums to invest in the development of Arizona. At least one Arizona bank noticed women with funds. Its advertisement in the *Arizona* magazine in 1912 offered "a comfortable enclosure . . . perfectly equipped and at their [women investors] service. Here you can transact your business in privacy."[30]

Women's legal inheritance rights were more extensive and more secure in Arizona than in other parts of the country at the turn of the century. The basis for this difference was the Southwest's reliance on Spanish law as opposed to English common law. English common law prior to Magna Carta placed heavy emphasis on tenure rather than title of property. In other words, because women were considered unable to perform the feudal duties of tenure, land was to be held by the husband. Spanish law allowed the usage of the woman's property only for "support of the family" and her inability to manage the property was not a foregone conclusion.[31]

All property acquired after marriage by either husband or wife in Arizona was presumed the gain of both and as such was common. This was the basis of community property law written in Arizona by the second territorial legislature in 1865. According to this precedent, upon the death of either, the survivor took one-half of the estate and one-half went to designated heirs.[32] The survivor also received the right to maintain the home against any sale or division.

Community property laws were based on the understanding that "each has an equal, present and existing interest therein, whether it originates entirely from the earnings of the husband, . . . from the wife, or partly from each."[33] In addition, with the enactment of the Married Women's Property Act in 1871, married women over 21 had the sole control and management of their separate property.

The widow's rights were also protected through her legal right to be appointed executrix of the estate and to retain guardianship over all minor children upon the death of the father.[34] And according to revenue statutes enacted before 1871, the property of widows and orphans, not to exceed the amount of $100 to any one family, was exempt from taxation (the tax rate at the time was 50 cents on each $100 value).[35]

It is quite clear from Pima County deeds and records books that despite community property provisions, a number of families attempted to limit inheritance taxes and legal entanglements on their estates. Pete Kitchen, in 1885, "granted title to their Tucson house and lot to [his wife] Rosa and her heirs in consideration of her years of love and devotion."[36] Hiram Stevens sold to his wife, Petra, eight different lots of property in the city of Tucson all "for one dollar and the love and affection which [he] bears."[37] Lyman Smith disposed of all of his property (probably to his wife) before he died.[38]

Like these men, aged or sick Pioneers often disposed of their halves of the community property before their deaths, thus simplifying the widow's legal tasks. This strategy offered the further advantage of allowing a freer use of the estate's assets after the death of the husband, rather than the restrictive use imposed by probate proceedings, which could be drawn out over a year or two if the community and separate property of the estate were plentiful and varied. This was also the case in situations where debts were high and property had to be sold. While the courts decided the destiny of the estate, widows were forced to live with the homestead and, theoretically, on half of what had previously been available to them. If these funds were insufficient for the intervening period, the widow could petition the courts for an allowance during probate proceedings. Lillie Marks Goldtree requested and received $125 a month for her and her two minor daughters when her husband Joseph died in 1897.[39]

The wills of Pioneers filed with the probate courts tend to be uncomplicated statements for the division of property. In Arizona, this meant the division of one-half of the community property since the other half went directly to the wife. In many instances wills read as Hiram Stevens's: "I, Hiram Stevens, of the City of Tucson . . . of the age of sixty, being of sound mind . . . give and bequeath to my wife . . . all of my property both real and personal."[40] A straightforward appointment of the widow as sole heir was common. Others, like Samuel Drachman, made provisions for his children only to have them return the inherited property to their mother after his death.[41]

Wills also indicate some interesting differences between the values of men and women. With the exception of one Pioneer will, all provided for the payment of debts and division of real estate. Little, if any, mention was made of church services, philanthropic donations, or the bequeathing of personal items. Women's wills consistently mentioned these items. Altagracia Elias de Ochoa was careful to leave $100 to the Orphans' Home of Tucson and another $100 to the Society of St. Vincent de Paul.[42] Petra Stevens bequeathed "one up-right piano of the make of Kranich and Batch of New York" to a sister. She also left her "good friend Sarah Sanchez, one silk home made crazy quilt" and to another friend "one large picture of our Lady of the Immaculate Conception." In this lengthy will, the majority of which dealt with personal items, she left St. Mary's Hospital $50 and the parish priest $126.50. The last quarter of the will finally came to the division of real estate.[43]

Altagracia and Petra both had considerable personal and real property, but it was not only these individuals who made such provisions. Petra Goodwin was a widow of modest means when she died in 1922, and she wrote a will that called for the division of personal property. She left a "filigree pin" to one daughter and "large earrings" to the other.[44] The meaning of these value differences between Pioneer men and women is unclear. Further research might indicate women felt that they had more control over the destiny of personal items than of property.

Bequests were not, of course, the widows' only means of support. Insurance companies were relatively new in Arizona, but several Pioneers had life insurance and at least one served as director of a life insurance firm. In some cases, the insurance money made a great deal of difference in the support of the widow. John Hart was a man of modest means. The 1870 census noted his worth at $720, which he had accumulated as a gambler, stagecoach driver, and occasional miner. When he died in 1893, he left his wife and daughter a $2,000 life insurance policy from the Ancient Order of United Workmen (nearly $9,000 in 1970 constant dollars).[45]

Pensions were also available to widows of former soldiers, although they did not appear to have been plentiful with this group of Pioneers. According to the *Vedette* of June 1888, the pension law allowed $8 a month to be paid to widows of soldiers who fought in the United States–Mexican War. Widows' pensions for other wars were approximately $12 around 1890. This amount was barely a survivable income given the costs of food and housing. The pension also appears to have been difficult to procure: Pioneer Frank Sullivan's widow and minor daughter persuaded the commander of Negley Post in Tucson in 1902 to write to the appropriate authorities in their behalf to try to secure a pension for them. Although she was described as in "destitute circumstances," the widow was unable to receive a pension because she had none of her husband's papers.[46]

Widows without bequests, insurance, or pensions could request county aid or housing in county poor houses.[47] In the case of APS Pioneers, it was significant that this aid was applied for indirectly, since the APS could and did recommend a number of Pioneer widows for county benefits based on their contributions to Arizona's development. Additionally, it probably did not hurt the cases of these women that many APS members served on the county board of supervisors, the decision-making body for pension allotments.

In addition to the APS, other benevolent societies were available to aid widows in distress. The Woman's Association for Mutual Benevolence, founded in 1872 to help the plight of destitute Hispanic women, the St.

Vincent de Paul Society, organized in 1890, and the Alianza Hispano-Americana, founded in 1894, were the major philanthropic organizations in the Tucson area. None of them seem to have aided widows of the Pioneers, since most of these women were not destitute.

Gary B. Nash, in an article on poverty in Philadelphia in the eighteenth century, points out, "When poverty was found it almost always seemed to be the result of ill chance within the social system fundamentally based on the family—the aged without relatives, widows and orphans without roots in the city or the mentally ill shunned by kin."[48] Indeed, in Arizona an interlocking of families through marriages, migrations, and adoptions was a way to become rooted in the newly settled area and to secure, physically and psychologically, the position of the family. Thus, Pioneers and their families avoided the ill chance Nash describes.

Familial networks were established in several ways. First, Anglos married into established Mexican families. The marriages between these two cultural groups also created linkages among the many Anglos themselves. For example, several APS pioneers married Mexican sisters. Each pair, Granville Oury and Adams Sanders, John Spring and Alex Levin, and Sam Hughes and Hiram Stevens, found themselves after marriage not only part of a large Mexican family but also brothers-in-law. Sisters who followed their brothers to Arizona and then married also helped to create familial networks. Louisa M. Toole was the link between her brother, Governor A. P. K. Safford, and her Arizona husband, James Toole. Children's marriages within the Pioneer network offered these same connections. James Speedy's daughter, for example, married Pioneer Frank Burke, and William Kirkland's married Thomas Steele. When marriage linkages were not available, cultural linkages could be made through religious ceremonies like baptisms. C. A. Shibell's child had as godparents Samuel and Atanacia Hughes.[49]

When families were not created through civil or religious ceremonies, they were imported. Brides meeting their new husbands in Arizona brought their mothers and other relatives with them. Lyman Smith's wife, Isabel Ballestero, was accompanied by her mother. Pete Kitchen's entourage was more elaborate. Pete returned to Arizona from a sojourn in Mexico with a new bride, Rosa, her brother, her sister and brother-in-law, and thirty Opata Indians.[50] The Pioneers created for themselves an interlocking system of families linked together for support. When the Pioneers were alive this often meant support in business ventures. When they died, the widows took advantage of this system more than any other option available to them.

Tamara K. Hareven has noted that solitary residence was most uncommon throughout the nineteenth century in all age groups. Except for western frontier communities and mining towns, only about 3 to 5 percent of the population lived alone. Many of the Pioneer widows maintained their residences in the old homestead after a husband's death, but few appear to have lived alone.[51]

Nellie Shibell and Concepcion Martinez Keen were among many who spent their widowhood in the old homestead; however, both lived with unmarried daughters. Other women stayed at home until their late years and then moved in with other relatives. Eva Mansfield spent most of her thirty-three-year widowhood at her home in Tucson, from which she also orchestrated the needs of the family business. "Her home for 30 years has been synonymous for glowing hospitality," but in the last few years of her life she moved in with her brother.[52] Jennie Drachman also moved to be with relatives after she was widowed; for her this meant going to California to be with her daughters, with whom she spent the last twelve years of her life.[53] Lizzie Steele was cared for in her later years by her son.[54] All of the Pioneer widows relied on the formal and informal familial ties in their late years, although most lived in the homestead until that time.

The APS proved to be a rich source of information for analyzing the circumstances of widows on the frontier. Its membership represented the economic and cultural orientation of development in Arizona from the 1870s through the early 1930s. Notably, APS interest in the preservation of history meant that it collected a variety of useful data on the early settlers and their families.

Demographically, the APS wives can be described as having been married in their twenties and widowed near 50. Variation in these ages is primarily dependent on whether it was a first or second marriage. Generally, women experienced a lengthy widowhood of twenty-five or more years. However, few spent this widowhood entirely alone since APS families averaged four children each.

The economic circumstances of these widows were dependent on several key variables related to the families' business endeavors and property ownership. APS families with government contracts and diversified businesses tended to be the wealthiest. Specialization or employment in the professions could not compare favorably to the gains made in transportation or mining, for example. Most APS families identified profitable sources of income, and when husbands died they left moderate to substantial estates for their widows.

Estates, however, varied not only in cash value but also in substance. Property, for example, included urban lots, ranches, and mining claims. Widows, especially the elderly, did not find the inheritance of a ranch advantageous. They often sold such ranches or allowed other family members to manage them. Urban lots, especially ones with housing, on the other hand, usually stayed under the direct control of the widow. The rents from these properties provided continual and predictable income.

APS widows appear to have been successful money managers, since their estates were of similar value to those of their husbands. In addition, there is little evidence that APS widows found it necessary to use the Society's widows' and orphans' fund nor any of the various philanthropic organizations available to them. Instead, they found support in the familial networks that their stability made possible. Formal and informal ties were created to protect individuals from the ill chance of being abandoned in widowhood or any other desperate circumstance.

The APS experience makes clear the advantages of Arizona's multicultural society. Mexican families provided kindred networks and Anglo settlers used this stability to foster economic growth generated from the railroad and mining. APS members and their families approached life in an ambitious, legalistic, and entrepreneurial manner that secured a comfortable existence for widows who acted in the same focused way until their own deaths.

NOTES

I thank Gary Hearn, Jenny Jensen, and Marsha Weisiger for their research assistance; the staffs of the Superior Court in Maricopa and Pima counties for their cooperation; and the staffs of the Arizona Historical Society in Tucson and the Arizona Foundation in Tempe for sharing their knowledge of those collections.

1. "Report of Arizona Census, 1864," cited in Howard Roberts Lamar, *The Far Southwest, 1846-1912: A Territorial History* (New Haven: Yale University Press, 1966), 437.

2. Various sources including the Carl Hayden Papers, Arizona Historical Society (AHS) Archive, Tucson; Pioneer Biographical Files, AHS; *Arizona Citizen; Arizona Star.*

3. Lamar, *Far Southwest,* 445.

4. APS minutes, Jan. 1, 1870, AHS Archive. All APS records are in this archive.

5. APS undated newspaper clipping.

6. Ladies Auxiliary of Arizona Pioneers, Constitution and By Laws, AHS Archive.

7. APS minutes, 1885.

8. See, for example, APS minutes, Mar. 1, Apr. 5, 6, 1885, Dec. 4, 1891, Dec. 29, 1892, Jan. 14, 1893, July 6, Dec. 30, 1895, July 3, 1904, July 4, 1905, Jan. 6, 1907, Jan. 5, 1908, Dec. 29, 1910, July 5, 1914.

9. *Abstract of the Twelfth Census of the United States: 1900, Bureau of the Census* (New York: Arno Press, 1976).

10. Ethnicity was determined by surname and verified by place of birth, which was derived from various files, including the Hayden Papers, AHS, and Pioneer Biographical Files.

11. T. A. Larson, "Women's Role in the American West," *Montana, the Magazine of Western History* 24 (1974):5, cites Ninth Census data, and defines the West as California, New Mexico, Utah, Idaho, Montana, Oregon, Arizona, Nevada, Wyoming, and Colorado.

12. First marriages $Q = 7.5$; second marriages $Q = 6.7$; Blaine T. Williams, "The Frontier Family," in Sandra L. Myres and Harold M. Hollingsworth, eds., *Essays on the American West* (Arlington: University of Texas Press, 1969), 52-57.

13. Quoted in Donna J. Guy, "The Economics of Widowhood in Arizona, 1880-1940," herein, from *Fourteenth Census of the United States: 1920* (Washington, D.C.: Government Printing Office, 1921), 2:398; *Fifteenth Census of the United States: 1930* (Washington, D.C.: Government Printing Office, 1931), vol. 3, part 1, 149. The median figures for age at widowhood and length of widowhood are as follows: 54 years at widowhood and 18 years for first marriages, 49 years at widowhood and 21 years for second marriages.

14. See Susan Grigg, "Toward a Theory of Remarriage: A Case Study of Newburyport at the Beginning of the Nineteenth Century," *Journal of Interdisciplinary History* 8 (1977):183-220; Robert V. Wells, "Demographic Change and the Life Cycle of American Families," *Journal of Interdisciplinary History* 2 (1970):282; and Wells, "Quaker Marriage Patterns in a Colonial Perspective," *William and Mary Quarterly*, 3d Ser., 29 (1972):425.

15. Female employment is not discussed because few APS widows joined the labor force. See also Guy, "Economics of Widowhood."

16. The statistics cited in this section are based on a compilation of data from sources that were entered onto a computer file. Occupational data were gathered from the Hayden Papers, Pioneer Biographical Files, family papers, census records, and Arizona newspapers.

17. Anthony Hubbard file, Hayden Papers.

18. Samuel Drachman, report of administration, docket no. 1177, Dec. 10, 1897, and Samuel Hughes, report of administration, docket no. 2428, both in Pima County Probate Court Records, Tucson.

19. Cash values of estates during this period have been adjusted for the fluctuation in the overall price level. According to the U.S. Department of Commerce consumer price index, constant-dollar purchasing power ranged from $21.50 to

$44.71 (100 = 1970) during the period from 1866 to 1929. Thus, the goods that could be purchased in 1898 for $21.50 would have cost $100 in 1970. All current-dollar values in the remainder of this essay have been converted to constant 1970 dollars to facilitate comparison. These are the latest comparative data available. For the relevant index, see U.S. Bureau of the Census, *Historical Statistics of the United States, Colonial Times to 1970,* Bicentennial ed., Part 1 (Washington, D.C.: Government Printing Office, 1975), 211.

20. This median dollar figure is based on current dollars reported during probate proceedings. *N* = 47.

21. Milton Friedman and Anna Jacobson Schwartz, *A Monetary History of the United States, 1867-1960* (Princeton: Princeton University Press, 1971), 135.

22. U.S. Bureau of the Census, *Statistical Abstract of the United States: 1971,* 92d ed. (Washington, D.C.: Government Printing Office, 1971), series K:256-85.

23. U.S. Bureau of the Census, *Statistical Abstract, 1971,* series N:259-61.

24. Calculation of Arizona housing prices for this period is difficult because only fragmentary data are available prior to the 1930s. Adjusting the price of housing in Washington, D.C., by the relative per capita income of mountain state residents is an approximation to the Arizona price that is sensitive to the income index use. A more geographically specific index developed by 1929 shows the ratio of per capita income between Washington, D.C., and Arizona as 2.18:1. Thus, the Arizona housing prices may have been even lower than those reported in the text (e.g., the 1920 price in Arizona may have been closer to $2,888). Aware of the potential bias in these estimates, I have reported the larger housing prices that tend to undervalue rather than overvalue the practical worth of the estates.

25. U.S. Bureau of the Census, *Statistical Abstract, 1971,* series E:187-202.

26. The historiography of probate records is extensive. Methodological problems remain, but the results of their use are intriguing enough to make the effort worthwhile. For information on the use of probate records, see Bruce C. Daniels, "Probate Court Inventories and Colonial American History," *Histoire Sociale/Social History* 9 (1976):378-405; Daniel Scott Smith, "Underregistration and Bias in Probate Records," *William and Mary Quarterly,* 3d Ser., 32 (1975):100-10; Gloria L. Main, "The Correction of Biases in Colonial American Probate Records," *Historical Methods Newsletter* 8 (1974):10-28.

27. "Instructions to Appraisers," Inventory and Appraisement form, Probate Court Records, Maricopa County, 1895, Phoenix.

28. M. G. Samaniego, report of administration, docket no. 1670, Aug. 8, 1907, Pima County Probate Court Records, and Biographical File.

29. *N* = 27.

30. *Arizona* (Feb. 1912):16.

31. William C. Wells, "Women's Property Rights in Latin America," *Bulletin of the Pan American Union* 59 (1925):22; also see Helen S. Carter, "Legal Aspects of Widowhood and Aging," herein.

32. Wells, "Women's Property Rights," 238.

33. John D. Lyons, "Development of Community Property Law in Arizona," *Louisiana Law Review* 15 (1955):522.

34. *Revised Statutes of Arizona, 1901,* 3, title 45, cited in *Arizona* (Feb. 1912):12.

35. Coles Bashford, comp., *The Compiled Laws of the Territory of Arizona, including the Howell Code and the Session Laws from 1864 to 1871, Inclusive* (Albany, N.Y.: Weed Parsons, 1871), ch. 33, sec. 5, 311.

36. Pima County Deeds and Real Estate, Book 13, 97-98, Tucson.

37. Hiram Stevens, Biographical File, Hayden Papers.

38. Lyman Smith, Biographical File, "Reminiscences by His Daughter," Hayden Papers.

39. Joseph Goldtree, petition to Probate Court, docket no. 1177, Dec. 10, 1897, Pima County Probate Court Records.

40. Hiram Stevens, last will and testament, docket no. 600, Mar. 21, 1893, Pima County Probate Court Records.

41. Samuel Drachman, report of administration, docket no. 1949, Dec. 26, 1911, Pima County Probate Court Records.

42. Altagracia Elias de Ochoa, last will and testament, docket no. 2129, June 3, 1907, Pima Probate Court Records.

43. Petra Santa Cruz Stevens, last will and testament, docket no. 2295, Dec. 15, 1909, Pima County Probate Court Records.

44. Petra Mercedes Moreno Goodwin, last will and testament, docket no. 3084, May 12, 1922, Pima County Probate Court Records.

45. John Hart, *Arizona Citizen,* Aug. 8, 1893, 4:2.

46. Frank Sullivan, pension records no. D4573, Sawtelle, Calif., Soldiers' Home, filed in Hayden Papers.

47. See Guy, "Economics of Widowhood."

48. Gary B. Nash, "Poverty and Poor Relief in Pre-Revolutionary Philadelphia," *William and Mary Quarterly,* 3d Ser., 23 (1976):5.

49. C. A. Shibell, Biographical File.

50. Elizabeth Rebecca Snoke, "Peter Kitchen: A Study in Successful Frontiering, 1819-1895" (Master's thesis, 1969), 36.

51. Tamara K. Hareven, "The Last Stage: Historical Adulthood and Old Age," in David D. Van Tassel, ed., *Aging, Death, and the Completion of Being* (Philadelphia: University of Pennsylvania Press, 1979), 178.

52. Eva Mansfield, undated obituary, AHS clipbooks, AHS Archive.

53. Jennie Drachman, *Arizona Star,* June 13, 1927.

54. Lizzie Steele, Biographical File, several letters dated 1924 and 1926.

10

Letting Go: Bereavement among Selected Southwestern Anglo Widows

ARLENE SCADRON

"Words cannot express the almost mortal agony which pierced my soul when the loved form of the best of husbands was brought home to me *dead,*" recalled Martha Morgan Graham about the murder of her husband, Jesse Morgan, during a squatters' riot in Sacramento, California, in 1850. "This word [dead] possessed great significance to me, blasting in a moment all my earthly hopes, nearly driving reason from her throne for a time." Sanity began to return "in season," wrote Graham, whose belief that she and her mate would reunite "in the land of souls" provided solace and support. Yet, in this life, she insisted, "My loss can never be made up to me, nor until such meeting ['in the land of souls'], when I believe full compensation will be awarded for every heartthrob of pain."

Suffering "still further trials and disciplines," during the next few months, Graham left the city rather than "daily [having] to live over again these melancholy scenes." The widow sold her belongings and, with her young daughter, boarded a ship for New Orleans via Panama. A letter of introduction from her husband's acquaintances to the ship's captain or to any Free Mason "greatly cheered" her in her "depressed condition." From New Orleans they proceeded to St. Louis, reuniting with her son who was working in a saw mill. Graham found a job paying $7 a month as a hotel cook for thirty to forty boarders. Finding this too taxing, she tried sewing and washing for a time, but after three years returned to San Francisco in the hopes of improving her finances. In early 1854, again feeling overburdened by exhausting labor, the widow relocated to the scene of her travail in Sacramento, where she found reasonably priced lodging, secured credit at the local hardware store (whose owner remembered her husband and responded sympathetically to her plight), and took in washing. Townswomen watched her daughter and bought her groceries, cooking utensils, and bedding, thus freeing Graham for wage-earning. She earned $12 from her first pile of washing and within three months had repaid creditors and placed her daughter in school. This arduous struggle faltered temporarily when Graham moved to a mining community and remarried. Her choice of mate was unfortunate. Unknown to her, he was a polygamist, who soon had Graham supporting him. After five years, she divorced her second husband, presumably seeking a more stable life.[1]

Since each bereavement is unique, neither Martha Graham's nor any other widow's experience epitomizes that of all widows in mid-nineteenth-century America. Yet her bereavement was partly shaped by the lawlessness and violence often associated with male-dominated gold rush towns that sprang up near mining sites in the West and Southwest. The response to unanticipated, untimely, and in this case, violent death usually intensifies bereavement, at least initially. Whether the proportion of widows suffering such a fate in this region was greater than elsewhere in America during this period would be difficult to establish, though it is not improbable. Some of the themes that emerge from Graham's widowhood were shared by other women in similar circumstances: the rootlessness and isolation of recent arrivals in unsettled communities, the resort to migration as a strategy for finding economic and social support, and the lack of developed social or kin networks. Reliance on working-age children to contribute to family income, the burden of dependent children, and the constraints on women whose only marketable skills were extensions of domestic activities characterized the experience of many widows, especially in less developed regions of the country prior to the twentieth century.[2]

Graham's story also encapsulates the wrenching psychosocial transition from being married to being widowed and traces the pilgrimage from her husband's death to the subsequent attempt to restructure her life, a journey involving "major changes in the heartland of the self."[3] Many women, including Martha Graham, whose stories are presented in this essay experienced widowhood as a period of challenge and readjustment and shared some responses to the stresses of grieving. And although coping with widowhood is partly determined by personal temperament and psychological makeup, it is also shaped by prevalent socioeconomic and cultural conditions. In the discussion that follows I explore these dimensions of bereavement among fourteen southwestern white women, widowed during the period 1857 to 1939, who represent different social classes, religious affinities, and range in age from their early twenties with young children to elderly women in their sixties to eighties. They were selected to illuminate individual experiences as well as recurring patterns of bereavement guided by the following questions: "How did widowhood change their lives and self-perceptions? How did they cope with their new situation? What constellation of factors—age, quality of relationships with spouse and circumstances of his death, age and number of dependent children, kin relationships, religious beliefs, social networks, previous work experience, social class, economic conditions, and other historical circumstances—fostered or impeded their adaptation to widowhood? Using primary sources such as diaries, family correspondence, reminiscences, oral histories, popular literature, newspapers, magazines, and the records of charitable societies and government agencies, I also use these women to convey something of the texture of this difficult passage in human experience.

In most Western cultures serious physical and psychological disorders often complicate bereavement, and the professional literature abounds with discussions about the course and outcome of the grieving process and suggestions for its effective management. According to contemporary experts, *grief* is "the sorrow, mental distress, emotional agitation, sadness, suffering, and related feelings" caused by loss, in this case the death of a loved one. *Bereavement* is "both the period of time following a death, during which grief occurs, and also the state of experiencing grief."[4] Loss of a loved one, such as a spouse or child, is one of the most significant and traumatic events a close survivor is likely to experience during a lifetime. And it is an experience not easily overcome. Yet grief is one of the painful costs of being human and forming intimate attachments.[5] Because culture modifies concepts of grief and loss as well as accepted responses to them, our notions of bereavement and experiences of widowhood are not universally valid.[6]

Recent studies of bereavement acknowledge "a wide variety of patterns of response to bereavement," noting that some people "recover from grief unscathed, or even strengthened, while others suffer lasting damage to body, mind, and spirit." Some people seem to recuperate quickly from their loss, others do so only with help, and still others never fully recover.[7] Although many experts insist that grieving proceeds through successive, identifiable stages whose desired outcome is successful reintegration into society equated with "letting go" of one's dead spouse, bereavement might be better understood as an emotional continuum in which survivors experience a host of feelings in the course of a day and often over many years. Further, it appears that as widows many women do forge a fresh identity and reintegrate without wholly or finally "letting go" of their deceased mate.[8] Nor is unwillingness to entirely "release" the deceased necessarily unhealthy.

Students of bereavement outline a full range of depressive symptoms and reactions that commonly follow the death of a loved one.[9] They include: (1) *impact* or *numbness,* usually lasting a few hours to a few days or even as long as a few weeks, characterized by automatic functioning in a kind of "daze," only vague memory later of events during this period, and a prominence of anxiety symptoms sometimes described as grief "pains." The bereaved may feel as if they lack appropriate feelings or any feelings at all, a sensation that usually passes within a few days. The pains include "sensations of somatic distress occurring in waves lasting from twenty minutes to an hour at a time, a feeling of tightness in the throat, choking with shortness of breath, need for sighing and an empty feeling in the abdomen, lack of muscular power, and an intense subjective distress described as tension or mental pain."[10] Sobbing and crying also accompany these pains, which usually occur less frequently in about two weeks and then recur occasionally, most markedly on the anniversary or some other reminder of the death. (2) *Recoil and/or depression* consists of two aspects—yearning and protest (of the death) followed by disorganization, with such symptoms as irritability, loss of appetite, restlessness, sleeplessness, anger, a sense of hopelessness and worthlessness, and even death wishes and suicidal thoughts. Among other persistent depressive reactions are sleep disturbances, anger, and diminished hope and self-esteem, as well as a conviction that someone is to blame for the death. Anger generated by guilt and the irrational sense that the deceased died deliberately to impose guilt or independence upon the bereaved is sometimes displaced onto scapegoats including doctors, God, family members, employers, and others.[11] (3) *Recovery* is connoted by an acceptance of the death and a return to a level of functioning established before its occurrence. This might involve willingness to seek new roles and relationships or perhaps strengthen those assumed prior to the death. The bereaved may also continue to cultivate a "sense of the deceased" and maintain "emotional involvement with the deceased"; they will often "sanctify" their former spouses, crediting them in death with qualities lacking in life and ignoring negative aspects of character or behavior. But even when the bereaved begin to reintegrate into society and develop new lives, experts regard depressive symptoms and continued grieving as normal.[12]

Whether psychiatrists would have regarded her behavior as "normal,"

Marietta Palmer Wetherill never stopped grieving over the death of her spouse, Richard Wetherill. A pioneer archaeologist, he discovered the cliff dwellings at Mesa Verde and Kiet Siel, the Basket Maker sites at Grand Gulch, Utah, and initiated excavations of Pueblo Bonito in Chaco Canyon, New Mexico, the largest prehistoric ruins in the United States. He was ambushed and murdered by a band of Navajos in Chaco Canyon on June 22, 1910. The excessively traumatic circumstances of her husband's death continued to evoke in Marietta Wetherill anger, frequent uncontrolled tears, and a vivid recollection of gory details during oral history interviews forty-three years later.[13] Her hatred for the U.S. Indian agents she held responsible for Wetherill's death was unmitigated. She told the interviewer: "There is no punishment, you know, that will pay for all the misery; . . . I just hope that Shelton and Stacher [the agents] would both live to be two hundred years because . . . they would be very old men and they would have to sit in a chair and lay in the bed and they'd have lots of time to think and they would be punished."[14] Regret that she had not murdered one or both of them remained undimmed. So painful was her loss that thirty-eight years elapsed before Marietta Wetherill could bear to hang her husband's picture in the house.

The leader among the agents in question was William T. Shelton, autocratic, ambitious, and a controversial figure since his appointment in 1903 as superintendent of the Navajo agency in Shiprock, New Mexico. That he was determined to undermine Wetherill's stature and influence with the Indians and among his own superiors in Washington, D.C., through misleading and deceptive written reports appears fairly evident. Using Samuel F. Stacher, another agent and superintendent of the Eastern Navajo Jurisdiction, initially headquartered at Chaco Canyon, as an aide in spreading misinformation, Shelton tried to force Wetherill from the region. The two men apparently succeeded in planting seeds of discontent against Wetherill among a few Navajos heavily indebted to him by overreliance on credit at his trading post. But the precipitating event that led to the ambush was a violent altercation between William Finn, Wetherill's cowhand, and a Navajo who rode to death a pony belonging to Wetherill's daughter, followed within hours by a second confrontation between Finn and Wetherill and a group of six Navajos. A coroner's jury convened two days after the killing indicted Chis-chilling-begay, who owed Wetherill much money. He was heard to brag about intentions to kill Wetherill and ultimately was convicted of Wetherill's murder. Five other Navajos were also indicted as accomplices, although eventually they were found not guilty. And at the insistence of

Stacher's deputies, William Finn was arrested for assaulting a Navajo named Hostine Nez-begay. Finn, whose shady past as Joe Moody cattle rustler was known to all but Marietta and Richard Wetherill (who had hired him about 1905 as an expert range rider and marksman for their Triangle Bar Triangle Ranch), may have been more of a liability than Wetherill realized. For Finn reputedly mistreated a few Indians and was accused of stealing stock from them, factors that may have helped turn some Navajos against Wetherill himself. Yet when a district court judge in Farmington dismissed charges against Finn, Shelton moved quickly to file another complaint in Aztec District Court, which ultimately ordered him to serve one year to 18 months in the penitentiary (a sentence that was suspended) and to pay almost $300 in costs on assault charges. Finn's countercharges against the Indian who abused the colt and against most of the other Navajos ultimately failed. Immediately after the murder, Shelton moved into Stacher's jurisdiction and organized the legal defense of the Navajos, while rumors circulated that he congratulated the murderer for doing a good job. His accounts of incidents preceding the murder, including predictions that there would be violence against Wetherill, conflict with other reviews of these events, even from Stacher and with presumably confidential interviews Shelton gave to the press, and later retracted.[15]

The morning after the killing, the thirty-three-year-old widow with five children ranging in age from a twelve-year-old son to a six-week-old infant daughter, described her mental state: "I lost my mind. I didn't know what to do. I didn't know what to do so I just had to be guided by other people." Decisions about retrieving the body from the ambush site—which Marietta Wetherill threatened to carry out herself—building a coffin, choosing an appropriate spot for burial, and organizing simple funeral services were made by a few household retainers, friends, and one of Wetherill's five brothers who arrived from Farmington, New Mexico. Mrs. Wetherill remained in seclusion during most of those first days, emerging only to testify as a witness at the coroner's jury and to inform her children about the death. But "everything was sorta in a commotion, you know naturally, and I couldn't think like anybody ought to for a few days or maybe for a week or two, I don't know," she recalled. Signs of depression, confusion, and even occasional hallucinations marked her immediate reactions. "Mentally confused and unable to sleep," she awakened in the middle of the night before Wetherill was buried and remembered him perched in the doorway, looking sad, shaking his head, and telling her: "I'm so sorry to leave you like this . . . with all these children." Later, interpreting this event, she believed

Wetherill was alluding to his heavy borrowing against an insurance policy that left her nearly penniless. She also recalled being unable for a long time to even look at the spot where her husband was buried underneath one of his favorite rocks. The Navajos, remorseful and guilt-stricken, would sneak to her home at night, tap on her bedroom window, beg her forgiveness, and offer help. They observed, "You have gotten very poor, you don't eat. . . . You cry too much."

While the shockingly violent and totally unexpected nature of Richard Wetherill's death undoubtedly complicated his widow's recovery, the stress of grief was further compounded by her precarious financial situation and naivete about these matters, an agonizing coroner's inquest, and harassment by Shelton and Stacher, who had been spreading lies about Richard Wetherill. They also took measures to deny Marietta Wetherill any help from the Navjaos in digging water holes and keeping control of her cattle herds—actions that eventually forced her to leave Chaco Canyon. In addition, Marietta Wetherill was one of the chief witnesses in the long series of legal proceedings involving criminal trials against the Indian indicted for Wetherill's murder, the countersuits against Finn, who had escaped when Wetherill was ambushed, her own suit against Stacher for loss of her stock and to enjoin him from interfering in operations of the ranch, and the tangled legal and financial problems concerning the administration of Wetherill's estate and collection of debts. Though a poor witness for the prosecution in the case against the Navajos, Finn remained loyal to Marietta Wetherill, undoubtedly contributing to her survival until his own death from influenza in 1918.

Tenacious, gutsy, and utterly determined to obtain justice, Mrs. Wetherill spent four or five years and most of her money in the courts. On several occasions, she even piled all of her children including the baby and a goat (to provide milk for nursing) into a wagon and proceeded to Aztec and Farmington for court hearings. To her great distress, the murder trial was deliberately delayed two years. "I thought I would lose my mind, I wanted to kill myself. I couldn't take much more of it," she recalled. A true test of fortitude occurred exactly one year after her husband's death when the baby she had been nurturing died suddenly. "I just thought I couldn't take it, I couldn't do it, it was just too much," she said. "But I did. I had my others, I had to." For twenty years Wetherill did not mention the child.

In the immediate aftermath of the murder, Marietta Wetherill was faced with the necessity of having to feed her family. Appearances of prosperity notwithstanding, Wetherill's estate, aside from the ranch property and numerous uncollected debts, totaled less than $75 deposited in an Albuquerque bank. Efforts to collect more than $12,000 owed him by Indians and other traders brought enough only to pay off debts against the estate and legal fees of $2,500, leaving a tiny nest egg. A few friends and employees of their ranch, several Wetherill brothers, as well as East Coast archaeologists in the area for summer expeditions, including Doctor T. Mitchell Prudden, offered assistance. With Prudden's help, Mrs. Wetherill desperately tried to salvage sheep, horses, and cattle grazing in the highlands above Pueblo Bonito, but before the year was out she left the area permanently, unable to sustain a living. Relocating temporarily to Aztec and then Farmington, Marietta Wetherill was assisted by the parents of one of her cowhands who offered cheap lodgings. Critical to her economic survival was the generous help of a prosperous rancher in the town of Cuba, Epermenia Miera, who bartered acreage in the mountains above the town for mules she and Richard Wetherill had raised from mares. In addition, he provided money for food, new stock to begin ranching, and aid in building a house. Miera also gave her a chance to earn additional money by pasturing horses owned by his friends, providing her with boarders, and paid for a couple to assist Marietta Wetherill with household and child-care chores. Her older children, who were experienced cowhands, also assumed some of the responsibilities of running the ranch. Prudden spent his last days in the area trying to clear Wetherill's reputation and clarifying the circumstances of his death; he demanded an official investigation from the U.S. Commissioner of Indian Affairs. In the end, however, he contended the government study was a whitewash with critical evidence either suppressed or deliberately uncollected.

Describing the area in the Jemez Mountains as heavenly, Marietta Wetherill slowly regained her mental health. After a few years, she returned to a characteristic pattern of her early life, becoming a "gypsy" and moving to a small ranch and trading post at Sanders, Arizona, then returning to New Mexico. When her children were grown, Wetherill settled near some of them on the outskirts of Albuquerque in a small house filled with a few of the baskets and rugs remaining from Pueblo Bonito. She died there of heart failure July 11, 1954, forty-four years after the tragedy.

The intensity and enduring quality of Wetherill's bereavement reflects the searing, totally shocking nature of Richard Wetherill's death but also the extreme sense of injustice surrounding the circumstances of his murder, which the widow believed never to have been satisfactorily resolved. Marietta Wetherill's difficulties in accepting her loss were similar to but more complex than Martha Graham's, compounded by the lengthy legal battle she clearly felt compelled to pursue. Not unlike Graham, she chose (or was forced by circumstances) to migrate from her isolated home to survive economically. She also relied on the help of men—brothers-in-law, colleagues of her husband, and a generous friend—as well as able-bodied children. Although she fared poorly in dealing with the law, Wetherill showed more determination than many widows in this arena. Finally, her instinct for survival and reliance on the skills she had developed as farmer and rancher carried her through.

For other young widows, the sudden death of their spouse and the need to support children provoked similarly intense but less constructive responses. If Marietta Wetherill contemplated suicide, others actually attempted it. During her journey from Salt Lake City to California, Martha Graham prevented a young wife with four children from jumping into the river to join her husband who had accidentally drowned.[16] Those who succeeded at suicide are difficult for historians to count. Most widows seemed to have stopped short of such measures.

Thirty-five years old when her husband died suddenly of a heart attack on the day he became a U.S. citizen in 1927, Anna Rauh, who eventually emigrated to the Southwest, was an Austrian immigrant living in Pittsburgh with two small children.[17] She suffered a nervous breakdown upon her husband's death. Although living in a large city, Rauh was nearly as isolated as Marietta Wetherill. While she could not recall the funeral, Rauh remembered the generosity of a Viennese physician who attended her husband in the last minutes of this life and later treated her as well as the kindness of an uncle, newly rich from bootlegging alcohol, who took her into his home. Bedridden for a few weeks, Rauh was also helped by a Negro woman employed in the small grocery store that provided the family's living. In the three to four months following her husband's death, she tried working but developed "nervous heart" and was advised by the doctor to quit these activities for at least a year. Rauh had already informed her parents of her inability to survive on her own, and in 1928 she returned to Europe to live with them. Nonetheless, she sought to attain eventual financial independence while her parents hired a governess to care for the children.

Anna Rauh first assumed control of a recently bankrupted store in a fine district of Czernowitz, her hometown, and two years later, moved to Vienna, starting a factory that produced men's shirts. When this failed, she borrowed $2,000 from her father, bought tapestries and fine linens in Vienna, Berlin, and Paris, which she then sold in Pittsburgh, to which she had returned to maintain her U.S. citizenship. Having doubled her money, and with additional orders for handmade drapes and linens, she traveled to Europe, purchased $4,000 worth of merchandise, and returned again to the United States with the materials and, this time, with her children. To fulfill her husband's dream of living as an American citizen and raising their children in this country, Rauh was committed to forging a livelihood in the United States. A wealthy Pittsburgh cousin helped introduce her to a clientele interested in buying this merchandise, and other contacts assisted in finding her rent-free lodging. She took a stab at the "rag trade," buying a cheap line of lingerie in New York City and selling it in Pittsburgh. She upgraded the merchandise, selling less for more, and was preparing to open a shop when, in 1937, she was asked by a brother, who had moved to Tucson because of an arthritic back condition, to give him temporary help at a guest ranch on which he held an option.

It quickly became obvious that her brother needed more than a brief assist, so within a few weeks Rauh returned to Pittsburgh to sell the remnants of her business, pack, and prepare her children for the trip west. While working at the guest ranch as cook, supervisor of the kitchen, and trainer of other chefs, Rauh also earned additional income by taking guests into her rented three-bedroom apartment.

Often advocated as the best coping mechanism for widows, remarriage didn't work for Anna Rauh. She tried it briefly at age 57 to a wealthy man who had been one of her boarders, but it lasted only a year. She said it was a big mistake because their values were too dissimilar. Although she had other opportunities, Rauh said she never thought about marrying a third time. Reflecting on this experience years later, she advised that marriage was an excellent alternative for young widows, but advocated it as soon as possible after the death of the spouse. However, she noted that when a friend tried to make a match between her and another young widower at precisely that time, she objected because she didn't feel ready to remarry.

Until 1960 when she retired at age 67, Rauh worked seven days a week at the guest ranch as a salaried employee, and eventually received about $10,000 as part of the proceeds from its sale. In her meager spare time, Rauh was active in Tucson's Jewish community. She provided financial support for a younger brother and her father who emigrated to Israel, and despite frail health, continued to live alone into her 92nd year. When interviewed at age 90, Rauh was clearly proud of her independence and somewhat impatient with those who complained about their lot. Thus, depite rocky beginnings and lack of preparedness for the world of work, Anna Rauh, driven by her husband's dream of raising his children in

America, ultimately adapted successfully through a combination of hard work, persistence, optimism, significant financial aid from relatives and a few friends, and a commitment to the ideals of her dead spouse.

Relocation to the parental household also provided succor and economic assistance to Helen Ivancovich[18] and her only child, a five-year-old daughter, when she was widowed for the first time at age 23. Before succumbing to familial pressure to return to Post, Texas from Los Angeles, where she and Ralph Ketchum lived for five years prior to his death from pneumonia, in 1917, Helen (then Ketchum) relied upon her musical talent to earn a living. She played piano first for exercise groups at a Los Angeles playground and later to accompany Hollywood films. Once in Texas, her parents managed her finances, and earnings from teaching music were used for travel to Los Angeles and elsewhere. "I was treated like a queen," she said.

Three years after Ketchum's death, as Helen Ketchum traveled to Los Angeles, she met John Ivancovich at a dance in Tucson. In a whirlwind summer romance that took the couple to Los Angeles, Helen Ketchum and this son of a wholesale immigrant grocer were married. Interviewed sixty years later, Helen Ivancovich's eyes twinkled when she mentioned her second husband, whom she described as a very nice person and a handsome playboy. After working briefly in El Paso and Los Angeles, the couple returned to Tucson under pressure from his family. There she worked part-time playing a pipe organ while he entered his father's wholesale grocery business. John Ivancovich insisted that his wife's eight-year-old daughter live with them and that Helen quit working, although he supported her association with voluntary musical groups. When his father sold the grocery business, John Ivancovich sought their livelihood in real estate.

Then, in 1932, just ten years after their marriage, John committed suicide, apparently despondent over business reversals and his father's refusal to lend him money. John Ivancovich's parting message to his wife was that he could not carry on. Reflecting on this loss, Helen Ivancovich declared, "John was my soul."

Ironically, though John Ivancovich was hardpressed for money, he left his widow relatively well off. Having once sold insurance, Ivancovich protected his wife with a policy that contained no suicide exclusion clause. Nevertheless, his business affairs were confused, and his widow was ill equipped to untangle them. Helen Ivancovich recalls, "I didn't even know what an insurance policy was." She turned for help to a bank, but settling the estate dragged on for almost twelve years, a delay Helen attributed to her lawyer's incompetence. Yet the security provided by the insurance policy permitted her to travel (to New York, the Caribbean, Japan), while her parents once again cared for her daughter.

Regarding her emotional state in the early stages of bereavement, Helen Ivancovich recalled that she was very concerned to resist domination by her mother-in-law. After the funeral, she went to her mother-in-law's home. "There I sat, and I would still be sitting there if I hadn't gotten up and left. My mother-in-law consumed me." After two marriages, a third no longer interested her, in part because she thought suitors were solely interested in her money, and she added, "I didn't want to wash anyone's socks." Helen Ivancovich resumed an active social life in Tucson and managed Arizona's exhibit at the Golden Gate Exposition in San Francisco in 1939, where she remained for ten years following her daughter's marriage to a San Francisco journalist. Eventually, however, she returned to Tucson where she lived in a communal housing project for financially well-off elderly people until her death at 90 in 1982.

Ivancovich's two experiences with widowhood were eased considerably by parents who were willing and able to assist her in providing a temporary home and economic support (not unlike Anna Rauh's parents). Remarriage—as long as it endured—proved a more successful solution to her first widowhood than it did for Graham or Rauh, both of whom were older (Rauh was thirty years older). Although she was no more successful in untangling the mysteries of the law involved in her husband's estate than Wetherill, she was more fortunate in having a solid financial basis through an insurance policy that helped her to live comfortably even during the Depression of the 1930s until John Ivancovich's affairs were settled.

Previous work experience and her husband's lengthy decline helped Mary B. Price adapt to widowhood during the Great Depression, after her husband, Charles, died in 1930.[19] An agent of the El Paso and Southwestern Railroad in Courtland, Tombstone, and Douglas, Arizona, Charles Price suffered from pneumonia and influenza for almost five years before his death. More realistic about his condition than was his wife, Charles Price prepared her for life without him.

Before their marriage, Mary Price taught school for several years, an occupation increasingly dominated by women. (By 1900 three out of four teachers were women.) In the early 1920s she served briefly as postmistress in Courtland. When Charles Price was stricken, his wife found a teaching position in Tombstone, despite the difficulties married women faced in obtaining such employment. (Many school boards required women to leave their jobs upon marriage.)[20] Each summer she also managed to escape Arizona's heat, taking Charles and their two young daughters to California, where she chaperoned young women and housesat for the wealthy. While Price found the sudden reversal in breadwinners difficult to accept, he encouraged his wife to work, save, and invest in blue chip stocks. Ultimately, these provided her with a small nest egg and along with $2,000 from an insurance policy, Mary Price bought a small home in Tombstone that she rented during her summer excursions. For $25, a lawyer settled the entire estate and obtained her full widow's exemption from property taxes.

On the day Charles Price died, his wife felt disbelief and disorientation. Yet within two days she resumed work and continued to prepare for a planned trip to California. Focusing on household chores such as baking hundreds of cookies for her daughters and their friends, she sought to maintain a happy household, lest she and her ten- and fourteen-year-old daughters lapse into depression. Mary Price was comforted by her minister, also a friend, who performed the funeral service; she found solace, too, in the belief that her husband would have preferred death to lingering on as an invalid. While Charles Price seemed certain that his wife would remarry, she differed: "I always knew that I wouldn't," she said later. In discussing three potential suitors, May Price remarked that marrying again did not appeal to her. "For years, I didn't have a social engagement with a man. I was a one-man woman with a very happy marriage," she explained. In retrospect, although she expressed no regret about her own decision, she urged other young widows to marry again soon after bereavement.

Following Charles's death, Mary Price pursued a long, successful career in public education. Her work and an extensive network of friends, many of them members of the teaching sorority Alpha Delta Kappa, absorbed her and provided sororal intimacy and support. She served as a school principal and held administrative posts in the State Department of Education, including director of Elementary Education and Curriculum Development, and state director of the School Lunch Program until her retirement in 1959 at age 70.

Anticipatory grieving over a period of several years helped ameliorate Mary Price's transition to widowhood, although she still found it difficult to accept her husband's death. Equally important, her prior education and experience positioned her to take advantage of the historic expansion of women into the teaching profession following the Civil War and thus to support herself and her family. Especially in the West, women teachers found it possible to advance on the administrative ladder and into educational politics, a situation that worked in Price's favor. The profession also provided her with a supportive network of female friends, which may have deterred any thoughts of remarriage. Finally, though necessity compelled him to suppress his own preference for the traditional sexual division of labor, Charles Price's encouragement of a sound economic strategy saved his widow from a bereavement complicated by severe financial pressure.[21]

Wealth, if it could not erase the blow of bereavement, certainly mitigated the economic and social dislocations of widowhood. A case in point is the experience of Gertrude Hill Berger, whose husband Charles expired less than two months after their marriage in 1890. Charles contracted diphtheria shortly after the socially prominent couple's wedding in Denver and was dead six weeks later. As soon as he fell ill, his mother and Gertrude's mother alternated in maintaining a round-the-clock vigil with Gertrude. Doctors and nurses attended him constantly, food was provided by servants of Alice Hale Hill, Gertrude's mother, and both women offered the young bride continual moral support. Though Charles rallied briefly, when he died, "Gertrude was prostrate."[22]

The two mothers then moved quickly, paying the nurse, hiring the undertaker, and ensuring that by evening "Dear Charlie lay in his coffin." The family's minister visited twice that day, and Alice Hill sat up all night relieving the elder Mrs. Berger and the nurse. The next morning letters, telegrams, and flowers started to arrive. The mothers provided proper mourning attire for the new widow and helped prepare her for the funeral service that began in the Hill's parlor and continued in a large procession of carriages to the cemetery where the dean, in white robes, led the burial service and laid Charles Berger to rest.

Gertrude Berger's grieving process soon had to compete with her own fight for life, for the day after the burial she was diagnosed with diphtheria. Once again, Hill and, to a lesser extent, Berger started the nursing process all over again, sitting up throughout the night, "spraying, gargling, painting, and dosing Gertrude." As for Gertrude Berger's progress, her mother recorded that she "keeps perfectly quiet and seems not to care whether she gets well or not." But in a week she improved, her survival no longer in doubt. Alice Hale Hill thus arranged to move her daughter from the household Gertrude Berger had so briefly inhabited with her spouse back into the family residence nearby. All the packing was dispatched to Hill household servants, including the sad task of packing "Dear Charlie's clothes," which were eventually dispersed to friends, family, and local charity organizations. Exactly three weeks to the day that Charles Berger died, his widow was safely ensconced in the parental womb where she continued her recovery. Maids unpacked her trunks, and additional mourning attire was fitted by dressmakers who also clothed Alice Hill. The family minister periodically called on Gertrude, and when she regained sufficient health, daily outings in the family carriage and visits with friends became a regular part of the schedule. Yet her emotional state was still precarious, indicated by an incident in late April when a family friend left a "sweet tribute to Gertrude and Charlie," and the mother withheld it from her daughter. A month later, however, Alice Hill departed on a trip to the East Coast where she shopped for herself and Gertrude, also purchasing a layette for the baby soon to arrive. On August 10, 1891, almost nine months after her marriage, Gertrude Berger gave birth to a baby girl. A new life had begun, and in the fall of 1900 she married. Her second mate lived for fifteen years following their union, and they had three children together.

Gertrude Berger is still another example of a young woman whose family provided critical support during her transition to widowhood and for a lengthy period thereafter. Unlike Rauh and Ivancovich, the decision to return to the parental home was made entirely by her mother. Gertrude, ill and distraught, appears to have had no role in the process. In her case, coping with widowhood did not necessitate self-support. Nor did she share the most advanced attributes of the "new women" who had emerged in the last decades of the nineteenth century with a college education and professional aspirations. Her primary goal, which also fit domestic ideology, was to raise her daughter properly and to make the essential social connections for remarriage. Yet following her mother's example, she also participated actively in several female associations through their church and projects to uplift and assist the poor—activities that typified the expansion of women's sphere into the public arena.[23]

Only a few months before Gertrude's second marriage, her father, Nathaniel Peter Hill, died at age 66, leaving Alice Hale Hill, age 60, a widow after forty years of marriage.[24] One of Denver's wealthiest, most prominent women, her experience and that of other upper-class older widows contrasts with the grieving pattern of the younger, less financially secure widows discussed here. Alice Hale Hill's husband was a U.S. Senator from Colorado and a presidential appointee to the International Monetary Commission, as well as president of a major smelting and refining company and owner of the *Denver Republican,* one of the town's major newspapers. Alice Hill spent her time with voluntary associations and social activities, including the YMCA, the Mt. Vernon Ladies Association, the creation of free kindergartens, church functions, and the Charity Organization Society, which distributed funds to smaller charities. Her daily journal, both before and after her husband's death, listed a constant round of social and philanthropic activity. Since he had been ailing and growing more feeble for several months, Nathaniel Hill's death came as no surprise. In fact, shortly before he died, Alice Hill cleared their safety deposit box. On the day of his death, two nurses were in attendance along with his daughter and daughter-in-law, and his wife was not far away.

Immediately upon Nathaniel Hill's death, Alice Hill, relatives, household retainers, and servants quickly undertook all necessary arrangements. Following the funeral the house was flooded with visitors, flowers, condolences, and editorial tributes, and the mourners were busy with numerous details. Though extremely tired, Hill noted in her journal the visit of a dressmaker to shorten her granddaughter's dress and to help prepare her own mourning attire. Within days she was running errands, although in public she remained in her carriage while Gertrude or a granddaughter made purchases or paid bills. Immediately before Nathaniel Hill's death, Alice Hill had been redecorating several bedrooms; afterward, her journal indicates, removing and replacing bedroom wallpaper became a major preoccupation, if not a fixation. She paid close attention to her estate but relied heavily on her son, Crawford, who also managed the family business. Several times her journal indicated general distress when she felt ill and retired early, but it included no evidence of severe somatic complaints. As did other members of the family, she visited the cemetery regularly. At the end of the year, in December, Alice Hill resumed an earlier pattern and sailed for Europe with a close companion, one of her daughters, and another couple.

The bereavement of women like Alice Hill appears relatively restrained, in part perhaps because their age accustomed them to expect death among friends, relatives, and spouses. Finances usually posed no problem, and the complexities of probate were frequently managed by older sons, family advisors, or legal counselors. Yet many of these women were shrewd, asking astute questions of their advisors and deciding important issues about their estates. Furthermore, widowhood was not followed by a decline in economic or social status. Equally important, their well-established social lives involving visits, charitable work, and extensive travel within and outside the United States continued almost uninterrupted and provided friendship, stability, and a sense of purpose. They relied on grown children, relatives, close friends, and extensive female social networks for emotional support during their widowhood, but the basic pattern of their lives and their identities remained unaltered.

Marriage to prominent men whose deaths evoked an outpouring of public memorials, laudatory obituaries, and declarations of sentiments about their nobility and importance may also have provided some solace to their widows. Elizabeth Byers, the wife of William N. Byers, the founder and publisher of Denver's *Rocky Mountain News* and an early settler of Colorado, was widowed at age 69 after forty-nine years of marriage.[25] Byers seems to have had a stroke several years before his death and manifested symptoms his wife colorfully described as "softening of the brain." Elizabeth Byers had been expecting his death, and when he died, she was in California where she often spent the winters. She returned by fast train for the funeral, and the press described her as under considerable strain. But at the end of the year in which he died, reflecting their mutual experiences in a letter to a daughter who had lost a child, Mrs. Byers considered herself lucky and wondered why she was so favored.[26] Her pattern of travel continued, and it was from Portland, on board a boat, that she recorded a scene in which her husband reappeared. She felt a hand on her shoulder and thought it was her son, who had accompanied her on the trip. "I turned to look and he was nowhere near *nor had he been.* I was *startled* at first then grew calm and peaceful. So often on this trip your father had seemed very near me, almost speaks to me. It is very strong. Frank has felt the Presence too."[27]

Martha Eliza Hale, another prominent Denver widow, was 76 in 1901 when Horace Morrison Hale died of a heart attack. Her son, Irving Hale, described the death as a "sudden blow" and remarked on his mother's "courage and calm" as she assured relatives that she "will continue to bare her great sorrow and loneliness bravely and cheerfully as she does everything."[28] A number of relatives arrived for the funeral and reported that they were keeping his mother bright and cheerful. In the last two years of her life, however, as she became more feeble, Martha Hale moved into her son's home and at the very end was under the daily care of a nurse. A member of the Universal Church, Hale died at 81, sustained not only by a loving and devoted son but also by the faith that "it will come out right in the end."[29]

These widows also reported vivid conversations with their dead husbands, loneliness and sadness, and among the most elderly, a desire to join the deceased as soon as possible in a world where death would exist no more. Religious beliefs in which the death of their loved ones served some larger purpose helped to support them (and some younger widows) and eased their grief.

Annie E. K. Bidwell, the wife of John Bidwell, the founder of Chico,

California, was prominent in her own right.[30] Widowed at age 60 in 1900, she survived her husband by eighteen years before dying of a stroke. Deeply religious, she was also a businesswoman who scrutinized the work of lawyers handling her husband's estate. After her husband's death, she remained active on behalf of numerous causes she had served before, including prohibition, equal suffrage for women, and Indian welfare. She bequeathed her large estate to the Presbyterian church, and upon her death the papers reported that 10,000 people paid her tribute.[31]

Immediately after her husband's death, Annie Bidwell displayed typical symptoms of somatic distress. According to her own description, while she was waiting for her sister to arrive from the East for the funeral, "My strength which had been remarkable suddenly failed, and my doctor ordered me to my room where I had not been since this sad event (and to bed) saying if I did not obey her strictly I would not be here upon my sister's arrival and she would not promise that I would even if I obeyed her, as she could neither hear my heart or feel my pulse. Also that no one must enter my room except to give the medicine and food precribed [*sic*] as I must be left entirely alone."[32] She went on to describe a vision that appeared immediately after her husband's death when she was "so completely prostrated from sorrow and loneliness." Her papers include several versions of this vision, which involved a friend whose husband had recently committed suicide and reiteration of faith in Christ, that left her with a sense of "exaltation, peace, adoration, gratitude and love." The dream included images of waves, birds, strong winds, lightning flashes, and then the departure of her recently bereaved young friend. For the widow, the scene "filled her soul" and made her realize that it was "Gods manifestation . . . of his inexpressible sympathy and love, and his desire that I should rest in His love."

A similar faith sustained Arvilla D. Meeker in enduring more than twenty years of widowhood following the massacre of her husband by the Ute Indians who also held her and her daughter captive. Nathan Cook Meeker, her husband, the founder of Greeley, Colorado, was murdered in 1881, but this was not the only loss that Arvilla Meeker suffered as she reflected upon her life at the time of her eighty-second birthday; she recalled the deaths of two daughters and a young granddaughter as well as a son. "The loss of these beloved ones added loneliness to my already lonely life. But I feel God knows best when to take his jewels home. In His mercy, He has still left me with a dutiful son and daughter as a comfort in my old age. For this blessing I cannot be too thankful. All these years, God has been purifying and fitting me for his Kingdom and now I am peacefully awaiting the summons of my Lord."[33]

In addition, formalized and often expensive mourning rituals requiring appropriate dress and accessories, jewelry, stationery, and other ephemera, coffins and tombstones, funeral and memorial services, and restrictions on social life provided a guide for these wealthier widows, and other women as well, through the early period of bereavement. Etiquette books of Victorian America focused almost exclusively upon the role of women as mourners, prescribed the attire of deep mourning (black crepe and bombazine dresses without ruffles and veils extending to the feet) to be worn by widows for at least a year followed by a change during the second and later years to lighter colors—from solid black to black and white, gray, or lavender. Some widows continued in deep mourning until their deaths. Black-bordered handkerchiefs, stationery, and calling cards, and black bonnets, straight pins, beads, and mourning pins constituted additional paraphernalia. While it is unclear just how extensively they were practiced or how long they persisted, nineteenth-century mourning customs offered at least some widows "a socially workable mechanism for dealing with the inevitable grief of death."[34]

Sentimental mourning—regarded by nineteenth-century middle-class culture as the quintessential expression of genteel social status—was notably absent in the response of Anna F. Haskell to her husband's death. Widowhood, for Haskell, was the denouement to a miserable marriage.[35] Estranged from her husband, Burnette, for almost nine years by the time of his death in 1907, she had spent years summoning the courage to try to survive on her own as she found it increasingly unbearable to remain married to the alcoholic, volatile lawyer and socialist who founded the communal society of Kaweah in Tulare County, California. She prepared for the separation by studying and obtaining a teaching certificate, then moving to the Shasta Mountains in Trinity County to teach elementary school. When she finally learned of his death four days after it occurred, Anna wrote in her diary, "Burnette is gone.—it seems when I write that, that there is no more to be said . . . but I think many thoughts." And the next day she recorded: "Of course it will make no difference in my life, but I shall miss him."[36]

Though Anna Haskell declared her independence before her husband's death, there were other women for whom widowhood was liberating. Formerly dependent upon their mates, immersed in their roles as wife and mother, generally removed from the affairs of the world, they were unleashed by the deaths of their husbands. Although they clearly had talent and the interest to enlarge their sphere beyond the home, it was widowhood that forced these women to assume responsibilities not only for their husbands' financial affairs but also in a few instances, such as that of Harriet Russell Strong, to launch their own successful careers in business. Harriet Strong, the mother of four daughters, was 39 and at the opposite end of the country, visiting a physician in Philadelphia, when her husband, Charles Lyman Strong, committed suicide over the loss of a "salted" mine in which he and others had heavily invested. Only nineteen when she married, their early, prolific correspondence during long stretches when Charles was frequently investigating mining possibilities in Arizona, Nevada, or Baja, California, reflects Harriet's consuming domestic interest and a great deal of affection.[37] But later letters included discussions of business and engineering as well. Their relationship became somewhat more tense near the end of his life as Charles encountered business difficulties and was increasingly depressed; at the time of his death in 1883, Harriet was under the care of the famous Doctor Silas Weir Mitchell for back pains, neuralgia, and anxiety over her husband's condition. Mitchell was reknowned for the extensive rest cures he prescribed for delicate, debilitated women. The recommended treatment included one to two months' confinement in bed, overfeeding, applications of electricity, and bodily massage under a physician's supervision. At the root of women's diseases, he believed, were female self-indulgence and moral laxity, and this "cure" was designed to repel the patients sufficiently that they would no longer regard bed rest as pleasurable.[38]

Whether or not Mitchell effected his goal in Strong's case, Strong did not return to California for months after her husband's death, leaving the funeral and burial to friends, relatives, and her older children. This behavior appears to contradict the sentiments expressed in response to a condolence letter. Strong wrote: "I cannot say much about how we managed to live without him: we waited long for his return to us, and it seemed just—being fulfilled—the long promised hope when everything was ended for us: . . . I do not realize that *he is gone,* my judgment and reason tell me it is so but my soul refuses to accept the truth and the sorrow grows in weight as time goes on—" She continued by looking for a future in which God's wisdom will guarantee that hopes and wishes will be realized in the other life.[39] But she did not wait for the afterlife to fulfill her needs and challenge her intelligence. Her widowhood marked the beginning of one of the most successful business careers in California. Harriet Strong developed a prosperous agricultural business in orange and walnut groves and cultivated pampas grass, originally exported to Europe and later sold in the United

States, patented a method of storing water, and developed an irrigation and water company in the San Gabriel Valley. Her death at 82, following an automobile accident, ended the career that may never have been launched without widowhood.[40]

A woman whose career was well established before marriage, Ina Sizer Cassidy was different from most widows then and now in another way. Cassidy was ten years older than her husband, Gerald, a New Mexico artist, who died at the age of 55 during the height of the Depression in 1934.[41] She seemed resigned and less shocked than many of her sympathetic friends about his accidental death from inhalation of fumes emitted by the spray paint he used in composing large murals. A native of Colorado, Ina Cassidy was an early crusader for women's rights, a lecturer, active in the Alliance of Unitarian Women, and a professional writer who had supported herself most of her adult life writing short stories, articles, and poems that were published in national literary journals. In 1931 she began writing a regular column for the *New Mexico Magazine on Art* about young artists in New Mexico and in the late 1930s served as director of the New Mexico Writers' Project under the New Deal's Works Progress Administration. Despite this lengthy professional career and a network of wealthy friends who congregated in Santa Fe, she still suffered under the combined impact of widowhood and the Depression. Most of her income derived from the sale of Cassidy's paintings, and a flurry of letters and telegrams sent after Gerald's death to the galleries that held them indicated they were not selling well. Several times toward the end of the decade, her letters sound desperate, as Ina Cassidy obviously feared losing her few properties, including her own home and some rental housing in the Santa Fe area, because she lacked the money to meet the mortgage payments. Her friends, many of them prominent artists and writers, came to her emotional aid with sympathetic letters of condolence—but not money. When she lost a job in 1939 as state director of the Writers' Project as part of a political shake-up, Cassidy's pleas to well-placed politicians were almost pathetic. Yet despite this difficult transition, she lived to age 96, relying on a combination of expertise and experience in the business and literary world, proceeds from the sale of Indian artifacts, Social Security benefits, and, as the economy improved, earnings from Cassidy's paintings.

"The pain of grief is just as much a part of life as the joy of love; it is, perhaps, the price we pay for love, the cost of commitment."[42] For most of the group of white widows discussed here, and for numerous others whose stories went unrecorded, this perception rang true, even though modern psychiatric descriptions of the grieving process were unknown to them. Whether one describes grief as an "illness" with defined symptoms and stages or as the " 'normal' " accompaniment of a major loss"—a response to the stress of a traumatic psychosocial transition—the expression of grief as well as its course and outcome in different individuals and cultures varies enormously.

Several of the women presented herein suffered great hardship as a result of their loss, and even years later continued to experience floods of sudden grief and deep, continuing sorrow. A few widows never truly recovered, while others eventually succeeded in sufficiently "letting go" of the emotional ties and roles that centered on their deceased spouses "to achieve a new and independent level of functioning."[43] Religious beliefs, mourning rituals, previous wage-earning experience, and/or preparation for work and opportunities in the labor market were also important determinants of the response to bereavement. And they reflected socioeconomic variables and cultural beliefs and practices. Individual resilience and the ability to handle stress, strength of character, and the quality of each marriage were some of the enduring personal qualities that also affected the bereavement process—yet also transcend historical conditions. In addition, lack of social support or perceived nonsupport, low socioeconomic status, young age, little previous experience with death, concurrent life crises, and unexpected or untimely death often contributed to impairment of widows' physical and psychological health.[44]

Certainly some of the widows presented here attest to this. Marietta Wetherill may be the best example of a widow who apparently suffered from chronic grief. Of course, the peculiar circumstances of Wetherill's death and Marietta Wetherill's geographical and personal isolation reflected frontier conditions and Indian policies of the time. Yet despite the severity of her reaction, persistent anger toward those she held responsible for her husband's untimely death, and inability to effectively continue her husband's work, she kept her family intact and alive, living into old age. That her responsibility for the survival of numerous, mostly young children posed an extreme burden but also a serious challenge raises a question pertinent for other widows as well: would they have had the fortitude to continue with their own lives without such pressing family responsibilities? Though we cannot "rerun an experiment" controlling for the variable of young children, the women here who were mothers of dependent young were all motivated by these family obligations to persist despite their intense grief.

For those who believed, religion and, at times, the expression of grief in stylized mourning rituals offered succor and comfort to help ease the pain of grieving. Older widows, particularly, who had personally suffered other grievous losses, including friends of their own age, were more accepting of death and regarded widowhood as a brief transition prior to their own deaths, which were welcomed as an opportunity to be reunited in the afterlife with their deceased spouses. But full participation in Victorian rituals was costly and restricted to those who could afford it. A number of widows could not, although they still found solace in God.

Bearing in mind the complexity inherent in any attempt to weigh the most critical factors determining the response to bereavement, socioeconomic conditions are probably the single most important element that runs through these accounts. None of the women here was dependent upon charitable agencies, and most of them, even the wealthy, relied upon varying degrees of emotional and/or economic help in the initial stages of widowhood, especially from relatives, close friends, informal support networks, and religious advisors. Migration to new communities with better wage-earning prospects, relocation to the family of orientation or occasionally to the home of relatives, and dependence on family for financial advice and support were alternatives that helped some of the younger widows cope effectively. Older widows frequently moved in with children. Few widows were truly independent, in the sense that they could immediately pick up the pieces of their lives and stand on their own.

What is notable about most of these widows who did not remarry or who did and were widowed again or had unsuccessful marriages is their eventual transition into breadwinners, heads of households, and independent human beings. The options available to single women during this period in history were predominantly extensions of their domestic roles, although wage-earning possibilities slightly expanded in the twentieth century in large towns and cities. Taking in washing and sewing, cooking and keeping boarders, domestic service and music instruction were all functions widows had learned as young women to fulfill their proper adult roles as wives and mothers. Even teaching school and running ranches or farms, which required additional preparation and knowledge, were well within the province of women's work. The widows who were better prepared to assume positions as heads of households because of advance warning or previous experience as wage earners usually did best. Yet given severe economic crises, the rarity of insurance or pensions, traditionally lower-paying jobs open to women, and the limitations of the southwestern economy prior to World War II, even skills and preparation were no guarantee of a smooth transition to earning a livelihood. Certainly Ina Cassidy, a seasoned professional, is but one example of a widow who found that economic circumstances beyond her control profoundly circumscribed her opportunity to support herself. Others discovered within themselves previously untapped talents and resources. They included a few extremely gifted, energetic, and hard-driving women who did more than merely make ends meet; they found new lives and built careers that far surpassed those of their husbands.[45]

In sum, most of the widows presented in these accounts were survivors who believed they had little choice but to persist in spite of their problems. "You can't be a beggar forever," Anna Rauh said. And she also noted, in a bit of philosophy translated from her native German, a fitting explanation for the adjustment of most of these women: "Need makes iron."[46]

NOTES

1. Martha Morgan Graham, *The Polygamist's Victim: or The Life Experiences of the Author During a Six Years' Residence Among the Mormon Saints* (San Francisco: Women's Union Printing Office, 1872), 52-69. For a description of this book in the Newberry Library, see Colton Storm, comp., *A Catalogue of the Everett D. Graff Collection of Western Americana* (Chicago: University of Chicago Press, 1968), 246.

Apparently it was not unusual for merchants to extend credit to women, particularly those with children, while denying it to men. See "Luzena Stanley Wilson, '49er. Memories recalled years later for her daughter Correnah Wilson Wright," in Christiane Fischer, *Let Them Speak for Themselves: Women in the American West, 1849-1900* (Hamden, Conn.: Archon Press, 1977), 152. Wilson, recounting her experience in Sacramento, noted: "There was no credit in '49 for men, but I was a woman with two children, and I might have bought out the town with no security other than my work." This excerpt also details the scarcity of women, the commonplace presence of death in early Sacramento, and the fact that the "rough" element came to Sacramento a little later. Ibid., 154-56.

The Masons, who assisted Graham on shipboard, were a secret fraternal organization that was part of the westward movement. For a brief description, see Richard A. Bartlett, *The New Country: A Social History of the American Frontier, 1776-1890* (New York: Oxford University Press, 1974), 345-46.

2. For a discussion of violence on the frontier, see Robert V. Hine, *The American West: An Interpretive History* (Boston: Little, Brown, 1973), ch. 19. Richard Max-

well Brown, "The American Vigilante Tradition," in H. D. Graham and T. R. Gurr, eds., *The History of Violence in America: Historical and Comparative Perspectives* (New York: Frederick A. Praeger, 1969), 154-225, calculates the number of people killed by vigilante groups, many of which were formed in the West. Other useful essays in this collection are: Brown, "Historical Patterns of Violence in America," 45-84, and Joe B. Frantz, "The Frontier Tradition: An Invitation to Violence," 127-54. Useful also is Howard R. Lamar, ed., *The Reader's Encyclopedia of the American West* (New York: Thomas Y. Crowell, 1977), 1227-28.

3. Colin Murray Parkes, *Bereavement: Studies of Grief in Adult Life* (Harmondsworth: Penguin Books, 1981), 13.

4. Ibid., 15-28. Also see Paul C. Rosenblatt, R. Patricia Walsh, and Douglas A. Jackson, *Grief and Mourning in Cross-Cultural Perspective* (New Haven, Conn.: Human Relations Area Files, Inc. Press, 1976), 2.

5. Colin Murray Parkes and Robert S. Weiss, *Recovery from Bereavement* (New York: Basic Books, 1983), 1-6.

6. Rosenblatt, Walsh, and Jackson, *Grief,* 3-5. Also see Joachim Whaley, ed., *Mirrors of Mortality: Studies in the Social History of Death* (London: Europa Publications, 1981), 14: "That men are more or less sad when faced with death is not something which historians can hope to measure. But the ways in which it is generally permissible for men to express grief are both constantly changing and linked to some of the most important characteristics of any human society." Whaley also notes that even within the same society, it is important to bear in mind that there is bound to be an almost infinite diversity of attitudes toward something as profound as death both among individuals and among groups. Ibid., 9.

7. Parkes and Weiss, *Recovery,* ix.

8. Private communication, Genevieve Ginsburg, Widowed to Widowed Services, Inc., Tucson. The founder of this support group has recently written: *To Live Again: Rebuilding Your Life After You've Become a Widow* (New York: St. Martin's Press, 1987).

9. I have relied heavily on a thorough, critical review of this sizeable literature by P. J. Clayton, "Bereavement and Its Management," in E. S. Paykel, ed., *Handbook of Affective Disorders* (New York: Guilford Press, 1983), ch. 30. Also useful is Richard A. Kalish, *Death, Grief, and Caring Relationships* (Monterey, Calif.: Brooks/Cole Publishing, 1981), 209-53.

10. Kalish, *Death, Grief,* 220, quoting the famous study by E. Lindemann of over 100 bereaved persons who lost family in a fire, "Symptomatology and Management of Acute Grief," *American Journal of Psychiatry* 101 (1944):141-48.

11. Kalish, *Death, Grief,* 226.

12. Ibid., 228.

13. The account that follows is based on oral history interviews conducted by Lou Blachly in Albuquerque, New Mexico, summer 1953, deposited at the Uni-

versity of New Mexico, Special Collections Library, Albuquerque. See specifically transcribed tapes 484, 485, and 486, passim. Extremely useful is Frank McNitt, *Richard Wetherill. Anasazi: Pioneer Explorer of Southwestern Ruins,* rev. ed. (Albuquerque: University of New Mexico Press, 1966).

14. Blachly interview, tape 485, 3. All direct quotes that follow are taken from the three tapes listed in note 6, unless otherwise noted.

15. McNitt, *Wetherill,* 248-318, provides a narrative account of Wetherill's murder and its aftermath.

16. Graham, *Polygamist's Victim,* 51.

17. The following account is based on an oral interview with Mrs. Anna Rauh, conducted by the author and Donna J. Guy, in Tucson, Nov. 25, 1982. Mrs. Rauh died in 1984.

18. This account is taken from an oral interview with Mrs. Helen Ivancovich, conducted by the author and Donna J. Guy in Tucson, Nov. 25, 1981. Mrs. Ivancovich died in 1982.

19. The information was gathered from Mrs. Mary Price, then 90, in two oral interviews, Nov. 11, 1981, and Jan. 22, 1982, conducted by the author and Donna J. Guy in Tucson. In addition, Mary Price provided us with a handwritten account of her life, entitled "Unwilling Pioneer: Mary Lee Bandy Price (Mrs. Charles D. Price)."

20. The issue of discrimination against married women in the work force, especially during the Depression, on the theory that they were displacing men and did not really have to work, is discussed by Winifred D. Wandersee, *Women's Work and Family Values, 1920-1940* (Cambridge, Mass.: Harvard University Press, 1981), 98-102. Despite the discrimination and job shortages of the 1930s, married women workers "were in the labor market to stay"; in fact, their participation increased during this period.

21. Sandra L. Myres, *Westering Women and the Frontier Experience, 1800-1915* (Albuquerque: University of New Mexico Press, 1982), 184-85, 248-52, describes the growing role of women in the teaching profession in the West. Their professional advancement into administrative and political posts connected with the schools provided a contrast with their experience in the East (except New England), the rural Midwest, and the South, where they did not then participate in public life.

22. Alice Hale Hill, Daily Journal, 1876-1891, 5 Nov. 1890–10 Aug. 1891, passim, and typed biography, Alice Hale Hill Collection, Colorado Historical Society, Denver.

23. Nancy Woloch, *Women and the American Experience* (New York: Alfred A. Knopf, 1984), 269-71, discusses the rise of the "new woman" and her enhanced roles.

24. Hill, Daily Journal 1899-1903, Alice Hale Hill Collection; biographical information, Nathaniel Peter Hill Collection, Colorado Historical Society.

25. Elizabeth Byers to Mary Byers Robinson, Dec. 3, 1901, box 2, f.f. 22, biographical sketch and scrapbook, William Newton Byers Collection, Denver Public Library.

26. E. Byers to M. Robinson, Dec. 31, 1903, box 2, f.f. 22.

27. E. Byers to M. Robinson, Nov. 28 or 29, 1903, box 2, f.f. 22.

28. Irving Hale to "Dear Friends," Nov. 3, 1901, Irving Hale Papers, box 5, f.f. 348, Denver Public Library.

29. Martha Elizabeth Hale to "Ever Dear Friends," Dec. 5, 1904, box 5, f.f., 366, Irving Hale Papers.

30. Bidwell Papers, part 1, box 6, Bancroft Library, University of California, Berkeley, includes a folder of clippings about Mrs. Bidwell. Articles on John Bidwell can also be found here. Memorial resolutions for John Bidwell are contained in carton 2, part 1.

31. Bidwell papers, part 1, box 6; regarding her will, see part 1, box 3, and part 1, box 6. Also see part 1, box 5, for correspondence with J. P. Edwards, Esq.

32. Bidwell Papers, Apr. 7, 1900, part 1, carton 2.

33. Arvilla D. Meeker to "My Dear Children," Mar. 5, 1897, Nathan Cook Meeker Papers, Letter 25, Denver Public Library.

34. For accounts of nineteenth-century mourning customs, see Martha Pike, "In Memory Of: Artifacts Relating to Mourning in Nineteenth-Century America," *Journal of American Culture* 3 (1980):642-59; Karen Halttunen, "Mourning the Dead: A Study in Sentimental Ritual," in *Confidence Men and Painted Women: A Study of Middle-Class Culture in America, 1830-1870* (New Haven: Yale University Press, 1982), 124-52, 229-33; and Ann Douglas, "Heaven Our Home: Consolation Literature in the Northern United States, 1830-1880," in David E. Stannard, ed., *Death in America* (Philadelphia: University of Pennsylvania Press, 1975), 49-68.

35. Diaries of Anna Fader Haskell, 1896-1910, box 4, Haskell Family Papers, Bancroft Library.

36. Diary of Anna Fader Haskell, Nov. 20, 1907. Also see the entry of Nov. 21, 1907, where she reveals guilt and depression: "It has been a long sad day. I feel so downhearted and dreary. I think of a thousand things about Burnette when he was young and gay and full of enthusiasm. — Then I reproach myself for this, that and the other and I know not what. — I do not wish to think of him at his worst. I remember when his mother died that he said he did not grieve at death but considered only that they had gone away on a long journey. I guess it is the best way to think." She also remarked that Burnette was "very lovable and was well loved," an interesting response in light of the bitterness she expressed many times during his life. This pattern of selectively remembering the good things about the dead mate is not uncommon.

37. Harriet Williams Russell Strong Collection, Henry E. Huntington Library,

San Marino, Calif., summary report, letters 73, 129, 149, 372, 374, 377-82, 386-87, 391, 399, 412-13, 415, 418, 801, 825-26, 828-29, 831-36.

38. Strong Collection, box 11, and Harriet Strong to daughter, Feb. 10, 1883, 846, "Notes on a Trip," June 1-5, 1883, 853. Sheila M. Rothman, *Woman's Proper Place: A History of Changing Ideals and Practices, 1870 to the Present* (New York: Basic Books, 1978), 34-36, discusses Mitchell's methods.

39. Strong Collection, Harriet Strong to Eben E. Olcott, Sept. 20, 1883, 786.

40. Strong Collection, box 18, newspaper clippings about and by her, including her obituary from the *Los Angeles Times,* Sept. 17, 1926. Also see references in Myres, *Westering Women,* 236, 262-63, 268-69. Isabella Greenway King, who buried two husbands but was survived by a third, was a rancher, businesswoman (who built the Arizona Inn in Tucson), and politician, the first woman elected to Congress from Arizona, where she served two terms as a representative beginning in 1933. Isabella Greenway King Collection, Arizona Historical Society, Tucson.

41. Cassidy Family Papers, Bancroft Library, especially cartons 1-2, boxes 1-4, 14-15. Also see Ina Sizer Cassidy Collection, Museum of New Mexico Historical Library, Santa Fe.

42. Parkes, *Bereavement,* 20.

43. Ira O. Glick, Robert S. Weiss, and Colin Murray Parkes, *The First Year of Bereavement* (New York: John Wiley and Sons, 1974), 299-300; Parkes and Weiss, *Recovery,* 5.

44. Clayton, "Bereavement and Its Management," 5-6. Also interesting is David Maddison and Beverley Raphael, "Conjugal Bereavement and the Social Network," in Bernard Schoenberg, ed., *Bereavement: Its Psychosocial Aspects* (New York: Columbia University Press, 1975), 26-40.

45. Lisa W. Waciega, "A 'Man of Business': The Widow of Means in Southeastern Pennsylvania, 1750-1850," *William and Mary Quarterly,* 3d Ser., 44 (1987):40-64, examines a group of propertied widows who succeeded in the propertied "male world" of business and finance, defying stereotypes about "the cult of true womanhood."

46. Oral interview with Anna Rauh; n 17 above.

11

Legal Aspects of Widowhood and Aging

HELEN S. CARTER

Although laws affect all persons, there is no universal legal system: groups of people in different areas at different periods of time have developed varying laws to confer basic personal rights and to regulate property rights. The laws concerning widows and the aging through the years reflect these inconsistencies and vary locally and nationally. In the southwestern region under study here, for example, two major legal philosophies prevail: the civil law system of Arizona and New Mexico, and the common law system of Colorado and Utah. (See table 1.)

In civil law countries an imperially written or a legislatively enacted code of laws is of primary importance, while law made by judges, reflected in decided cases, is secondary. Conversely, common law has been defined as "those principles . . . which do not rest for their authority upon . . . declaration of the will of the legislature."[1] Common law rose "from usages and customs of immemorial antiquity . . . particularly the ancient unwritten law of England."[2]

In this account of the legal aspects of widowhood and aging I focus on these two major legal systems, the laws in effect in the mid-nineteenth century, the subsequent legislatively enacted laws, and on the reported cases interpreting those laws. I review each legal system's provisions for widows and aged persons, with specific scrutiny of selected territorial, state, and federal laws and the relevant cases that interpreted these statutes. I also discuss the differences in civil law and common law over property rights, widow's dower rights, women's property rights, intestate deaths, and concomitant descent and distribution statutes, with the question of heirship;

Table 1. Comparison of Features of Civil Law and Common Law

Civil Law			*Common Law*	
Arizona	New Mexico		Colorado	Utah
		History		
Spanish Derivation		*Principles*	*English Derivation*	
Use of text of law & scholarly legal commentary for decisions			Use of decided cases (*stare decisis*) as binding precedent for decisions	
One-half ownership to each spouse (community ownership of property)			Husband obtained interests in both real & personal property of wife (old English feudal obligations)	
Valid ceremonial marriage required			Common law marriage recognized	
Case law held each spouse had present, vested, & equal interest in community property			As territorial/state laws developed, either spouse could acquire separate property	
Husband deemed manager with control of community (but not separate) property			Husband controlled property until enactment of married women's property laws	
Husband & wife each had testamentary rights over ½		Husband, only (until 1973), has right to will his ½ of community property. Wife's ½ went to husband automatically if she predeceased him.	Wife had testamentary rights over her property	
		Dowry		
Goods or wealth wife brought to marriage as her prior contribution to the relationship			Wife acquired legal rights to some property of her husband if she survived him	
		Changes		
		Dower rights abolished / Legislative succession acts passed by territories/states		
1865	1907		1868	187
		Married women's property laws enacted		
1971	1897		1874	1895-9

testate deaths; estate debts; homestead exemptions; and widow's allowances and rights of election.

I review a series of laws affecting the financial status of many widows, including welfare, pension, and employer-employee legislation, disability, and compensation laws, and the Social Security Act. All indicate legal changes dictated, at least in part, by changes in public social consciousness both prior to and during the 1930s Depression and reveal a shift in the care, support, and maintenance of individuals from the family or privately supported agencies to local, then state, and finally the federal government.

Since federal policies and laws, rules and regulations promulgated by the U.S. Department of the Interior and the Bureau of Indian Affairs, and tribal law historically have controlled "reservation" Indians, they are an exception to the territorial and state legislation discussed herein.

There is no adequate way to encompass ninety-two years of law in a single essay. Yet, as U.S. Supreme Court Justice Oliver W. Holmes, Jr., contended, "The history of what the law has been is necessary to the knowledge of what the law is."[3] Guided by his postulate and using selected statutes and cases, I also survey some of the major legal problems, solutions, differences, and universalities concerning widows and aging persons in the Southwest from 1848 through 1939.

Civil Law and Common Law

Early English judges used prior case decisions as guides for current similar disputes; over time this became the doctrine of *stare decisis* and is fundamental to English common law. When a court applied a principle of law to a set of facts, and where subsequent case facts were substantially the same, future cases followed the prior decision. By contrast, the Roman civil law relied both on legal writings from authoritative legal scholars and on texts of enacted laws to guide their case decisions. The American legal system evolved using both case law and statute law, not one system to the exclusion of the other.[4]

The legal systems of Arizona and New Mexico, colonized by Spain and Mexico, were based on civil law. Colorado and Utah, settled largely by migration from the eastern United States, followed English common law (table 1). The existing property systems prescribed different legal entitlements upon the provider's death for his widow, children, and aged parents. English common law court rules of practice and decision not repugnant to nor inconsistent with regional laws then in effect were adopted by Arizona

(1864), Colorado (1861), New Mexico (1876), and Utah (1898).[5] Arizona's first territorial legislature enacted the Howell Code in 1864 (effective January 1, 1865), which went even further, in fact, and adopted some of the separate marital property theories of English common law, taking no notice of the Spanish community property system. However, the second territorial legislature repealed this portion of the law (December 30, 1865) and restored the community property system to Arizona.[6] In general, these enactments adopting common law for use in the courts did not abolish the civil legal system then in use in Arizona and New Mexico.[7]

Civil Law—Community Property

Under civil law, concepts of community property developed from familial ownership in which a husband and wife constituted a marital community. The community property system required a valid ceremonial marriage, nullifying the validity of common-law marriage in establishing a marital community. Spanish law opposed common-law marriage; in Arizona and New Mexico it was invalid for accrual of property rights during cohabitation.[8] In contrast, Colorado recognized common-law marriages; case law there held that a common-law wife would inherit the estate of her common-law husband.[9]

Brought to Spain by the Visigoths, the community property system prevailed in the territories acquired by Spain and in many of the states originally under Spanish rule.[10] The *Fuero Juzgo*,[11] a code fusing Spanish and Visigothic law, recognized a marital community ownership in which husband and wife held *acquêts* and *gains* as a common property during continuance of the marriage, that is, it belonged to both by halves. Acquêts in civil law were estates in property, acquired during marriage either by donations made jointly to husband and wife or by purchase, even if the purchase was in the name of only one of the two, and not of both, or in any other similar way (or otherwise than by succession); they also included profits or gains from their property as a product of the joint industry of both husband and wife, including profits from all property (other than his separate property) that the husband administered and enjoyed, either of right or in fact. *Bienes gananciales*, in Spanish law, is property acquired or gained during marriage, held in common by husband and wife.[12] This ganancial system, with some modifications to suit local customs, prevailed in Arizona and New Mexico.[13]

Community property is property other than separate property that is acquired by husband or wife or the two of them together during marriage.[14]

A person bringing separate property to a marriage, or acquiring it by gift or inheritance during marriage, could maintain its separate character. In general, a spouse could manage and control his or her separate property so long as it was not comingled with community property.

Arizona and New Mexico courts held that separate property became community property when it was "confused, intermixed, and comingled with the community property so that such separate property lost its identity."[15] This doctrine could adversely affect a woman who owned much valuable property and married a man with little. If during marriage her property was comingled and presumed by law to be community property, and her husband died intestate, then the widow would be entitled only to a community half-interest instead of the major portion she brought to the marriage. The other half would pass to heirs of the deceased.

A characteristic of original Spanish property law deemed the husband head of the household, head of the marital community, and gave him sole power to manage and control community property. Arizona statutes of 1865, as well as New Mexico territorial law prior to 1901, granted the husband the right to manage, control, and dispose of both real and personal community property, including earnings of the wife, without her consent.[16]

By the latter part of the nineteenth century and the beginning of the twentieth, the women's rights movement had made limited gains in the area of legal rights. In particular, the movement stimulated legal enactments requiring less deference of wives to their husbands in property management. As they became more active in family business concerns, women began to acquire more power within marriage. Arizona in 1871 and New Mexico in 1907 enacted statutes stipulating that a wife could manage and control her separate property.[17] Legislation in Arizona in 1913 and in New Mexico in 1901 provided that a wife must join her husband to transfer title to real property. However, the Arizona Supreme Court as late as 1923 in *Pendleton v. Brown* considered the husband the head of the community with power to manage and dispose of its assets and with exclusive control of proceeds from the sale of community property, notwithstanding the requirement that his wife must join in conveyances of community realty.[18]

Community property law presumes each spouse to own a present, vested,[19] and equal half-interest in their common property. Arizona's landmark case on this issue, decided in 1914, established in part that the husband and wife had equal legal rights in their community property. The court held that the law gave hubands no higher or better title than their wives and recognized a marital community where both were equal. The court said the law plainly expressed as policy the endowment of a wife with dignity equal to that of her husband and recognized her familial contributions as an equal factor in matrimonial property gains whether or not she contributed actual cash to acquire the property. The Arizona court held "that the wife in her station [was] as much an agency in the acquisition as the husband and [was] entitled to just as great an interest."[20]

By contrast, a New Mexico court in 1908 held differently on this same question of present, vested, and equal community property rights for a wife. The husband and wife in this case were married in 1857. In 1889 and 1893 the husband bought land that became community property. In 1902 (after the 1901 New Mexico law requiring both spouses to join in executing a deed transferring title to property), the husband, without his wife's participation in the conveyance, sold the land in question. The New Mexico Territorial Supreme Court held that the husband was in substance the owner, with the wife having a mere expectancy of ownership at the termination of the marital community if she survived her husband. The court based its holding largely on the ground that the husband had acquired vested rights in the property before the passage of the 1901 statute, rights that would be taken from him if that statute were allowed to apply to previously acquired land. A strong, well-reasoned dissenting opinion by Justice Ira A. Abbott pointed out that the wife had an actual ownership existing during the marriage, subject only to the managerial powers of her husband. On appeal, Justice Abbott's view was approved by the U.S. Supreme Court in 1911.[21] Subsequently, the New Mexico court in 1919 recognized that a wife, with her husband, has vested and existing ownership during marriage,[22] which continues to be the law in New Mexico.

In both Arizona and New Mexico either spouse had full and complete power to dispose of his or her separate property by will,[23] and in Arizona either spouse could will his or her half-interest in community property.[24] In New Mexico, however, only a husband had testamentary power over half the community estate, and he could will his half to whomever he chose; wives had no such testamentary rights. A wife's interest in the community property, although held by case law as noted above to be "present and vested," passed immediately on her death entirely to her husband if he survived her.[25] Thus, in New Mexico, a wife could not will her half of the community property, although, if widowed, her acquisition of her husband's half of the property depended on the terms of his will. This anachronistic legal aberration persisted in New Mexico until 1973, when after many years of effort by women to effect such change, a law was enacted that allowed wives the same testamentary rights as husbands.[26]

Common Law

The English common law property system, with its feudal rather than familial origins, lacked the concept that property rights arose from the marital partnership. Common law also ignored the equal ownership of husband and wife in acquisitions and gains during marriage. While under community property the fact of ownership is paramount, under English common law prior to the colonial period, the technical matter of who was named in the title took precedence.[27] The origins of this stipulation lay in English feudal allegiance and military obligations to the sovereign, liege, or lord who granted title to the property owner. Because a woman was considered incapable of fulfilling military responsibilities associated with property ownership, as a married woman she could not own land in her own name.

Under English common law transplanted to America and eventually westward to Colorado and Utah, during marriage the husband and wife were considered as "one person in law; that is, the very being or legal existence of the woman is suspended during the marriage, or at least is incorporated and consolidated into that of the husband, under whose protection, wing, and cover she performs everything."[28] Under this theory the wife was considered as another chattel or item belonging to her husband; there was no recognition of her as an individual having a separate character, mind, or personality.[29] In explaining this theory, an 1889 federal court opinion, in a Colorado case, stated a wife "was absolutely under the control of her husband, and without his consent she could neither act nor contract with reference to any right of property."[30]

This old English common law concept held that through marriage a husband acquired interests in both real and personal property of his wife; personal property owned by a wife at marriage, which under civil law would have remained her separate property, became under common law the property of her husband. She could not alienate her land without her husband's concurrence and consent; it was administered for her by her husband, and he was entitled to the usufructs (advantages and profits) from it. In return, the husband had a duty to support his wife, and she had a duty to render services to him.[31]

A somewhat modified form of common-law property ownership developed in Colorado and Utah. No property was owned in common unless the couple chose to assume joint title. The separate property of each spouse generally included property owned at marriage, property acquired separately by gift or inheritance, and all personal earnings during marriage. At the death of an intestate spouse, the survivor received a statutory share—one-third or one-half—of the other's separate estate. As for benefits to the widow, there was little to distinguish this common law separate property system from the community property system.

The separate property system of Colorado and Utah was ostensibly impartial in its recognition that either spouse was free to accumulate separate property, but its effect was discriminatory since it ignored women's actual role in the society of the time. A woman's primary responsibility was assumed to be in the care of the home and children. Thus, while women were legally free to accumulate their own separate property, realistically they were hampered in acquiring it unless they had a separate source of income.

The community property system of Arizona and New Mexico was highly advantageous to women in this respect because it gave each spouse a present, vested, and equal interest in community property acquired by either spouse during marriage. This system considered the work of the wife in caring for the home and children to be her contribution to the acquisition of marital property. Her labor was accorded "dignity and equality,"[32] as a collaborative effort with her husband, and "entitle[d] her to a one-half interest in her husband's earnings."[33] As pointed out by William DeFuniak, a prominent authority on community property law, "This recognition of the wife as a person in her own right is one of the outstanding principles of the civil law and is one of those in which it diverges sharply from the common law."[34]

Dower Rights

Another area of readily apparent difference between common and civil law systems is the concept of the widow's dower right. The dowery of biblical history was actually a bride price, a gift from the suitor to the father or other near relatives of an intended bride. It had no resemblance to what was later known as dower in the common law. Neither is common law dower similar to the dower, called "dos," of the civil law (or the "dot" in France).[35]

Common law dower was the legal right that a wife acquired by marriage in the property of her husband if she survived him. It consisted in her use, during her surviving lifetime, of one-third of all real estate her husband held during marriage as a freehold estate (which could be inherited by a child born of the marriage).[36]

Dower was provided especially for the sustenance and protection of the widow and for the nurture and education of the children of the marriage.[37] Until the husband died, dower was not a full or complete interest in property but was "an inchoate right during coverture. . . . It was not an estate in land, vested or otherwise, but a mere expectancy or possibility incident to the marriage relation, contingent on the wife surviving the husband."[38] Inchoate dower was inalienable by the wife without her husband's consent.

As the territories and states enacted laws of succession providing for the descent and distribution of property, the right to dower was abolished in Arizona (1865), Colorado (1868), New Mexico (1907), and Utah (1872).[39] Descent and distribution statutes then prescribed the intestate share a surviving spouse received. Generally this benefited widows, since they received a fee simple (absolute ownership with unrestricted rights of disposition), instead of only a life estate in one-third or one-half the property owned by the deceased.

Married Women's Property Rights

The drive to gain women's suffrage and other legal rights for married women constituted critical goals of feminism in the latter half of the nineteenth century. The National Woman Suffrage Association and the American Woman Suffrage Association, each organized in 1869, attacked these problems using two differing methods: the former, by working at the federal level for a U.S. constitutional amendment, and the latter, by lobbying the territorial and state legislatures for voting rights and legal changes expanding property rights for married women. By 1860, when New York passed the most comprehensive Married Women's Property Act yet enacted, fourteen other states had already approved some form of this legislation. The Southwest responded more slowly. Colorado (1874) and Utah (1895-96) altered common law property rules to enable married women to retain, manage, and control their own real and personal property.[40] Arizona (1871) and New Mexico (1897) passed similar emancipatory legislation, generally known as Married Women's Acts, which granted married women the right to appear in court, to make contracts and conveyances, and to manage their own property.[41]

Suffrage was a more arduous battle, but complete voting rights for women were achieved in Colorado (1893), Utah (1896), and Arizona (1912) before the passage of the Nineteenth Amendment in 1920.

Intestate Succession—Descent and Distribution Statutes

Legal problems frequently aggravated the difficult position of widows, children, and aged parents of the deceased and contributed to their sorrow and emotional distress. As noted above, all our territories/states in early law gave husbands the right to control and manage marital property. In many cases the bereaved survivors had been denied participation in any active or meaningful way in management of family property during the life of the deceased. As a result, the survivors might have little or no knowledge of legal provisions made by the deceased or their rights to share in the distribution of or succession to the estate.

Succession is the devolution of title to property under laws of descent and distribution. Intestate succession is the succession of an heir at law to property and estate of an ancestor when the latter died without a will, or left a will that was set aside as legally null and void.[42] From earliest historical time, intestate inheritance systems evolved incorporating the principle of succession to or devolution of an estate to a blood-related heir. Transfer of property at death gave heirs not only the right to step into the place of the deceased to control, enjoy, and administer the estate but also passed the obligations (including debts) of the deceased to the heirs.

A widow was not considered an heir of her husband by either common law or civil law.[43] Case law defined heir as "he who is born or begotten in lawful wedlock" and held that "the words 'my heirs-at-law'. . . include only his heirs-at-law by blood and not his widow."[44]

Although a widow had no hereditary share in the estate of an intestate deceased husband, under common law, if a wife died first, her surviving spouse succeeded to her entire personal estate. In a partial attempt to correct this inequity, a seventeenth-century English act[45] gave the widow a one-third share in the personal property of her intestate deceased husband if issue (child or children) was born of the marriage; if no issue resulted, the widow received half his personal estate. However, since land interests (realty) and not personal property generally made up the major asset of an estate, and land descended to heirs, a widow, in many cases, continued to be poorly provided for by the law. By the nineteenth century, laws began to advance the idea that marriage established a bond, similar to kinship, between husband and wife. The most significant feature of subsequent intestate succession laws was the striving for substantial equality in the share received by a surviving spouse. Specific intestate succession laws from each of the four states reflect legislative provisions to provide for widows, children, and, in some cases, parents of the deceased.

For example, an Arizona intestacy law of 1865 gave one-half of the community property to a surviving spouse, and the other half, after payment of debts, to descendants. If there were no descendants, the entire estate, after payment of debts, passed to the surviving spouse. In 1887 another Arizona law provided that when an intestate husband left a surviving widow and child, children, or their descendants, his widow received one-third of his separate personal estate, and the issue, two-thirds. The surviving widow was also entitled to an estate for her lifetime in one-third of the deceased's land, with the remainder to their issue. If they had no issue, the widow was entitled to all deceased's personal estate plus one-half the lands, in fee simple, with the other half of the lands to pass to the mother and father of deceased. If the deceased husband left no issue, and no mother or father, then everything passed to the widow.[46]

In Colorado an 1876 law provided that when an intestate left a surviving spouse and child, children, or their descendants, one-half the estate passed to the surviving spouse and the other half to issue or their descendants. If there were no issue or descendants of issue, the entire estate, subject to payment of debts, descended to the surviving spouse as his or her absolute estate, according to an 1891 statute.[47]

Under an 1872 New Mexico law, "when either the husband or wife dies without legitimate children, the one surviving shall be heir to all the acquired property of the marriage community."[48] Ten years later this law was changed to define heirs of an intestate as "legitimate children and descendants" and further stated explicitly that "the widow of the deceased . . . [is] not an heir."[49] A likely reason for this change was to expand the descent and distribution law to provide a more complete plan for property devolution.

An extremely complicated statute, the 1882 New Mexico law provided that each marital partner should pay his or her private debts from his or her private property and that community debts would be paid from community property. The balance of the estate was styled "Acquest Property" and was divided into equal halves. One-half was added to and became a part of the private property of the wife; the other was added to the private property of the husband and became the total amount of his estate with complex provisions for distribution. In 1889 an intestacy law stipulated half the common property to the widow, and of the remaining half, half to the widow and half to children or their heirs. Further changes in 1897 held that if there were no issue, or their descendants, the widow received the entire estate.[50]

In Utah under an 1898 law,[51] if children were born of a marriage, the widow was entitled to the equivalent of a child's share, but not less than a child's one-third share. If there were no issue, but the deceased left a surviving parent, brother, or sister, his widow received a half share, and the other heirs, the other half. If none of the foregoing survived except a widow, she received all of deceased's estate up to $5,000 plus half of any residue above that.

By 1917 Utah law provided "one-third in value of all the legal or equitable estates in real property possessed by the husband at any time during the marriage, and to which the wife had made no relinquishment of her rights, shall be set apart as her property in fee simple."[52] Additionally, if there were no issue, and the estate, real and personal, did not exceed $5,000 exclusive of debts and expenses, the widow took the entire estate; if it was over $5,000 she took $5,000 plus half the excess, with the remainder to the deceased's father, mother, brothers, or sisters. If there were no issue, father, mother, brother, nor sister, the widow received the entire estate.

Testate Succession

Testamentary disposition or the right to arrange before death for postmortem transfer of property has ancient origins. "Solon is said to have introduced wills into Greece B.C. 594, and testamentary bequests were first regulated at Rome by the laws of the Twelve Tables, B.C. 450."[53] The right to transmit property at death is not a fundamental right, not a property right, nor a natural, inherent right; it is purely a statutory creation, subject to complete legislative control, available only in strict compliance with statutory requirements, and can be accomplished only by means of a valid will.[54] The law, as a general rule, favors testacy. Less evidence is necessary to authenticate a will than to disprove one. The courts generally try to protect the rights of widows and children and to keep them from being defrauded either by the terms of a will or by prior acts of the deceased.

For example, an 1861 Colorado law[55] prohibited a married man, in the absence of a marriage settlement agreement, from devising more than half his property away from his wife. Also general rules of law provide that wills made by single persons are presumed revoked by marriage unless the spouse, by a marital settlement, agrees and knowingly contracts away his or her future rights. In a 1902 Colorado case, one Peter Magnes, with little explanation of his financial condition to his prospective bride, a Scandinavian with little learning or sophistication, had her sign a marital property agreement. The court opinion, in part, stated,

> An ante-nuptial agreement will be sustained when fairly made, but will be regarded with rigid scrutiny, and where the circumstances establish that the woman has been deceived, or in the absence of a full and complete knowledge and understanding of her rights, entered into such a contract it will be held null and void. . . . The husband or his representatives [must] show perfect good faith . . . especially where the provision made for the wife is inequitable or unreasonably disproportioned to the means of the husband. . . .
>
> . . . The parties to such an agreement stand in a confidential relation. . . . Marital rights of the widow should have been disclosed to her. The failure to do so would constitute an undue advantage, for which such contracts have been repeatedly annulled.[56]

In another Colorado case in 1897,[57] a husband deeded property to his children from a former marriage, but he kept control and use of the property. His children did not record the deeds until after their father's death four years later. The court disallowed this as a fraudulent transfer, which attempted to defeat the rights of the widowed second wife.

In a New Mexico case, decided in 1890, a husband bequeathed to his wife "all articles of goods in my house, personal furniture, household furniture, and all that therein exists."[58] The court held that clause sufficient to include $25,000 contained in a household iron box and safe, which only the testator knew was there; neither the money nor its location was specifically mentioned in the will. The deceased's nephew, named administrator by the will, took possession of the money against a claim by the widow. The court ruled that the testator owed his wife protection and support, and this obligation, together with evidence that he had sufficient means of fulfilling it, raised a presumption that her deceased husband intended to make ample provision for her through his will.

Another New Mexico case in 1911 protected a widow against a fraudulent attempt to dispose of property rightfully hers.[59] A 1919 New Mexico case held a purported property settlement was an attempt to defraud the wife.[60] The wife had transferred to her husband property valued at between $100,000 and $200,000, while in exchange he paid her $4,000. She had agreed to this inequitable settlement while under accusation of adultery, without receiving any independent legal advice and without full knowledge of her legal rights to the marital property. The court set aside the settlement as presumptively fraudulent. The court also declined to follow Spanish law, which held that an adulterous wife forfeited her right to community property, thus overruling earlier New Mexico decisions on this point.[61] By contrast, a 1923 Arizona case acknowledged, as a "well-recognized rule,"[62] that an adulterous wife who unjustifiably abandoned her husband lost her community property rights to property acquired after the abandonment; however, this decision was based, at least in part, on the court's finding that the separation agreement of the parties, containing a division and partition of their community property, was evidence of their intent to abolish the marital community and was an implied contract that subsequent acquisitions of each party would remain the separate property of the one acquiring it.

Estate Debts and Homestead Exemptions

In all estates debts must be paid before the estate is closed and distribution of property made. Administration costs, medical and funeral expenses, allowances for the widow and children, taxes, and other debts are paid first from personal property of the deceased. If the personalty is insufficient, real property of the deceased becomes liable. The debts of a deceased landowner, in that event, may become a lien on that land.

Most states provide statutory exemptions for specified amounts of an estate to pass to surviving spouses free of the liens just noted. A probate homestead is a "homestead set apart . . . for the use of a surviving husband or wife and the minor children out of the common property, or out of the real estate belonging to the deceased."[63] The purpose of a homestead is to ensure a home for a surviving spouse and minor children. Homesteads are always creations of constitutions or statutes and not of common law. Ordinarily these statutes allow a debtor as head of a family to keep specific property of a certain value or quantity and not be forced to sell it to pay debts. When a husband died, leaving a widow and family, his homestead exemption was legally available for his widow as a life estate, with the remainder to the decedent's children.[64]

Homestead exemptions generally entitled a widow and minor children to remain in the homestead, to keep all family clothing, all household furniture, and to receive a judicially determined reasonable provision for their support. The value of homesteads varied through the years in each state and provisions varied from state to state.

For example, in 1883, Colorado law limited the homestead value to $2,000.[65] A New Mexico law of 1897 allowed a widow to keep all wearing apparel, beds, bedsteads, bedding, cooking stove, warming stove and sixty days' fuel, one cow (or furniture of $40 value), two swine (or furniture of $15 value), six sheep and their wool (or furniture of $20 value), food for sixty days for animals, Bibles, hymn books, Psalm books, school books, family pictures, one sewing machine, one knitting machine, one gun or pistol, and tools and implements necessary for trade or business (not exceeding $150 value). The law further provided that this widow's exemption "shall be set apart to her as her property in her own right, and shall be exempt in her hands as in the hands of the decedent."[66] Utah law in 1898 limited the homestead value to $2,000 plus $250 for each minor child.[67] Case law in Utah held that real estate set apart for the use of the widow and minor children did not vest in the widow absolutely; she had no power to convey it to the exclusion of other family members of the deceased because she was entitled only to an estate in the homestead for her lifetime.[68]

Widow's Allowance

It was common practice during the late 1800s and early 1900s for the male-dominated legislatures of the territories and states of the United States to provide for a "widow's allowance." In their legislative wisdom, manifested in the male viewpoint that a wife was little more than the "property" of her husband, apparently it seemed inconceivable to legislators that a widow might be able to provide for herself and her children, if any, without the generosity of a legislative enactment providing an allowance to free her from debts incurred by her husband before his death. Indeed, the proverbial "widow's mite" probably was at least a portion of the widow's allowance concept. Thus, under laws enacted as public policy, a widow was given her widow's allowance of money or property from her deceased husband's estate.[69]

At the judge's discretion, the widow and children were entitled to a reasonable allowance according to the finances of the deceased's estate. This was to provide a maintenance allowance for her and any children, to support them during administration of the probate estate. It was regarded as a substitute for the support previously provided by the deceased husband/father.[70] A Utah court in 1904 viewed the allowance as an "absolute right" of the widow "during the administration of the estate. In fixing the amount of the allowance, the age of the survivor or survivors, their health, their social position and standing, the education of their children, the value of the estate, and its solvency or insolvency" were considered by the court.[71] An Arizona court in 1941 held that an allowance of $100 per month for the widow was "not excessive."[72]

Widow's Election

In the four states of this study, statutes and case law gave surviving widows a legal right known as "widow's election."[73] Under such a law a widow had two alternative choices, which were basically the same under community property or common law jurisdiction. She could choose to accept what her husband provided for her in his will, or she could choose—elect—to take, instead, what the statute law in her jurisdiction provided. The latter, commonly, was an amount equal to what she would have received had her husband died intestate.

Development of Welfare and Pension Laws

Widows, children, and aged parents left unprovided for by the death of their main provider might find themselves dependent on public support systems as those functions became established by law. Welfare assistance originally was a privilege, not an entitlement. Individual citizens had no legal duty to provide for the general poor, and common law duty to support dependents was limited. Common law required that a husband support his wife, their minor children, and older children too weak in mind or body to support themselves. A child might have a moral duty to support its parents, but there was no common law requirement that an adult child support needy or indigent parents.

From the legal viewpoint, the duty for primary support originally rested on morally obligated consanguineous relatives, who by the "law of nature" should provide for their own. However, since the "law of nature" offered no method of enforcing such moral obligations, governing bodies in conformity with public policy precepts enacted enforceable statutes either to provide assistance from the government or to compel assistance from closely blood-related persons or both.

The poor laws of England, which acknowledged the government's obligation and public duty to support the general poor, were designed to suppress vagrancy and begging. America's poor laws, passed in the colonial period, were based on English laws. Later, state governments assumed responsibility and delegated it to local governments. There was little uniformity from state to the state, county to county, or city to city within a state. In general, counties were authorized by territorial enactments and early state statutes to provide such welfare and relief as the public good might require to the aged, indigent, or others who were unable to care for and provide for themselves with any degree of sufficiency.

Toward the end of the nineteenth century and in the early twentieth century, state governments became more active in assuming and enlarging their social welfare responsibilities. They enacted legislation establishing state welfare, retirement, and pension systems. Selected public assistance and pension laws reveal affirmative efforts to provide government-financed assistance to widows, dependent children, and the indigent elderly.

The Arizona Constitution, for example, gave a mandate to the government to "protect and maintain individual rights."[74] An 1895 Colorado law provided:

> The county clerk of each county shall keep a book, to be entitled "record of County Poor," which shall be so ruled as to conveniently show in separate columns the date of registration, name of person, age, sex, place of birth, date of immigration to the United States, date of immigration to Colorado, from what county in Colorado, and the date of arrival in the county of record, cost of maintenance in poor house, cost of maintenance in hospital, cash furnished, other aid and a description and value of the same, total value of all aid, total time of maintenance, cause of poverty or distress, and remarks.[75]

Colorado counties were authorized to levy taxes to provide this care.

New Mexico 1882 statutes created a Board of Charities & Industrial Schools, funded from the territorial treasury; an 1884 law established an orphans' home, and a 1913 law provided funding "for the relief of deserving indigent persons who are objects of charity."[76] Laws of various states to provide "mothers' pensions" or "mothers' allowances" can be traced to pioneering efforts in the 1911 legislatures in Missouri and Illinois.[77] These laws, one outcome of the White House Conference on Dependent Children in 1909, recognized an economic benefit to society to help a widow to care for her children at home instead of the governments' having to assume the expense of maintaining them in orphanages or foster homes. It was believed to be a public benefit to provide aid to a widowed mother to enable her and her children to live at home in reasonable health and comfort. These laws foreshadowed the later federal "aid to dependent children . . . in . . . their own home," language in the Social Security Act Amendment of 1939.[78] An Arizona Initiated Act of November 3, 1914, providing old-age and mothers' pensions, was enacted by the 1915 Arizona legislature;

however, it was held by a 1916 case to be null and "violative of [Arizona Constitution] mandate."[79] The opinion was based on a technicality in the act, with the court holding that if the wording in the act, which would have abolished almshouses, was construed to include state institutions, it would be unconstitutional.[80]

To provide for elderly retired teachers, a 1912 Arizona law established an annual teachers' pension of $600, after a teacher had taught twenty-five or more years in Arizona.[81]

A 1903 Colorado law established a firemen's pension for paid (but not volunteer) firemen with twenty or more years of service, their widows, and dependent children under age fourteen. And in 1909 Colorado statutes established a public school teachers' retirement fund, paying up to $40 per month "to any *man* teacher *sixty* years of age or any *woman* teacher *fifty* years of age" with twenty-five years service[82] (emphasis added).

New Mexico provided pensions for firemen in 1927. It created a state department of public welfare in 1937. The 1941 New Mexico Statutes Annotated included a state excise tax on cigars and cigarettes, which designated the proceeds for old-age assistance.[83] A 1907 Utah law provided pensions for teachers.[84]

During the same period when these expanded benefits were being legislated, all four states broadened legal liabilities to provide for reciprocity of support between husband and wife, and between adult child and parent. As the common law duty of a husband to support his wife was recognized by enactment of state laws mandating such support, similar duties were imposed on a wife, requiring her to support her needy or infirm husband when she was financially able.[85] All four states also enacted laws to compel support from other relatives able to support but refusing to do so. One of the provisions of the 1939 Arizona Old-Age Assistance Act established relatives' responsibility to support the elderly. The 1912 Colorado Annotated Statutes stated, "Every poor person who shall be unable to earn a livelihood in consequence of any bodily infirmity, idiocy, lunacy or other unavoidable cause, shall be supported by the father, grandfather, mother, grandmother, child or grandchild, brother or sister of such person, if they or either of them be of sufficient ability."[86] This same law also allowed counties to levy a fine of $20 per month on financially able relatives refusing to support a poor relative and provided that the money collected be used by the county to support the indigent relation. The duty to support poor relations was always dependent on ability, both at common law and under statutory enactments.[87] These laws sought to transform an imperfect moral responsibility into a legally enforceable liability.

Employer/Employee Legislation

Under common law an employee was assumed to agree to and take on all ordinary risks of employment. This rule of law regarding employer/employee relations was attacked as being too pro-employer to provide even a modicum of protection for employees; it efficiently protected employers to the detriment of employees. As in the earlier lobbying for married women's property rights, it took a number of years before legal safeguards and protective laws for workers were finally attained.

All four states during the years 1912-33 enacted workmen's compensation, employer's liability, and unemployment insurance laws.[88] Workmen's compensation laws provided payment for disability or death from accidental industrial injuries sustained by a worker when such disability or death arose out of and in the regular course of employment. In case of death, payment went to the widow or dependent heirs. These laws encountered resistance in early court cases. In *Ives v. South Buffalo Ry.*, a 1911 New York case, the court held that state's 1909 Workmen's Compensation Act was unconstitutional; it ruled that the liability sought by plaintiffs to be imposed on employers constituted "a taking of property without due process of law."[89] Other authorities have viewed *Ives* as an "aberration" even at the time it was decided, and laws providing compensation for workers ultimately prevailed.[90]

Social Security

As pressure mounted for an expanded system of welfare, assistance for the needy began to shift from a familiar and personal level to cities or counties, then to state and federal governments. In response to these demands and to alleviate the extensive suffering of many persons during the Depression of the 1930s, the federal government became involved more inclusively in the administration of social welfare.

In 1935 Congress passed the Social Security Act,[91] which established a public benefit system, offering to the states the assistance of the federal government in providing financial aid to qualified recipients. Basically, this was a compulsory, contributory, old-age annuity program for employed workers. It established annual appropriations and guidelines to enable each state to allocate funds more adequately and effectively for the needy aged, dependent and crippled children, maternal and child health, child welfare, public health, vocational rehabilitation, and unemployment compensation. The theoretical basis of this was a belief that public policy is promoted by protection, welfare, and assistance of the aged and others in need, and that economic insecurity is a serious menace to the health, morals, and welfare of the entire populace. The primary purpose of the act was to provide general welfare benefits, but perhaps it is known best as a system of compulsory old-age insurance that pays benefits proportional to earnings to those over sixty-five with sufficient earnings during the required time period in jobs covered by the act.

Like earlier workmen's compensation laws, the Social Security Act was attacked. In the several *Social Security Act Cases* of 1937, the courts construed congressional legislative powers broadly, holding that under U.S. constitutional provisions, Congress could spend money from the public treasury and impose taxes to provide old-age benefits and unemployment insurance as a means of promoting the general welfare. In one opinion, the U.S. Supreme Court included an illuminating 1937 statistical study by the Social Security Board to indicate the need for benefits to aged workers:

> One-fifth of the aged in the United States were receiving old-age assistance, emergency relief, institutional care, employment under the works program, or some other form of aid from public or private funds; two-fifths to one-half were dependent on friends and relatives, one-eighth had some income from earnings; and possibly one-sixth had some savings or property. Approximately three out of four persons 65 or over were probably dependent wholly or partially on others for support.[92]

The original act provided for federal old-age benefits payable to qualified individuals on retirement after reaching age 65. In 1939 amendments to the act[93] added immeasurably to the future economic welfare of women aged 65 or over and widows, dependent children, and dependent parents aged 65 or over of deceased individuals covered under the original act. The amendments provided monthly benefits for two classes not covered by the original act: (1) wives and dependent children of those entitled to primary insurance benefits, and (2) widows and dependent children (or dependent parents, if deceased left no widow or dependent children) of properly qualified insured deceased individuals.[94]

Supplementary monthly benefits were provided for eligible wives (aged 65 or over, living with her husband, and not entitled to receive the same amount or more from an account of her own if she was also a covered worker) of workers entitled to primary benefits and to their unmarried dependent children under age 18. Both classes were entitled to monthly benefits equal to one-half that of the husband/parent's primary benefit.

The survivors' monthly benefits program was of major importance to widows, dependent minor children, and aged dependent parents of qualified deceased individuals. The new amendments established monthly benefit payments for eligible survivors of qualified workers who died after December 31, 1939.

An unremarried widow, aged 65 or older, who was living with her husband at the time of his death, and who was not entitled to a monthly payment equal to or greater than three-fourths of that of her deceased husband under her own workers primary insurance coverage (if she was also a covered worker), would receive three-fourths of the primary insurance benefit of her deceased husband.

The unremarried widow, under age 65 of an insured worker, who was living with her husband at the time of his death and who had in her care their dependent child who was entitled to survivors' benefits, was entitled to receive three-fourths of her husband's benefit rate so long as she continued to have the care of their dependent child. While under age 18 each unmarried, dependent child of an insured deceased would receive monthly benefits of one-half the rate of the deceased parent.

If there were no surviving widow or eligible dependent child, each dependent parent, aged 65 or older of the insured deceased, after filing proof of complete dependency on their deceased child and who was not entitled to receive other monthly insurance benefits of more than one-half that of deceased, was entitled to a monthly survivors' benefit of one-half the rate of the deceased.

These 1939 amendments, providing that a proportion of the monthly benefit payments of qualified workers who died after December 31, 1939, would be paid to survivors, established financial assistance for them when their need was most urgent. The new laws assured continuing monthly financial assistance, thus enabling survivors to remain in a home or family relationship rather than forcing them into institutions or possible destitution.

Conclusion

Legal theory in America through the first quarter of the twentieth century tended to favor restriction of governmental power in public welfare laws. However, state pension laws, employer-employee legislation, and early welfare laws, along with unemployment compensation and other provisions of the Social Security Act of 1935, all ran contrary to this viewpoint. Many of these laws required litigation in the courts to determine their constitutional validity. Not until the *Social Security Act Cases* of 1937 did the courts fully recognize that governmental legislative and administrative decisions regarding public welfare belonged to Congress and state legislatures. The judiciary then approved legislative assumption of broad powers to tax and spend to promote public welfare. This resulted in a shift of welfare services from family and local levels of government to federal and state agencies and institutions. It also raised expectations and dramatically increased support for widows and the aged.

The growth of aggressive, affirmative government action, particularly regarding public assistance, brought major benefits to aging persons. The Social Security Act in 1935 was of paramount financial importance for aged employed persons. After age 65, it provided monthly benefit payments for insured workers funded by government appropriation and by prior contributions from the worker. At a time of life when the earnings of other workers were likely to decline or disappear, these monthly benefits supplied income vital to the survival of some individuals.

The legal rights of women and widows underwent major changes from 1847 to 1939. While many significant differences have been pointed out between the original laws in the civil law states of Arizona and New Mexico and the common law states of Colorado and Utah, these differences, at least regarding rights for women in general, and for widows in particular, have narrowed considerably during the years under study. This is not to imply uniformity of the law in all four states but to point out that time, legislation, Congress, and judicial opinions led to fewer disparities in the laws of civil and common law states.

From having literally no rights under common law, and relatively few managerial property rights under civil law, married women progressed to having rights to manage and control their own property, to sue and be sued in their own names, and to make contracts and other legal documents. Married Womens' Property Acts provided women the necessary legal authority to control their property. State laws granted widows homestead exemptions, allowances, and election rights. Dower was statutorily abolished. Intestate succession laws clarified methods for the devolution of estates. Legal provisions were made for payment of estate debts. While there remained differences in the legal systems of each state, the provisions for homestead exemptions, widows' allowances, and elections were similar. Legislation, in effect, evened out the practical differences.

The amendments to the Social Security Act in 1939 brought major financial benefits to widows and certain other survivors of covered workers. The amendments provided monthly benefits to widows and surviving dependent children or to aged parents of unmarried deceased covered workers without dependent children. One consequence of the act and its amendments was a proliferation of welfare assistance programs at state and federal levels. To quality for federal aid, states enacted new laws or amended assistance laws already in effect and created bureaus and departments to administer them. Although statutes differ from state to state, there is also considerable uniformity in the provisions due to the compliance requirements of the act. Thus, over time public welfare law in each state became more uniform.

Under our system of government, law is not static; it changes and adapts to the needs of the populace. The responsiveness and adaptability of the U.S. legal system was demonstrated during the time period of this study by the many legislative and judicial changes that benefited women, widows, and aged persons. Socioeconomic changes and the imperative of response to an economy brought to the brink of collapse in the 1930s hastened a major shift of legal opinion that recognized and accepted the power of federal and state governments to regulate every essential aspect of economic existence. Major positive changes in laws affecting women and the emergence of legally enforceable social welfare laws were two of the most important legal and governmental administrative developments that fundamentally improved the status of widowed and older women during the period 1848-1939.

NOTES

1. Bishop v. United States, 334 F.Supp. 415, 418 (S.D. Tex. 1971).
2. *Black's Law Dictionary* 250-51 (5th ed. 1979).
3. O. Holmes, Jr., *The Common Law* 37 (1881).
4. B. Fisher, *Introduction to the Legal System* 104, 147 (2d ed. 1977); *Id.* at 35-38; B. Schwartz, *The American Heritage History of the Law in America* 15-37 (1974).
5. 1864 *Howell Code,* ch. LXI, § 7; 1861 Colo. Laws, p. 35 (rep'ld. 1868 and re-enacted with limitation that common law be "applicable" and of general nature); 1868 Colo. R.S. p. 105; 1850 Organic Act, establishing N.M. Terr., Act of Sept. 9, 1850, 9 *Stat.* 446, 31st Cong., 1st Sess.; 1875-76 N.M. Laws, ch. 2, § 2, 1898 *Utah*

R.S. & 1907 *Utah* C.L. § 2488; *see* R. Clark, *Community of Property and the Family in New Mexico* 6, 7 (1956).

6. Lyons, *Development of Community Property Law in Arizona,* 15 *La. L. Rev.* 512 (1955), reprinted in *Comparative Studies in Community Property Law* (J. Charmatz & H. Daggett, eds., 1955).

7. The 1876 case, *Browning v. Estate of Browning,* held in part that the 1846 Kearney Code and 1850 Organic Act did not adopt the entire English common law system for the Territory of New Mexico, specifically stating, "[T]he legislature intended . . . to adopt the common law, or *lex non scripta,* . . . not in conflict with the constitution or laws of the United States, nor of this territory, which are applicable to our condition and circumstances"; other cases in all four states consistently upheld the adaptation of common law only insofar as it was applicable and appropriate to the local legal provisions in existence in each territory and state. 3 N.M. 659, 675, 9 P. 677, 684 (1886); Luhrs v. Hancock, 181 U.S. 567, 570-71, 21 S.Ct. 726, 727-28, 45 L.Ed. 1005, 1007 (1901) (Arizona case); Kroeger v. Twin Buttes R. Co., 13 Ariz. 348, 114 P. 553, 554 (1911); Morris v. Fraker, 5 Colo. 425, 432 (1880); Crippen v. White, 28 Colo. 298, 64 P. 184, 186 (1901); Bent v. Thompson, 5 N.M. 408, 423, 23 P. 234, 238 (1890), *aff'd* 138 U.S. 114, 119, 11 S.Ct. 238, 240, 34 L.Ed. 902, 904 (1891); Hatch v. Hatch, 46 U. 116, 148 P. 1096, 1099 (1915).

8. 1865 Ariz. Laws, ch. XXX §§ 1-11, & ch. XXXI, § 19; 1928 *Ariz.* R.C. § 2170; 1929 N.M. *Stat. Ann.* §§ 87-102, 87-123; *In re* Gabaldon's Estate, 38 N.M. 392, 394, 34 P.2d 672, 673-74, 94 A.L.R. 980, 983 (1934); *see* Clark, *supra* note 5, 15, n. 75; 1 W. DeFuniak, *Principles of Community Property,* § 55 (1943).

9. Brewer v. Brewer's Estate, 68 Colo. 84, 188 P. 725, 726 (1920); *see* G. May, *Marriage Laws and Decisions in the United States* 72 (1929).

10. 1 W. DeFuniak, *supra* note 8, § 1; *see* J. Murphy, *The Spanish Legal Heritage in Arizona* (1966).

11. Fuero Juzgo, *Libro IV, Título II, Ley XVII* (*A.D.* 693); 1915 N.M. *Stat. Ann.* § 2764; *see Black's Law Dictionary* 40 (4th ed. 1968); 1 W. DeFuniak, *supra* note 8, §§ 2, 23, 24; 3 W. Holdsworth, *A History of English Law* 522 (1923); R. Huebner, *A History of Germanic Private Law* 639, 656 (1918); G. Lee, *Historical Jurisprudence* 383, 384 (1900); J. Vance, *The Background of Hispanic American Law* 43-60 (1942); Hamilton, *Germanic and Moorish Elements in Spanish Civil Law,* 30 *Harv. L. Rev.* 303 (1917).

12. 1 W. DeFuniak, *supra* note 8, at n. 2; *see Los Códigos Españoles, Tomo Noveno* (1850), reprinting, in Spanish, *Novïsima Recopilaciön de las Leyes de España, Libro X, Titulo IV, Ley IV* (1805), stating *"[L]os bienes que han marido y muger, que son de ambos por medio,"* loose translation, "The property acquisitions that husband and wife have are shared by both in halves."

13. 1865 Ariz. Laws, ch. XXXI, § 2; 1846 Kearny (var. Kearney) *Code of Laws* (N.M.), Administrations, § 1; La Tourette v. La Tourette, 15 Ariz. 200, 137 P. 426,

428 (1914); Blackman v. Blackman, 45 Ariz. 374, 43 P.2d 1011, 1014 (1935); Barnett v. Barnett, 9 N.M. 205, 209, 50 P. 337, 340 (1897); Crary v. Field, 9 N.M. 222, 229, 50 P. 342, 344 (1897); *see* Clark, *supra* note 5; Murphy, *supra* note 10, 31; Clark, *New Mexico Community Property Law: The Senate Interim Committee Report,* 15 *La. L. Rev.* 571, *reprinted* in J. Charmatz, *supra* note 6. *But see* Lyons, *supra* note 6.

14. 1865 Ariz. Laws, ch. XXXI, § 2; 1887 *Ariz. Civ. Code,* par. 2102; 1928 *Ariz.* R.C. §§ 2171-73; 1846 *Kearny Code, supra* note 13; 1851 N.M. Laws, p. 176; 1884 N.M. Laws, §§ 1410-22 (descent & distribution laws, expressly rep'ld by 1889 N.M. Laws, ch. 90, and replaced by other law continuing the existence of community property); 1901 N.M. Laws, ch. 62, rep'ld & replaced by 1907 N.M. Laws, ch. 37, § 10, reaff'd at 1912 statehood, N.M. *Const.,* art. XXII, § 4; *see* Compiler's Notes to N.M. *Stat. Ann.* 57-4-1 (1953); Horton v. Horton, 35 Ariz. 378, 278 P. 370, 371 (1929); Blackman, *supra* note 13; Barnett v. Wedgewood, 28 N.M. 312, 317, 211 P. 601, 604 (1922); Carron v. Abounador, 28 N.M. 491, 494, 214 P. 772, 773 (1923); G. Schmidt, *Civil Law of Spain and Mexico,* Arts. 43-50 (1851). *But see* Jones v. Rigdon, 32 Ariz. 286, 257 P. 639, 640 (1927); Rundle v. Winters, 38 Ariz. 239, 298 P. 929, 931 (1931) (both holding presumption of community property could be overcome by contrary evidence).

15. Brown v. Lockhart, 12 N.M. 10, 18, 71 P. 1086, 1088 (1903); Rundle, *supra* note 14, at 298 P. 931 ("when separate and community funds are mingled, the comingled funds are presumed to be community").

16. 1865 Ariz. Laws, ch. I, § 2 (effective Jan. 29, 1866); 1887 *Ariz.* R.S., par. 2102 ("common property . . . during coverture may be disposed of by the husband only"); 1901 N.M. Laws, ch. 62, § 6(a); 1907 N.M. Laws, ch. 37, § 16; Pendleton v. Brown, 25 Ariz. 604, 221 P. 213, 218 (1923); Munger v. Boardman, 53 Ariz. 271, 88 P.2d 536, 539 (1939) (holding wife may act as agent of the community with husband's consent); *see also* Charauleau v. Woffenden, 1 Ariz. 243, 260, 25 P. 652, 657 (1876); Woffenden v. Charauleau, 1 Ariz. 346, 25 P. 662 (1876); Woffenden v. Charauleau [*sic*], 2 Ariz. 44, 8 P. 302 (1885); *id.* 2 Ariz. 91, 93, 11 P. 117, 118 (1886); and interesting, informative explanation of community property problems in these four cases in Lyons, *supra* note 6, at 15 *La. L. Rev.* 514-18 or J. Charmatz, *supra* note 6, at 5; W. DeFuniak & Vaughn, *Principles of Community Property* § 113 (1971); G. Schmidt, *supra* note 14, Arts. 40-42, 51-55.

17. 1871 Ariz. Laws, p. 18; 1907 N.M. Laws, ch. 37, §§ 8, 29 (§ 29 said wife could be judicially appointed head of community if husband was incapacitated); Fidel v. Venner, 35 N.M. 45, 46-47, 289 P. 803, 804 (1930); *see* Clark, *Management and Control of Community Property in New Mexico,* 26 *Tulane L. Rev.* 324 (1952).

18. 1913 *Ariz.* R.S. K 2061; 1901 N.M. Laws, ch. 62, § 6(a); 1907 N.M. Laws, ch. 37, § 16, *as amended by* 1915 N.M. Sess. Laws, ch. 84; Pendleton, *supra* note 16, at 221 P. 218; Cook v. Stevens, 51 Ariz. 467, 77 P.2d 1100, 1102 (1938); Munger, *supra* note 16, at 88 P.2d 538; Baca v. Village of Belen, 30 N.M. 541, 545-46, 240

P. 803, 804-05 (1925); *see* Bendheim, *Community Property: Male Management and Women's Rights, Law and the Social Order* 163, 173 (1972); *The New Columbia Encyclopedia* 934 (W. Harris & J. Levy, eds., 1975).

19. Present interest takes effect immediately and not at some future time, a now existing interest. Vested interest is noncontingent, is more than a mere expectancy of a future interest, and one where there is an immediate fixed right.

20. La Tourette, *supra* note 13.

21. Reade v. de Lea, 14 N.M. 442, 466, 95 P. 131, 139 (1908), *rev'd sub nom.* Arnett (de Lea) v. Reade, 220 U.S. 311, 320, 31 S.Ct. 425, 526, 55 L.Ed. 477, 481 (1911).

22. Beals v. Ares, 25 N.M. 459, 499, 185 P. 780, 793 (1919).

23. 1877 *Ariz.* C.L. p. 250 § 1; 1913 *Ariz.* R.S. par. 2058; N.M. *Stat. Ann.* §§ 30-1-1, 57-3-3 (1953).

24. 1913 *Ariz.* R.S. par. 1100.

25. 1907 N.M. Laws, ch. 37, § 26; 1915 N.M. *Stat. Ann.* §§ 1840, 1841; 1929 N.M. *Stat. Ann.* § 38-104; *Re* Chavez's Estate, 34 N.M. 258, 262, 264, 265, 280 P. 241, 242, 69 A.L.R. 769, 772, 773 (1929); Brown v. Brown, 53 N.M. 379, 393, 208 P.2d 1081, 1090 (1949); Ingram, Jr., & Parnall, *The Perils of Intestate Succession in New Mexico and Related Will Problems,* 7 *Nat. Res. J.* 555 (1967); Jones II, *Community Property—Power of Testamentary Disposition—Inequality Between Spouses,* 7 *Nat. Res. J.* 645 (1967).

26. 1973 N.M. Laws, ch. 276, § 2.

27. 1 W. DeFuniak, *supra* note 8, 3; G. McKay, *A Treatise on the Law of Community Property* §§ 1121-26 (2d ed. 1925).

28. 1 T. *Cooley's Blackstone* 387 (4th ed. 1899); 3 C. Vernier, *American Family Laws* § 167 (1935).

29. 1 W. DeFuniak, *supra* note 8, § 2; W. Buckland & A. McNair, *Roman Law and Common Law* 31, 32 (1936).

30. Daniels v. Benedict, 97 F. 367, 371 (8th Cir. 1899).

31. 1912 Ariz. Sess. Laws, ch. 64, § 2; 1921 *Colo.* C.L., G.S. §§ 5566, 5567, 8879; 1887 N.M. Laws, ch. 21, § 2; 1907 N.M. Laws, ch. 37, § 1, 18; 1933 *Utah* R.S. §§ 103-13-1, 103-13-2; *see* D. Pomeroy, *Business Law* 746 (3d ed. 1948); 3 C. Vernier, *supra* note 28, §§ 161, 162; Bingaman, *The Effects of an Equal Rights Amendment on the New Mexico System of Community Property: Problems of Characterization, Management and Control,* 3 *N.M.L. Rev.* 13, 14 (1973); Sayre, *A Reconsideration of Husband's Duty to Support and Wife's Duty to Render Services,* 29 *Va. L. Rev.* 857 (1943).

32. Sayre, *supra* note 31, 859.

33. Bingaman, *supra* note 31, 18.

34. 1 W. DeFuniak, *supra* note 8, § 2.

35. 25 *Am. Jur.* 2d *Dower and Curtesy* § 12 (1966).

36. Mayburry v. Brien, 40 U.S. (15 Pet. 21) 21, 10 L.Ed. 646 (1841); 25 *Am. Jur.* 2d *Dower and Curtesy* § 1 (1966).

37. Beals, *supra* note 22, at 185 P. 789.

38. *Id.*

39. 1865 Ariz. Laws, ch. I, § 2 (effective Jan. 29, 1866); 1868 *Colo.* R.S., ch. XXIII, § 1; 1907 N.M. Laws, ch. 37, § 17; 1872 Utah Laws, p. 27, (Utah dower was restored by 24 Stat. § 18, pp. 638-39, Edmunds-Tucker Act, eff. Mar. 13, 1887, & by *Utah Const.* art. XXIV, § 2 [1896], but later was modified by 1898 *Utah* R.S. §§ 2826, 2831, 2832); Hanna v. Palmer, 6 Colo. 156, 160 (1882) (citing 1861 Colo. dower law, and stating, "The dower act, which bore little resemblance in character to common law dower, was repealed . . . by the revision of 1868"); Norton v. Tufts, 19 Utah 470, 57 P. 409, 410 (1899).

40. 1874 Colo. Laws, p. 185; *Utah Const.* art. XXII, § 2 (1896).

41. 1871 Ariz. Laws, p. 18; 1897 N.M. Laws, ch. 73, § 8; *see* L. Foster, *The Legal Rights of Women* (1913); *The New Columbia Encyclopedia, supra* note 18, 3000; H. Platt, *The Law of Property Rights of Married Women* (1885); 3 C. Vernier, *supra* note 28; §§ 150, 167.

42. *Black's, supra* note 2, 1283.

43. Kircher v. Murray, 54 F. 617, 626 (1893), aff'd 60 F. 40, 50 (1894); Branch v. Texas Lumber Mfg. Co., 56 F. 707, 709 (1893); 23 *Am. Jur.* 2d *Descent and Distribution* § 109 (1965); *Person Entitled to Devise or Bequest to "husband," "wife," or "widow."* 63 *A.L.R.* 81 (1929).

44. Meadowcroft v. Winnebago County, 181 Ill. 504, 54 N.E. 949, 950 (1899); Black v. Jones, 264 Ill. 548, 106 N.E. 462, 466 (1914).

45. An Act for the better Settling of Intestate Estates, 1670, 22 & 23 Car. II, c. 10, §§ V, VI, at 335, enacted for seven years, re-enacted for similar period by an Act for . . . continuance of . . . Act, . . . , 1677, 30 Car. II, c. 6, at 371, made permanent by An Act for reviving the Continuance of several Acts . . . mentioned, 1685, 1 Jac. II, c. 17, § 5, at 388; 3 *Statutes at Large, Great Britain* (MDCCLXXXVI); *see* I. Loeb, *The Legal Property Relations of Married Parties* 161 (1900).

46. 1865 Ariz. Laws, ch. XXXI, § 11; 1887 *Ariz.* R.S. § 1460; *see* I. Loeb, *supra* note 45, 163-67.

47. 1876 Colo. Sess. Laws, p. 65, § 1; 1891 M.A.S. § 1524; Hanna, *supra* note 39.

48. 1872 N.M. Laws, ch. 17, § 1.

49. 1882 N.M.G.L., art. II, ch. V, §§ 1-8.

50. 1889 N.M. Laws, ch. 90, §§ 1410-13; 1897 N.M.C.L. §§ 2031, 2033; *In re* Teopffer's Estate, 12 N.M. 372, 382, 78 P. 53, 56 (1904); Girard v. Girard, 29 N.M. 189, 196, 221 P. 801, 803, 35 A.L.R. 1493, 1496 (1923) *reh. den.* (1924); *see* I. Loeb, *supra* note 45, 164.

51. 1898 *Utah* R.S. §§ 2826, 2828.

52. 1917 *Utah* C.L. §§ 6406, 6408(3), 6408(5).

53. De Morgan, *Wills—Quaint, Curious and Otherwise,* 13 Green Bag 567, 571 (1901); *See Genesis* 25:29-34, 27:1-40, 48, 49:1-28; 79 *Am. Jur.* 2d *Wills* § 1, n. 5 (1975); Schouler, *Origin and Policy of Wills,* 20 *Amer. L. Rev.* 502 (1886).

54. 1901 *Ariz.* R.S. pars. 4217-4221; 1913 *Ariz.* R.S. §§ 1209-1213; 1861 Colo. Sess. Laws, pp. 246, 398, § 1; 1868 *Colo.* R.S. p. 642, § 1; 1883 *Colo.* C.S. p. 1020, § 3483; 1891 M.A.S. §§ 467, 4654; 1851-52 N.M. Terr. Legis. p. 352, § 1 (Art. First of Last Wills and Testaments); 1884 N.M.C.L. § 1380; 1897 N.M.C.L. §§ 1947, 2031; 1917 *Utah* C.L. §§ 6326-28; Hernandez v. Becker, 54 F.2d 542 (10th Cir. 1931) (N.M. case); *In re* Tyrrell's Estate, 17 Ariz. 418, 153 P. 767, 768 (1915); McNabb v. Fisher, 38 Ariz. 288, 299 P. 679, 682 (1931); *In re* Wilkins' Estate, 54 Ariz. 281, 94 P.2d 774, 776 (1939); Wolfe v. Mueller, 46 Colo. 335, 104 P. 487, 489 (1909).

55. 1861 Colo. Laws, p. 153, § 9; 1891 M.A.S. § 3011.

56. *In re* Will of Peter Magnes, Deceased (1902) *reprinted in* 1900-1902 *Colorado Nisi Prius Decisons* 322, 369-70 (1937).

57. Smith v. Smith, 24 Colo. 527, 52 P. 790, 791 (1897). See generally W. MacDonald, *Fraud on the Widow's Share* (1960).

58. Garcia y Perea v. Barela, 5 N.M. 458, 472-75, 23 P. 766, 770-71 (1890).

59. Arnett, *supra* note 21, at 220 U.S. 320, 31 S.Ct. 426, 55 L.Ed. 481 (1911); see *Novísima, supra* note 12, *Ley V;* G. Schmidt, *supra* note 14, Art. 51.

60. Beals, *supra* note 22, at 25 N.M. 507, 185 P. 796.

61. 1 W. DeFuniak, *supra* note 8, § 189.

62. Pendleton, *supra* note 16, at 25 Ariz. 611, 221 P. 216.

63. *Black's, supra* note 2, 661.

64. 1877 *Ariz.* C.L. ch. 37, §§ 1, 2; 1868 *Colo.* R.S. p. 385, § 60; 1897 N.M.C.L. § 1737; 1876 *Utah* C.L. § 850; Hancock v. Herrick, 3 Ariz. 247, 29 P. 13, 14 (1891); Weller v. City of Phoenix, 39 Ariz. 148, 4 P.2d 665, 666 (1931); Barnett v. Knight, 7 Colo. 365, 370 (1884).

65. 1883 *Colo.* G.S. § 1049, 1634, 1635.

66. 1897 N.M.C.L. § 1737.

67. 1898 *Utah* R.S. §§ 2829-30.

68. Rands v. Brain, 5 U. 197, 14 P. 129, 130 (1887).

69. 1877 *Ariz.* C.L. p. 252, § 18; 1901 *Ariz.* R.S. §§ 1727, 1728, 1731; 1883 *Colo.* G.S. §§ 1049, 1050; 1891 M.A.S. §§ 1534, 1535; 1912 M.A.S. *Rev. Ed.* §§ 1817, 8012; 1915 N.M. *Stat. Ann.* § 5893; 1898 *Utah* R.S. § 3846; 1917 *Utah* C.L. § 7643; Hanna, *supra* note 39, at 6 Colo. 159-61; Wilson v. Wilson, 55 Colo. 70, 77, 132 P. 67, 68-70 (1913); Deeble v. Alerton, 58 Colo. 166, 143 P. 1096, 1098 (1914); Grover v. Clover, 69 Colo. 72, 169 P. 578, 579 (1917); *In re* Remington's Estate, 72 Colo. 95, 204 P. 802 (1922); *In re* Williams' Estate, 101 Colo. 262, 72 P.2d 476, 477-78 (1937); Western Nat'l. Bank v. Rizer, 12 Colo. App. 202, 204, 55 P. 268, 269 (1898).

70. *In re* Bubser's Estate, 71 Colo. 95, 204 P. 333 (1922) (where wife was

supporting herself while voluntarily living apart from husband, she was not entitled to widow's allowance).

71. *In re* Pugsley, 27 U. 489, 76 P. 560, 562 (1904).

72. *In re* Nolan's Estate, 56 Ariz. 366, 108 P. 2d 391, 392 (1941).

73. 1883 *Colo.* G.S. § 2270; 1891 M.A.S. §§ 1536, 3011; 1912 M.A.S. *Rev. Ed.* § 7868; 1898 *Utah* R.S. § 2827; 1917 *Utah* C.L. § 6407; La Tourette, *supra* note 13, at 137 P. 429-431; Crandell v. Sterling Coal Mining Co., 1 Colo. 106, 110 (1898); *In re* Will of George Tritch (1900), *reprinted in* 1900-1902 *Colorado, supra* note 56, 43, 44; Hanna, *supra* note 39, at 6 Colo. 156, 160; Logan v. Logan, 11 Colo. 44, 17 P. 99, 100 (1888); Owens v. Andrews, 17 N.M. 597, 604, 605, 607-09, 131 P. 1004, 1005, 1006 (1913).

74. *Ariz Const.* art. 2, § 2; 1909 Ariz. Laws, ch. 3, § 1; 1912 Ariz. Sess. Laws, ch. 57, §§ 1-3; 1913 *Ariz.* R.S. §§ 2481, 2486, 3577, 3588.

75. *Colo. Const.* art. 8, § 1; 1874 Colo. Laws, p. 180; 1876 Colo. Sess. Laws, p. 15, § 6; 1883 *Colo.* G.S. § 2343; 1895 Colo. Sess. Laws, p. 226, § 1; 1912 M.A.S. *Rev. Ed.* §§ 609, 1343, 1346, 5390.

76. 1882 N.M. Laws, ch. XLI; 1884 N.M. Laws, ch. 55, § 1; 1913 N.M. Sess. Laws, ch. 8, §§ 1-2; 1915 N.M. *Stat. Ann.* §§ 4044-4045; 1929 N.M. *Stat. Ann.* §§ 101-102; *see also* 1898 *Utah* R.S. § 511(40-43); 1917 *Utah* C.L. § 1400x40; People *ex rel.* v. Scott, 9 Colo. 422, 426, 12 P. 608, 614 (1886); Bd. of Saguache Co. Comm'rs. v. Tough, 45 Colo. 395, 400, 101 P. 411, 413 (1909); Zollman, *The Development of the Law of Charities in the United States,* 19 *Columb. L. Rev.* 91 (Pt. I), 286 (Pt. II) (1919).

77. 1911 Ill. Laws, p. 126; W. Trattner, *From Poor Law to Welfare State: A History of Social Welfare in America* 186 (2d ed. 1979).

78. Pub. L. No. 379, 53 *Stat.* 1360, 1380, §§ 402(b)(2)(B), 403 (a) (1939).

79. Initiated Act of Nov. 3, 1914, enacted by 1915 Ariz. Sess. Laws, p. 10; St. Bd. of Control v. Buckstegge, 18 Ariz. 277, 158 P. 837, 839 (1916); 1937 Ariz. Sess. Laws, ch. 69 (created state social security & public welfare board).

80. See Donna J. Guy, "The Economics of Widowhood in Arizona, 1880-1940," herein, 195-223.

81. 1912 Ariz. Sess. Laws, ch. 95.

82. 1903 Colo. Sess. Laws, ch. 172; 1909 Colo. Sess. Laws, ch. 214; §§ 1-3.

83. 1927 N.M. Sess. Laws, ch. 94; 1929 N.M. *Stat. Ann.* §§ 90-4301 to 90-4317; 1937 N.M. Sess. Laws, ch. 18, §§ 12-15; 1941 N.M. *Stat. Ann.* §§ 73-101 to 73-139.

84. 1907 *Utah* C.L. §§ 1966x1 to 1966x18.

85. *See* statutes, cases, and authorities cited notes 31 & 58, *supra.*

86. 1939 A.C.A. § 70-214a; 1912 M.A.S. *Rev. Ed.* §§ 5378-80; 1880 N.M.C.L. p. 392, § 12; 1907 N.M. Laws, ch. 37, §§ 18-20; 1915 N.M. *Stat. Ann.* §§ 2744, 2746-48; 1929 N.M. *Stat. Ann.* §§ 68-101, 68-103 to 68-105; 1907 *Utah* C.L. §§ 2499, 2500; 1917 *Utah* C.L. §§ 5853, 5854; Bd. of County Com'rs. of Phillips Co.

v. Kohrell, 100 Colo. 455, 68 P.2d 32, 33 (1937); see Clark, *supra* note 17, 327; 1 W. DeFuniak, *supra* note 8, § 133; 79 *Am. Jur.* 2d *Welfare Laws* §§ 75-83 (1975). See generally authorities cited notes 31 & 58, *supra.*

87. 79 *Am. Jur.* 2d *Welfare Laws* § 77; *see* authorities cited note 76, *supra.*

88. *Ariz. Const.* art. XVIII, §§ 7, 8; 1912 Ariz. Sess. Laws, Reg. Sess. ch. 89, §§ 1-11; 1912 Ariz. Sess. Laws, 1st Spec. Sess. ch. 14, §§ 1-17; 1913 *Ariz. Civ. Code,* §§ 3153-79; 1912 M.A.S. *Rev. Ed.* §§ 2181-83; 1917 N.M. Sess. Laws, ch. 83; §§ 1-24; *as amended by* 1919 N.M. Sess. Laws, ch. 44, §§ 1-18; & *as amended by* 1921 N.M. Sess. Laws, ch. 184, §§ 1-18; & *as amended by* 1929 N.M. Sess. Laws, ch. 113, §§ 1-28; *as amended by* 1933 N.M. Sess. Laws, ch. 51 & ch. 178, §§ 1, 2; 1929 N.M. *Stat. Ann.* §§ 156-101 to 156-217; 1921 Utah Laws, ch. 67.

89. Ives v. South Buffalo Ry., 201 N.Y. 271, 94 N.E. 431, 448 (1911).

90. B. Schwartz, *supra* note 4, 195; *see* Gonzales v. Chino Copper Co., 29 N.M. 228, 222 P. 903 (1924).

91. Pub. L. No. 531, 49 *Stat.* 620 (1935).

92. Helvering v. Davis, 301 U.S. 619, 640, 57 S.Ct. 904, 908, 81 L.Ed. 1307, 1315 (1937) (citing *U.S. Const.* art. 1, § 8); Social Security Board, *Economic Insecurity in Old Age* 15 (1937); see B. Schwartz, *supra* note 4, 204.

93. Pub. L. No. 379, 53 *Stat.* 1360 (1939) (codified, for the most part, in 42 U.S.C. beginning at § 301 (1976); (Social Security Act amendments since 1939 have changed qualification requirements; for current regulations, see *Unemployment Insurance Reporter* (CCH) vols. 1, 1A, 1B, 1C).

94. Pub. L. No. 379, *supra* note 93, § 202(b)-(f); *see* Abbott, *The Social Security Act and Relief,* 4 U. *Chi. L. Rev.* 45 (1936) (gives historical perspective from Elizabethan times to mid-thirties); Carstens, *Social Security Through Aid for Dependent Children in Their Own Homes,* 3 *Law and Contem. Prob.* 246 (1936); *Social Security Act Amendments of 1939,* 28 *Geo. L. J.* 211 (1939); tenBroek, *The Impact of Welfare Law Upon Family Law,* 42 *Calif. L. Rev.* 458 (1954); Waldron, *Social Security Amendments of 1939: An Objective Analysis,* 7 U. *Chi. L. Rev.* 83 (1939).

Conclusion

ARLENE SCADRON

This book began with contributors asking what it was like to be a widow in the American Southwest during the ninety years before 1940. It is clear from the many answers that there is no such thing as "a typical widow." Although the experience of widowhood is one of the constants of female lives—which most women will undergo, usually later in life—it is multidimensional, shaped by many variables, including that of historical time.[1] This study of widowhood in the Southwest suggests that "widowhood means many different things, both emotionally and functionally, to different women and that there are many ways of coping with it."[2] While the lives of some widows discussed herein do mirror aspects of the stereotypic "sorrowing widow" or "merry widow" of mainstream Western culture, these images do not capture the authentic experience of the majority of widows—many of whom were poor but not pitiable—nor do they offer adequate guidance for innovative responses to changing circumstances.

Yet these women, living in the Southwest during this particular time in history, experienced and coped with widowhood differently than they would today, or if they had resided in New England or the South then or now. Additionally, interdisciplinary, multicultural comparisons with groups outside the western tradition permit us to extend our understanding of widowhood and enrich our conception of its significance.

For example, the essays on southwestern Indians (chapters 1 and 2) in this volume demonstrate how different widowhood can be in non-Western cultures and provide a basis for challenging facile assumptions about the universality of the experience of widowhood. During most of the period under study, Hopi society—which did not have a word for widow—had more widowers than widows. This demographic difference, due to high maternal mortality, reinforced by matrilocal residence, and the importance of household and kin, the practical arrangements of daily life, as well as marriage patterns and expectations very different from those of Western society, underline fundamental cultural divergences. Hopi widowhood was more problematic for men than for women. The identity and social status of a Hopi widow was not threatened by loss of spouse. Nor did widowhood endanger continued possession of her home or basic economic sustenance. Data from tribes other than the Hopi, including other matriarchal societies, suggest an inverse correlation between the social and economic penalties of widowhood and a woman's autonomy prior to widowhood and raise important implications for women in Western culture, where status and economic loss resulting from widowhood generally are more severe.

The work on Mormon women (chapters 5 and 6) scrutinizes widowhood in a cohesive Anglo society where deep-seated religious beliefs, particularly about the meanings of marriage and death, might be expected to provide greater comfort and support for the bereaved than in other groups. The institution of polygynous marriage, though it endured a relatively short time and at its peak comprised approximately 20 percent of total marriages in Utah, as well as a close-knit community support system, offered widows various types of sororal assistance. Still, we find a range of response to spousal loss, from the permanently grieving widow to the independent widow, with the majority lying somewhere in the middle of the spectrum. Interestingly, some Mormon women who wrote autobiographies ended their accounts with the death of their husbands, sometimes twenty years earlier than their own deaths, leaving the impression that once their husbands had died, nothing more needed to be written about their own lives.

Among Santa Fe's Spanish-surnamed widows (chapter 3), we find that an array of roles prior to widowhood—mother, relative, and friend—supported a balanced identity afterward. In northern New Mexico before 1880, widows constituted a sizeable proportion of the population and may have formed one of the more stable cultural and social groups within this frontier region. Yet even within this patriarchal society, women lived frequently on their own and often headed large families. While widowhood probably forced many of them to depend at least partly upon others, these women were the primary supporters of their children, which almost surpassed in importance their husbands' deaths.

Not unlike some Mormon widows, Hispanic widows of the rural Mesilla Valley in southern New Mexico (chapter 4) early in the twentieth century also relied on kinship ties, including distant relatives by blood or marriage, religion and its prescribed mourning rituals, cultural values, a broad interpretation of socially defined roles, and resourcefulness in tapping whatever help was available to keep their families together. In these small Catholic communities, institutionalized rituals and customs surrounding the death of a spouse dictated procedures for funerals, wakes, various religious observances, and appropriate mourning behavior for widows and their families; they provided emotional support that helped some widows work through their grief, reinforcing the reality and acceptance of death. Similarly elaborate customs among wealthy Protestant widows have been documented in this study. Both differ sharply from the experiences of women widowed while crossing the frontier or those in isolated settings, where on the surface at least, just after the burial, life proceeded as it had before. Neither the time, the money, nor the institutional support of church and kin essential to such rituals were available to these widows who stoically continued with their lives.[3]

While these examples underscore the diversity of the experience of widowhood, they should not obscure a significant common factor: the critical importance of a woman's economic situation in determining her experience of widowhood. Undoubtedly, the stereotypic "poor widow" more accurately captures the dire economics of widowhood. In most cases, the loss of spouse, traditionally the primary breadwinner, not only ruptured the family but also caused serious financial dislocation. The few exceptions occurred among already wealthy widows whose economic situation may actually have improved as they gained control of property and assets formerly shared with their husbands. Historians have noted the power that rich widows acquired in controlling property, as well as the lives of their children, after their husbands' decease in early modern Europe. One finds in the Southwest an occasional, remarkably successful widow, such as Harriet Russell Strong, who was left in decent but not plush circumstances and used her autonomy to build a new life as a businesswoman. Another group from this study includes the middle and upper middle-class widows portrayed in chapter 9 on the Arizona Pioneer Society—women whose economic status was negatively affected by widowhood but who were better protected than most through prudent investments in urban property to provide for old age and widowhood. Even where strong religious or kinship networks provided support, a widow was nearly always worse off economically after her spouse's death.

In addition to provisions made by the dead spouse for support of the widow, and perhaps their children, a widow's economic status is also affected by other important variables: her preparation for work, opportunities for women in the paid work force, her age, the presence or absence of children, and the availability of institutional supports. To take advantage of options in the paid labor force, women needed some preparation; by the twentieth century many middle-class women had worked for a few years before marriage. As the century progressed, and as high school education became more common, more women were prepared for work and more worked before marriage. However, then as now, widows' occupational attainment and remuneration did not rise correspondingly. Many of the occupations open to women during this period of study, such as laundress, seamstress, domestic servant, and boardinghouse keeper, were extensions of traditional domestic responsibilities and were generally unremunerative. As is still the case, age, time, and prejudice all worked against women on their own.

Generally, the widow in the worst circumstances was the relatively young, poor widow with small children, who could not contribute financially to family coffers. During the years 1848 to 1939, such poor women might seek assistance from fledgling, erratic, and often unreliable local charities, orphanages, or welfare institutions. Those who had no choice but to work and no one to care for dependent children sometimes placed these so-called half-orphans in institutions. And elderly widows, who were unable to maintain an independent household and lacked familial support, often were forced into the few existing homes for the destitute. Others may have received modest assistance from local charitable organizations, most of which coupled meager aid with ample moral judgment. Racial and ethnic exclusiveness and patronizing moralism marred the relief efforts for many widows and elderly, mitigating their effectiveness. And even then, only a few of the needy were reached.[4] Most of these widows would have been eligible for today's federal welfare programs, such as Aid to Families with Dependent Children (AFDC), whose roots can be traced to passage of mothers' pension laws during the Progressive Era. But this legislation was designed primarily to promote the welfare of children and the stability of the family by encouraging widowed mothers to care for their offspring at home; it did not aim to assist widows per se.[5]

Another common thread evident among poor and middle-class widows, especially earlier in the period, before population growth and economic expansion, is their reliance upon "multiple strategies" to survive. Many had to piece together several "jobs"—serving as domestics and cooks, taking in laundry, sewing, and boarders, and running hotels and restaurants. Some undoubtedly turned to criminal occupations—such as prostitution or thievery. Because most of these jobs were marginal, holding several simultaneously protected at least part of the widow's income if one or even two were lost; this allowed her to survive until she found a substitute, a strategy also favored by some contemporary Third World women.

The domestic ideology and its bias against women working outside the home certainly influenced many women who earned money doing domestic chores but did not perceive it (or report it to census-takers) as work. For example, profits from handmade articles sold through women's exchanges were rarely reported as income. In the Denver census of 1880 analyzed in chapter 7, thirty-seven women identified themselves as boardinghouse keepers, but the same census shows that 150 women who took in boarders were not recorded as working.[6] Thus, there are major difficulties in identifying the sources of income of widows who were not in the paid labor force and who did not perceive themselves as working women. Another example of unreported and unrecorded work was older widowed women looking after grandchildren for working daughters in exchange for food and housing.

Widows have not usually been regarded as a migrant people, and when their economic and social needs are met, they usually are not. Certainly, widowhood is less disruptive when the widow need not relocate; still, mobility has been an important means of adjustment. Geraldine Mineau's demographic study of Mormon women (chapter 6) found that of widows who survived their spouses by at least twenty years and did not remarry, more than 50 percent made some kind of move—across county or state boundaries. From these data, however, one cannot easily determine whether widows moved to obtain employment, live in households of relatives, including adult children, or perhaps to share households with others. In an essay on widows in eighteenth-century Woburn, Massachusetts, Alexander Keyssar suggests that the high percentage of widows in Boston and other cities of eastern Massachusetts reflected inmigration from agricultural areas for potential urban employment.[7] Without a detailed analysis of household structure before and after migration, one can only speculate on actual motives for relocation. It is evident, however, that for Anglo women who usually live in neolocal families, widowhood has usually meant the end of the old family form and, very often, a less desirable living arrangement, whereas for women with matrilocal residence, widowhood's disruptions of the living situation are minimal.

The efficacy of strong kinship networks, especially among American Indians, Hispanics, and Mexican-Americans, in providing support for widows is usually assumed without close scrutiny. And there has been a tendency to romanticize the welfare available to the person embedded in a family or clan, obscuring its drawbacks. Where one has classificatory or ritual kin, as among Hopi, the widow has "claims" on those kin. But we have no statistical evidence to demonstrate that Hopi widows made those claims in greater frequency, for example, than did Mormons on the Relief Society or Hispanics on their kin. In the case of the levirate or the sororate, there is a very real expectation that the family a woman marries into is going to provide support or that there will be automatic provisions for remarriage. Yet there is a big difference between claims on kin (and claims on voluntary charities), which depend on the willingness of kin (or volunteers) to fulfill them, and legally enforceable claims on the state. Although reliance on federal bureaucracy by society's dependents, including widows, often provokes severe criticism, governmentally regulated programs serve them better than informal support systems. Whereas kin and voluntary support can be highly discretionary, federally mandated assistance has often taken on the status of a right, enforceable by the courts.

Anglo-American law (chapter 11) has long recognized widows, but not always out of concern for their specific needs. Laws that in one way or another have constrained or protected widows and later the elderly have often been directed toward other groups—children, for example—or other goals, such as the orderly descent of property. Exemption of specified amounts of property from debts owed by the deceased was designed to ensure that widowed mothers would have some protection against destitution and dependency. Careful analysis of the intent behind certain statutes as well as their application in case law is necessary to chart the changing status and autonomy of widows and older women in the law. One clear trend is the movement of support for the poor from the informal and local level to federal jurisdiction, a shift solidified during the Depression of the 1930s when local resources could no longer bear the welfare burden. Yet a special group of widows—those of war veterans—had been receiving federal protection since 1836, when Congress broadened enactments applying to Revolutionary War veterans. Examination of widows' pension applications following all American wars would reveal much about these widows and society's commitment to them.[8]

While it is more difficult to recover personal experiences of widowhood among any but literate, middle- and upper-class women who have left written records of their feelings, pension applications by widows of war veterans, case reports of social workers, and oral histories of more contemporary widows should help us recover the perspectives of less privileged widows. Using the impersonal but not always accurate records of census-takers or tax-recorders, we can reconstruct widows' living arrangements, household composition, sources of income, family and kin relations, age at marriage and at death of spouse, cause and circumstances of spouse's death, economic status, education, and work experience.

The effect on widows of loss of sexual consortium is an elusive but important topic. Accounts of widowhood in early modern Europe and the American colonies suggest that the young widow, much more than the unmarried virgin, was considered dangerous sexually, creating intense pressure on her to remarry. That she was alluring and in need of sexual fulfillment is aptly summarized in this proverb for potential suitors: "He that wooeth a widow must go stiff before."[9] That older as well as younger widows very likely suffered from the loss of consortium may be less obvious in light of historical notions about the lack of sexuality among women past menopause[10] and contemporary emphasis, especially in America, on youthfulness. Some widows in our study talked about loneliness though not about loss of consortium. While historical sources of this type may be scarce, we cannot expect to find what we do not seek. Furthermore, the work of historians on sororal relationships among women in Victorian America,[11] which occasionally included sexually intimate ties, suggests that in some cases, widows may also have relied upon them for fulfillment. Sexual deprivation did have its positive aspect for women still capable of conception; death of a spouse was their only relief from the threat of further pregnancy at a time when contraception was far from effective or simply unavailable. Finally, polygyny, practiced by some Mormons, may have provided a sexual partner for widows who remarried without threatening other wives already part of the marital arrangement.

The widow's status as a single woman raises questions about the problems she shared with other women alone, including the spinster, the deserted woman, and the divorcée. Economic deprivation is commonly associated with singleness and is generally more severe if young children are involved. We have not explored in this book the similarities and differences between widows and other single women, although chapter 3 (on Santa Fe's unmarried women) exemplifies the difficulties researchers face in distinguishing among them when census-takers failed to do so. At times or in places where the stigma of divorce or desertion was prevalent, widows were usually more highly regarded than these women, if literary sources and other evidence are a guide. For example, in her study of Helena, Montana, during its boomtown days as a mining center, Paula Petrik matched some of the women in divorce records with census information and found that many of the divorced women (ranging from four to seven out of ten) described themselves to census-takers as widows. Although this amount of deception may be anomalous, one suspects it occurred elsewhere.[12]

While historians have learned to tread cautiously in using prescriptive literary sources and the ideology they embody as a direct reflection of behavior, these materials "may supply a context for behavior and clarify the boundaries between acceptable and deviant acts."[13] Accordingly, one area of fruitful research would be to compare the images and stereotypes of widowed women in fiction, advice literature, and ladies' magazines with what we know about the actual roles, status, and experiences of widows.

Historians are rarely comfortable predicting the future. Caution is especially called for when forecasts must be based on knowledge of so tiny a slice of the past. Yet this inquiry does raise salient points about present and future policies.

1. Any nostalgia for an earlier "golden age of widowhood" in which informal mechanisms of support, an idyllic family and kin network, and the local community took care of older (and younger) dependent widows cannot be sustained by the available evidence. Many widows and older women, through sheer hard work, resourcefulness, courage, and a great deal of suffering, kept their families together and survived. That other lives were destroyed by widowhood is clear but more difficult to document.

2. Some now advocate paring away numerous features of the welfare state to reduce bureaucratic encumbrances and taxation. The burden of responsibility to support the dependent elderly would then devolve on young and middle-aged children, kin, and local communities. At a time when the percentages of widowed elderly women (and men) have significantly increased, the burden on younger generations becomes increasingly disproportionate. Ironically, the present system, with all its flaws, was instituted because local and familial resources could not support the needy.

3. The economic support currently available for widows through Social Security survivors' benefits, Aid to Families with Dependent Children, and other government programs, in addition to private pension and retirement programs, life insurance policies, and opportunities to accumulate savings, provides minimal levels of financing unavailable in the period prior to 1940. Yet because some of these programs were motivated more by concern for children than for widows, they continue to overlook some basic needs. The well-known "blackout period" in Social Security, for example, provides no support for widows who do not have dependent children and who have

not yet reached retirement age. If these women have not worked or cannot find or qualify for gainful employment and have no other source of income, they face privations similar to their forebears—at least until they qualify for minimal survivors' benefits.

4. Advances in women's educational attainment coupled with increasing representation of younger women in the paid labor force (who work and remain joint or single heads of households throughout their adult lives) should mitigate some of the financial burden of widowhood. We can also expect problems associated with role loss to diminish as women's self-esteem is reinforced by their careers. Still, on the average, women earn only 60 percent of what men do and remain in lower-paying, lower-status jobs, with only token representation at the policy-making levels of most professions. As long as gender-based economic inequities persist, we anticipate that the trauma of spousal loss will entail disproportionate financial and social losses for women.

5. While it has many negative implications and unforeseeable results, ironically the increasing frequency of divorce may better prepare women for widowhood—should they remarry. Such an emotional break forces most divorcées to cope with financial stringency, independent living, and decision making; they learn to live as single women (and often as single parents) in a society whose social life focuses on couples. When divorce was rare and socially unacceptable, widowhood had its "beneficial" side: the severing of poor marriages. In affording a release that only death provided in the past, divorce has become a contemporary analogue of widowhood.

6. Successfully working through bereavement may have been somewhat easier in the past for women who relied upon elaborate religious customs or mourning rituals that carefully prescribed widows' appropriate role and behavior. Now, in the face of an increasingly antiseptic relationship with death, we "let go" of our dead in greater isolation and with less grace than formerly. Consequently, our grieving mechanisms have become attenuated and ineffective. As a society, we seem to be searching for new responses to death and, specifically, to spousal loss. Some contemporary innovations include development of support networks such as widowed-to-widowed programs, growth of the hospice movement, recognition of the importance of anticipatory grieving in long-term illness, and replacement of some "clergical" functions by psychologists and psychiatrists. The durability and efficacy of these developments, however, remain to be evaluated.

7. During this period of diminishing public resources and change, we are challenged to innovate while coping with stringency. Increasing life

expectancy portends a society populated by higher percentages of the elderly, especially older widowed women. Thus, it behooves us to recognize the effectiveness of these women in adapting to limited resources, surviving and sometimes flourishing under substantial stress. Needed historical and contemporary studies of the triumphs as well as the tragedies of many older widows ought to inspire and instruct us. For whether or not we accept the contention of an historian that "grandma" is a most logical revolutionary leader for the future, it unquestionably merits increasing scholarly attention.[14]

The essays in the volume treat various facets of widowhood in the plural society of the Southwest from several disciplinary vantages. They have illuminated the striking resilience of women under trying circumstances. The findings about the experience of widowhood in one region of the United States suggest some of the ingredients for a larger framework to guide further historical research. Above all, they have intensified our awareness of the complexity and importance of a traumatic and increasingly frequent experience affecting the lives of contemporary women. While the subject of widowhood has been terra incognita for historians, and to a lesser extent, other social scientists, it promises rich dividends for explorers in the interstices of the history of the family, the history of women, and the history of aging.

NOTES

1. See Tamara K. Hareven, "The Last Stage: Historical Adulthood and Old Age," in David D. Van Tassel, ed., *Aging, Death, and the Completion of Being* (Philadelphia: University of Pennsylvania Press, 1979), 165-89, for a discussion of "the correlation of historical and individual time [especially 170-74] and for the conceptualization of 'old age' and 'aging' as social and cultural phenomena in relation to historical change." She points out that the social experience of each cohort is influenced not only by the external conditions of its own time but also by the cumulative experience of its earlier stages in life (171).

2. Unpublished comments of Janet Roebuck, department of history, University of New Mexico, at the Western Social Science Association Meeting, Albuquerque, New Mexico, Apr. 27-30, 1983, on preliminary versions of several of the essays included here. Roebuck's remarks have been useful in formulating some of these conclusions.

3. Lillian Schlissel, "Family on the Western Frontier," Jan. 13, 1984, presented at "Western Women: Their Land — Their Lives," a conference in Tucson, describes the ordeal of the Malick family, 1848-67, part of the vanguard who crossed the

Oregon Trail; also see Schlissel's *Women's Diaries of the Westward Journey* (New York: Schocken Books, 1982), and examples of Marietta Wetherill and Mrs. Graham provided in Arlene Scadron, "Letting Go: Bereavement among Selected Southwestern Anglo Widows," herein.

4. A useful comparison to the material on Denver and Arizona in this book can be made with the Home for Aged Women in Boston, described in Brian Gratton, "Labor Markets and Old Ladies' Homes," in Elizabeth W. Markson, ed., *Older Women: Issues and Prospects* (Lexington, Mass.: Lexington Books, 1983), 121-49. The flavor of these moral overtones are captured in social workers' reports in appendix 1 to Mary E. Richmond and Fred S. Hall, *A Study of Nine Hundred Eighty-Five Widows Known to Certain Charity Organization Societies in 1910* (orig. publ. 1913; New York: Arno Press, 1974).

5. For some of the documents revealing the thinking behind this legislation, see Robert H. Bremner, ed., *Children and Youth in America: A Documentary History,* vol. 3: *1933-1973* (Cambridge, Mass.: Harvard University Press, 1974), 519-38. Background on the social welfare system is provided by Walter I. Trattner, *From Poor Law to Welfare State: A History of Social Welfare in America,* 2d ed. (New York: Free Press, 1979), esp. 93, 184-87. Also excellent is James T. Patterson, *America's Struggle against Poverty, 1900-1980* (Cambridge, Mass.: Harvard University Press, 1981), 27-34. Also, Helena Z. Lopata and Henry P. Brehm, *Widows and Dependent Wives: From Social Problem to Federal Program* (New York: Praeger Publishers, 1986), 56-86.

6. It is not possible to determine whether the widows themselves did not perceive taking in boarders as "work" to be reported or whether the census-taker made this judgment.

7. Alexander Keyssar, "Widowhood in Eighteenth-Century Massachusetts: A Problem in the History of the Family," *Perspectives in American History* 8 (1974):88-94.

8. Very suggestive in this regard is the work of Constance B. Schulz, "Revolutionary War Pension Applications: A Neglected Source for Social and Family History," *Prologue* 15 (Summer 1983):103-14.

9. Lawrence Stone, *The Family, Sex, and Marriage in England, 1500-1800* (New York: Harper & Row, 1977), 280; also cited in Laurel Thatcher Ulrich, *Good Wives: Image and Reality in the Lives of Women in Northern New England, 1650-1750* (New York: Alfred A. Knopf, 1982), 97.

10. Peter N. Stearns, "Old Women: Some Historical Observations," *Journal of Family History* 5 (1980):44-57.

11. Carroll Smith-Rosenberg, "The Female World of Love and Ritual: Relations between Women in Nineteenth-Century America," *Signs* 1 (1975):1-29.

12. Paula Evans Petrik, "The Bonanza Town: Women and the Family on the Rocky Mountain Mining Frontier, Helena, Montana, 1865-1900" (Ph.D. diss., State University of New York, Binghampton, 1981), and private communication. It is

unlikely, however, that many of Santa Fe's single adult women household heads in early censuses were divorced.

13. Nancy F. Cott and Elizabeth H. Pleck, eds., *A Heritage of Her Own: Toward a New Social History of American Women* (New York: Simon and Schuster, 1979), 14.

14. Janet Roebuck, "Grandma as Revolutionary: Elderly Women and Some Modern Patterns of Social Change," *International Journal of Aging and Human Development* 17 (1983):263-64.

Notes on the Contributors

LAVINA FIELDING ANDERSON completed her Ph.D. at the University of Washington in 1973. A dissertation in American literature, "Attitudes toward Landscape in Western Narrative Traditions," pulled her toward the study of history, and proximity to Mormon materials in Utah, where she moved after finishing her doctorate, led her to focus attention on Mormon women's history. She now runs her own company, Editing, Inc., and is associate editor of *Dialogue: A Journal of Mormon Thought.* Together with Maureen Ursenbach Beecher, she has edited *Perspectives on Mormon Women* (University of Illinois Press, forthcoming).

DEBORAH BALDWIN is associate professor of history at the University of Arkansas, Little Rock. She received her Ph.D. from the University of Chicago and specializes in twentieth-century Mexican history. Her most recent book is *U.S.–Mexican Energy Relationships* (1981). She has also authored several articles on modern Mexico, including "Broken Tradition: Mexican Revolutionaries and Protestant Allegiances," *The Americas* (1983), and "The Mirror of Mexican Modernization: International Style Architecture," *Mexican Forum/El Foro Mexicano* (1985).

MAUREEN URSENBACH BEECHER is associate professor of English at Brigham Young University, Provo, Utah, and research appointee with the Joseph Fielding Smith Institute for Church History there. She has been writing on Mormon women's history since 1973, when she finished her dissertation of the picaresque in literature for the University of Utah. Her edition of the diaries of Eliza R. Snow will soon be published, as will *Perspectives on Mormon Women,* which she has edited with Lavina Fielding Anderson (University of Illinois Press, forthcoming).

HELEN STRICKLER CARTER, who died in 1985, earned a B.A. from the University of New Mexico in 1947 and a J.D. from the University of Utah in 1951. Admitted to the Washington, D.C., Bar in 1951, she served as staff attorney for Sen. Clinton P. Anderson in 1951-52 on the U.S. Senate Subcommittee on Indian Affairs. Licensed as well by the New Mexico Bar, she conducted a private practice in Albuquerque from 1954 to 1966, and was a faculty member and librarian at the University of New Mexico School of Law from 1966 until her retirement in 1981. She was also a legal consultant to the City of Albuquerque's Ad Hoc Committee for Environmental Concerns in the 1970s, and to the American Civil Liberties Union from 1967 to 1980.

DEENA GONZÁLEZ is a member of the department of history at Pomona College, Claremont, California. She received her Ph.D. in history from the University of California, Berkeley, where she has also taught. She now teaches courses in Chicano history and is revising her manuscript on the women of Santa Fe for publication.

JOYCE D. GOODFRIEND, who received her Ph.D. from the University of California, Los Angeles, is associate professor of history at the University of Denver. A specialist in American colonial history and American women's history, she is the co-author of *Lives of American Women: A History with Documents* (1981) and "Women in Colorado before the First World War," *Colorado Magazine* (1976), and author of *The Published Diaries and Letters of American Women: An Annotated Bibliography* (1987). In 1982 she was the recipient of a Radcliffe Research Support Grant.

DONNA J. GUY is associate professor of history at the University of Arizona, Tucson, and specializes in the history of industrialization in Latin America and its impact on women. She has published a book on the political economy of sugar in Argentina, articles on commerical, family, and tariff law, and is currently working on a study of the sociocultural implications of legalized prostitution in Argentina, 1875-1936.

MARTHA OEHMKE LOUSTAUNAU is associate professor at New Mexico State University, Las Cruces, where whe has taught sociology since 1973. She received her M.A. from the University of Illinois in 1966 and her Ph.D. from the University of New Mexico in 1973. She has been actively involved with the New Mexico Health Systems Agency since 1976, serving in various capacities, including chair of the governing body. She is currently working on an analysis and description of the development of medical and health care in southern New Mexico.

CAROL CORNWALL MADSEN is a research appointee of the Joseph Fielding Smith Institute for Church History of Brigham Young University, Provo, Utah. Before completing her dissertation, she and Susan Staker Oman published *Sisters and Little Saints* (1979), a history of the children's organization of the Church of Jesus Christ of Latter-day Saints. The dissertation itself, completed in 1985 for the University of Utah, was a biographical study, "Emmeline B. Wells: A Mormon Woman in Victorian America." She has published widely on aspects of the history of Mormon women.

GERALDINE P. MINEAU is a co-investigator on the Mormon Historical Demography project and research associate professor in the department of sociology at the University of Utah, Salt Lake City. Her interests include historical demography, the fertility transition, family sociology, and family and household formation and dissolution.

SARAH MILLEDGE NELSON holds Ph.D. (1973) and M.A. (1969) degrees from the University of Michigan and a B.A. degree from Wellesley College (1953). She is chair of the department of anthropology and director of women's studies programs at the University of Denver. Her work has several different foci: women, archaeology, Asia (especially Korea), and quantitative methods. These interests are reflected in several publications, including chapters in books and journal articles: "Recent Progress in Korean Archaeology," in *Advances in World Archaeology*, 1 (1982); "Korean Archaeological Sequences," in *Chronologies in Old World Archaeology*, 3d ed. (1987), and "The Origins of Rice Agriculture in Korea," *Journal of Asian Studies* (1982).

ARLENE SCADRON is a graduate of the University of California at Berkeley, where she received an A.B., M.A., and Ph.D. in American history. She also holds an A.M. in journalism from the University of Arizona and has worked as an education reporter for the *Tucson Citizen*, a daily newspaper. In 1985-86 she was a Fulbright Fellow in India, where she lectured in U.S. history and women's studies. She is a research associate in the department of surgery, University of Arizona, and teaches journalism at Pima Community College, Tucson.

ALICE SCHLEGEL is professor of anthropology at the University of Arizona. She has conducted fieldwork among the Hopi since 1956. Along with southwestern ethnology, her areas of research include the family, community organization, and gender in society and culture. Her publications include *Male Dominance and Female Autonomy* (1972) and *Sexual Stratification* (1977); she is now writing a book on adolescent socialization across cultures.

Index